Commander of All Lincoln's Armies

Commander of All Lincoln's Armies

A Life of General Henry W. Halleck

John F. Marszalek

The Belknap Press of Harvard University Press
Cambridge, Massachusetts, and London, England, 2004

Library of Congress Cataloging-in-Publication Data

Marszalek, John F., 1939–
    Commander of all Lincoln's armies : a life of General Henry W. Halleck /
John F. Marszalek.
        p. cm.
    Includes bibliographical references (p.) and index.
    ISBN 0-674-01493-6 (alk. paper)
    1. Halleck, H. W. (Henry Wager), 1815–1872.
2. Generals—United States—Biography.
3. United States. Army—Biography.
4. United States—History—Civil War, 1861–1865—Biography.
5. United States—History—Civil War, 1861–1865—Campaigns.
I. Title.
E467.1.H18M37 2004
973.7'41'092—dc22
[B]   2004047614

Designed by Gwen Nefsky Frankfeldt

For Mississippi State University students

1973–2002

Contents

Illustrations

Prologue

THE UNION ARMY had suffered a horrendous defeat at Fredericksburg, Virginia, on December 13, 1862. Under orders from General Ambrose Burnside, the courageous soldiers of the Army of the Potomac had charged directly into entrenched Confederates on Mayre's Heights and had fallen in droves. A major Union army had suffered a bloody setback. President Abraham Lincoln was consumed with grief and worry, and fellow Republicans in the Senate were demanding the dismissal of the cabinet and Commanding General Henry W. Halleck. Lincoln hurried to Halleck's house, taking with him Herman Haupt, the Union railroad coordinator, who had just returned from Burnside's headquarters. Something had to be done quickly to deal with the crisis.

Halleck had come to Washington less than six months earlier, when the nation was confident that he was the man to bring victory in the East, as he had done in the western theater. He had never been physically impressive, and the burdens of command had ravaged his body and his psyche, and he looked exhausted when he faced the President. Pasty and overweight, he had dark circles around his blank and bulging eyes. His hair, though it still covered his large ears, had receded severely, and the long sideburns he affected merely called attention to his double chin. Certainly, he looked older than his forty-eight years, and he exuded unhappiness and discomfort.

Lincoln, whose face and physique also showed the wear of the war, spoke first after the three men sat down. Lincoln told Halleck to order Burnside to take his army back across the Rappahannock River to avoid being trapped by the victorious Confederates. Halleck listened impassively, and then stood up and began pacing up and down the room. After a few minutes, he stopped in front of the President and responded forcefully: "I will do no such thing." He went on: "If we were personally present and knew the exact situation, we might assume such responsibility. If such orders are issued you must issue them yourself. I hold that a general in command of an army in the field is the best judge of existing conditions." In the midst of a major Union military crisis, Henry W. Halleck, the Union Army's commanding general, refused to command.

Halleck's reaction was inexplicable. He was a man of impressive accomplishments who had been brought East to gain victory for the Union. He had graduated from the United States Military Academy near the top of his class and then had had an outstanding career as an army engineer. He had published the major American books on military theory, international law, and land litigation. He had fought courageously in several battles during the Mexican War. As a founding father of the state of California, he had built one of the nation's largest buildings and become a member of the leading land-law firm in San Francisco. When he reentered the army in 1861 and commanded the military effort in Missouri, he produced the only string of victories that the Union Army experienced in those early days of the conflict. He was a respected intellectual, a prolific writer, a brave soldier, a practical statesman, a brilliant attorney and businessman, an efficient organizer, and a no-nonsense man of action.

Yet when historians consider his performance in the Civil War, they write him off as an inconsequential failure, neglecting to examine him more closely. The man who made so many contributions to American history, and who served as commanding general longer than any other officer during the Civil War, has not previously inspired a historian to write his biography. The only substantial book about him was written by Stephen Ambrose, initially as a master's thesis, and it is not an investigation of Halleck's entire life and his many achievements. No historian has compared the successes of his pre–Civil War life with his lackluster performance during the conflict itself.

Yet understanding Halleck provides important insight into the history of the Civil War and into the attributes of those whom we call leaders. In some cases past success is a valid predictor of future achievement, but in others it is not. Sometimes, faults or tendencies that once seemed relatively innocuous or inconspicuous assume critical proportions in other circumstances. Grasping exactly who an individual is and how he has been shaped by earlier experiences may well be a more valid indicator of future success than past achievements.

In this biography, therefore, I will attempt to demonstrate that although Halleck indeed enjoyed considerable success before he assumed command of the Union armies in 1862, he had also developed personality traits and health problems that markedly affected his record as commanding general. Halleck's life demonstrated no strict dichotomy between success and failure, action and inaction, decision and indecision. In the early success, the early actions, and the early decisions lay the seeds of Halleck's later failure, inactivity, and indecision. To understand this man, we must not simply try to make sense of such episodes as his encounter with Lincoln after Fredericksburg; we must get to know him from his earliest days as a youngster in Westernville, New York, in the early nineteenth century.

1

Born to Gentility, Educated to Elitism

LIKE MANY other frontier boys of the early nineteenth century, Halleck was stuck behind a plow but his head was full of dreams. He hungered to replace his hard manual labor with mental activity. He wanted to be sitting in a classroom learning, not walking in the hot sun behind a plow. His family was prominent in its thriving backwoods community in upstate New York, but theirs was not the life he wanted, and he saw no way to escape except to run away from the father who kept him at the work he so disliked. Henry Wager Halleck was born into property, but it was freedom from that land that occupied his young mind.

In the early colonial period, what later became the Halleck family farm in Oneida County, New York, had been a wilderness, far from New Amsterdam (later New York City), and even distant from Fort Orange (eventually Albany), the Dutch colony's capital on the Hudson River. This was the home of the powerful Iroquois Confederacy, the lords of a vast territory extending in all directions. When the Dutch arrived in 1613, they took uneasy possession of some of this Indian empire, mostly land along the Hudson River.

The broad central valley of the Mohawk River and its connecting waterways were the geographic features that dominated Oneida County's development. The valley was at first heavily wooded, but white inhabitants methodically cut down the hardwood and pine trees to provide fuel for heat and cooking. Many of the fifty to sixty species of native animals, including the moose, elk, panther, and fox squirrel, gradually disappeared as more and more settlers felled the forests.[1]

As people migrated into the region, communities sprang up. In the 1790s, in the north central portion of the area, settlers founded the town of Western, so named because it was carved out of the western part of the town of Steuben. Western town land was slowly sold off to interested migrants from the eastern part of the state. The first white settlers in the town were Asa Beckwith and Henry Wager (pronounced Waygur). The nearby community of German Flats produced grain and seed potatoes, so Beckwith and Wager walked there, each returning with a bushel of potatoes. These were the first vegetables planted in Western. It was said that Wager himself harvested seventy bushels that fall.[2]

Within this town, the village of Westernville came into being, and once again Henry Wager was among the first settlers. In the spring of 1788, he joined with Reuben Beckwith and David Hicks to purchase some farmland, and for a while they had the only three teams of oxen in the region. Among other projects, they used these animals to build the area's first bridge across the Mohawk River. Around 1794, the first store opened in the village. Over time, several hotels came and went, providing space for public meetings, school programs, social events, and voting. In 1812 the first post office opened its doors. Methodists established several churches and cemeteries, and there was even a small Quaker (Religious Society of Friends) congregation. The first school began in 1802 in a small wood frame building. In 1811 another school was started, this time near Henry Wager's home; the teacher's salary "consisted of a third grain and two thirds cash." The village of Westernville prospered, but it was a small community in an overwhelmingly rural region. As late as 1878, Westernville consisted of only five stores (two mercantile, one millinery, and two shoe), three blacksmiths, two tinsmiths, and one wagon shop, a tannery, a schoolhouse, a post office, and a Lodge of Good Templars.[3]

Into this fertile valley watered by the Mohawk River and filled with migrants from New England and eastern New York came two families who were to produce the future Civil War general. Henry Wager himself was of German stock, born in the Hudson River valley town of Ghent, descended from Barent and Elizabeth Sheffer Wager of Baden-Baden. In 1781, although only seventeen years old, Wager became a member of the Eighth Albany County Regiment in the American Revolution, serving in the Mohawk River Valley that was later to become his home. In 1784, he married Laetitia Ismond, a native of Dutchess County, New York, and he brought her with him when he settled in Westernville. Their union produced five children, the oldest of whom was Catherine, born on February 18, 1796.[4]

Catherine Wager married into another famous New York family. The

Hallocks, as they then spelled their name, traced their ancestry back to one of the early British-American colonists, Peter Hallock. In 1640, Hallock landed at New Haven, Connecticut, with a group of Puritans seeking refuge from religious conflict in England. Almost immediately, this band continued on to the northeastern shore of Long Island near Southold, where they hoped to settle permanently. The story was long told that when the ship sailed into Peconic Bay, the sixty passengers refused to step ashore for fear of the Indians. Peter Hallock disembarked alone to demonstrate that there was nothing to fear. In tribute, his thankful fellow travelers named that place of landing Hallock's Neck and Hallock's Beach.

The Hallock family lived in nearby Mattituck for over a hundred and fifty years. Peter Hallock eventually died there as did his son, Peter, Jr., and grandson Major Peter. Major Peter's son, Joseph, died in the American Revolution while commanding an American warship, but he sired Jabez, the first family member to begin spelling his last name Halleck. It was Jabez who in 1797 migrated to Westernville. His marriage to Sarah Wines resulted in a large family, including, in 1785, the first-born, Joseph Halleck, who became a lieutenant in the local militia and served a year in the War of 1812.

Catherine Wager and Lieutenant Joseph Halleck, descendants of these two leading New York families, met in Westernville and married on March 7, 1813. Their union was exceedingly fruitful, producing fourteen children. The first born were twins, a boy and a girl, the latter dying just after birth. The boy, named after his maternal grandfather, was to become the most famous family member of all. Henry Wager Halleck was born on January 16, 1814.[5]

The young Henry knew from his earliest years that he came from important stock. His maternal grandfather, Henry Wager, had a large farm near Westernville, in what today is the artificial Lake Delta. An early friend of the Revolutionary War luminary Baron von Steuben, Henry Wager maintained a consistent leadership role in the community, serving as town supervisor from 1800 to 1824. During the same period, Henry Wager Halleck's fraternal grandfather, Deacon Jabez Halleck, served as a church officer for forty-five years, using the title Deacon or Dea as practically his first name. He founded Westernville's Presbyterian Church in 1818, and throughout his long life was a farmer, an imposing man capable of hard manual labor until a few years before his death at the age of 103. He settled on land just across the bridge from Westernville, where Joseph and Catherine Halleck raised their family, and where Henry Wager Halleck spent his boyhood days.[6]

Young Henry lived on a farm, but he could easily walk the short distance to the bridge that crossed the Mohawk River into the small Westernville village. The entire town consisted of only 1,557 people the year he was born and grew to only 2,500 during his lifetime.[7] Here he probably went to school for whatever limited time a farming community allowed its boys to leave the fields, and if his fraternal grandfather had any influence, he attended church on Sunday with the Presbyterian congregation. Although most farmers' families tried to make do with what they produced on their own farms, Henry probably went to the Westernville stores often enough to experience the excitement of the small variety of products available. He must have hunted in the area's fields and forests and fished its river and streams. Most of the time, however, he had a job—even as a young boy—and that job was to help with the hard work on the farm. There was always something to do, and every hand was essential.

There were books in the spacious farmhouse where the large family lived, and Henry must have read and reread them often because the family could not have owned many. Surviving today are three books that were in the family's possession in those early years. There was a Bible, a copy of John Bunyan's *Pilgrim's Progress,* and J. and R. Bronson's *Domestic Manufacturer's Assistant, and Family Directory, in the Arts of Weaving and Dyeing . . . ,* published in 1817. Written in the inside leaf of this last book is the name of Henry's sister Elizabeth with an indication that the book had originally belonged to Grandfather Wager. Written in bold script on the endleaf are the words: "Henry Wager's Book[.] Who ever borrows it will please return it when they get threw with it &c &c be sure to do it &c &C."[8]

Halleck's father, Joseph, was a hardworking man and expected his family, particularly his boys, to work hard too. Not only did he tend his farm, but he also served for thirty years as a town magistrate, and in the early 1840s he served one term in the state legislature. Other than leading a three-county appeal against the governor's veto of a local canal bill, he played a minor role in the legislature, his desk situated about as far from the speaker's podium as possible. According to a local historian, however, as a judge he "had a county reputation for the wisdom and justice of his legal decisions, and was held in the highest honor by his fellow citizens."[9] But he was also a strict taskmaster within his family, and he and his oldest son did not get along. Apparently, Joseph Halleck bore down hard on his first-born, creating conflict between the two.

The young boy had to deal with several family issues that his father's strictness exacerbated. The death of his twin sister, Catherine, at birth must have raised the inevitable survivor's question: Why did I survive and she die? Was he in some way responsible for her death? Henry's mother, like so many women of that time, was very often pregnant and regularly giving birth, and thus was not able to give him the parental attention that children need in the critical early years. Before he was two years old, for example, his mother had delivered two more children, followed by ten more in the next fourteen years. Her childbearing and its physical and emotional demands did not allow her to compensate for the unbending strictness of an excessively demanding father.

Neighbors later remembered Henry "as a studious, manly boy, with a decided predilection for mathematical studies."[10] He clearly thirsted for an education, but beyond what he could get from his mother, other family members, and the community school, there was little available to him. Around 1831, when Henry was seventeen years old, he had a significant confrontation with his father. Perhaps Henry demanded the opportunity to go to school. If so, it is likely that the elder Halleck accused his son of a lack of interest in the family farm. Not enough information has survived to provide a definitive answer, but Henry must have been very upset because he ran away from home, depriving his family, which then consisted of father, mother, and nine children, the youngest less than one year old, of his labor.

Others must have understood, because Grandfather Henry Wager took him in and, along with Uncle David Wager, lent him support. David Wager, a Utica lawyer and politician who exerted an important influence on the young runaway, provided the only existing explanation for the disagreement. He later said: "His father has been unfortunate and is unable and unwilling to give him an education suited to his natural abilities."[11] Financial problems prevented the father from educating his son as the young man wished, but money was not the ultimate source of the difficulty. Joseph Halleck did not want his boy to leave the farm and go away to school. The young man was fortunate to find allies in a strong-willed grandfather and a bachelor uncle willing and able to support his aspirations. When his brother Jabez was eighteen years old and hoping to go to school himself, Henry urged him to work that summer on one of his grandfather's farms in a distant town. "If you are like me," Henry explained, "it will be more agreeable, under existing circumstances, for you to be away from Western for a while."[12]

Henry was angry at his father, and he remained angry for the rest of his life. When he returned to Westernville for a visit some years later, he noted that "circumstances have rendered my stay at Western so peculiar that my visits there are not as agreeable as they otherwise would be." Henry's fractured relationship with his stern father remained a source of unhappiness as the young man struggled to maintain close ties with his mother and the rest of his family. When he received a letter from his mother in 1840, after not having heard from her for a long time, he poured out his feelings. "I was very glad, Dear Mother, that you wrote to me, for I had not heard from you in so long a time that I almost feared that you had forgotten me. I feel, however, Mother, that you still love me and will pardon all my faults. It shall ever be my highest aim to merit your esteem and hope by an honest and upright course of life to make myself as worthy as I can of your affection. Although circumstances have separated us in the world[,] still you shall ever be before me and the image of your love remain deeply engraved on my heart."[13] Despite his anguish, there is no evidence that he ever regretted his departure. And he never again mentioned his father's name.

Information on the young Henry's education is sketchy. He first attended Hudson Academy in Hudson, New York, thirty miles or so below Albany on the eastern side of the Hudson River. Founded in 1805 through the subscription of the community's nine leading citizens, the school consisted of a three-story brick building that looked down on the Hudson River. Henry lived in town with a man named Bassett, a friend of his uncle's whom he clearly did not find intellectually stimulating. The school itself proved much more to his liking. Expressing himself in the florid style that characterized his youthful writing, Henry wrote, "It was at Hudson that I first began to rub off the rusticity of uncultivated youth and to acquire a relish for the beauties of nature and art, and particularly a taste, if I ever had any, for the beauties of discourse and writing. It was there," he continued, "where I formed youthful attachments and friendships which of all others are likely to be long lasting." He had already taken a very big step away from the mindless labor on his father's farm.[14]

The new friends he made were stimulating. One in particular, Theodore Miller, became his closest correspondent. It was with Miller that Henry shared his innermost thoughts and feelings as a young man. Miller had lost his father at the age of six, so that like Henry he lacked a parental role model. Relatives helped him as they helped Henry Halleck. Miller went on to become a lawyer, district attorney, and eventually a judge on New York's Court of Appeals, its highest court.[15] The two men drifted apart in later life, but their youthful correspondence sheds light on Henry's thoughts and aspirations during his early years.

Henry's disdain for his father was manifest when he registered at Hudson Academy as Henry Wager, abandoning his father's name in a clear act of defiance.[16] Although he soon reverted to calling himself H. Wager Halleck, his initial action sought to wipe away all vestiges of relationship with the father who (in his view) had treated him so severely. He now saw himself as a member of his grandfather's and his uncle's family.

After his stay in Hudson, Henry returned closer to his uncle's home in Utica to attend David Wager's alma mater, Fairfield Academy. Only eighteen miles away, Fairfield, New York, was then a small village, and it remains that today. But, like its newest resident, Fairfield had ambitions. In 1802, a large crowd gathered from throughout Herkimer County to erect a school building for a new educational institution. Except for the Hamilton Oneida Academy in Clinton (today's Hamilton College), there was no other academic institution in New York state west of Schenectady's Union College, and Fairfield hoped to fill that gap. In the early 1830s, the Reverend David Chassell was Fairfield's principal. A native of Scotland, he graduated from Dartmouth College in 1810, was ordained a Presbyterian minister in 1819, and later gained his Doctor of Divinity degree from Union College. He served three terms as Fairfield's leader. But though he was a great teacher, he was an indifferent money manager.[17]

When he arrived at Fairfield, Henry found everything to his liking. "The village is not large but pleasently [sic] situated," he said. In addition to the academy, which consisted of a chapel and two other buildings, there were three stores, two taverns, three law offices, several doctors, and a number of boarding houses. Henry found the academy "flourishing," the students "between the ages of 15 and 25" (Henry himself was in his late teens), and the main teacher, no doubt Chassell, "one of the best in the country."[18]

Henry was also excited about becoming a member of the Calliopean Society, a club named after Calliope, the Greek goddess of poetry and speech. The purpose of this organization was self-improvement. The students debated a variety of topics in the hopes of becoming great thinkers and speakers. They wore a red K insignia and regularly participated in songfests. Henry was proud to be a member, considering this organization "by far the best" when compared to the other two student groups: the Philotechny and the Ciceronean Club. He found his society's debates "on the whole interesting and instructing" and was pleased that, when they took place, "our room . . . [was] generally crowded with auditors." He was also thankful that his society had access to a six-hundred book library.[19] Henry obviously enjoyed the intellectual elitism of this organization on his school's campus.

All during his time in Fairfield, Henry boarded with the Waterman family, and here he particularly enjoyed being around the "2 fine daughters—

one—Mary—[who] was quite pretty." He also enjoyed walking to a grove on top of a hill about a mile east of the village, where he could view "the beautiful and variegated country which surrounds it" and reminisce about a similar hill in Hudson and the friends who used to accompany him there. "Oh that I could live those times [at Hudson] over again!!" he lamented. But he added, "I like living here very well—it is a delight[ful] place in the summer season." When his younger brother Jabez later attended Fairfield, Henry wrote him: "I was very much attached to old Fairfield, I shall be pleased to hear from you respecting all the good folks of the village. I believe I am acquainted with most of the families there & still feel an interest in their welfare."[20]

Despite his affection for Fairfield and its academy, however, either he, his grandfather, his uncle, or all three of them decided that it was time for him to move up the educational ladder. In the fall of 1834, he moved to Union College in Schenectady, New York, close to Albany, the state capital. He continued calling himself H. Wager Halleck, and he listed himself as a ward of his uncle David Wager. He no longer claimed Westernville as his home, giving Utica, where his uncle lived, as his place of residence.[21]

On arrival at Union College, he passed a faculty examination and was happy to be placed in the junior class. He was pleased with the appearance of the campus, but he said he had "not been here long enough to form a very correct opinion of college life." Then, in the same sentence, he expressed his apprehension: "But from what I have seen I am not as well pleased as I anticipated." Certainly he realized that "I came here prejudiced in favour of the place which I left . . . the most pleasant place I ever resided in." He was worried because "our studies this term are very hard," and there were three recitations per day: at 7:00 A.M., 11:00 A.M., and 4:00 P.M. He wished he could be "spending the long evenings of autumn with some favourite *fair one.*" Happy to leave home to gain the education he had pined for, Henry had found it provided in a congenial way in Hudson and Fairfield. Now, this same education was proving difficult in the more competitive environment at Union, and his confidence retreated as his intellectual insecurity increased.[22]

Henry's new school was the preserve of one of the pioneers of American education, a Presbyterian clergyman and inventor named Dr. Eliphalet Nott. Having gained wide notice because of a sermon he had delivered during Alexander Hamilton's funeral in 1804, Nott became president of the school that same year, serving until his death in 1866. He stamped his personality and philosophy on the institution during a time when American education was trying to find its purpose in the new American democracy. When Henry began his studies at Union in 1834, Nott was forty-eight years old, around six feet tall, and in excellent physical shape, the result of his long walks through the fields and forests around the campus. Although his students loved him, he was a controversial figure in wider educational circles. At a time when a college education meant learning the classics, he introduced into the curriculum the practical study of the sciences and substituted modern languages for Latin and Greek. (He held thirty patents himself, being most famous for his invention of the first self-feeding base-burning anthracite coal stove). Whereas other educators maintained a disciplined authoritarian control over their students and readily suspended or expelled them, Nott saw his relationship with his charges as that of a father toward his children. He believed in positive reinforcement of a student's talents rather than negative punishment for shortcomings. Even though it was accepted practice not to admit anyone expelled from another institution, Nott gave such students a second chance at Union, much to the disgust of other colleges' officials.[23]

In the nineteenth century, the college president was the principal teacher on the campus, and Nott fulfilled this role admirably. When he entered the classroom, the students saw a man in love with learning. He exuded contentment and frequently joked with his charges, who laughed along with him. His lectures were more informal than those the students were used to in other classes. A later colleague said that "the recitations of Dr. Nott were of the nature of conversational lectures." To put it another way, he led discussions, guiding the students but allowing them to contribute to the learning process themselves. In return, students loved him for his wit, wisdom, and forbearance.[24]

Henry was especially susceptible to the sway of this marvelous teacher and administrator. He roomed in "South College, No. 6, Dr. Nott's section," so he may very well have seen the great man more often than most of the other students. He was drawn to Nott as a son is drawn to a father. Halleck remarked soon after arriving at Union that he had already heard Nott speak several times "and was much pleased with him." When Nott gave a lecture on cholera, which had infected several people in town, Henry thought "he made some grand remarks." More significant, Henry seemed to be expressing Nott's philosophy when he wrote to Theodore Miller about the purpose and direction of study. Nott was, according to a historian of Union College, "a student of men and of nature, rather than of books." Henry advised his friend Theodore that "the study of human nature is the main thing after all. Books may inform us what men of such and such dispositions and inclinations will do, but it is from observation alone that we learn what men possess these dispositions and inclinations."[25] Nott could not have made that point better. Henry clearly admired his mentor, a man much more approachable than the father he had left behind.

Henry completed three semesters in less than a calendar year. He took many classes in mathematics, the subject in which his Westernville neighbors had said he excelled. He studied algebra, trigonometry, "conic sections" (geometry), two semesters of analytic geometry, and calculus. In addition he took rhetoric, Italian, two semesters of Cicero, two semesters of mechanics, French, political economy, and two semesters of Greek. He did so well in his studies and in his behavior during his first semester that the college merit roll indicated that he had earned 499 points out of a possible 500. Because others made a perfect score, however, his rank was sixth out of a class of fifty-nine. He also became a member of Phi Beta Kappa, an honor, like his diploma, bestowed on him only after he had already departed the institution.[26]

Despite such an excellent performance, Henry was uncertain about his future. A college degree did not guarantee escape from "indolence and obscurity." Before a man began a career, he believed, "the mind ought to be thoroughly disciplined, so that it can grasp with vigor any subject, and in its investigation of truth, like a strong and mighty torrent, bear down every thing that may oppose its course." He thought the study of mathematics and languages could certainly provide such *"preparation,"* but that was all it was, preparation. "The graduate so far from having arrived at the Empire of fame is only shod and clothed for the journey."[27] Henry may have been parroting Nott again or, more probably, he realized that he had a long way to go before he could be content with his learning.

When Henry left Union College in the summer of 1835, he had indeed gained a healthy portion of the preparation he so desired. His mind had been broadened in a way that he had only dreamed of while tilling his father's fields. He had studied the classics, but he had also spent a great deal of time gaining knowledge of mathematics, modern languages, and science. His contact with Dr. Nott and this educator's philosophy exposed him to a wide definition of learning and a genial interaction with a man he could look up to. Those who studied under Nott's guidance frequently said that the best part of their education consisted of his informal talks about a variety of practical subjects. They left Union College, they believed, prepared to deal with everyday problems. Alumni who later distinguished themselves in a variety of fields, but especially in public service, believed they were successful because of what they had learned from Dr. Nott. Their education, they argued, prepared them for successful leadership.[28]

H. Wager Halleck had only a year under the tutelage of Dr. Nott. But it is fair to say that Nott and Union College expanded the horizons of the Westernville farm boy far more than anything he had experienced at Hudson and Fairfield academies or with his grandfather and uncle, and Nott certainly provided him with a strong intellectual role model. Union gave him a rigorous academic experience, and Henry rose to the occasion. He was gaining the education that he had left home for. But Union College, as it turned out, was only a way station on the road to his final educational destination, the U.S. Military Academy at West Point.

David Wager may have taken the lead in seeking a West Point appointment for his nephew. On December 31, 1832, while Henry was a student at Hudson Academy, Utica's Samuel Beardsley, a member of the U.S. House of Representatives, recommended him for admission to West Point. He cited Halleck's "good English education" and his knowledge of Latin and Greek, and reported that "in all respects [he was] a very suitable person for that station." Andrew Jackson's Secretary of War, Lewis Cass, acknowledged the congressman's letter, but a clerk in his office made an error that Beardsley immediately corrected. "There is a mistake in the name," he wrote back to Cass. "His name is *Halleck* not *Calleck*."[29]

Nothing further happened, so David Wager took it upon himself to write Vice President Martin Van Buren, asking for his help with the application. He received a promise of support in return. But when again nothing happened, in February 1834, when Henry was at Fairfield, Beardsley wrote Secretary of War Cass once more. There was still no response, so Beardsley tried a third letter, then a fourth, then a fifth. Pressured by David Wager, who contacted Cass himself, Beardsley wrote the Secretary of War still another letter telling him that Henry was over nineteen years old and "that it is therefore desirable to have him enter the academy at West Point the present year if at all." This correspondence finally bore fruit. Henry received news of his appointment, and he accepted immediately. Grandfather Henry Wager, acting as his guardian, concurred.[30]

Politics played a role in Henry's successful application. Besides being a bright young man, he was a solid Democrat from a solidly Democratic town. A later Wager descendant described Beardsley as "a Democrat of the strictest sect," and Henry was an avowed supporter of Andrew Jackson. In the midst of traveling between Fairfield Academy and Union College, he had attended the Democratic state convention in Herkimer and had approved the proceedings. He urged Theodore to keep him informed about politics at his end of the state "as I am something more of a politician than when at Hudson. Political news is always acceptable."[31] H. Wager Halleck was a Jacksonian through and through, and this fact not only helped get him his appointment to West Point, but would also influence his later life.

As he prepared to travel down the Hudson River to the U.S. Military Academy in the summer of 1835, he must have felt good about himself and his future. He was twenty-one years old, quite a bit older than the other new cadets, but he had a solid academic preparation, something most of them lacked. He also suffered no homesickness, his departure from his home four years previously having long ago insulated him from any anxiety about going off on his own. He was a mature young man who had experienced the world around him. He had military blood in his veins, so he had to be excited about his future education in the best military school the United States could offer. His future was promising, but his family life remained fractured. The major influences in his life so far had been a stern unbending father, a distracted mother, a no-nonsense grandfather, a caring uncle, a school friend, and two intellectual teachers. All had put their stamp on him, and they would continue to do so far into the future.

At West Point, Halleck faced new challenges that would mold him further. In the previous four years he had experienced intellectual excitement at Hudson Academy, Fairfield Academy, and Union College, but he confronted the strict military regimen of the army's officer school. This was clearly education of a different sort from what he had experienced at the civilian institutions. He adapted, however, at first reluctantly, but eventually completely. The farm boy had matured during his earlier studies; now he purposefully trained to be a military engineer. He would never turn back.

The academy was located in Henry's home state, not far from his former schools. Unlike them, however, the military academy was not in a town; it was isolated on a plain overlooking the Hudson River. He was entering a military world all its own. The first sight of the military academy that most cadets received was looking up, from the river wharf below to the plain above. A steamboat full of aspiring young men would land there in June or September, the human cargo having traveled from all over the United States. Stepping on shore, these teenagers would see a soldier with a slate board, recording everyone's arrival. Immediately they would walk up the steep road from river to plain, reporting to the adjutant's and then the treasurer's office, officially signing in. Given their room assignment, the nervous civilians reported to a twelve foot by twelve foot room and met the upperclassmen, who would help torment them into becoming soldiers, and other future cadets who would share their misery. A visit to the quartermaster provided the necessary room equipment and military clothing. Before November 1838 and the introduction of bedsteads, they were given mattresses for sleep on the floor. An examination for physical and mental suitability by the post physician and academic faculty followed soon after. The knowledge requirement was minimum: "must be able to read and write well, and to perform with facility and accuracy the various operations of . . . Arithmetic."

First, however, the new cadets were herded together and, though still in civilian clothes, marched in what could loosely be called a military formation. "The first day after my arrival," one cadet later remembered, "I was taken out to drill & sure you never saw a more awkward creature in your life than I was." When they saw the veteran cadets on parade, the newcomers marveled at their precision and no doubt wondered if they could ever match such a spectacle.[32]

The young men were not issued their uniforms until later, usually on July fourth. This was a momentous occasion, demonstrating that they had reached an important milestone in their new careers. Now, at least, they looked like the veteran cadets, even though they hardly marched like them. Each cadet donned the gray coat with bright metal buttons and a high collar, gray pants in the winter and white in the summer. A white belt held up a bayonet and a cartridge box, and on top of his head he wore the dress hat complete with brass eagle on the front. When the weather was rainy or cold, he covered himself with a gray cloak.[33]

It was not a comfortable outfit. The tight-fitting trousers posed a particular problem because they were not anatomically correct: the buttons were located at the side. Change did not come until the future Civil War General John Pope returned from furlough in the fall of 1840 wearing uniform trousers with the opening in the front rather than on the side. The superintendent recognized the utility of this innovation, though he had to overcome his wife's shocked protests to implement the change.[34]

If they arrived in June, the new cadets, called plebes, first went into summer encampment, living in tents pitched on the parade ground. If they arrived in September, they missed this annual rite and went immediately into the classroom. There, they faced their imposing instructors and the recitation system, which required them to be prepared to receive a grade every day. On the basis of this daily performance, the teachers placed them into sections, the worst-performing cadets, for example, being placed together in the lowest section. At the end of each academic year, there was also a final examination, oral and public, in each course. The cadet's life at West Point was under constant scrutiny and evaluation.

The cadets' days were long, full, and demanding. The reveille bugle or drum sounded at dawn, immediately followed by thirty minutes of policing the room that each cadet shared with several other young men, not necessarily all from the same class. There was then time for study and thirty minutes of breakfast beginning at 7:00 A.M., followed by thirty minutes of recreation. From 8:00 A.M. to 1:00 P.M., cadets were in class or studying, then lunch, then more classes until 4:00 P.M., and then marching and recreation until the sun went down. It was then time for supper, more study until 9:30 P.M., a final thirty minutes of recreation, and lights out at 10:00 P.M.[35]

Cadets were expected to conduct themselves as gentlemen at all times. Anyone deviating from the rigid prescribed military behavior during this busy day received demerits, and 200 such marks led to "deficiency" and the threat of dismissal. Cadets therefore had to be sure that their rooms were cleaned and that they themselves were properly dressed and that they were not caught drinking or sneaking off to the nearby Benny Havens saloon, or doing anything else that violated the many rules and regulations governing them. They could march off demerits during free time on weekends, although a particularly egregious infraction of conduct might result in dismissal. It was a hard life, and most cadets probably agreed with their fellow cadet John Pope, who "about 3 o'clock at night walking Post both cold and dark and raining . . . thought of my Dear Mother & home & wished that I were with them. But as the old saying is," he philosophized in his misery, "whatever is, is right, and with that I console myself, although it is but poor Consolation."[36]

When H. Wager Halleck arrived at West Point in June 1835, records listed him as being twenty years, five months old. Actually, he was one year older than that, having been born on January 16, 1814. Academy regulations set no age limit for admission, but Halleck may very well have felt sensitive about his true age, compared to that of the other plebes, some of whom were as young as fifteen. So he shaved a year off his actual age. From that time on, this incorrect age became a standard part of his resume.[37]

Halleck underwent the summer encampment on the parade ground from mid-June through July and into August, but this experience elicited from him no surviving comments. In his first year, he ranked third in mathematics, ninth in French, and fourth in overall standing out of 57 plebes. He was seventeenth in conduct among all 215 academy cadets. Each year his standings improved. By the time he reached his final semester, he ranked third in civil and military engineering, third in ethics, fourth in infantry tactics, artillery, chemistry, mineralogy, and geology, and third in his class among the 32 who had survived the grind to that point. He was second in conduct among all the academy's 231 cadets.[38]

Similarly, he advanced steadily in cadet military rank. At the end of his plebe year, he, along with thirteen others, was promoted to cadet corporal. After his second year, he made sergeant, and after his third year, he was named captain, the commander of one of the companies in the corps. These were not automatic promotions. William T. Sherman, who graduated the year after Halleck, never held any cadet rank during his entire four-year academy career. Halleck also belonged to the Dialectic Society, a group that met regularly to discuss and debate a variety of intellectual, military, and political topics. Since it resembled the Calliopean Society he had so enjoyed at Union College, he must have been eager to participate in these meetings of the mind amidst the strict military regimen on the Hudson River. And, in his senior year, he took fencing lessons, ranking at the beginning of that year as a member of the "first squad." But since that unit consisted of the academic leaders of the class, Halleck's ranking was not an indication of any particular proficiency with the sword. Dancing lessons were also offered, and, according to academy financial records, Halleck paid each July and August for these lessons and the ball that ended the summer encampment. Significantly, he spent less money on dancing than did many of the other cadets, apparently demonstrating that he kept his good times to a minimum.[39]

Halleck's four years at West Point coincided with the presence there of a host of others who were to make reputations for themselves in the Civil War. Besides Sherman, future Union generals were Joseph Hooker, George H. Thomas, Don Carlos Buell, William S. Rosecrans, and John Pope. It is interesting to note that Halleck had difficult relations with all these future Union leaders at some time during the Civil War. Future Confederates included James Longstreet, P. G. T. Beauregard, William Hardee, Braxton Bragg, and Jubal Early.[40]

His two closest West Point friends appear to have been Jeremy Gilmer of North Carolina and Schuyler Hamilton of New York. Not only did Gilmer and Halleck graduate in the same class, but they were also detailed together in June of 1837 to tutor West Point candidates in arithmetic, and later they shared faculty status and common assignments in the Engineer Corps well into 1846. Between 1858 to 1861, they were next-door neighbors in San Francisco. When the Civil War began, however, Halleck stayed with the Union, and Gilmer joined the Confederacy. This difference fatally affected their friendship.[41]

Halleck's relationship with Hamilton was his closest of all. They roomed together for two years, although Hamilton graduated two years after Halleck. The grandson of Alexander Hamilton, Schuyler Hamilton came from a distinguished American patriot family in Halleck's home state of New York. After graduation in 1841, Schuyler made a reputation for himself in the Mexican War and, from 1847 to 1854, he was aide-de-camp to Commanding General Winfield Scott. He resigned his commission in 1855 to enter civilian life and lived in San Francisco, where, for a time, he worked for William T. Sherman's bank in San Francisco at the same time that Halleck was one of that city's leading lawyers. When the Civil War began, Hamilton served as Winfield Scott's aide until that general's retirement in November 1861. He then briefly served as Halleck's aide, before commanding a division in several western theater campaigns. During Halleck's advance on Corinth, Mississippi in 1862, Hamilton contracted malaria, and this chronic illness forced him to resign from the army in 1863. In the end, however, his most important influence on Halleck was not their friendship or their military relationship; it was his introducing Halleck to his sister, Elizabeth, whom Halleck married in the 1850s.[42]

From surviving records, there is no indication that Halleck made many other close friends. In later years, Hamilton described their relationship and Halleck's lack of other friends delicately: "Halleck was my roommate at West Point for two years, and he was very kind to me. We never had any disagreements. He had few intimate friends, but they were of the best." Joseph Hooker, who later had major disagreements with Halleck, said that Halleck's relation with the other cadets was "of the most formal and distant character." Halleck himself recognized that he had few close friends. In his continuing correspondence with his Hudson Academy fellow student, Theodore Miller, he mulled over this fact but took no responsibility for it. "During my residence in different places, I had formed an intimate acquaintance with 3 or 4 young men of about my age," Halleck told Miller. "These were close friends," he said, "to them I was free to unbare my bosom." "But where are they now?" he asked. One died and others married and "by thus selecting a friend from the other sex have deemed it proper to absolve all connexions with ours. . . . Thus Death & Hymen have left me but few confidential friends, in fact you now stand almost alone in my affections," he concluded. "God grant that no unforseen event may soon sever that bond that connects our hearts."[43]

As graduation from West Point approached after four years of isolated life with fellow cadets to whom he never drew close, Halleck continued to look to the friends of his youth, and not to his classmates at West Point. His lack of friends among the cadets was partly due to the fact that he did not approve of them. During his four years at West Point he received only sixteen demerits, and all of these were for minor infractions, ranking him among the most strait-laced cadets at the academy. Most of his colleagues could not match that record, and he knew it. As early as his first year at West Point, he expressed his disapproval. "The education here acquired," he wrote, "is of the highest order but the habits usually contracted are de-cidedly bad." "If parents [only] knew the hardships & privations their children would have to undergo . . . & the inducements to vice they must meet," he predicted, "I think they would not be so anxious to get them ap-pointments." "Christmas and New Year's here passed in drunkenness [sic] and rioting," he reported to Theodore Miller with no attempt to hide his disgust. "It is strange to me that men of talents & education will make beasts of themselves." "I think it very doubtful about my remaining here," he concluded. Perhaps Halleck had assimilated his father's stern and judg-mental nature and found it hard to accept the vices of others.[44]

Yet, at least once, Halleck put himself in possible harm's way by sup-porting other cadets. The West Point chaplain during Halleck's last year at the academy regularly gave two-hour long sermons during the mandatory Sunday church service. Such extended discourses resulted in the cadets' having to eat a cold lunch instead of a more appetizing hot dinner. One Sunday, they rebelled. As the chaplain droned on, Mess Call sounded on the plain; the first captain immediately ordered his Company A to rise and march out of the church. Halleck, as commander of Company B, and no doubt angry at the chaplain's lack of proper form, quickly followed suit. Soon the entire corps of cadets was leaving the chaplain in mid-sentence in the middle of a long sermon. Furious, he demanded a court of inquiry, but fortunately Winfield Scott, who chaired the court, did not punish the ca-dets, calling instead on the chaplain to consider switching to a civilian min-istry.[45]

Halleck wrote a letter to his uncle singing the praises of a fellow New Yorker, Alexander H. Dearborn, for his willingness to give up his cadet-ship in order to help his parents through a financial crisis. (Dearborn never did resign and graduated sixth in his class.) Halleck asked his uncle, who had helped him when he had left his own parents, to find gainful employ-ment for Dearborn, a fellow academic leader whom Halleck revealingly called a "friend." In this same letter, Halleck proudly talked about West Point seniors petitioning to be sent, before graduation, into the field to battle the Seminole Indians in Florida. They wanted revenge for an Indian ambush of an army unit containing several recent West Point graduates. Halleck might not have many friends at West Point, and he might not approve of much cadet behavior, but he was still a proud member of the corps.[46]

Politics continued to captivate Halleck at West Point. In his letters to Theodore Miller, he gave detailed disquisitions on the political scene in New York and the nation. He remained a staunch Democrat, but was terribly upset at the direction President Martin Van Buren was taking the party. When the Whigs gained success in the 1837 New York election, Halleck attributed it to Van Buren's support of the sub-treasury system. The only hope for the Democratic party and the President, now battling the Panic of 1837, Halleck said, was to take the "medium," what later generations would call the middle of the road. "The elements of the party in this state need *continuing* in one solid mass—the knife must not be applied. If straggling parts are lopped off[,] the balance of power is gone," Halleck said. He harked back to the days of Andrew Jackson: "give me neither a national Bank nor a Sub treasury." The forthright and bold Andrew Jackson remained his political ideal, and Halleck was unhappy with subsequent party leaders.[47]

His discussion of Congress's passage of a new army bill, however, demonstrated that he did not accept Jacksonian democracy when it came to the military. He believed that bill would give him, upon graduation, "a better situation" than the old one did, "provided that the President does not fill up the present vacancies with citizens. It is hard for us [cadets] to be placed under citizens who have spent no time in preparation for their commissions, while we have spent four or five years here at hard toil fitting ourselves for the various duties of our stations." Halleck was clearly expressing the military academy's party line: only West Pointers made real officers. Militia members and political appointees did not. This hardly sounded like the rhetoric of a Jacksonian.[48]

Showing that West Point was indeed having an influence on him despite his unhappiness with some aspects of his life there, Halleck always ended his passionate comments on politics with a caveat: "I have no great confidence in these opinions, not being so situated as to become acquainted with the views of the people. We [military people] are but little affected by those political surges that sweep over the land. The waves dash at our feet, but do not bear us away. Not being allowed to vote, we are more free from party sympathies & prejudices." Making a similar point later, he wrote: "I am no politician & probably cannot enter into the feelings & motives of a partisan."[49] Halleck accepted the West Point dictum. He had become a military man and, as such, had to stay clear of politics. It was hard for him, but he was trying to make the difficult transition from strong partisan to political neutral.

Of all his West Point experiences, Halleck's exposure to Dennis Hart Mahan, Professor of Civil and Military Engineering and the Art of War, seemed to have had the greatest influence on his later professional life. Mahan was himself a graduate of the academy and later joined its faculty, serving from 1832 until long after the Civil War. He was a prolific writer, publishing books on a variety of engineering topics, but was most famous for his book on strategy and tactics, *An Elementary Treatise on Advanced-Guard, Out-Post, and Detachment Service of Troops and the Manner of Posting and Handling Them in Presence of an Enemy . . .*, known succinctly and familiarly as *Out-Post*. He was a demanding teacher who struck fear into the hearts of his students with his exacting standards and rigorous demands on their time. He expected them to spend three to four hours a day on the homework he gave them. They even had to sit perfectly straight in his classroom; he would chastise a sloucher with the stern rebuke: "the body at attention, so will be the mind." If a cadet did not know his lessons to Mahan's satisfaction, he would have him report on Saturday afternoon for special tutoring during what was normally free time. One cadet remembered him as "the most particular, crabbed, exacting man that I ever saw. He is a little slim skeleton of a man and is always nervous and cross." But another said that cadets "thought it impossible that any one head could carry more than he knew."[50]

Mahan's key course on military engineering and strategy was squeezed into one semester; the first half of that same year the cadets busily studied civil engineering. As a young man, Mahan had visited France, where he learned first-hand that French military thought stressed engineering and fortifications. In later years, Mahan read mostly French books on engineering, and he founded the Napoleon Club.[51] Thus it is not surprising that he taught engineering and strategy together, basing his course on the French model. Indeed, his first publication in 1836, during the time Halleck was a West Point cadet, was a book on field fortifications in warfare.

Throughout all his writing and teaching, Mahan emphasized the importance of history, and Halleck took notice. "It is in military history that we are to look for the source of all military science," Mahan believed. He found no sense in the long-held American Minute Man view of warfare that anyone, without any prior training, could successfully lead men in battle. In a passage that would have particular resonance twenty-five years later in the midst of a civil war, Mahan wrote: "Let no man be so rash as to suppose that, in donning a general's uniform, he is forthwith competent to perform a general's function; as reasonably might he assume that in putting on the robes of a judge he was ready to decide any point of law."[52] Mahan was clearly an early advocate of military professionalism, and the cadets imbibed a major dose of this attitude with their engineering and strategy lessons. Halleck's letters to his friends demonstrated this influence.

Mahan so dominated the West Point faculty, and his impact on the cadets was so powerful, that even a one-semester exposure to his teachings had a major influence on his students. As his biographer put it, he "plant[ed] the seeds of curiosity and dedication" in his charges.[53] Surely no medium was more fertile than the curious brain and determined purposefulness of Henry Halleck, already partially prepared during his time at previous schools.

The West Point faculty, perhaps prodded by Mahan, recognized Halleck's ability and rewarded it. When he completed his third year at the academy in June 1838, Halleck was given the honor of making the Fourth of July oration. There is no record of that day, but there is enough information on earlier such celebrations to provide insight into what happened in 1838. At dawn, as the sun began to appear over the surrounding hills, the cadets fired a thirteen-gun salute. The rest of the day they listened to a cadet oration and drank much claret and champagne in response to several exuberant toasts. In 1837, separate salutations and responses were shouted in honor of the President of the United States, the memories of Washington, Lafayette, Kosciuszko, the navy, and, among many more, to the "Associations connected with our profession—Whatever may be the vicissitudes of our fortunes, never shall we cease to remember with other than the most exquisite pleasure, those friends with whom we have shared the terrors of the blackboard and the hardships of a camp. A long life of health and happiness to each and all of them.—Auld Lang Syne. 3 cheers." At each toast, everyone stood and took a generous drink of the appropriate wine. Between drinking bouts, the cadet orator of the day presented his address.[54]

It was in the midst of such substantial toasting and drinking, therefore, that Halleck, who disdained rowdy behavior, rose to address the corps. The presentation has been lost to history, but Halleck spoke on a similar theme elsewhere and that address suggests the ideas that he no doubt offered to his semi-inebriated classmates.

Demonstrating the continuing influence of Union College's Eliphalet

Nott, Halleck announced that a West Point education was "necessarily of an elementary character," and that "the practical uses of the elementary principles which are taught here you must learn elsewhere." The military academy, he said, "only professes to teach rudiments and elementary principles; to discipline the mind, to form habits of study & thought, to establish a substantial basis for your future usefulness and success in the military profession." It was true, he said, that "the principles of attack and defense which you have learned from Vauban and the other great masters of military engineering, are as unalterable as the laws of gravitation; but the practical rules must necessarily change with the ever varying circumstances of time and place." All aspects of the military art had this in common, he insisted, but then, echoing Mahan, he said that "in order to fully understand these rules, one must be well versed in military history, and have a critical knowledge of the details of battles and campaigns. Such knowledge can only be acquired by years of study," again a Mahan principle. He also told the cadets they would have to learn "subordination and discipline," "the habit of *courtesy*, and a high and delicate sense of *honor*." In short, Halleck was telling them that, as officers, they were to be educated gentlemen.

It was not true, however, that those who did well at West Point would necessarily become the most successful officers in the army, he continued. Those who were critical of the constant grading of cadets did not understand the merit system. That was the *"measure of Academic proficiency, but not the gauge of talent."* "The aptitude of the boy does not determine the ultimate success of the man," Halleck said, again sounding like Eliphalet Nott. "From one of the numerous fountains and rills that form a river, who can predict the nature and magnitude of the future stream!" Sometimes those best prepared get lazy, he said, while "the ignorant, rude and awkward boy becomes the learned professor, the skilled officer, the accomplished gentleman." Then, too, the seniority system of promotion did not encourage ambition, and "the isolation of frontier service–the hardships of the march & camp, and the monotony of garrison service" sometimes led to "a career of intemperance." "The young man who once embarked upon the sparkling stream of social indulgence glides merrily but swiftly along with the increasing rapidity of the current." "As a preservative against this danger," he concluded, "permit me to urge upon you the importance of cultivating those habits of study which it has been the object of this institution to form."[55]

Given these serious warnings, it is doubtful that many of the cadets gave him their complete attention. The very evil that he was warning them against, the overuse of alcohol, was in evidence right before his eyes as he spoke. Most cadets, warning or no warning, probably shared the thoughts of one of their number. "We had a glorious time on the fourth," Cadet Edwin Wright Morgan wrote in 1835. "Nearly the whole Corps, and invited Citizens too, were quite patriotick, or to speak unequivocally, most celestially *fuddled.* All passed off very well and the next day we were all as sober and as wise as if we had not had the exquisite felicity of being *independent.*"[56] Most cadets were hardly as serious as Halleck was or he wanted them to be.

Halleck was very proud of being asked to do what he called the "speechification" on the Fourth of July and, although disappointed that it would prevent him from going to see his friend Theodore Miller, he tried to compensate for his disappointment by inviting Miller to come to West Point instead. Miller did not make it, but Halleck hoped he would still come some time before the end of the cadet summer camp. Halleck continued to reach out to Miller, even as he lectured his recalcitrant fellow cadets about proper behavior. He reflected Dennis Hart Mahan's ideas about military life,[57] and Eliphalet Nott's belief that experience is a major element of learning. Ironically, he also demonstrated his unbending father's stern seriousness.

Halleck caught the faculty's eye in several other ways. He served as a tutor for incoming cadets preparing for the entrance examination; and in December 1838, although still six months from his graduation and commissioning, he was named assistant professor of chemistry and ordered to report to Professor Jacob W. Bailey. According to academy regulations, such an appointment was "an honourable distinction" carrying with it an additional "ten dollars per month as a compensation for extra services." There were other privileges, too, that made such appointment desirable. As an assistant professor, Halleck was excused from having to march with his section and perform many other cadet military duties; he received one of the larger rooms in the more modern of the two cadet barracks; and, finally, his uniform had more glitter to it than did the regular cadet issue. The fact that Professor Mahan had once also served in this position made the appointment even more rewarding.[58]

Halleck also had the good fortune to teach under the supervision of an understanding faculty member. Until 1838, there had been no professor of chemistry, mineralogy, and geology. That first professor was Jacob W. Bailey, a native of Massachusetts, and himself an 1832 graduate of West Point. Although he was responsible for chemistry and geology, Bailey became world renowned for his studies in botany, particularly for his use of the microscope and his study of freshwater algae. He wrote articles in leading journals, published reports on American coastline harbor bottoms, and, from material sent him by graduates, established one of the nation's largest collections of minerals and rocks. He was a model intellectual.

Unlike Mahan, Bailey was a kindly figure, a cadet favorite because of his willingness to try to stimulate the cadets to learn rather than forcing them to memorize massive amounts of material. He applied the principles of science to practical situations that cadets might encounter while on active duty. He hated to fail anyone and worked with those having academic problems in the hopes of somehow getting them to succeed.[59] He must have reminded Halleck of Dr. Nott.

Bailey was responsible for two courses: one on chemistry to the second class (juniors) and a class on mineralogy and geology to the first class (seniors). Presumably Halleck was in charge of a recitation section of second classmen in chemistry. He had to evaluate each cadet in his section of about ten cadets, and at the end of each week he ranked everyone. These weekly reports were consolidated each month, and a report was sent to the parents or guardians of each cadet.[60] Although only a cadet himself, Halleck had a major responsibility; he fulfilled the role of faculty member because there simply were not enough officers available to do the job. This burden did nothing to lessen his seriousness or his unhappiness with the other cadets. The military had told him by orders what he had always believed: that he was superior to these other frivolous young men.

He was very pleased with his position. "I am now as agreeably situated as I ever have been here," he wrote to Theodore Miller; "I now hold the office of Asst Prof of Chemistry which relieves me from all military duty & somewhat increases the severity of my studies." He qualified his contentment somewhat by adding that he could not expect much more satisfaction at West Point "considering my impatience of restraint," but overall, he enjoyed working under the kindly Professor Bailey.[61]

In June 1839 Halleck graduated third in his class, saying in his subsequent handwritten résumé that he had graduated "with distinguished honors." He was commissioned in the Corps of Engineers, the most prestigious branch assignment a West Pointer could receive. Only the highest graduates became engineers; those lower in class standing went into the artillery and those at the foot of the class became infantry officers.[62]

Normally June graduation meant a furlough for the newly commissioned officer before assignment to his first post. Such was not the case for Halleck. Granting him only a shortened leave (although he later insisted that he had never received any time off), the army ordered him, his friend

Jeremy Gilmer, and another graduate to remain at West Point on the teaching faculty. This time he became assistant professor of engineering. Halleck was now going to be directly under the supervision of Dennis Hart Mahan, the faculty's most influential member and a man whose sternness contrasted starkly with Jacob Bailey's kindness.[63]

Since he did not have to report until August 28, Halleck took advantage of the free time to purchase a silver watch fob and chain, proudly engraving his name, his incorrect birth date, and "Engineers U.S.M.A. 1839." He visited his home town of Westernville and, no doubt, visited Theodore Miller in Hudson. As he had promised in March, he evidently brought some books home for his brother Jabez, who was planning to begin classes at Fairfield Academy in the fall. He also gave Jabez some money to help with his expenses. He told his brother: "Whenever you want money[,] ask me before any body" else. He also pushed for his sister Catherine to attend school, which she did at the Rome (New York) Female Seminary, much to Halleck's delight. Only his relationship with his father remained conflicted; his "visits there are not as agreeable as they otherwise would be," he told Jabez.[64] His encouragement to other Halleck siblings to follow his example and leave home to gain an education did not help heal the breach with his father.

Mahan's engineering and the science of war course was considered the most important class military academy's cadets took. In his classes, Mahan assigned a heavy reading load, consisting entirely of his own writings. In two semesters he taught the cadets civil engineering, field fortifications, permanent fortifications, and the science of war. If the course description in the *Military Regulations* for that era is any guide, the cadets spent most of their time studying civil engineering, while field and permanent fortifications shared second place, and the science of war received the shortest shrift. All these topics were important for the cadets' future military careers, so they had to pay close attention throughout the year to be sure they took everything in.[65] Mahan tried to make sure that they did, and no doubt he intensified Halleck's determination to make the cadets take their work seriously. He demonstrated to Halleck that earnest seriousness was the key to life as a military intellectual.

By the time he began working for Mahan, Halleck had passed the course himself and knew the material his section of cadets was to recite before him. In addition, he supervised thirty or forty civilian workmen building a road on the academy grounds. He also had the responsibility of "drawing plans for models of Forts &c which are to be made during the coming winter for the instruction of the Cadets." He boarded at a nearby hotel, unhappy at the expense, but pleased with the "large parlour & 3 bedrooms which," he added parenthetically, "will be as much as one Bachelor will want." Wistfully, he added, "If I get married sometime or other I may get more rooms." He said nothing about any prospects for the altar, and the military academy was hardly a favorable place to be prospecting for a future wife.[66]

For the first time here, he mentioned the possibility that either he or his friend Theodore might eventually marry. In the past, the only time he had broached the subject was in disgust over how marriage caused his friends to cease communicating with him. This time, he seemed more willing to consider the institution—for his friend and obviously even for himself. "Our old friends are fast becoming husbands. Go thou and do likewise," he told Theodore, "that is when you get in *love*—not before. From my own observation," he waxed poetically, "I am fully convinced that Love-matches are the happiest. Pecuniary considerations should have but little to do with this matter. For myself, I am sure that I never have felt the 'volcanic earthquake bringing all consuming fire' of true love. But when it shall flame forth in my heart," he promised, "I intend to allow it room for all the bursts of splendor of which it may be capable." He insisted that there was only one true love for each person, "but for myself I see no immediate prospect of anything taking fire in me."[67]

Though no flame consumed him, Halleck obviously now looked more kindly on love's fire than he had done before. He was unable to attend the wedding of his beloved uncle David Wager because of examinations at West Point, and he regretted missing the event. When he met his new aunt, he expressed pleasure "with Uncle's choice and . . . [had] no doubt that she is a most worthy and amiable lady."[68] Marriage was becoming something to investigate rather than castigate.

His professional life as an engineer was very much to his liking. It was hard, but "my duties are agreeable," he said. "I am well pleased with the members of the corps & the nature of the duties that I shall probably remain in it." Halleck apparently found his engineering colleagues to be serious people, and he felt more comfortable with them than he had ever been with the other cadets. Yet he worried about his health. He told a brother he believed he had "much injured" his health "by neglecting exercise," though not indicating the nature of the problems. Other than four colds and some kind of joint pains, he did not seem to have any particular physical ailments during his youth, but psychological stresses certainly stemmed from his strained relations with his father.[69]

Halleck suffered a major loss when his Grandfather Wager died in the fall of 1840. He wrote his mother, "I hardly know how I may address you without exciting rather than pacifying your feelings, and increasing rather than assauging your grief." "May we be faithful to our duties as he was to his, that we may meet him in Heaven!" "How different Western is becoming to me!" he sighed. "The loved place of my birth is becoming the burial place of all that I hold dear."[70]

In fact, Halleck's entire life was in flux. He had graduated from the military academy with the cachet of a respected scholar, evidenced by his two assistant professorships. The grandfather who had saved him from farm life under a demanding father was gone, while the uncle who had served as his guardian and confidant now had a new wife. Only Theodore Miller still remained of his old friends, and he, too, would soon disappear from Halleck's life. Perhaps realizing that it would only be a matter of time before Theodore married, Halleck began talking of marriage for himself.

"As to politics," he wrote his close friend, "I do not take much interest in them. I remain as I ever hope to, a Democrat, but I am not well pleased with the new-fangled views and coat-turning operations of the Administrative Party." On the positive side, however, "I think that the Whigs have properly ensured their own defeat by the [presidential] nomination of Old Granny [William Henry] Harrison." He was wrong. As his personality grew ever more military, Halleck continued to be interested in the political arena, but he grew increasingly dissatisfied with what he saw there.

Most of all, however, Halleck began to realize that he had to rise to meet the future. "I sometimes look mournfully back on old times and on my own separation from old friends and associates, but I am beginning to learn wisdom." Then paraphrasing something he had read, he cited the words he said he tried to live by: "'Look not mournfully upon the past; it comes not back again. Improve the present; it is thine. Go forth to meet the shadowy future with a firm step and a manly heart.'"[71] These were apt words for the twenty-five-year old H. Wager Halleck. He was about to leave the cocoon of West Point for the larger army in the wider world. He would never return again. Until then, his life had been spent in the same region in the same state. That was all about to change. He took with him into the army the austere influence of his father, the warm intellectualism of Eliphalet Nott, and the demanding brilliance of Dennis Hart Mahan.

2

Army Engineer at Home and Abroad

On April 5, 1840, Second Lieutenant H. Wager Halleck formally signed himself out of the U.S. Military Academy.[1] Unlike his classmates, Halleck had remained at West Point as a faculty member, but that term of teaching was now over; and the elite Engineer Corps had other plans for him. Over the next six years, he worked in Washington on the national Engineer Board and in New York Harbor, where he planned and constructed a variety of military fortifications. He reported to Congress on the status of the nation's national defense and traveled to France to investigate the state-of-the-art fortifications there. Most important for his military career, he lectured at Boston's prestigious Lowell Institute and published a book that would make him one of the leading American military theorists of the pre–Civil War period. In those years, Halleck went from being a junior officer under the tutelage of West Point Professor Dennis Hart Mahan to becoming one of the most renowned officers in the U.S. Army. All the while, however, he continued to experience family problems and to exhibit the unbending personality that would become his trademark in the years ahead.

Halleck's first assignment after he left West Point sent him to the Board of Engineers in Washington, the central military bureaucracy for the Corps of Engineers and its national activities. It was an excellent assignment for a young officer because it gave him the opportunity to meet and work with the army's leaders, such as Commanding General Winfield Scott, and it gave him the chance to see the national government in action. He also found the city rich in opportunities for an active social life, and in contrast to his years at West Point, he had a wide group of friends.

He felt as though he was living again the good times he had enjoyed at Hudson and Fairfield. He lived in a house with six other men, most of them army officers. They facetiously called themselves the Grape Club, probably because they enjoyed drinking but also perhaps because they frequently loaded down their table with the bounty of "beautiful peaches, pears, melons, grapes, etc.," that they found available in the nearby market. The house was less than a mile from Halleck's office, and his work day followed a typical nineteenth-century pattern. He had breakfast at eight o'clock in the morning, then walked to his office where he remained on duty until three in the afternoon. After returning home, he had tea and dinner at the same time. At night, he visited acquaintances, finding "the people of Washington very sociable and agreeable." He became "charmed" with the family of former Secretary of State John Forsyth and even visited the White House, although he apparently never met President John Tyler. He hunted with friends and regularly toured the area on horseback, perhaps with another group he belonged to known as the Hope Club.[2]

Much of his social life in Washington revolved around the "many young ladies here of great beauty and accomplishment," the daughters of Washington society. He attended parties and dinners, these festivities normally not beginning until around nine at night. He and his friends would "chat and partake of the refreshments till one or two, and then retire." He also enjoyed horseback rides with his female acquaintances, expressing particular delight at his ride to the great falls of the Potomac River with the women of the John Forsyth family. On most days, his engineering duties prevented such extended trips, but he frequently took shorter excursions at four in the afternoon with a group of young women who, he found, could "generally ride very well." Keeping a horse in Washington proved expensive, but "if it were not for riding I am sure that I should never be able to perform the sedentary duties of an office," he said.[3]

He found another older man to admire in John Forsyth. A Georgia politician who had served both Andrew Jackson and Martin Van Buren as Secretary of State, Forsyth was the kind of warm, sophisticated man that Halleck's own father was not. Halleck respected the southerner for his oratory, but particularly believed that "in him were combined, in a most enviable degree, great talents, elegant persona and manners, a placid temper, and a warm generous heart." He "always greeted with a happy smile those who visited his house, making the most diffident person perfectly at their ease," something Halleck's father could never do. "I have there passed," Halleck said, "the happiest hours of my life." Cruelly, however, Forsyth died within the year, and Halleck lost a potentially valuable mentor. Had Forsyth lived and Halleck spent more time with him, perhaps the Georgian's open and congenial personality would have afforded Halleck greater social ease. Instead, Halleck found himself spending more of his time among other officious West Point–trained engineers who, like himself, had been professionalized by the irascible Dennis Hart Mahan and socialized by the military school's rigid code of conduct and ethics.[4]

Had Forsyth lived, Halleck might also have gained wider experience in politics, a passion that continued to consume him. As it was, Forsyth encouraged Halleck to study the law in his spare time, advice that Halleck followed. His army career precluded any participation in politics, but he nonetheless remained a staunch Democrat. He was most unhappy with the direction the party had taken during the Van Buren presidency and believed it was responsible for Van Buren's loss to the Whig candidate William Henry Harrison in the 1840 presidential election. He blamed Van Buren's defeat on his fellow New Yorker's embrace of "Loco Focoism," an unbending hard-money policy, and on his continued support of those shrill Jacksonian newsmen Francis Preston Blair and Amos Kendall. As far as Halleck was concerned, John Forsyth was "probably the most pure and able politician in the party" and should have been the party's presidential candidate instead of Van Buren. "These opinions," Halleck concluded, in a letter to Theodore Miller, "have been formed after due reflection upon what I here see and hear." And most of what he saw and heard was at Forsyth's welcoming home.[5]

Despite his continued separation from his father, Halleck maintained regular contact with the rest of his family in Westernville. In particular, he portrayed himself as the worldly wise elder brother to his siblings. He sent his brother Jabez, then studying at Fairfield Academy, a check for thirty dollars, apologizing for the smallness of the sum. "I am poor," he insisted, "but will always assist you to the best of my ability." His expenses in Washington, he lamented, "leave me almost empty handed." Despite such financial limitations, he made an agreement with Uncle David Wager, the relative who had helped save him from the farm, that he would repay any funds Wager made available to the other Halleck children. Halleck was deliberately adopting the role of family benefactor, mimicking Uncle David, in the hope that his own siblings might receive an education. He urged Joseph to go to school, warning him not to go to New York City and try to find a clerkship because "you write and spell too badly to keep any accounts." When Joseph did go to Fairfield, Halleck was pleased, but when the brother could not survive academically, Halleck reluctantly agreed on the suitability of his trying to find work. Having done all he could for Joseph, Halleck immediately switched his attention to helping another younger brother get an education. In all this activity, Halleck encouraged his brothers to follow his own example rather than their father's. Amazingly, however, he sighed, "a farmer's life is the one I should choose if I were to begin again"—no doubt, with a different father. Halleck clearly was both repelled by and compelled by his home.[6]

Halleck worked hard at the variety of engineering projects his army superiors assigned him. He completed his work competently and continued to learn about the practical side of his trade. His official correspondence, however, makes no mention of his labors. The few surviving letters from this period read like the one he wrote during the fall of 1840 to Colonel Joseph G. Totten, the army's chief engineer, blandly acknowledging that he had received a copy of a manual entitled *Totten on Mortar.*[7]

In the summer of 1841, Halleck's official life took a new direction when he was temporarily sent to New York Harbor. There he made detailed measurements and drawings of Fort Wood on Bedlow's Island (later the site of the Statue of Liberty). He had barely returned to Washington from this temporary duty when he was ordered back to New York permanently to serve under the harbor's chief engineer, Major John L. Smith. The major gave Halleck orders to repair the fort; and because Smith was more preoccupied with his health than with his duties, he allowed Halleck to become the driving force in the evaluation and improvement of Fort Wood as well as the other fortifications in the harbor.[8]

Halleck moved into temporary quarters on Bedlow's Island and went to work. The fort, which was key to the defense of New York Harbor, was "so completely delapidated [*sic*] as to be entirely defenceless," the result of what Halleck called "the ruinous policy our government pursues of postponing the construction of their principal defences till war is actually forced upon us and then hastily building miserable tumble-down concerns." He worked steadily on the project, and by the end of September 1843, the army's chief engineer could report to Congress that the sea wall and advanced battery, suitable for forty-five of the army's largest artillery pieces, was almost completely repaired. Halleck had done well. The next project was the fort itself.[9]

For most of the year, Halleck resided on this military island in the middle of the harbor, though he spent winters in Manhattan. He found he did not have the same ready access to the social life he had enjoyed in

Washington. Adding to his isolation was a long bout with influenza, the so-called Tyler grippe, named after the sitting president, John Tyler. For nearly two months he suffered with the malady, which caused a "severe inflammation" in his eyes, perhaps the result of streptococcus pneumonia. A pleasant aspect of his island life was his dog Little Toe, who apparently was a constant companion.[10]

The lack of social life, his chronic sickness, and his intellectual bent led Halleck to use the time when he was not supervising repairs to write articles, reports, and even books. All were related to his career, and all were both technical and extremely dry. It is a measure of Halleck's personality as well as his mind that he spent his days and nights composing such material. He compiled a review article of congressional reports that he published in the October 1840 *New York Review*. He included a call for a nationally trained militia, because he thought raising one was the only way to assure having a military force sufficient to counter all threats to American security. He also wrote a slim book called *Bitumen* that discussed the military use of asphalt. He countered a critique of the chief engineer's recently published report by presenting a blizzard of technical details. Finally, in a professional military journal, he published an annotated bibliography of foreign military magazines, urging other officers to translate articles contained in them for publication in English. Though his writings were pedestrian compilations rather than innovative analyses, he was becoming a published scholar. In 1843 he received an honorary M.A. degree from Union College and wrote a "Report on the Means of National Defence," which Congress published. That work brought national attention to this young army officer only five years out of West Point.[11]

Halleck did not say anything particularly new in his report to Congress, but he buttressed his points with a plethora of detail that lent his statements an authoritative tone. With Dennis Hart Mahan's influence clearly evident, he called for the nation to prepare for war during peacetime, not on the brink of conflict or during the war itself. "To postpone the making of military defences till such time as they are actually required in defence, is to waste the public money and endanger the public safety," he said. He called for increased military training, citing the present-day militia as undependable because it was poorly trained. The only valid permanent means of defense, he said, were the army, the navy, and fortifications. He pointed out that some argued that fortifications were unnecessary given the existence of a navy, but Halleck ridiculed this notion. No navy could defend the entire U.S. coastline, but strategically positioned fortifications could. Besides, he argued, a navy's job was to go on the offensive, not passively repel enemy attacks. As for those who insisted that a ship could overwhelm a fort, they were clearly misreading history. To make sure they understood this point, Halleck presented page upon page of historical examples to demonstrate just the opposite. Forts regularly repelled naval attacks and forced the attacking ships to withdraw. "But we will not further specify examples," he concluded, "the whole history of the wars of the French Revolution is one continued proof of the superiority of fortifications as a maritime frontier defence." He argued similarly for fortifications inland, a position supported by both historical facts and the recorded opinions of the best military men of modern ages.[12]

The only question, Halleck said, was *where* to build such essential inland fortifications. The obvious place in the United States, he said, was on the Lake Champlain line of attack from Canada into New York. The Engineering Board had already recommended one fort for that area, but he insisted that at least three lines of fortifications were necessary, once again citing earlier authorities. After his great victory at Austerlitz, Napoleon had called for the fortification of Paris. "It was in five short years afterwards that the bitter consequences of national vanity, which prevented his design from being carried into effect, were experienced by the Parisians." Paris was overrun, and, Halleck seemed to be warning, the United States would suffer the same fate if it too refused to fortify. In this report to Congress, therefore, Halleck justified the work he was doing on Fort Wood and that which his engineering colleagues were doing throughout the nation. He made use of the European military experience to support the existing American defense system of extensive fortifications all along the Atlantic coast, and to call for more of the same.[13]

In November 1843, with his appetite for more military information whetted by his scholarly efforts and also in hopes of ridding himself of the flulike symptoms that continued to plague him, Halleck decided to apply for overseas duty in France, thus retracing the steps of his teacher Mahan. He wanted to see for himself, as Mahan had, how the ~~French,~~ the leaders in fortifications and military writing, did it. He repeatedly wrote to Chief of Engineers Joseph G. Totten asking for a leave of absence. To his frustration, he received no response. He sent a fourth inquiry saying that a leave was "a matter of great importance" to him, and that he was "greatly disappointed in receiving no answer." Before that complaining letter reached Washington, however, he received authorization to travel to Europe immediately. The leave authorized him to remain abroad until spring.[14]

In the nineteenth century, an overseas tour was considered good for one's health and an advantage for an ambitious officer. From 1815 until the beginning of the Civil War, there were one hundred and fifty foreign military missions, trips by individual officers and groups traveling together. Some of these missions were official—that is they were part of an officer's duty—while others, like Halleck's, were undertaken on the officer's own time during a leave of absence.[15] Despite Halleck's rising military reputation, the army did not consider his trip important enough to make it an official observer mission. He had to travel to Europe on his own.

His relationship with Dennis Hart Mahan certainly influenced his decision to go overseas. As a young officer, Mahan had been an official observer in France between 1827 and 1830. He had toured the nation, carefully observing every civil and engineering project he could find. He had even enrolled in the French military school for engineers at Metz, all the while imbibing French theory and practice and developing what his biographer calls "his life-long Gallic bias." He infused all his West Point courses with the French way of doing things. And no doubt Halleck had heard even more glowing tales about France while he served under Mahan on the West Point faculty. It is no surprise, therefore, that Halleck was determined to visit France and gain all the advantages of first-hand contact with the nation that his major professor said was home to the leading military thinkers of the age.[16]

The thirty-year-old Halleck bid adieu to New York Harbor on November 24, 1843, sailing past Bedlow's Island and his own repair work at Fort Wood. Ocean travel was never easy during the nineteenth century. Ships went down more often than passengers cared to believe, and a trip between August and March was particularly hazardous. "The North Atlantic is the earth's most dangerous ocean," one writer has correctly asserted, "often storm-tossed and bitterly cold." Even if no iceberg damaged a wooden hull, violent seasickness was a terrible problem for most ocean travelers. Crowded accommodations could also make life miserable, and the varying quality of food added to the discomfort. Yet despite the danger and unpleasantness, by the 1840s Europe was luring some three hundred Americans to its shores every month.[17] Halleck excitedly joined the exodus.

His voyage, happily, was not dangerous; indeed, it was professionally and personally fulfilling. He had the good fortune to spend time with a fellow passenger, General Henri Gratien Bertrand, who was a famous military engineer and one of Napoleon's generals. Bertrand took such a liking to the young American that when they arrived in France, he introduced

Halleck to Marshall Soult, war secretary for King Louis Philippe. Soult gave Halleck "full authority to examine everything of a military character in France." Through Bertrand, Halleck also received permission to visit French military schools, and he immediately planned a visit to Metz, the school Mahan had attended, and after that he planned to tour the fortifications in southern France. Because his time was short, however, he did not think he would be able to see the vast entrenchments on the German frontier.[18]

His time in Paris proved to be especially exciting. Because of the entrée into French society Bertrand provided, Halleck was presented to King Louis Philippe and his queen, both of whom he found to be "old, but very fine looking." The king spoke English, but the queen did not, so Halleck had to use the French he had learned in college and at West Point to carry on a conversation with her. He thought he had managed well enough and noted that the French were much more polite about foreigners mangling their language than Americans were about the French fracturing English. He guiltily recalled how his family had laughed at some French people who had purchased land near them in Westernville. He also noted the profusion of flowers in Paris. The market, he said, had "more than a thousand pots of most beautiful flowers exposed for sale at the same time." Somewhere else, perhaps nearby, he purchased a candelabra and an ornate clock for his family. He also went to the debtors' prison to visit Chaplain Thomas Warner, a former West Point faculty member incarcerated there because of a disagreement with a wealthy military man in Paris.[19]

Nevertheless, Halleck spent most of his time in France on military business. Through his French contacts, he was allowed to study the fortifications defending Paris, finding "French Engineer officers exceedingly polite on all occasions, making up," he pointedly told his superior back in Washington, "by their kind attentions, for the want of letters which *might* have been afforded me by our government." He feared that his lack of formal letters of introduction might yet prove to be a problem when his French patron, General Bertrand, died suddenly. He was now on his own in France and resented his own government's lack of support.[20]

All went well on his military tour, but the inefficiency of the U.S. army bureaucracy frustrated him. He visited military schools and key fortifications, receiving from French officers "several new Lithographic pamphlets on the different branches of the profession, and also maps, plans, & buildings &c which have been prepared exclusively for the corps & consequently are not for sale." He even reached the German frontier but had to rush back to England to catch his ship back to the United States. To his dismay, when he arrived in England he found that his ship, the *Great Western,* was out of service, so he had to wait ten days for another vessel. Even more frustrating was his discovery when he returned to duty in New York Harbor that, without his knowledge, his leave had been extended by two months to July 1. He could have stayed in France longer and done a more thorough job of inspecting the fortifications on both sides of the French-German border. The army's slipshod communication and its mishandling of his leave angered him. He pointed out that the extension had not been sent from Washington to Europe until April 1. "Of course it could not have reached Paris previous to my leaving that place for the United States in accordance with former instructions from the Engineer Department," he said. "I am much gratified at the kindness of the Department in its unsolicited extension of my leave of absence," he said with no small hint of sarcasm, "although its action was too late to be of any use to me." And that was doubly bad, he concluded, because he had been near some key fortifications with letters of introduction from Minister of War Soult and a leading general. The disorganization at Engineer Corps headquarters, as much as the loss of time in Europe, irritated Halleck.[21]

Despite his annoyance at the unnecessary brevity of his visit to France, he felt sure he had brought back significant information for the American army. He had obtained "detailed drawings of the new system of barracks for infantry and cavalry; the general plans and much detailed information respecting the new defences of Paris and . . . all necessary information and documents respecting the details of organization, government, and instruction in the several military schools of France." And, he added happily, the trip "entirely restored my health."[22]

The chief engineer agreed that Halleck had indeed collected worthwhile information. In mid-1845, Totten ordered him to send a detailed outline of "French regulations for the construction, repairs and preservation of Barracks." This material was hardly as significant as that resulting from the 1840 board of officers' visit to France, which caused major modifications in American artillery practice, but, for the engineers, Halleck provided important data.[23] Halleck was thankful enough to send his acquaintances in the French army copies of several of Dennis Hart Mahan's engineering manuals, demonstrating yet again his old professor's influence on him.

By May 1844, Halleck was back in his accommodations on Bedlow's Island, and presumably Little Toe was happy to see him, but he was not content to be back. After the novelty of the ocean crossing, the chance to meet a legendary general and a reigning monarch, and the opportunity to travel throughout France, Halleck's daily work at Fort Wood and similar activities on Staten Island and Governor's Island were mundane. He was back to scrawling receipts for circulars and manuals, estimating costs of repairs, recommending the purchase of a new crane, and testing masonry strength. When his commanding officer took leave, he became interim commander, and this temporary position increased the paperwork on his desk. The numbing bureaucracy he faced is evident in one of the letters he wrote to the chief engineer: "I have to acknowledge the receipt of Engineer Order No. 3, inviting attention to Paragraph 1292 of Army Regulations, and expressing a hope 'that no officer of the Corps of Engineers will show himself less mindful or less observant than his brother officers of other corps of any Regulation however unimportant it may by some be deemed which has been regularly published for the government of the Army.'" In short, Halleck acknowledged an order ordering him to obey orders. His daily life could not have been duller.[24]

Fortunately, he had diversions. His proximity to New York allowed him to turn his attention regularly to considerations of the fairer sex, and in the process he showed a seldom-seen sense of wit. He sent updates on the New York social scene to George Washington Cullum, an army officer he had grown close to in New York and who would remain a friend for the rest of his life. Halleck reported to Cullum, then stationed elsewhere, that he had not seen "Our New York Sweethearts" for several weeks because bad weather had kept him from reaching the city. Fortunately, he said, his old West Point roommate and native New Yorker Schuyler Hamilton kept him informed of their activities. He happily related to Cullum how, at a party during his last visit to the city, he had successfully teased a fellow officer, Alexander J. Swift, about Swift's pursuit of a young woman named Wolfe, a woman Cullum also admired. Halleck pointed out that "the [courting] race was not always to the *Swift*," jokingly warning the officer that Cullum had said "that he was on the *Wolfe* track." "Seventeen devils with a regular broadside could not have produced more consternation!" Halleck laughingly reported. "Swift looked for a knothole . . . and I, the cause of all the disturbance, was the only one who remained cool."

Then Halleck turned his humor on Cullum. "How is that about your falling over board and having to be rolled on a beer-barrel in the Sutler's Shop! If I ever get drowned in that way I shall most obstinately refuse to be resuscitated on a *beer-barrel*. The only proper method of restoring a drowned person is to rub his belly with a champaign bottle—of course the bottle should be a full one."[25]

Another example of Halleck's levity even when aimed at himself was his playful reference to himself as Tustennuggee. In Florida during the 1840s, an Indian leader by the name of Halleck Tustennuggee had the reputation of displaying a superior intellect and pleasant disposition, but also a merciless streak. He killed his own sister over a disagreement and once bit off a rival's ear. Halleck jokingly signed a number of his letters to Cullum "Tustennuggee," and a friend later referred to Halleck's son as the "Young Tustennuggee." Clearly Halleck enjoyed bantering with his friends, but his official correspondence demonstrates that he was growing increasingly irritated with his job despite his promotion to first lieutenant on January 1, 1845. Halleck was never one to suffer fools gladly, and he grew upset when appropriations for repair work on a fort were sent to him when he believed they should have been sent to his commanding officer. "It is difficult to understand," he lectured the chief engineer, "why the money was asked for in *my name* after the receipts had been passed in the name of Major Smith and especially after I had requested Capt. Dutton not to use my name in any estimates for funds." When the chief engineer spoke about the corps establishing a purchasing office "through which the corps are to be *obliged* to make any purchases," Halleck responded sharply: "I think the project would be objectionable, and I should be unwilling to be in any way connected with it."[26] Halleck was clearly upset at the lack of precision in Engineer Corps procedures, even when the matter in question was minor.

Almost every official letter demonstrated Halleck's growing impatience with army bureaucracy. A more careful reading of this correspondence, however, shows that it was not bureaucracy per se he objected to but inefficiency. He demanded that the Engineer Corps do its job correctly, so he would know exactly where he stood on every issue. Nothing short of such perfection was acceptable. Halleck was becoming a demanding bureaucrat, and his insistence on procedural precision was coming to dominate his personality. The tension between his father's and Mahan's influence and that of Eliphalet Nott and John Forsyth seemed to be tilting toward the former.

Before he could push his perfectionist demands too far, however, he had more good fortune in his professional life. He published another article, this time unsigned, not surprisingly trumpeting the predominance of engineers in Napoleon's army. More important, he also received an invitation to give a series of lectures at the Lowell Institute in Boston. On November 29, 1845, the Corps of Engineers granted him a thirty-day leave, and he moved into the U.S. Hotel in Boston to prepare for his important public appearances.[27]

The Lowell Institute was an outgrowth of a New England phenomenon:

the popular public lecture.[28] Organizations and individuals in the region had long presented lectures in all kinds of venues, on all kinds of topics, to a variety of audiences. The person who took this phenomenon to a new level, however, was John Lowell, Jr. Having entered Harvard at the age of thirteen, where he studied under the famous orator Edward Everett, he became a bank director by the age of twenty-three. He was also treasurer of several cotton mills and a leading member of the Harvard Corporation, the governing body of the university. Drawing on these experiences, Lowell established the Lowell Institute to bring organization and efficiency to the New England lecture. His aim was to establish a regular lecture series that would provide occasions for the best minds of the age to speak on important topics before a public audience of average citizens desiring to learn.

When H. Wager Halleck gave his twelve lectures on "the Military Art" in December 1845, the institute was only in its sixth year of operation, but it had already hosted a distinguished group of lecturers. Edward Everett had given an inaugural talk, and later speakers, each on stage twelve times, included Yale University's Benjamin Silliman, the founder of the *American Journal of Science,* lecturing on geology; the Reverend John G. Palfrey, Unitarian minister, Harvard professor, and editor of the *North American Review,* speaking on Christianity; professor and later Harvard president Jared Sparks, talking about American history; and Harvard professor and later leading American Darwinian Asa Gray, discussing biology. Halleck's invitation was thus a recognition of his standing as one of America's leading scholars.

Like all the lecturers, Halleck was treated royally. In addition to being housed in one of Boston's leading hotels, he was also wined and dined on Beacon Hill and in Cambridge. The remuneration was excellent. Halleck received a thousand dollars for his twelve presentations, an amount that exceeded the annual salary of most college professors.[29]

Early on, Lowell established precise rules for the lecturer and the audiences, mostly male. The lectures were held in the Odeon Theater, a facility with excellent acoustics and a seating capacity of two thousand. Lowell and his curator, the efficient Dr. Benjamin E. Cotting, advertised the lectures widely to ensure a packed house. Many of the lectures were oversold; often eight to ten thousand people sought seats and, as a result, tickets were sold by lottery. There was never an introduction; the lecturer simply walked on stage, told the audience who he was, and began speaking. The time limit was one hour. The moment a lecturer began his oration, all the theater doors were closed and they were not opened until the speech was over. The only time the audience applauded was at the beginning and at the end. Speakers frequently commented on the intelligence of the audience and thus responded with presentations of high quality. When Bostonians began expressing interest in owning printed copies of these addresses, Lowell paid for their publication.

The lecturers considered a Lowell invitation to be an honor. Benjamin Silliman viewed his appearances on the institute's stage as the high point of his distinguished career, "both as regards my reputation and my pecuniary resources," he said. Halleck shared this enthusiasm. After he completed his stint in Boston and returned to New York City, he received a letter from Cotting that contained Lowell's payment for all expenses, ("*sans hesitation*," as Halleck put it), and "a check for a clean thousand" besides. Beyond that, Halleck happily noted, Cotting told him that Lowell "seemed well satisfied with my *performance* on the Lowell stage."[30]

Halleck's good fortune did not end there. Whether through Lowell's sponsorship or on Halleck's own initiative, in 1846 the important New York publishing house of D. Appleton and Company published Halleck's combined lectures in book form, under the grandiose title: *Elements of Military Art and Science; or, Course of Instruction in Strategy, Fortification, Tactics of Battles &c; Embracing the Duties of Staff, Infantry, Cavalry, Artillery, and Engineers. Adapted to the Use of Volunteers and Militia.* The book came to be known briefly as *Elements of Military Art and Science* and was essentially a compilation of other authors' writings. In his preface, Halleck stated that "no pretension is made to originality in any part of the work"; it basically consisted of "hastily thrown together . . . lectures" for the Lowell Institute, previous publications including the congressional report, and "well established military principles." This book demonstrated again that "H. Wager Halleck, A.M., Lieut. Of Engineers, U.S. Army," as the book's title page identified him, was one of the army's most famous officers. The book became must reading for all interested in continuing the education they had received at West Point. It long remained the major American publication on military theory.

In an appropriate coincidence, Dennis Hart Mahan published his own book the following year and it too had a long title, even longer than Halleck's but came to be known simply as *Out-Post*,[31] Mahan's and Halleck's books were not really in competition, although both men in their prefaces said they had published them in response to the needs of militia officers. Mahan concentrated on tactics and fortifications and did not even have a chapter on strategy, while Halleck placed his emphasis on broad military topics such as strategy.[32] There were similarities in their thought, of course, for both men had been influenced by European thinkers. And Mahan of course had also directly influenced Halleck, with the latter emphasizing the importance of fortifications in strategic thought. He said, for example, that "all military writers agree that fortifications have heretofore exerted a great and frequently a decisive influence on the operations of a war." Halleck, indeed, specifically praised Mahan's 1836 book, *Field Fortifications*.

Both Mahan and Halleck owed an enormous intellectual debt to Antoine Henri Jomini, the Swiss general on Napoleon's staff and the leading nineteenth-century military theorist before the Civil War. Jomini had written numerous books, the most famous being his last, *Précis de l'art de la guerre* (1838). In *Précis*, Jomini explained Napoleonic strategy by presenting several rules of war that, he argued, would never change no matter who the commanders were or what the battlefield conditions were. According to Jomini, these strategic rules required a commander to send masses of his troops into the decisive area of a theater of war and to attack the enemy's communications while protecting his own communications; he was to maneuver to cause masses of his troops to fall upon smaller numbers of the enemy's troops; he should maneuver tactically so as to place his forces at "the decisive point of the field of the battle, or upon that part of the hostile line which it would be important to overwhelm"; and finally, he should be sure to engage his troops simultaneously. It was essential, Jomini held, for a commander to use interior lines so that he could most efficiently concentrate his army against separated enemy forces.[33]

An earlier book of Jomini's, published in 1806 and entitled *Traité des grande operations militaires,* influenced Halleck more than the *Précis*. When he later translated Jomini's four-volume life of Napoleon, Halleck concluded that the *Traité* was "the most important of all his [Jomini's] works, as it embodies the main principles of the military art, with numerous illustrations drawn from the campaigns of the great captains of different ages."[34] The *Traité* had originally analyzed Frederick the Great and his military activities during the Seven Years' War, but later Jomini added a discussion of Napoleon's activities. In short, this book expressed the eighteenth-century military thinking of Frederick more than it did that of Napoleon. Accordingly, the book's emphasis is on a united army attacking as a whole rather than on the Napoleonic concept of concentration of separated units in the face of the enemy. Consequently, what Halleck learned from Jomini included lessons from an earlier time, too.

There is no doubt that Jomini significantly influenced Halleck's thought and writings. Yet so did many others, including of course Mahan, the other European writers Halleck read, and the French officers he met during his tour. But paramount in shaping his writings were Halleck's own experiences in preparing and repairing fortifications. Though his book was a compilation of writings by a variety of European military thinkers, it was Halleck who selected the works to include and Halleck who interpreted those works. Since the book was readily available in English, it was probably even more influential on American army officers than were Jomini's works, which long remained untranslated. It became a essential reading for military men.[35]

Halleck's *Elements of Military Art and Science* consists of fifteen chapters, most of which discuss military matters in the broadest terms. The first chapter, for example, is a defense of warfare itself against those who said that religion condemned it. "Few events rouse and elevate the patriotism and public spirit of a nation so much as a just and patriotic war," Halleck argued. "It raises the tone of public morality, and destroys the sordid selfishness and degrading submissiveness which so often result from a long-protracted peace."[36] Having thus established that war is good, Halleck proceeded to discuss, in detail, how to fight it. He wrote about strategy, the importance of fortifications, logistics, tactics, military policy, seacoast and northern frontier defense, permanent fortifications, field engineering, military education in Europe and the United States, and he even included four chapters on army organization.

Throughout these chapters, Halleck's positions—one might argue his prejudices—are clear. He believed in a professional military, castigating the poorly trained militia in general and amateur officers in particular. Like Mahan, he believed the militia was effective only behind fortifications. It was useless in the open field because it had not been properly drilled for combat. He insisted that political favoritism in the administration of an army led only to disaster. Military schools such as West Point were absolutely necessary to produce the kind of educated professional officer who could fight wars most successfully. The Engineer Corps was the heart of any army because fortifications were major determinants of battle results, and excellent field engineering allowed an army to maneuver most efficiently. The French were the leading military thinkers of the day, and they and other European writers had to be studied and emulated. "War is not as some seem to suppose," he wrote, "a mere game of chance. Its principles constitute one of the most intricate of modern sciences; and the general who understands the art of rightly applying its rules, and possesses the means of carrying out its precepts, may be morally certain of success."[37]

The two chapters that students of war and later historians have particularly studied in order to understand Halleck's thinking are Chapter 2, "Strategy," and Chapter 5, "Tactics." In these two sections, Halleck discusses how all the other things analyzed in his book come together to produce victory.

On strategy, Halleck stated that "the first and most important rule in offensive war is, to keep your forces as much concentrated as possible." But, he added a bit later, "This rule does not require that *all the army should occupy the same position.*" All elements of the army should, however, be close enough to support one another. The next important rule, he said, was for a commander to keep an army "fully employed." "Your movements must be more rapid than his. Give him time to *breathe,* and above all, give him time to *rest,* and your project is blasted." "As a general rule," he continued, *a line of operations should be directed upon the centre, or one of the extremities of the enemy's line of defence.*" Only in the most unusual circumstances was an attack possible on the middle and flank at the same time.[38]

Halleck particularly warned against carelessly advancing against and gaining the rear of the enemy army because while this might allow a commanding officer to threaten his opponent's communications, it might also end up endangering his own. An army had to move in such a way as to "preserve its communications and be able to reach its base." Flanking movements were fine, but "*as a general rule,* a central direction will lead to more important results." Interior lines "have almost invariably led to success," he said. And, "if the field of battle be properly chosen, success will be decisive."[39]

When it came to tactics, Halleck again emphasized the offensive because "the attacking force has a moral superiority over the defensive." He presented twelve orders of battle, or "particular disposition[s] given to the troops for a determined manoeuvre on the field of battle," that he had culled from the writings of European thinkers, especially Jomini. He discussed how to use the infantry, artillery, cavalry, and engineers in battle, emphasizing that "all offensive operations on the field of battle require *mobility, solidity, and impulsion;* while, on the other hand, all defensive operations should combine *solidity* with *the greatest amount of fire.*" Like Jomini and Mahan, Halleck believed a commanding officer on the defensive should go on the offensive as quickly as he could, but he also insisted, as a modern historian has noted, that "inside an enemy's territory celerity of movement is less important than concentration, than keeping one's own force united and well in hand against surprise." Jomini, Mahan, and Halleck all advocated tightly packed rather than loose formations for the attack.[40] Halleck's one field command during the Civil War, the Corinth campaign of 1862, would exemplify these concepts exactly, especially his emphasis on concentration over speed of movement.

Though he frequently agreed with Jomini and Mahan, Halleck's theories actually stood between those of the two men. He "was an outspoken champion of Jomini's strategic emphasis on the direct concentrated approach," but he also "accepted Mahan's dictum that the natural field of battle for militia was from behind a breastwork." He emphasized both the concentrated advance of Jomini and Mahan's emphasis on fortifications. By reading Halleck, therefore, an aspiring military officer was able to get an excellent distillation of contemporary military thinking. As two modern historians separately put it, "Halleck's *Elements* may be taken as a broad but basic treatment of the art of war as understood in America in 1846." He "made an exhaustive and imaginative attempt to adapt European principles to the American scene." Or to put it even more broadly as another twentieth-century study does: "Mahan and Halleck initiated American strategic studies and consciously promoted professionalism, arguing that military science was a specialized body of knowledge understandable only through intense study, especially of military history."[41]

Once his book was published, Halleck tried to make sure that people bought it. He cleverly sent a free copy to his West Point classmate Isaac I. Stevens, then stationed as an army engineer in Maine, hoping that Stevens would recommend it to others. Halleck worried that unless his friends bought copies the publisher would not even meet the printing costs. Stevens should notice, Halleck said, that the book called for the army to have more engineers, and he hoped that this call would elicit a favorable response from the authorities. And, of course, he hoped such advocacy would convince his fellow engineers to purchase and publicize the book. In a letter to the chief engineer, he called for the Corps of Engineers to put more emphasis on having its officers write learned articles, thus emulating his example. He did not want them to have to pay for such publication out of their meager stipend, however. "Deduct[ing] $50 per annum from the expense of clothing might make of some of us, veritable *sans culottes*," he said.[42]

Although Halleck was gaining important attention for his theories of war, he was infuriated that his position as an engineer officer might deny him the opportunity to practice his profession in combat. The war with Mexico had begun in 1846, and Halleck expressed his growing anger and that of other engineers that Colonel Totten, the chief engineer, was keeping them working on fortifications instead of allowing more of them to participate in the war against Mexico. His low tolerance for views with which he disagreed was evident in his letters. "This is a most suicidal policy," Halleck complained, "calculated to injure us individually and to ruin the reputation of the corps." "In all matters of *policy*," he said, "the colonel is but a child—the weakest men in the army outwit him." Halleck had no respect for Totten; unlike paternal authorities such as Mahan, Forsyth, or Eliphalet Nott, Totten was a "child."[43]

Then, without warning, Halleck received orders to accompany an expedition traveling to the Pacific Coast, to one of the theaters of the already raging Mexican War. He realized that this was not where the action was, but at least the orders enabled him to leave New York, where he had nothing to look forward to but more fortification building and paper shuffling. All he knew about his assignment in California was that it would include "surveying and examining the country," and that he would probably be gone for two years. There were to be six officers and somewhere between a hundred and two hundred men on the expedition, and this number gave him hope for some kind of military action. He carefully gathered the engineering equipment he would need in California. Perhaps not to worry his mother, he said nothing about the war in a letter home. "The country is described as being very delightful, and I have no doubt we shall have a pleasant time," he wrote her.[44]

H. Wager Halleck the renowned engineer could not have imagined what faced him in California. Like all career officers, he hoped for the glory of war, and was clearly bored with having to spend time on Bedlow's Island completing routine matters or reading books such as Thomas Carlyle's *Cromwell,* which he found "well calculated to put a man to sleep . . . an excellent substitute for opium."[45] The future would see him garner new laurels, but these were to come not primarily from battle, but from that which he said he disliked the most—bureaucracy and paper shuffling. Like Mahan, Jomini, and his previous civilian professors, Halleck gained fame behind a desk rather than through the wielding of a sword or musket. All the while, he demonstrated an increasingly rigorous perfectionism. Moreover, his offhand reference to opium might have been just another example of his humor, or it might have been an indication of something more serious.

3

War and Peace in California

As important as Halleck's time in France and his lecture series in Boston were to his professional development, they could not rival his voyage to the Pacific Coast and participation in the Mexican War. A descendant of New York pioneer stock, Halleck would become a Californian and a founding father of that state. And eventually he would become one of the wealthiest and most influential attorneys on the Pacific Coast. While he was there, his character and personality would solidify into the harsh and demanding persona that marked his adult years.

All this lay before him as he stood on the site of one of his engineering projects, Fort Columbus on Governor's Island, preparing to board the U.S. Navy ship the *Lexington*. Originally built as a sloop of war, this vessel was now serving as a supply ship, with only six guns and a crew of thirty-five sailors. On board for the voyage to California was Company F of the Third U.S. Artillery Regiment, consisting of 113 men and 5 officers, including two who later became famous Civil War leaders: William T. Sherman and E. O. C. Ord. Ord's brother, the civilian physician Dr. James L. Ord, and Halleck completed the list of passengers. On July 14, 1846, the *Lexington* slipped out of New York Harbor and set sail. The mission of the soldiers was to capture Monterey or San Francisco from the Mexicans, depending on circumstances. While aboard the ship, the orders read, the army men were "*passengers* not *marines*," but should the ship be attacked, they were "to show themselves at least as efficient as any equal number of marines whatsoever." Though as an engineer, Halleck was not part of the artillery company, he was attached to it, so he had to be pleased by the uncompromising sternness of Commanding General Winfield Scott's order. He might finally get to see combat.[1]

The *Lexington* was all that these men were to know for most of the next six months, and it was not large —127 feet from stem to stern and 34 feet, 7 inches across. There were three decks on the ship: the upper, or spar, deck where the guns were located and the sailors did their work, the berth deck where everyone slept, and well below the water line the cargo hold. Halleck shared accommodations with the five other army and navy officers, the ship's captain having his own cabin. The officers' wardroom was about 15 feet wide, with eight tiny rooms off to both sides, each containing minimal sleeping space for two officers. In pleasant weather, the officers usually went up to the deck above. When the weather turned foul, however, they sat around the mess table in the wardroom talking, reading, playing cards, and entertaining themselves any way they could. There they shared their two meals a day and enjoyed the company of the ship's cat.[2]

Halleck spent as much time as he could with his nose buried in a book. Like Sherman, who also did a lot of reading, Halleck devoured every book he could find on the ship, regardless of its topic or worth. He read, for example, *American Military Laws* and reveled in dissecting it in a letter to a friend, especially disdaining the section that said that the Engineer Corps was "nothing more than a body of scientific architects." At one point, Halleck became so desperate for reading material that he read his own book, and to his horror found that his publisher had not made the corrections he had noted on the galleys. He also spent a great deal of time translating Jomini's four-volume life of Napoleon. Sherman remembered with awe how persistent Halleck was in working on that task regardless of bad weather. "When the sea was high & ship rolling, the sky darkened so that daylight did not reach his state room, he stood on a stool, his book and candle on the upper berth and a bed strap round his middle secured to the frame to support him in the wild tossing of the ship."[3]

Halleck hated the whole shipboard experience. "I am heartily tired of the sea," he wrote ten weeks into the voyage. "I think seriously of testing the constitutional right of the Secty of War to send a *soldier* to sea. I never enlisted as a sailor." He particularly missed New York, or more accurately, the women there. He told his friend George Cullum: "I shall expect to be particularly remembered by you to 'Beach St.' and 'University Place,' not forgetting our little friend in Bond St." He especially hoped for "a smile just now from somewhere about 10th St." And to make sure that Cullum looked out for his romantic interests, Halleck warned him: "I have only to caution you in visiting 'them diggins,' that in saying one good word for me you don't put in two or three for yourself. If you should, when I return from California burnt brandy wont save you!"[4]

When the ship was within 150 miles of Cape Horn, a monstrous storm roared in. "The waves rolled up like mountains," Halleck wrote. "The ship staggered and plunged and rolled tremendously; the masts and bulkheads creaked fearfully, while the heavy timbers cracked and groaned as if tasked to the very utmost of their strength. Occasionally the seas broke heavily on the ship's bow, sounding like great sledge hammers, and making her tremble from stem to stern." For twenty-six days, the *Lexington* battled the elements, "vainly endeavouring to round that dreaded promentory," Halleck said. Snow fell, "making everything cold, damp, and uncomfortable." The voyagers' hands and feet swelled and everyone "suffered very much from the cold."[5]

The most pleasant parts of the trip were the stops in South American ports, Rio de Janeiro on the Atlantic and Valparaiso on the Pacific. After months on the ocean, the *Lexington*'s soldiers were ecstatic to arrive in Rio, reacting like a young naval officer on another ship. "Rio! Rio! At last at Rio. . . . Ho! What a nice place is land—sound good earth I mean—with lots of big houses, and bright cheerfull, strange faces moving about—with good solid tables and chairs, when one may put down his glass and seat himself, without fear of plunging a summersault [*sic*] backwards, and the glass getting away from reach."[6]

Though happy to be on land, Halleck viewed Rio with a professional eye. He analyzed the fortifications on the way into port and in the harbor itself. He found them all "very poorly constructed, the walls are much delapidated and the parapets (nearly all of masonry) thin and low, only partially covering the gunners." Halleck the military engineer saw the great city as a defense site to be analyzed rather than a place to be enjoyed.[7]

When the ship anchored for a week, however, Halleck did join his officer friends in exploring the city's attractions. He relished the food after months of surviving on the ship's boring fare. He visited the churches and museums, viewed the fine residences, and marveled at the variety of people on the city's crowded streets. But true to character, he gave special attention to one of its engineering marvels. Having climbed up the area's highest mountain with Sherman as his companion, Halleck enjoyed the view, but spent more time analyzing the aqueduct that supplied the city's drinking water. Like the fortifications, the aqueduct might teach Halleck lessons useful for his military career. Just as on the ship he read and translated while others were thinking of ways to entertain themselves, in port he could not seem to take himself away from his work. He might dream about New York women, but he showed little interest in those in Rio. Continuing to learn his trade was more important to him than enjoying the new urban sights and the exotic females.[8]

During the course of their meanderings, Halleck and Sherman bumped into several Americans, including the U.S. minister to Brazil, Henry A. Wise. After a brief introduction, the diplomat invited the two officers to the legation for dinner. After seating them on his veranda, he unexpectedly disappeared, returning soon to apologize for leaving them alone and apologizing even more for the absence of his wife. Dinner was then served, and afterward the men returned to the veranda for cigars and coffee. There they met a Brazilian doctor who diverted them with stories told in broken English. The physician seemed in no hurry to leave, but Halleck and Sherman did not want to overstay their welcome. They profusely thanked their host and departed.

It was only years later that Sherman learned more about that evening, although Halleck apparently never did. The reason the host was so apologetic, his wife never made her appearance, and the doctor seemed in no hurry to leave was that Mrs. Wise was in labor, and the doctor was waiting to make the delivery. Less than fifteen years later, Wise was to become a Confederate general, and the erstwhile young lieutenants served as leaders of the opposing Union Army.[9]

On the way to Valparaiso, the ship experienced the terrible month-long storm that had Halleck, Sherman, and everyone else aboard worrying that the ship might not survive the pounding seas. The *Lexington* finally made the turn around Cape Horn into the Pacific and within a month was sailing into the harbor at Valparaiso, Chile, on November 23, 1846. Halleck and the other officers carefully studied the city as they sailed in and quickly compared it unfavorably to Rio.[10]

Halleck immediately announced his plans to go to Santiago, the nation's capital, located about a hundred miles inland, in order to visit the Chilean national military academy. He and E. O. C. Ord retained a *bilache,* ten horses that were, on the fly, interchangeably hooked and unhooked to the wagon. They also hired three "peons" to control the entire operation. It took less than twelve hours to cover the hundred miles between the two cities because of this efficient transportation system. "The Chileans drive with frightful velocity both up hill and down," Halleck marveled, "changing their horses without even breaking the gallop."

He and Ord stayed in Santiago for several days. Halleck visited the country's military academy and took detailed notes on everything he saw.

"In its arrangements and course of instruction," he believed, "it redounds greatly to the credit of the Chilean government." He noted that, unlike West Point, it taught both commissioned and noncommissioned officers. A cadet might reside there from three to seven years, with the engineers, much to Halleck's satisfaction, remaining the longest time. Each day, the morning "is devoted to theoretical studies and recitations, and the afternoon, to drills and practical operations," he said. Each of the cadets had a private room, again in contrast to West Point, and building ventilation was much better in Santiago as well. Halleck seemed to feel his alma mater could learn lessons from this Chilean institution.[11]

With everyone back on board and all the supplies loaded, the *Lexington* put to sea for the final leg of its trip to California. A nautical error sent the ship forty miles past Monterey, but 57 days out of Valparaiso, on January 26, 1847, a cool fog-filled day, the ship glided into Monterey harbor. Everyone on board strained to get a glimpse of California. The travelers saw a circular harbor with wooded hills reaching up into the interior, and they could barely make out a few adobe buildings near the landing. California, the land they had been sailing toward for the past 198 days, did not look like much upon first sight.[12]

Following orders, Halleck immediately reported his arrival to the chief engineer in Washington. He was happy to find two U.S. Navy ships, the *Independence* and the *Dale,* already in port. "We hear various rumors of hostilities further south," he said, "but the reports are so contradictory that I do not deem them worth communicating." "Of what we are to do here I am perfectly ignorant," he continued sourly. He reported that the engineering equipment he had received in New York had been so badly packed that it was "considerably injured." Even the paper that had been supplied was of inferior quality. Halleck was unhappy about where he was, about his lack of definitive orders, and about the damage to equipment he would need to accomplish any necessary engineering work.[13]

California had only recently come under American army and navy control, and the two services and elements among each were battling over who was in charge. The army general Stephen W. Kearny was in disagreement with the navy admiral Robert E. Stockton and the famous army explorer John C. Frémont. Eventually orders would arrive from Washington to settle the matter, but when Halleck and his ship arrived, there was much tension and uncertainty. Halleck and the artillery unit he came with had the job of fortifying the newly acquired California territory against any Mexican attempts to retake it. There was little danger of that happening, but no one could be sure at the time and the interservice rivalry exacerbated American apprehensions.

Halleck and the other army officers on the *Lexington* met with the ranking U.S. military officer in the region, navy Commodore William B. Shubrick, to discuss whether they would fortify Monterey or get back on the ship and travel to San Francisco, farther up the California coast. They quickly decided to remain in Monterey. The soldiers began unloading their artillery pieces, ammunition, muskets, gunpowder, shovels, pickaxes, saws, and gristmill equipment. Halleck made a reconnaissance of the area and pointed out the sites the government would need for forts and fortifications. There were buyers already angling to purchase that property, so almost from the moment he set foot on California's soil Halleck became embroiled in a land dispute. He could not know it at the time, but such controversy over property would in later years provide him with the opportunity to gain new fame and substantial fortune.[14]

Monterey was hardly a place of beauty, the soldiers quickly discovered. "There is nothing very inviting or even pleasing in the general appearance of the country," a naval officer on the *Independence* reported, with the land "destitute of timber, and the mountains rising in too gentle slopes to be in the least picturesque." Yet a navy chaplain who became a civic leader in the city thought the citizens of Monterey were extraordinary. "I have never been in a community that rivals Monterey in its spirit of hospitality and generous regard," he said.[15]

Halleck expressed no such enthusiasm. When the army units disembarked, they pitched tents on a hill above the town where the navy had constructed a small blockhouse. "They called it a *Fort*," he derisively said, "but it had none of the properties of a fort, and hardly deserved to be named even a *redoubt*." Since it was the rainy season, "we were not only pretty well drenched every night but had to stand half-leg deep in the water to dress ourselves in the morning." To keep up their spirits, Halleck and another officer in an adjoining tent bellowed out the song "'A soldier's Life is always gay!—is always gay." As for Monterey itself, "the great capital of California," Halleck said sarcastically, it was "a miserable little town of about a thousand inhabitants living in mud or rather *adobe* houses scattered along the shore with little or no regularity. The streets were half leg deep with soft mud." Everything cost too much too. "I just paid $1 for a miserable little *chamber pot* which [Lt. Lucien] Loeser can fill at *one* pumping after a good glass of whiskey!" he complained. He even found the women lacking. "The California Senoritas have beautiful black eyes, but not equal to some soft blue eyes that I remember to have seen [in New York] once upon a time!"[16] Halleck found fault with everything he saw.

As an engineer officer, Halleck was in charge of constructing fortifications in Monterey, including what came to be called Fort Halleck, but he quickly inherited more responsibility. Army General Stephen W. Kearny, the recently arrived commander of the district, attached him to his staff so he could inspect the entire California coastline and recommend new fortifications.[17]

After sailing up to San Francisco, Halleck inspected the condition of existing fortifications on the bay. What he saw was not encouraging. He found the military works crumbling from lack of care. After returning to Monterey, he and an entourage traveled on horseback the 540 miles south to San Diego, the "roads in California being mere paths" and not wide enough for wagons. He was gone for seven weeks, and during that time he covered nearly fifteen hundred miles. He was proud of his achievement. "I have thus traveled over nearly all the settled parts of California and have probably seen more of the country than any officer in it, with the exception, perhaps, of famous explorer [John C.] Frémont," he gloated. The Pathfinder's maps were "exceedingly inaccurate," Halleck discovered, so he "made a map of the coast which I believe to be pretty accurate." When he returned to Monterey, he found that another regiment had arrived, but "how long I am to stay here or what I am to do I know not.[18]

Halleck was clearly bored and unhappy in Monterey. He had "neither men nor means for constructing fortifications," and thus he was "left almost without occupation." "I do not think my services are any longer required in this country, until means are provided for building fortifications, which I suppose will not be [done] till the close of the war," he complained. Having completed his long inspection trip, he felt frustrated with having to return to petty bureaucracy. For example, he had to send a letter to the chief engineer acknowledging his receipt of some government circulars and reporting that "a copy of Treasury Dept circular relative to the 20th & 21st Sections of the act establishing the constitutional treasury" had not arrived. All this was distressing when there was a war going on, and martial glory to be gained.[19] He might as well have stayed in New York.

Exacerbating his sour disposition was the news that an army engineer major had written an "official letter" to the chief engineer "abusing" Halleck's recent book and calling him "beneath criticism." Halleck was perplexed: "What on earth can have made the Major so bitter against me I cannot imagine." He was missing the chance for combat glory, and now even his literary reputation was under attack.[20]

Halleck's disappointment crested when it became apparent that he was to remain where he was. He had hoped that as a member of Kearny's staff he would accompany the general back to St. Louis to recruit troops for the war in Mexico. That way, he thought, he could get into the main theater of the conflict. Kearny, however, did not believe that he was authorized to allow Halleck to accompany him without the Secretary of War's explicit permission. Halleck unsuccessfully tried to expedite matters by writing the chief engineer in Washington. "Most of my classmates are now far ahead of me, though I am certain that I have done as good and efficient service as any of them," he complained to his brother. No matter. The chief engineer ignored his request. Kearny left, and Halleck remained in Monterey.[21]

Colonel Richard Mason, a blunt army veteran, arrived at the end of May 1847 to take command of the Tenth Military District, as California was now officially called. He was "one of those men," a contemporary said, "who mistake rudeness for decision, and who look upon the courtesies and amenities of life as incompatible with the character of a soldier." He was, in short, a hard-bitten soldier and, like Halleck, had little taste for frivolity. On August 13, 1847, Mason named Halleck secretary of state of the district with authority to deal with public law issues, while Sherman served as adjutant in charge of implementing military orders. Halleck now began signing his paperwork H. W. Halleck, no longer emphasizing his connection to the Wager family.[22]

Halleck's immediate military future thus was in California with a commander whose disposition must have reminded him of Mahan's. Sherman remained too. He and Halleck had enjoyed a friendly relationship during the long trip from New York and since their arrival in Monterey. Both shared frustration with the dullness of their duties and their distance from the major fighting. Halleck surmised bitterly that "my new office yields plenty of labor, but neither honor nor profit," and Sherman felt the same way.[23] Sometime after Mason's arrival, their unhappiness spilled over into a serious disagreement.

The incident was petty. In June 1847 Sherman sent Halleck a note in which he said that he "hoped or expected" (Halleck could not remember which) that some guns would be mounted on the hill overlooking Monterey by July 4. Halleck responded that he could not complete the task that quickly with the soldiers available to him. Sherman disagreed, and Halleck remembered saying that "I thought I knew my own profession best," indicating to Sherman, the artillery officer, that he had no business telling Halleck, an engineer, how to do an engineering project. Halleck then told Mason about the conversation, and the commanding officer authorized Halleck to use more men. There the matter rested until a few days before July 4, when Sherman noted that he had been right about the project all along because Halleck was clearly going to meet the July 4 deadline. Halleck disagreed. He was not going to get the job done despite having three times more men and despite pitching in himself. He told Sherman that he "did not 'object' so much to any error in his estimate as . . . [he] did to . . . [Sherman's] making an estimate at all. . . . It was neither proper nor delicate in others to do the duties that legitimately belonged to him." Halleck remembered later that "one word brought on another till some rather bitter and perhaps improper remarks were made on both sides."

Halleck recalled that Sherman had shown a similar lack of respect on the occasion of planning a blockhouse. Becoming increasingly irritated with Sherman's seeming lack of deference, Halleck "concluded that he no longer wished to act towards me as a friend, and I therefore determined thenceforth to treat him with the respect due to him as an officer and gentleman, but to discontinue all intercourse as friends." From then on, relations between the two men remained cool. Halleck's rigid sense of status had cost him a friend.[24]

Others who had dealings with Halleck at the time generally came away from the experience impressed. When a new arrival in California delivered a letter to Halleck, he "was much pleased with him; he is a young man & has a high reputation." Halleck invited the newcomer to dinner and even took him to view the Indian gambling grounds just outside town. Another American characterized Halleck as "distinguished" and "a man of calm, judicial mind, fitted to handle questions of public law, of which he had made a study."[25] As long as visitors granted him the deference he felt was due him, Halleck could be agreeable, but he remained professionally prickly. He retained the tension in his personality between the purposeful disciplined self that was unbending and distant and the more generous and good-humored self that reached out to others.

Halleck successfully accomplished a variety of tasks in his capacity as secretary of state. He ruled that land titles obtained from the Mexican government would remain inviolate, despite the call from some Americans to nullify them all. He ordered all those who occupied former mission property to produce copies of their land contracts. He tried to deal with the native Indian tribes and their disagreements with Mexican and American settlers. He established rules and regulations for customs collectors. He worked to establish procedures for the alcaldes, the Mexican officials who were the towns' judge, jury, and executive officers. He made sure that the orders of the governor (Colonel Mason) were published in the press so the public was informed. He conducted an informal census of California in the absence of an official one. Paperwork flowed from his desk; he might as well have been back in New York Harbor, for California was not getting him to closer to martial glory.[26]

He blamed everything on the Corps of Engineers. "I have been most heartily disgusted with the management of our affairs for the last two or three years," he confessed to his friend Cullum. "If God spares my life till the war is closed, I will leave the corps, and if I cannot do better in some other corps I will leave the army. I am not disposed to toil all my life, and receive no reward." Had he gone into the artillery, he believed, he would now be a captain, at least. Instead "I am now ranked by men, three or four classes after me, and whom I taught the first rudiments of their profession at West Point—men who did literally nothing while I was made to work night and day for the benefit of government. . . . You cannot appreciate the peculiarity of our position till you are made to serve under your *inferiors.*" Halleck was chafing at the bit.

He also continued to miss the women of New York, and he jokingly but tellingly said so to Cullum. "Don't forget me when making love to *my* sweethearts! Just drop in a word for me now and then at the *sandstone* edifice, or at Beach Street. I wish to heaven you would send one of them out here directed to me 'this side up with care'! I am heartily tired of California belles. Some are pretty, but most terribly ignorant."[27]

Even as he wrote, Halleck's military life suddenly changed to his liking. A navy squadron under Commodore William B. Shubrick was preparing to take the war to the Mexicans farther south, and Shubrick wanted Halleck to go along as his chief of staff. On October 16, 1847, the flagship *Independence,* with Shubrick and Halleck aboard, sailed out of Monterey Bay for Baja (Lower) California accompanied by the sloop *Cyane* and the storeship *Erie.* The plan called for the flotilla to link up at La Paz with several other ships to attack Mexican-held Matzatlán, one of the most important ports on the Pacific Coast. At last, Halleck was going to war.[28]

After disembarking at Palmilla Bay, the sailors and marines trudged five miles down a sandy road to San José del Cabo. Clearly excited, Halleck rhapsodized: "Our way was enlivened by the songs of birds, and the woods by the roadside were filled with the most beautiful flowers. . . . The fragrance of these flowers and of the odoriferous shrubs . . . filled the air with the most grateful [sic] perfumes." Shubrick relied heavily on Halleck, agreeing that, before anything else was done, a party of thirty sailors and marines, with Halleck along as an advisor, should conduct a reconnaissance of Todos Santos, a Mexican outpost commanded by Manuel Pineda, who as well as having his own cavalry expected support from local guerrillas.

Starting out on November 1, 1847, the Americans immediately received warnings from Mexican civilians that Pineda had a force of seven hundred men ready to decimate their small unit. Undeterred, the Americans pushed forward along the rocky mountainous roads, their mission being reconnaissance not combat. Along the way, Halleck and his unit stopped at a ranch on November 3, the night before a possible battle, where some women fourteen to nineteen years old took the Americans' minds off combat. Halleck reported with relish in his journal that these women were "wearing dresses without sleeves and low in the bosom like our belles at home when they wish to display their charms in the ballroom." The Americans were invited to dinner. "Each of us shared a block of wood with a fair companion, and it was necessary for the gentleman and lady to sit in close proximity . . . and one arm tightly about her waist lest she slip off the chair while the other hand did the double duty of feeding the entertained and the entertainer. . . . We were deficient in knives and forks but then fingers were invented before either—and we used these to advantage and held up the chicken to the rosy lips of our sweethearts while they delicately nibbled off the fleshy meat." Dancing followed dinner, but sentinels were necessary outside the door to warn of any surprise attack, and "it was slightly fatiguing to dance with revolvers in each pocket, horse pistols in the belt, and a heavy saber buckled to the side," Halleck said. It all ended at eleven o'clock, and the soldiers "slept soundly on the ground outside," Halleck said, "notwithstanding the close proximity of our sleeping beauties, and the strong probability of a fight before morning." When the Americans reached Todos Santos the next day, the city's insurgents, under a Padre Gabriel, were nowhere to be found. Halleck and his troops had avoided catastrophe despite their evening of enjoyment. For a brief time, Halleck had forgotten his New York belles and his military duties. He found titillation, though no satisfaction, in this faraway place. The expedition returned to San José and the men reported what they had seen, no doubt also bragging about their new female friends.

Shubrick decided to leave behind a small unit of marines to protect those who had helped (and entertained) the Americans and ordered the three ships to proceed to Mazatlan. After arriving on November 9, 1847, Shubrick put his ships into an attack formation and sent in a truce party, including Halleck, to demand the surrender of the principal Mexican commander, Colonel Rafael Telles. From a town twelve miles away, Telles sent word of his refusal. Not waiting for the Mexican's response, Shubrick sent forward seven hundred marines and sailors and five artillery pieces under navy Captain Elie A. F. LaVallette and Halleck. This force captured the Mexican army barracks at Mazatlan on November 11 without firing a shot. LaVallette became governor and Halleck lieutenant governor of the city. Halleck immediately began building fortifications to protect the new American enclave. His mind was once again focused on his duties; the temporary female distraction was gone.

Telles was furious at the American capture of the barracks and marched his seven hundred–man force toward Mazatlan. Governor LaVallette responded by ordering a hundred sailors, with Halleck along as advisor, to drive these Mexicans away. He deployed another sixty men to cut off any possible retreat. The main American force attacked a small group of Mexicans outside the city, and when night fell Halleck and a few others fixed the enemy's position, making contact with the American blocking force. At dawn, at Halleck's signal, the two American units attacked and drove the Mexicans back so quickly that the encircling force could not get in position fast enough to cut off the Mexican retreat. At the end of December, Pineda tried to fortify Palos Prietos, but fifty sailors, with Halleck once again providing leadership, drove the Mexicans out.

His appetite whetted by this taste of combat, Halleck now joined a friend, army Brevet Lieutenant Colonel Henry S. Burton, as second in command of the army units involved in further fighting in Baja California. Finally, in early February 1848 when he returned to La Paz, Halleck expressed amazement at what the war had done to the city and its population. "War, on the smallest scale," he said, "is not without its horrors; and even in this bye-place of the earth, many a suffering female and helpless orphan live to call down the vengeance of heaven upon the heads of profligate statesmen who involve nations in useless and unnecessary wars." For the next month, Halleck refrained from adding to this misery, firing no shot in anger. The enemy always melted away before him. He did more sight-seeing than fighting. But plans were again afoot to capture Pineda and to rescue some American prisoners of war held at San Antonio.

A force of thirty-one officers and men, under army Captain Seymour Steele, was preparing to move out against San Antonio when Halleck volunteered to go along as second in command.[29] The unit left La Paz late in the evening of March 15, 1848, rode 120 miles in twenty-eight hours, and smashed into San Antonio and its force of several hundred Mexican soldiers, easily rescuing the prisoners of war and locating the governor's archives. They failed to capture Pineda, however, who, according to Halleck's later autobiographical sketch, "barely" escaped "in his night clothes." "This," Halleck said with obvious pride and hyperbole, "was regarded as the most brilliant operation of the war on the Pacific Coast." Pushing forward, the soldiers ran into an ambush, but Halleck led them out of it. "Boys, slide off your horses," he shouted, "divide into sections, and get into the brush; don't give the enemy any advantage over you." The soldiers obeyed, rallied, and drove fifty Mexicans from their positions outside town.[30] Three Mexicans were killed and eight wounded, while only one American died and none of the rest suffered injuries.

On March 27, 1848, Halleck led another force, which finally captured Pineda, and at the end of the month he led still another successful assault at Todos Santos. Except for chasing the enemy for another month, Halleck's fulfilling combat experience was over. In April 1848, he sent Colonel Mason a detailed report about Baja California in compliance with his original orders to determine the proper locations for new fortifications. He also took the occasion to point out the absolute necessity for the United States to maintain control of the region in any postwar settlement.[31]

In June 1848, Halleck returned to Monterey, where good news awaited him. He had received a brevet promotion to captain, based, it was said, on his exemplary combat performance, but it was backdated to May 1, 1847, before his departure for the field of battle. Certainly the army was rightly impressed with his performance on the battlefield; he had shown personal bravery and tactical insight. He had applied the military theory he had written about, but the skirmishes he fought were so small and against such weak opposition that his "genius" was hardly tested. At the least, however, he had demonstrated successful reaction to the dangers of battle. The engineer had shown himself to be an able and decisive small unit commander.

Halleck did not impress everyone, however. He made a decidedly mixed impression on a naval officer with whom he had served, a man who would later become nearly as well known in the Civil War as Halleck himself. Samuel Francis Du Pont, the commander of the U.S. Navy ship *Cyane* had read Halleck's *Elements of Military Art and Science,* found it "interesting and instructive," and was therefore eager to meet him. But Du Pont found Halleck "selfish, covetous of renown, unfriendly to and jealous of all naval doings . . . but . . . an officer of ability, more, of genius; very brave and spirited and energetic." In sum, Du Pont believed Halleck was a great soldier with a nasty disposition. The dual nature of Halleck's personality was becoming increasingly evident to those around him.[32]

In the end all Halleck's military successes went for naught. When the Treaty of Guadalupe Hildalgo ended the Mexican War, Baja California was returned to the Republic of Mexico, much to Halleck's disgust. "Our government is guilty of the basest deception towards Lower California," he wrote, "and [it] will be the means of ruining all the respectable people of that country." Halleck felt strongly enough about this American withdrawal to compose a letter demanding protection for those Lower Californians who had aided the American forces. Whether he included the Mexican senoritas he had coveted is unknown.[33]

Ironically, the end of hostilities in May 1848 created greater problems for the army in California than it had experienced in combat. Colonel Mason remained military commander of the region, but the extent of his peacetime authority over the 26,000 civilians in the new American territory was uncertain. To make matters worse, his volunteer troops were being mustered out as required. And then, in 1848, gold was discovered at Sutter's Mill, and a wave of greedy prospectors from the East and throughout the world poured into the territory, while soldiers deserted in droves to join them in the search for riches. The population jumped to over 92,000. "If the orderly mind of Governor Mason was sorely tried with the perplexities of his office before, it was ten times more so now," an American civilian commented. Sherman, the adjutant, even worried about total societal collapse. On August 26, 1848, he told a fellow officer that Mason wanted to do all he could to maintain order in the territory, but he did not have the manpower to do so because of desertions to the gold fields. "All the women of the lower country may be ravished & men killed, horses stolen & houses burnt & you couldn't get a dozen men to leave the Gold district to go to their aid," he said.[34]

As secretary of state, Halleck was equally concerned about maintaining the territory's institutions while the U.S. Congress decided what to do with the newly acquired territory. He doggedly sent letter after letter to military men throughout California, encouraging them to stay on the job until civilians could replace them. In the meantime, he wrote, they should stop collecting the military tariff and begin enforcing the customs laws of the United States. He instituted the use of American legal weights and measures, a move particularly important because of the discovery of gold and the sale of gold dust. In telling officials how to register a ship, he freely cited chapter and verse from international law books, indicating that he was keeping up with his professional reading. To give these officials some further specific direction, Mason had Halleck promulgate a code of laws for the military government. Halleck himself set a personal example of duty by refusing to leave California to accept a September 25, 1848, offer of an engineering professorship in the Laurence Scientific School at Harvard. He must have been tempted, but he loyally remained at his post.[35]

While Mason, Halleck, and Sherman worked to maintain peace and order in the territory, they became involved in a private war. The wounds from Halleck's 1847 touchiness about his status as an engineer remained unhealed and festered openly in early 1849. To his shock, Mason learned that Sherman and Halleck had not been speaking to each other for the past two years, and that discovery provoked another argument about which of the two men had taken this issue up with their disbelieving commander. Sherman accused Halleck of complaining to Mason about their "unfriendly feelings to each other" and demanded: "Am I to understand thereby, that you think my private feelings influence my official conduct?" Halleck immediately denied being the first one to bring the matter up with Mason. "My complaint was entirely of an official character," he said, and if Sherman had not spoken about their disagreement, "Mason would have ever remained ignorant that our private relations were not of the most friendly character."

Angry letters flew back and forth between the two men. Mason tried to mediate the conflict by pointing out to Halleck that Sherman had supported his appointment to his present position and had written the note that Mason had sent to the adjutant general in praise of Halleck's job performance. "Let me entreat of you," Mason pleaded, "that this matter may be settled amicably as I am sure it can be honorably to both parties."

After more correspondence, Sherman finally asked Mason point blank who had first told him that he and Halleck were not on speaking terms. Mason responded that it had been Halleck and "that was the first I ever knew of the existence of any unkind feeling." When Sherman demanded that Halleck now admit his culpability, Halleck demonstrated the tenacity of a cornered bureaucrat with an evasive response. "I am perfectly aware that on the 25th I not you, first mentioned to Col. Mason that we were not on speaking terms; and I am also equally certain that you first used the word 'personal' in reference to the remarks I had just made, whereupon I spoke to previous private relations." This is all he had been saying, Halleck insisted. "I however am not disposed to discuss [further] this point nor . . . any [other] issues or collateral questions." Halleck then composed a statement explaining the 1847 dispute, which Sherman apparently never responded to, and there the matter rested. Having to work together on California's problems, Halleck and Sherman were unable to solve their own feud and remained distant personally.[36] Halleck could tolerate no perceived affront to his professional standing or personal honor and thus continued to sacrifice the friendship of a respected military colleague.

Even as he pettily argued with and snubbed Sherman, Halleck generously reached out to his family in Westernville. The hope of riches had lured several of his brothers to California, and he promised his mother that he would "help them get along until they get established in some business where they can support themselves." He did just that. For brother Jabez, he obtained the positions of collector and harbormaster of Monterey and quickly followed that with further sinecures as notary public and commissioner of deeds. By summer, Jabez had also completed, no doubt with Halleck's help, a translation and digest of the 1837 Mexican land law, which the military government had printed for civil officials. Halleck no doubt also obtained jobs for brother William, but he asked his mother to keep A. J. (Jack) from coming west because Halleck did not think that brother's health could survive the rigors of the territory.[37]

Meanwhile, as everyone continued to wait for Washington to establish a civilian government for California, Mason and his advisors proved ingenious in keeping the military administration solvent. To deal with the financial problems, Mason ruled that customs duty collections should be put into a "Civil Fund" under the exclusive control of the military governor and used to pay government expenses. In fact, Halleck coordinated this activity as well, a job that he remembered amounted to dealing with "several millions of dollars" which he "examined + audited . . . before they were forwarded to Washington."[38]

In December 1848, when news arrived that Congress had adjourned without taking action on California's future, the disappointed military leaders pressed forward with the military government, while civilian grumbling increased. A major source of controversy was the issue of land ownership in the new American territory. Did Mexican land grants and laws have any validity now that California was part of the United States? Under what legal principles were alcaldes and other civil officials to settle land disputes, especially those between long-time Californians and more recently arrived Americans? Mason ordered Halleck to collect whatever Spanish and Mexican archives he could find, which Halleck did with such zeal that he even confiscated a map that belonged to his one-time land lady and her husband. In effect he created the first archive in California history. He studied all the documents and translations he had gathered and, on March 1, 1849, produced a "Report on the Laws and Regulations Relative to Grants or Sales of Public Lands in California." When this report was sent to Washington, Congress published 100,000 copies of it, and it remained a basic source on the land question from then on.[39]

In this seminal report, Halleck concluded that, according to the Mexican law then in effect, any grant made within ten leagues of the coastline or any grant larger than one league square anywhere was invalid; no land grant was valid unless a territorial assembly or the Mexican national government had approved it; mission lands or any other land, for that matter, remained in government hands unless legally sold. Halleck recognized that boundaries were a problem because the old grants cited lines as lying between streams, hills, and other changeable or unclear geographic boundaries. Although he did not agree with the comment, Halleck seemed to realize what Walter Colton, the alcalde of Monterey, explained with a few lines of poetry. "The only rule which appears to have governed the military and civil authorities in these [land] matters seems to have been that of Rob Roy":

> The simple plan,
> That they shall take who have the power,
> And they shall keep who can.

In short, Halleck's report concluded, as he later said to San Diego city officials, that "what had been previously granted in accordance with law, remains, as before, the property of the persons or corporations to which it was given. . . . It must be remembered, however," Halleck continued, "that the general government of Mexico reserved to itself whatever lands might be required for fortifications, arsenals, and other public structures; this reserved right now belongs to the government of the United States, and it is believed that no territorial or municipal authority can interfere with or limit this right." In short, Halleck found that Mexican-American land grants were not conclusive, even according to Mexican law.[40]

Busy as he was, Halleck continued to find his life unfulfilling. "I am willing to remain here so long as I can get anything of a professional [engineering] character to do, but I do not like to be kept in this country merely to perform civil duties." If he "were not bound to serve the Government, he told his mother, "I believe I could make a fortune in a few years. But as it is," he concluded unhappily, "I fear I shall have to leave the country as poor as I came into it."[41]

So he remained at his post. Writing to his mother again eight months later, however, he seemed less sure how much longer he would stay. He had "not yet dug a single penny's worth of gold," he said, but hoped to travel to the mines during the summer if his duties allowed it. He had speculated successfully in land, and these profits would carry him over until he found gold. At the same time, however, he was very pessimistic about the gold rush itself. "It is difficult . . . in this whirlpool of excitement, dissipation, and vice [to see] what will be the result of these wonderful discoveries of gold, but I do not . . . [predict] much good from them, either to the country or to the gold-diggers."[42]

In February 1849, a change in military administration further complicated Halleck's life. Brevet Major General Persifer F. Smith became commander of a newly established Third Division (Pacific Division), which included the Tenth Military District (California Territory) and the Eleventh Military District (Oregon Territory). Mason left for the East in April 1849, when Brevet Brigadier General Bennet Riley arrived with a regiment of soldiers previously stationed in Buffalo, New York.[43]

Halleck was sorry to see Mason go because he admired the man. Such good feelings quickly evaporated, however, when Halleck received a copy of a letter that Mason wrote the chief engineer in July 1849 refusing to support a second brevet rank for Halleck until Sherman and another officer received their first such honors. Halleck felt his professional standing had been diminished and, characteristically, he lashed out. "This is the first time, in a military service of more than ten years," he wrote Mason, "that I have ever complained of the conduct of a commanding officer, but I do complain of your treatment of me in this matter." Clearly upset that Sherman, whom he continued to treat coolly, should receive his first brevet before he could receive his second, Halleck was brutally blunt to his former superior. "I have never asked of you, either directly or indirectly, any favor or reward. But when I find you stepping in between me and my friends to prevent my receiving my reward, *unless certain others should be first promoted,* is it strange that I should be both surprised and mortified?" Halleck's anger had no effect. He did not receive the promotion he desired, and Mason died soon afterward of natural causes. By the time Halleck wrote this letter to Mason, he was already serving under a new commanding officer. According to a contemporary, Bennet Riley "was a man of ripe experience, a soldier from his youth."[44] Perhaps Halleck would have more promotion luck with Riley than with Mason.

If he thought about it, Halleck had to be amazed by all that he had experienced since stepping aboard the *Lexington* in New York Harbor in July 1846. He had demonstrated why the army viewed him as one of its brightest stars. He had met every professional challenge successfully. Nonetheless, his relationships with those around him continued to deteriorate. He guarded his career so ferociously that he damaged personal relationships in the process. He could enjoy life but only occasionally and only if that enjoyment did not impinge on his profession. He had become harshly demanding like his father and Dennis Hart Mahan. The benign examples of Eliphalet Nott and John Forsyth had faded away.

4

From Soldier to Businessman

In 1849, when Congress failed yet again to act on California's status, the territory's residents were outraged. There was gold to be discovered, land to be bought and sold, and an exploding population to be incorporated into what, most hoped, would become the newest state in the American nation. Angry Californians held meetings threatening to take matters into their own hands. As secretary of state, H. W. Halleck shared their frustration.[1]

The military governor, Bennet Riley, had also reached the end of his patience. In late May 1849, he told Halleck that if no word came from Washington on the next steamer, he would act on his own. Word did not come and on June 3, 1849, he issued a "Proclamation to the people of California," a document that Halleck certainly drafted. Denying that he headed a military government, which, of course, he did, Riley insisted that he was, in actuality, "the executive of the existing civil government." Since Congress had failed to deal with the situation, he said, he would continue in office and complete appointments to necessary civil positions. "At the same time a convention, in which all parts of the Territory are represented, shall meet and frame a State constitution, or a territorial organization, to be submitted to the people for their ratification, and then proposed to Congress for its approval." He set August 1 as the day for delegate election.[2]

Eager for an immediate end to military rule, Californians quickly accepted the proclamation. The August 1 election was held as scheduled, and thirty-seven delegates were elected, nine more being added during the convention itself to bring the total to forty-eight. One of those originally selected was Halleck, officially chosen to represent Monterey, but obviously also selected as a delegate sure to protect the interests of the military.[3]

The delegates ranged in age from twenty-five to fifty-three. Halleck was only thirty-five. Nine of the delegates had Spanish as their native tongue; Halleck was able to speak both English and Spanish. Twenty-eight, including Halleck, had arrived in California before the gold rush, with fourteen coming from slave states and twenty-three, Halleck included, from northern states. Halleck was the only army man in the group, although seven had formerly been volunteer army officers during the Mexican War. Democrats, like Halleck, outnumbered Whigs two to one, but personalities more than politics drove the deliberations. Because of his position in the army and as secretary of state, Halleck knew most of the delegates, and this familiarity, his wide reading, and his many governmental, military, and archival experiences gave him a decided advantage over everyone else at the gathering.[4]

The site designated for the convention was Colton Hall in Monterey, which according to one contemporary was "the only plastered house in the new territory." Built of stone and originally used as a schoolhouse, it had a spacious second-floor hall measuring sixty-five by twenty-five feet. The delegates sat at four long tables, and on one wall were two American flags and a picture of George Washington. A specially constructed railing separated the dignitaries from the spectators, and a door in the middle of the room opened onto a balcony where delegates could go to clear their heads. The hall's builder, Walter Colton, Monterey's American alcalde, quipped that the structure had been constructed through "the labor of convicts, the taxes on rum, and the banks of the gamblers." It was an ironic place to write a constitution, but no one seemed to notice.[5]

Monterey was a city of some twelve to fifteen hundred residents when the convention began. The delegates, most of whom arrived on horseback, had to find accommodations wherever they could. Some slept outdoors at least part of their time there, because the lone hotel was still under construction. The town's inhabitants opened their doors to the strangers, however, and Halleck himself offered hospitality in his "little log hut" to J. Ross Browne, the man slated to become the convention's clerk. Halleck even took Browne to a party at the home of one of Monterey's leading citizens. Several restaurants opened their doors during the meeting, but their fare was notable for its quantity more than for its quality. Except for the spacious and pleasant meeting room, therefore, the delegates did not have a luxurious setting for their important work.[6]

The convention was taking place at a time when the nation was in turmoil over what to do with the land, California included, gained from Mexico in the recent war. The so-called Wilmot Proviso, supported by freesoilers, insisted that slavery be excluded from all territory gained in the Mexican War. Conversely, advocates of slavery demanded that the institution be permitted everywhere, with no restrictions. A rising number of compromisers called for the rule of popular sovereignty—the people in each territory should decide whether or not to allow slavery. The national outcome of this debate would influence California's fate, but its residents were in no mood to delay their deliberations. They pushed forward with their convention within the context of both national and their own uncertainty about the future of slavery.

The meeting opened on Saturday, September 1, 1849, with only ten members present since delegate election returns were still being counted. Halleck immediately assumed a leading role and moved that a temporary chair be elected. In his capacity as secretary of state, Halleck continued to receive delegate election returns, which he then compiled for the convention chairman. In his report he also called for "a spirit of harmony." "You have an important work before you," he told his fellow delegates, "the laying of the corner-stone of the State structure; and the stability of the edifice will depend upon the character of the foundation which you may establish. Your materials are good: let it never be said that the builders lacked skill in putting them together."[7] Halleck had, after all, been secretary of state for a long time, and he knew more about the inner workings of government than did most of the other delegates. He seemed determined to add to his professional laurels by becoming a founder of a new state.

On September 3, during a debate on the seating of some disputed delegates, Halleck successfully proposed the establishment of a committee on privileges and elections, to which he and nine other delegates were appointed. He insisted that it was "absolutely essential to the progress of business that each member should do his own voting," and asked for and was granted a recess so that absent members might have time to arrive. The convention chose a permanent president, and it was Halleck, in his role as secretary of state, who swore him in.[8]

Halleck continued his prominent role the next day by demanding that the convention immediately decide a central issue. Was it to compose a "plan of a State government," or should the convention "propose to Congress a plan of a Territorial Government"? By a vote of twenty-eight to eight, the convention delegates said they wanted to establish a state government. The convention voted to establish a twenty-person "Standing

Committee on the Constitution," consisting of two people from each district. Not surprisingly, Halleck was one of these members. This committee's task was to provide the convention with a draft of the new constitution.[9]

As the convention continued to work toward establishing a civilian state, Halleck continued to play a key role. Because he was secretary of state, his word initially carried more weight than that of the average delegate, but not everything he said was automatically accepted. He was treated with respect, but the convention quickly demonstrated that the military, in the person of Halleck, should not expect to dictate policy. After all, the convention was in session to move California *away* from military rule.

The delegates were particularly worried about the issue of slavery. A Sacramento delegate introduced a statement excluding slavery from California as an amendment to the "Declaration of Rights" Halleck's committee had composed. Halleck immediately moved that "a declaration against the introduction of slavery into California shall be inserted into the bill of rights." This was surprisingly uncontested, and became Article 1, Section 18 of the completed constitution. But numerous delegates insisted that neither slaves nor former slaves be allowed to enter California. Most delegates understood, however, that free blacks, because they were constitutionally protected in other states, could not be excluded. Halleck took a pro-southern antiblack position, the first such indication of his prejudices. "I wish to know why a difference should be made between a free negro and one who was formerly a slave. If you want to keep them out, I say keep them all out. I am opposed to any such distinction."[10] Either as slaves or as citizens, Halleck did not include blacks in his vision for the new state of California. He saw them as a stumbling block impeding the establishment of a successful new government. In this regard, he shared the racist view of most Californians and white Americans. His inability to see blacks as human beings in the antebellum era foreshadows his later difficulties in recognizing the human dimension when order and organization were at issue. To him, the individual was less important than the process. The convention did not accept his extreme antiblack position, however, and put the issue of slavery and black people in general behind them.

Halleck went along with the convention in approving voting rights for the future state's Mexican residents, and believed that the provision for excluding Indians had violated the Treaty of Guadalupe-Hidalgo. He supported the inclusion of tax-paying Indians as citizens. This idea was narrowly voted down, and the convention eventually decided to leave that issue for later legislative decision. The idea of the legislature meeting only once every two years elicited a strong response from Halleck: "If there is a country in the world, at the present time, that requires the legislature to meet at least once a year, that is California." Limit the length of each session if necessary, he argued, but make it a yearly event. As for revenue to finance the new state government, he opposed a state lottery, and the convention agreed. "We may be a gambling community," he said, "but let us not in this Constitution create a gambling State." In fact, he wanted to see a section included in the new constitution preventing any future legislature from establishing any sort of lottery, but the convention disagreed.[11]

During the discussion about convention expenses, especially delegates' salaries, Halleck made an impassioned plea for economy. As one who had been dealing with public accounts for a long time, he knew, even without consulting General Riley, that Washington would never pay the costs of the convention if they were exorbitant; such expense would have to come out of whatever taxation system the first state legislature established. "Let us set an example of economy to the legislatures that will follow us," Halleck implored. Jacksonian that he was, he successfully supported a prohibition on "the circulation of bank paper, properly so called," and to save substantial start-up costs, he supported, unsuccessfully, the naming of Monterey as the first state capital. He was also adamantly opposed to allowing any future legislature to tamper with federal lands, the income from which was set aside for education. Throughout, Halleck supported a lean but decisive government.[12]

The most controversial debate during the entire convention focused on the location of California's eastern boundary, with the slavery issue playing a major role. While it was part of Mexico, California had never had a definite eastern boundary, but almost all contemporary maps included the modern states of Nevada, Utah, and Arizona within the former Mexican province. A special convention committee recommended that the eastern boundary be drawn along the Sierra Nevada Mountains, but Halleck and William Gwin, another key player in the convention, called for a more distant boundary, one that reached the Rocky Mountains. Halleck's argument was straightforward. By establishing the farther boundary, he said, the convention "closes forever this agitating question of slavery in all the territory this side of the Rocky Mountains." If that extended territory was not included in California, he predicted, Congress would be kept from organizing it for a long time, and its inhabitants would have "to resort to lynch law for the punishment of crime." If Congress proved adamant in refusing to accept the proposed eastern boundary, however, Halleck offered a proviso that gave the later state legislature authority to compromise on a Sierra Nevada line. The most important consideration for Halleck and the other delegates was to get Congress to accept the California constitution and admit the state to the Union. No one wanted slavery, the boundary issue, or anything else to get in the way of that basic goal.[13]

After a spirited debate that lasted several days, the Gwin-Halleck boundary and proviso passed, twenty-nine to twenty-two. Shouts of protest ensued. "Your constitution is gone! Your constitution is gone!" a delegate yelled, and others agreed vociferously, worried that Congress would refuse to accept California as a state if it insisted on being such an enormous land. The convention adjourned in confusion, and the next day delegates suggested a number of alternative proposals to try to change the previous day's decision. There seemed to be little agreement, and Halleck, in disgust, warned that if it was determined "not to adopt any of the [boundary] propositions, he would move that the constitution go without any fixed boundary, leaving the question to be decided by the Congress of the United States." This ultimatum forced the delegates to settle on the Sierra Nevada line, and Halleck unhappily accepted the decision. His desire for the largest possible state, he saw, could not be realized, and understanding that further debate would hurt California's chances of admission to the Union, he went along with the Sierra Nevada boundary. In a rare departure from his characteristic combativeness, he demonstrated a pragmatic willingness to compromise.[14]

Halleck also demonstrated an occasional sense of wit. Regarding separate property rights for women, he said: "I am not wedded either to the common law or the civil law, nor as yet, to a woman; but having some hopes that some time or other I may be wedded, . . . I shall advocate this section in the Constitution, and I would call upon all the bachelors in this Convention to vote for it. I do not think we can offer a greater inducement for women of fortune to come to California. It is the very best provision to get us wives that we can introduce into the Constitution." When another delegate wanted the definition of a California citizen to exclude anyone "who has left his family elsewhere," Halleck wondered if such persons "were not [already] included under the head of 'idiots and insane persons.'"[15]

The final major issue for the convention was timing the establishment of a new civil government: Was it to be set up immediately or only after Congress gave permission? This debate occasioned criticism of some of General Riley's actions as military governor, and Halleck quickly jumped to the defense of his commanding officer. If Riley had violated any orders,

Halleck said pointedly, then his superiors in Washington, not this convention, should censure him. As for when the new government should be activated, "I, for one, shall vote to put the new Government in operation as soon as may be convenient . . . I am very certain (I give it only as my opinion) that no opposition will be made, either from Washington, or any party here, to that course."[16]

Halleck believed, however, that Washington had to be handled tactfully: "We cannot bully the Congress of the United States; and as for our Senators and Representatives going there and forcing themselves into the hall of Congress and saying: We come here to take our seats by force; you must receive us; you are compelled to receive us, and we will take our seats in defiance of your authority—I say that is bad policy. Let us pursue the moderate and usual course." As a good military man, Halleck respected congressional authority and was determined to abide by it. The convention accepted his suggestion that elected senators and representatives take the ratified California constitution with them to Washington, "requesting California's admission into the Union."[17]

"So it went," a later historian concluded. "There was controversy, intrigue, acrimony, bitter debate and occasionally flaring tempers, and humor, but by and large the convention moved seriously and steadily through its work. Major problems between great interests were compromised successfully, if seldom easily. In general, the document produced at Monterey was a good one." Halleck would have been pleased to hear such an evaluation. As in military so in constitutional matters, he believed that tried and true principles, not innovation, should guide, and his leadership took the convention in that direction. "He sat near the door, where he could overlook the whole body, and nothing was done that escaped his notice," a contemporary noted. "No survivor of that body [convention] fails to declare that his judgment was sound and that his services were invaluable because of his intimate knowledge of the country," another contemporary concluded.[18]

Halleck perceived his role in the convention as essentially political rather than constitutional. His goal, he wrote later, had been to "relieve Congress and General Taylor's [presidential] administration from the difficulties which they were involved in by the free soil and pro slavery parties of 1849." More than anything else, slavery drove Halleck's behavior inside Colton Hall. He later wrote that his antislavery, antiblack activities at the convention "saved California from anarchy."[19] Halleck recognized the threat that slavery posed to government in the United States, and he believed his leadership in the convention in avoiding an emergency over the slavery issue in California that might have created a national crisis was significant in keeping the nation calm. The enslavement or freedom of black people was not as important as the future of governments, he clearly thought.

The convention finished its work on Saturday, October 13, 1849, voting pay of $11 a day for the delegates and a $10,000 salary per year for General Riley and $6,000 per year for Secretary of State Halleck. Neither man protested this generosity. Cannon at Monterey's Fort Halleck boomed in celebration of the convention's end, and in a fit of excitement the delegates marched, en masse, to General Riley's house. There, amid repeated cheers, they thanked Riley for "the great and important services" to the nation in general and California in particular. Overcome by this show of support after earlier criticism, the military governor responded: "This is a prouder day to me than that on which my soldiers cheered me on the [Mexican War] field of Contreras." More cheers from the delegates, and then Riley said: "I have but one thing to add, gentlemen, and that is, that my success in the affairs of California is mainly owing to the efficient aid rendered by Captain Halleck, the Secretary of State. He has stood by me in all emergencies, to him I have always appealed when at a loss myself; and he has never failed me." The delegates responded to Riley's praise of his subordinate with three cheers, simultaneously and justifiably recognizing Halleck's major contribution to their own deliberations.[20]

The delegates then talked about possible future governors, and Halleck's name was always prominently mentioned. He was not nominated, however, partly because some people argued that the U.S. Senate was a better place for him. He certainly had significant support when, on December 20, 1850, the state's first legislature selected two senators: the "Old Pathfinder" John C. Frémont and the leading convention force William Gwin. Halleck came in a close third. The governor offered him a seat on the California supreme court, but he declined that position. His army commission complicated his candidacy for all these offices. He had himself pointed out that "no officer of the U.S. Army can now be a member of the ayuntamiento [legislature]," so the possibility of his serving as governor or senator or state supreme court justice was certainly in question as long as he wore the captain's bars.[21]

Halleck was distracted from the politics of the senatorial election because of the sudden death, from fever, of his brother Jabez, the sibling he had helped put through school. Halleck grieved and pondered what he should do with his own life. He thought "very possibly" that he might "go home during the winter," but he changed his mind immediately. If he gained the chance "to make some money in California," he told his mother, "I shall remain some months longer." His army obligations had kept him from any "opportunity to profit by the gold discovery, but I hope during the coming winter not only to get some pay for my services here, but also to make some money in other ways." Halleck was still unsure what he should do now that the convention was over. On December 12, 1849, in a proclamation no doubt written by Halleck, General Riley announced the ratification of the constitution in the November 13 popular election. He also resigned as governor in favor of a civilian. The new civil government of California took over and H. W. Halleck ceased being secretary of state.[22]

Halleck's uncertainty dissipated quickly, and he soon moved into a new career. While secretary of state, Halleck had possessed the power of patronage, so he had been able to grant family members government positions. Numerous acquaintances had also gained favor at his hands. For example, he had used his influence to have an attorney named Frederick Billings, a Vermonter who had arrived in California in April 1849, appointed the San Francisco recorder of deeds, later an inspector of a special election, and finally the state's attorney general. Similarly, A. C. Peachy of Virginia, who had also come to California in 1849, received the position of San Francisco notary public.[23] Now that Halleck no longer held high military office, these two men would return the favors he had extended to them.

Billings was involved in numerous business deals, and was apparently the first attorney to hang out his shingle in San Francisco. His tenure as attorney general proved important because he defended the military government's land claims, even ejecting squatters when necessary. The experience convinced him that he could make a fortune in land law and he turned to his friend, Archibald Carey Peachy, as a partner. Peachy, a southerner to the core, had been a candidate for a faculty position in moral philosophy at Virginia's College of William and Mary, but a split in the faculty and the fact that Peachy had challenged the school's president to a duel doomed his chances. He decided to come to California for a fresh start, and he met Billings en route. Debonair and with an eye for attractive women, Peachy was an effective advocate before a jury: "tall, straight, proud, dressing elegantly and tastefully, carrying a cane and wearing large gold-rimmed eyeglasses." The Vermonter and the Virginian combined to form the California legal firm of Peachy and Billings to practice land law.[24]

The partnership soon expanded into Halleck, Peachy, and Billings. Leaning against a fence outside a hotel in San José one day, Billings had suggested to Halleck that he join the law firm. Halleck's experience as secretary of state and convention delegate had provided him with a statewide reputation, and his ability to read Spanish aided his research into the land records in the state archive he had personally assembled. He was *the expert* in California land law. He could expound on the arcane material in the old documents so well that one acquaintance even characterized his comments on such dry facts as fascinating. Halleck was an excellent addition to a law firm hoping to specialize in land-title litigation. Billings was delighted when Halleck agreed to join the firm.[25]

The three new partners were, as one contemporary put it, "as incongruous and dissimilar in disposition, manners, and habit, as any three men . . . [he had] ever known. Halleck was thrifty and persevering, but his distinctive characteristics were obduracy and laboriousness . . . Peachy was a Virginian, aristocratic in deportment, magisterial in manners, and fairly learned in the law. Billings, the businessman of the concern, was active, ambitious, cheerful, and was always lavish in his charities." They were all young: Peachy and Billings were only twenty-nine and Halleck was thirty-five.[26] The pooling of their diverse talents proved to be their law firm's strength.

The three men announced the formation of their partnership in letters sent in Spanish to non–English-speaking Californians and in announcements in San Francisco's major English-language newspaper. In editorially praising the new firm, the newspaper particularly lauded the talents of Halleck: "His fondness for research, and the duties entailed upon him by virtue of his office, have enabled him to obtain a vast amount of information which will be of great service to his clients in all matters where the question of titles is under consideration." The U.S. Federal Court for the Northern District agreed. Although Halleck had never received any formal legal training and had never had any connection with a law firm before, he was admitted to practice in federal court on October 25, 1851. John Forsyth's advice in Washington many years ago to study the law had finally paid off for Halleck.[27]

San Francisco was a fascinating place. In 1848, when it was called Yerba Buena, it had been a sleepy village of 800 people, but by the time Halleck made it his home in 1850, it was a bustling, unkempt metropolis of 40,000 calling itself San Francisco. Everyone there seemed to want to make a fast buck, and everything else seemed secondary. The streets were muddy, unless they had been planked, and most people used the thoroughfares to dispose of garbage or anything else that they wanted to discard. In 1849–50, 1,214 ships arrived in port with men seeking gold, and by 1850, some 300 ships sat abandoned along the waterfront, their crews having raced off to the gold mines. Facetiously said to be famous for its "rats, fleas, and bottles," "San Francisco was [actually] the funnel through which . . . [wealth seekers] had to pass to get to the gold," and manufacturing of all kinds sprang up to supply their needs. Hungry men had come to make money, but many never found the riches they sought, so they limped back to San Francisco. Those who became wealthy frequently settled in the booming city too because "there were fewer rules and regulations [there] than in well-established cities back East. And, for everyone with an entrepreneurial spirit, the possibilities were limitless." One resident summarized it best: "San Francisco is a miserable place [,] all but for money making."[28]

Like many San Franciscans, Halleck yearned for financial success. He still felt the tug of his New York home, but he did not want to return penniless. San Francisco promised him the chance to become wealthy. He toyed with the idea of going to the gold fields himself, but his military and political experiences demonstrated to him that he had other talents for making money. He became the senior member of the law firm of Halleck, Peachy, and Billings in the bustling city of San Francisco because opportunities to exercise his talents seemed greater there than anywhere else.

Because of California's need to retain army personnel in the wake of the gold rush mania, Halleck could keep his army commission while he practiced land law. He needed the double salary, he believed, because living expenses in California were very high. "I have hired a very good house in this place," he reported to his mother, "and am living quite comfortably, but pay most enormous rent." This financial drain did not keep him from regularly sending his mother money for her use in the education of his siblings. Throughout this time, however, he never wrote his father or even mentioned his name in any letter home. He could not forget nor forgive the man who refused to accept who he was.[29]

The struggle for land ownership made California a fertile place for a law firm with the expertise of Halleck, Peachy, and Billings. In the 1848 Treaty of Guadalupe-Hidalgo, the U.S. government had annexed California and the rest of the Mexican Cession, promising, in return, to respect the rights of Mexican citizens in those areas. The gold rush, however, soon became a land rush, and problems resulted. The American newcomers found that Mexican-Americans held all the best land, some twelve million acres, in eight hundred Mexican grants. When the avaricious Anglo-Americans found that the boundaries of these tracts were haphazardly drawn and that some might have been gained improperly, they demanded that Congress act on their behalf. In his 1849 land report, Halleck had found that many grants had not specifically followed Mexican law and thus were questionable, but a report by the Washington attorney William Carey Jones supported the validity of most of them. Not surprisingly, Congress found Halleck's arguments more convincing than Jones's and passed the Land Law of 1851, introduced by Halleck's convention cohort and now California Senator William Gwin. This law said that for United States officials to validate the titles of Mexican grant holders, these individuals had to prove the legality of their land ownership under the Mexican law existing before the Treaty of Guadalupe-Hidalgo.[30]

A three-member U.S. Land Commission became the governmental body that ruled on this legal question. Mexican grant holders had two years to prove their ownership or they would forfeit the land to the American public domain. If dissatisfied with a commission decision, either a grantee or the U.S. government could appeal to the federal judiciary all the way to the U.S. Supreme Court. Halleck and his law firm represented these Mexican grant holders before the Land Commission and in the federal courts, such litigation requiring detailed research in documents that Halleck himself had gathered and knew intimately. Long, hard work was necessary to overcome the anti–Mexican grant attitude prevalent in California, ironically buttressed by Halleck's 1849 report. The fees Halleck, Peachy, and Billings charged, therefore, were steep. While a carpenter made $5 to $7 a day in San Francisco and beef and butter each cost 20¢ a pound, Halleck and his colleagues charged anywhere from $50 to $1,500 per case. If an appeal went to the courts, the firm assessed an additional fee. Clients frequently complained that "the charges appear[ed] to be excessive" but Halleck replied that he thought the charges were "exceedingly low." Because clients were often slow in paying, the firm regularly had to send reminders, such as the one a clearly irritated Halleck wrote to several people in default: "Having spent nearly two years in defending these land titles, almost without remuneration and continually paying money out of our own pockets for the benefit of our clients, we are compelled now to call on them not only for payment in cases already decided but also in others for past payment in advance." He also angrily accused other lawyers of not charging enough. "I shall decline all offers for paltry fees, & let the petty foggers take the cases." Money normally flowed into the firm's coffers, however, and Halleck, Peachy, and Billings quickly became one of the state's wealthiest law firms.[31]

Because the Land Commission met in San Francisco and in Los Angeles and because the firm's clients and their land were located throughout the state, the three lawyers were frequently away from home on business.

They communicated by mail among themselves and with Pablo de la Guerra of Santa Barbara, the state's leading Mexican-American and an agent for the law firm. In late 1852, Halleck complained from Los Angeles about his health, telling his colleagues that he was suffering from intestinal problems. His bowels had been "unwell since I came here, and [I am[still too sick to do much." He got over his illness, however, and gathered documents, witnesses, and depositions to submit with petitions to the Land Commissioners for their decision. He, Peachy, and Billings alternately attended these commission sessions in Los Angeles or San Francisco to safeguard their clients' interests. Each "expediente," as the petition was called, was similar to the one Halleck prepared in his own hand for José Antonio de la Guerra in support of his ownership of Rancho Las Pozas. In the document, Halleck stated that one José Carrillo had received a grant of land from the then governor of California on May 15, 1834, that he later conveyed to de la Guerra on June 27, 1846. Supporting de la Guerra's petition were legal documents in Spanish and English "wherefore he prays the commissioners to confirm to him the aforesaid tract of land."[32]

The problem with most petitions was their lack of adequate documentation, especially a clear statement of the grant's boundaries. Such an indefinite diseño, or map of the boundary lines, usually included imprecise text that read something like: "To commence at the junction of dry creek or bayou with the San Jauquin river—up the middle of which the line shall move to the distance of about two miles or so as to extend from one to two hundred yards above our house or bend where there are two small oak trees standing within a few rods of each other and only a few rods from the bank of the river (left bank)." The Mexican-American unfamiliarity with U.S. legal exactness in documents and on the witness stand frustrated Halleck, with his penchant for bureaucratic precision. Typically, he found his job of representing these individuals very difficult, but he loved researching the archives. As one contemporary put it, "To him legal work was what poetry was to Coleridge–its own exceeding great reward." The fact that it made him a wealthy man did not hurt either. If only he could have avoided dealing with incompetent people.[33]

A further frustration for Halleck was the Land Commissioners' leisurely promulgation of decrees. The board did not begin sitting until January 1852, and its first decision was not announced until the late summer. When Franklin Pierce replaced Millard Fillmore in the White House in 1853, the new President relieved the old board and appointed an entirely new one. Halleck complained bitterly that there was no way of knowing when the commissioners might even arrive in California, and then "they must *learn* their duties [and] *study* Spanish Law; so the wheels are blocked again for 5 or 6 months at least!" It was all part of a scheme, he insisted, to allow squatters to maintain land they had illegally taken from proper grant holders like his clients. "This cursed land business takes all my time and runs me half crazy with anxiety," Halleck complained. "We do everything in our power for our clients, & if their claims are rejected it shall not be our fault." Halleck insisted that the commission rejected about half the claims it ruled on, but in truth it certified about 60 percent of them. It was a frustrating life for Halleck, nonetheless, and he had no compunction about reprimanding a client who questioned his professional competence. "As you seem to understand the matter so well yourself . . . It is strange that you ever employed us as counsel at all. If such is your opinion of our services, we certainly have no desire to serve you any longer." Yet he maintained his sense of humor to his friends. "I think we shall soon remove our office to the Insane Asylum and advertise as *Lunatics* instead of *Lawyers.*"[34] Personally pleasant but professionally prickly, Halleck practiced his lucrative legal business as he had conducted his military career.

Busy as he was in his law practice, he continued to serve in the army, too. He was now a judge-advocate, trying cases nearby and traveling all over California and as far away as Oregon, where he remained for several months in early 1850. In December 1851 he was named an inspector of fortifications; in December 1852, he became a lighthouse inspector for the Pacific Coast; and in April 1853, he became a member of the Board of Engineers for Fortifications on the Pacific Coast. These military positions required extensive travel from the Mexican to the Canadian borders and the preparation of reports for both army and navy use on site and in the nation's capital. Indeed, Halleck was the father of California lighthouses and fortifications. He planned and helped oversee construction of the first coordinated series of these facilities on the furthest western frontier of the United States. And, on July 1, 1853, he was made full captain in the Corps of Engineers, the promotion being granted because of his fourteen years of excellent service, almost all of it administrative in nature.[35]

Such time-consuming military and legal activities were not, however, the extent of Halleck's busy life. He was also supervising his law firm's construction of what was, for a long time, the largest building west of the Mississippi River. Sometime in mid-1852, a group of San Francisco's leading businessmen met in the offices of Halleck, Peachy, and Billings at 90 Merchant Street. The city was still reeling from the last of six devastating fires that had flamed out of control between December 24, 1849, and June 22, 1852. San Francisco had risen out of the ashes each time, but by erecting new wooden structures it had produced fuel for the next fire. Halleck himself had lost all his papers in the gigantic May 3, 1851, conflagration, so he came to believe that it was time to construct more permanent buildings. He called for the construction of an office building that would cover an entire block, be made of flame-resistant brick and iron, withstand earthquakes, and thus be a symbol of the city's permanence.[36]

Worried that the repeated fires were allowing Oakland and other nearby cities to steal a march on San Francisco, the city's major businessmen listened with eagerness to Halleck's presentation. Someone inquired about the cost of such a magnificent "Washington Block," as Halleck had named his proposed structure, and Halleck and his architect, Gordon P. Cummings, estimated the bill at about three million dollars. The response was a shocked silence. One businessman called Halleck "a fool" and walked out. But Halleck was undeterred and, with the aid of Billings and Peachy, began soliciting investment money for the project on "the Wall Street of San Francisco," Montgomery Street between Washington and Merchant Streets. Construction began on October 3, 1852, after the law firm had purchased, for $100,000, the site, a sand- and dirt-filled extension into San Francisco Bay on which sat several small buildings. As late as 1849, the property had been under water, so it was a weak foundation for a large building.[37]

Halleck and his architect devised an ingenious way to solve the problem. After leveling standing buildings and removing the pilings, Halleck had hundreds of Chinese laborers wade out hip deep into the muck left by the low tide and, using baskets, scoop out the mud. In the basin these workers constructed, he placed redwood logs, dovetailed and topped by ship planking and tied together with iron bands, all interlaced into a wooden floating foundation, 22 feet thick and 122 feet by 138 feet in area. Upon this wooden mat, he erected a U-shaped building made of brick, iron rods and beams, cement, and glass, with a fire wall across the open end. What at first was called Halleck's Folly now became the Floating Fortress. Cynics were sure that "it would sink into the ooze of the tidelands or float across the Bay on its foundation of redwood logs."[38] The ridicule did not stop Halleck; he kept pressing forward doggedly. He regularly walked out into the mud himself to direct the construction.

The work took fourteen months to complete, and the result was a building that lasted over a hundred years and withstood the famous 1906 San Francisco earthquake, only to fall to the wrecker's ball in 1958. It was a huge five-story structure including the basement. Its fortress-like appearance no doubt sprang from Halleck's training and experience as a military engineer and inspector of fortifications. There were twenty Doric columns across the building's Montgomery Street front, with the windows of each succeeding floor diminishing to the top. Each window had an iron shutter for use in the event of fire. The main entrance consisted of massive bronze and iron doors with a head of Washington above them. Inside were suites of rooms that were bright and airy, with heat available from gas grates. Drinking water was piped into all the hallways from a well in the building's courtyard. In front of the back firewall there was a solarium and steam bathhouse. The formerly skeptical populace of San Francisco now gaped in awe at the new building.[39]

The structure was opened with a lavish ceremony on December 23, 1853. Soon it came to be called not the Washington Block, as Halleck had planned it, but the Montgomery Block, and even later it was facetiously known as the Monkey Block. Despite the high rental costs of $2,000 a month for upper-floor suites and $200 a month for second-story inside offices, tenants readily moved into its 150 offices and 28 basement and first-floor stores. Halleck, Peachy, and Billings at first occupied rooms 72, 73, 74, and 75 on the third floor and rooms 89, 99, 100 and 101 on the fourth floor. Later, the entire firm moved to the second floor. Several important businesses and people had offices in the building. The Adams Express Company operated a mint in the basement complete with a smelter oven and vault. The Bank Exchange, actually a saloon on the first floor, had a staircase connecting it to the second-floor billiard room and the lobby, where businessmen lounged and informally conducted financial transactions. A number of newspapers, at one time or another, were located in the building. In later years, the building became home to a variety of artists and such leading writers as Bret Harte, Mark Twain, Frank Norris, and Jack London.[40]

Halleck kept busy overseeing the construction of this building, maintaining his law practice, and fulfilling his military obligations. He also began to reassess his life. His military duties were increasingly interfering with his civilian money-making pursuits, while remaining a bachelor for the rest of his life was an unhappy prospect. In the fall of 1853, he asked for a six-month leave of absence from his military duties so he could travel east the following spring. At the same time, he requested permanent relief from his lighthouse inspection duties because they were too time consuming. The Secretary of the Treasury relieved him from the lighthouse board on December 21, 1853, and the Army's Adjutant General also granted his request for time off. The leave commenced on February 1, 1854.[41]

Having cleared the way for his travel, Halleck still debated the wisdom of the trip east: "For a man to leave his business for six months or more is certainly no easy matter, and I find a great deal of difficulty in getting everything arranged to be absent so long a time." He knew he had to go, however, having already made an important decision. Although Halleck did not discuss the matter in any of his surviving letters, an official in the Corps of Engineers headquarters in Washington knew he was planning to resign from the army. When he arrived in New York City, however, his main thoughts were not about the military but about matrimony. The fall of 1852 had seen a marriage mania in San Francisco society, and Halleck had obviously caught the fever.[42]

Forty years old now, he returned to the East to shop for a wife. He quickly looked up the female friends that had been so much a part of his daydreaming for so long, and to his dismay he found that "most of my old sweet hearts have from 2 to 3 children to show me." They asked him, he noted with satisfaction: "'Don't you wish you were the father of this fine boy or girl?'" Halleck said he simply "look[ed] blank . . . and inquire[d] for the younger sisters whom I left as school girls." "I am not yet engaged," he reported back to Billings and the rest of the law firm, "but fall in love nearly every day. The ladies here are very beautiful, but really there are so many of them that I don't know which I like best. I would be willing to take a dozen at least," he concluded with relish.[43]

As was always the case, his professional responsibilities never strayed far from his mind. As he looked for a wife, he also tried to influence the land cases back in California. He met with Senator Gwin, attended at least one session of the Supreme Court, and even had an evening's discussion with a justice of the high court. Although he spent a great deal of his time socializing, he could not seem to find that perfect mate. "I am pretty tired of visiting and if I don't soon get in love or married or with child, or something of the kind, I will start back for California," he complained. But he kept trying, grumbling all the while. "As I am not yet married nor engaged I fear I shall lose my bet with Billings," he reported back to San Francisco. "It really is getting too warm to get married," he then joked. After a visit home and to West Point, about which he said nothing, he concluded: "I give up the bet—they say I'm too old—not sufficiently good looking—and can't humbug them with 'Montgomery Block.'"[44]

It seemed that he would remain a bachelor, but as for the army, he took a fateful step. He resigned his commission, sending letters to the chief engineer, Joseph G. Totten. He tried to make up for all the times he had complained about the head engineer. "It is with extreme regret that I thus sever my official connexion with a chief from whom I have received every kindness, and from a corps of officers I so highly respect and with whom my relations have always been of the most friendly character." Soon afterward, he took another surprising step and became secretly engaged. A Washington friend learned of this and sent congratulations on Halleck's engagement to a "Miss H" of New York, the union "to be consummated some years hence." Halleck apparently kept the news to himself when he returned to California, not even sharing it with Pablo de la Guerra. In a letter to him, Halleck said only that he "found it quite hard to break away from my old friends in New York and return" after only three months. He had no choice, he said: "I had been obliged to run in debt considerably in building 'Montgomery Block,' and it was important for me to get back and earn some money, or the interest would eat me up."[45]

It was not until the spring of the following year that it became clear just who "Miss H" was. Born in 1831, she was Elizabeth Hamilton, the younger sister of Schuyler Hamilton, one of Halleck's West Point roommates and, in 1854, a clerk in William Tecumseh Sherman's San Francisco bank. She was the daughter of John Church Hamilton, attorney and author, and the granddaughter of Alexander Hamilton, one of the nation's founding fathers. She was certainly not one of the women he had been dreaming about all these years, but a younger sister who had been a schoolgirl the last time he had seen her in the 1840s. The circumstances of their whirlwind courtship never came to light, but certainly her brother Schuyler must have played some kind of matchmaking role.

In the spring of 1855, Halleck traveled back from California to Westernville and to New York City to prepare for the wedding. He was obviously happy about his forthcoming marriage to a woman seventeen years his junior. Expressing exasperation with his law partners for not having written him, he said: "My heart, however, just now is a little too large, and my feelings of too kind a nature to take offense at such neglect." With his friend George Washington Cullum as one of his groomsmen, Halleck became a married man on April 10, 1855. Bad weather unfortunately kept his mother and perhaps others of his family from traveling to New York City for the wedding. The bride missed having Catherine Halleck present and, as always, Halleck's father was not even mentioned. The new bride was extremely pleased at the Bible that Halleck's mother had sent her and happy at the permission to call her mother-in-law Mother.[46] The couple seemed content as they planned their return trip to San Francisco.

Other than several photographs that show a dark, thin, attractive woman and bits and pieces of other data, there is little historical information about Elizabeth Halleck. She was apparently "especially expert in horsemanship" and was able to travel to California by ship during rough seas without getting seasick. She was twenty-four years old when she and her forty-one-year-old husband arrived in San Francisco on May 16, 1855. She was leaving her family and her many friends in eastern society and moving into a less established network of acquaintances in a rough-hewn city on the Pacific Coast. The change had to have been difficult for her, but she seemed to have taken on the challenge without complaint. Halleck may have resigned from the army, but his full-time civilian occupations continued to keep him busier than ever. Now, at least, he could share his life with a wife and, he hoped, a family. Perhaps she could temper his perfectionism and bring to the fore his more humane and sociable aspects. Perhaps marriage would bring him the family happiness that the break with his father had precluded in Westernville. Elizabeth Halleck had no easy task before her, and she must have been a strong, adventuresome woman to undertake it. Halleck himself was so excited about his life with Elizabeth that he uncharacteristically blurted out to his partners: "I feel too comfortable and happy to quarrel with anyone."[47]

5

From Peace to War

With no worries about lighthouses and fortifications and no longer facing lifelong bachelorhood, Halleck could now expand his many business ventures on the Pacific Coast. Like the rest of California, San Francisco was experiencing severe economic dislocation, with many bank failures and a changing economy, and such economic fluctuations certainly affected Halleck. Because his interests were so diversified, however, he continued to do well financially. He remained a leader in the city's business class and, with Elizabeth at his side, he increasingly participated in its social life.

He continued to litigate a large number of land cases, and ownership of the Montgomery Block provided him and his law firm with the ability to exert enormous influence in the city. The building was a major gathering place, so Halleck, Peachy, and Billings had insight into most of what was going on in San Francisco. The firm was also involved in a railroad project and a quicksilver (mercury) mine. On his own, Halleck had purchased a large tract of land in Marin County, and he lived in San Francisco's fashionable Rincon Hill district. He became involved in politics, hosted or attended social functions of all kinds, helped found a historical society, wrote books on land title litigation, military theory, and international relations, and became one of the leaders in the state's militia. He also fathered a son, who would become the pride and joy of his life. He was finally a happy and successful businessman, husband, and father.

His major occupation continued to be the law firm, but he also remained general manager of the world's largest quicksilver mine, located south of

San Francisco, near San José. His responsibilities there and in the legal firm merged when he and his law partners became involved in what became the state's largest and most spectacular litigation over land ownership. The New Almaden Mine was an essential part of the gold rush. The state's major producer of quicksilver, this mine provided the most efficient means for separating gold from crushed rock and sand. Gold bonded with the quicksilver, in what one historian has described as "the magnetic-like phenomenon of 'amalgamation.'" It is no exaggeration to say that quicksilver made the wealth of the gold rush accessible, and it was the New Almaden Mine that produced the vast preponderance of this essential ingredient.[1]

The discovery of quicksilver's importance in mining was relatively recent. For a time, the Indians in the hills near San José used pulverized rock containing quicksilver to make a paste they called moketka to color their bodies red for ceremonial purposes. They found it burned the skin, however, so they stopped the practice. Then in 1845, a Mexican Army officer named Don Andres Castillero lay claim to the area, thinking at first that he had discovered silver and gold and then realizing that his claim actually contained quicksilver. He began a mining company, issued stock, and hired a New Yorker to develop the area for him. He received a Mexican government loan, but the outbreak of the Mexican War hindered his efforts to repay the money. Consequently, he sought help from an English bank, Barron, Forbes, and Company, already operating in Mexico. This financial institution took out a sixteen-year lease on the operations and gave the mine the grandiose name New Almaden, after the then largest mercury mine in the world at Almadén, Spain.

The mine was fifty-six miles southeast of San Francisco, some twelve miles past San Jose. There were brick buildings, including business offices, storehouses, and smelting furnaces, and another mile and a half up the mountain along an excellent road, "like every other part of this valuable property, intended for all time," stood the mine entrance.[2] Each day, workers entered the mine by riding one of the ore cars of an underground railroad propelled by Mexican or Indian laborers. Reaching the end of the line, they walked a short distance to ladders that led down to the darkness below, where flickering candles provided the only light. Two hundred feet below the entrance and six hundred feet below the summit of the mountain, the miners reached the site of their work. There, with the help of blasting powder, the "barateros" dug away at the rock. "Tanateros," or carriers, brought the ore-laden rocks up the ladders to the mine railroad above for transport to the "upper works," or "patio." Wearing a large sack on his back with a strap around his forehead, each ore bearer carried two hundred pounds of material per trip, making anywhere from twenty to thirty such trips a day up the steep ladders. Another group of laborers deposited the ore into a wagon for transport to "the works" below for smelting.

It was near the lower "works," or "hacienda," an area of about four acres surrounded by the mountains, that the smelting was done. There stood sixteen furnaces, forty feet long, ten feet high, and eight feet wide, each set about eight feet from its neighbor. The ore was deposited by wheelbarrow in the top of one of the furnaces. Constant heat caused the quicksilver to vaporize and pass through twelve compartments, leaking through numerous small holes into covered troughs located on the outside of the furnace. Much metal, however, escaped into the air or onto the ground either as vapor or liquid, and as a result the roofs of nearby buildings were covered with what one author called "mercurial soot." Other workers poured the captured liquid mercury into giant wrought iron flasks imported from England, each flask holding seventy-five pounds. These flasks were securely closed and shipped by wagon to San Francisco for sale around the world. One ton of ore produced one flask of quicksilver, a very favorable return.

Each furnace had a forty-foot chimney, and from these chimneys, according to a visitor, "there are constantly pouring clouds of arsenical vapors. . . . The tops of these chimneys are quite coated with cakes of white arsenic, hanging around their mouths like masses of ice about a house spout in winter." Even worse, this visitor noted, what escaped from the chimneys "withers all green things around. Every tree on the mountain side above the works is dead. . . . Cattle feeding within a half a mile of the hacienda sicken, and become salivated; and the use of the waters of a spring rising near the works is guarded against." Those working near the furnaces could do so only every fourth week, and even then they "frequently salivated, and are liable to palsy, vertigo, and other disorders of the brain." Visitors noted that "pale, cadaverous faces and leaden eyes are the consequence of even these short spells" near the furnaces. "To such a degree is the air filled with the volatile poison, that gold coins and watches on the persons of those engaged about the furnaces become galvanized and turn white."

Exposure to the arsenic vapors of mercury can indeed be lethal. Modern research has demonstrated that the symptoms of such poisoning include a wide variety of gastrointestinal problems, diarrhea/constipation, allergies, fatigue, insomnia, irritability, low self-confidence, anxiety, and timidity, conditions Halleck did exhibit, though only later in his life. Mercury poisoning can also cause swelling of the gums and malignancies of the skin and internal organs, which Halleck never experienced. One of his contemporaries was quite right in concluding that "in such an atmosphere one would seem to inhale death with every respiration," but there was no indication of such a lethal effect on Halleck during the 1850s.[3]

It was March or April 1850, after the close of the constitutional convention and after the founding of the law firm of Halleck, Peachy, and Billings, that Halleck became New Almaden's director general, at a salary of $500 every thirty days. He was not paid if his legal or military duties kept him from traveling to the mine. Before the end of 1850, Halleck built the first of the brick furnaces and made a variety of other improvements to boost productivity. He even spent New Year's Day of 1851 there. In 1852 he began building brick buildings to replace the existing wooden structures.[4] Halleck traveled to the mine every several weeks, in the meantime leaving direct administration of operations to the resident superintendent, John Young, a former ocean trader with whom he had a good professional and personal relationship. William R. Hutton, who later was the chief engineer on numerous projects including the Holland Tunnel in New York City, was an assistant to Halleck both at the mine and in the San Francisco law firm. Another engineer and later a charter trustee of the University of California, Sherman Day, was also superintendent under Halleck, and, according to one historian, he "was one of the first to use scientific methods in locating ore bodies." Halleck and his cohorts took what had been a primitive operation and made New Almaden into an efficient, money-making enterprise.[5]

Although Halleck was the mine manager and his law firm its legal representative with a $30,000 retainer, he never owned any part of the mine. Yet he was the driving force in the construction of what came to be known as Casa Grande, the major building on the property. At first, it was to be a one-story hotel, but quickly it became a three-story, twenty-seven-room residence-hotel. It was ready for occupancy in early 1855, by which time Halleck had resigned from the army and was on the verge of getting married. He proudly brought his bride to the massive and elegant structure, which, like the Montgomery Block, had a fortress-like quality, reflecting Halleck's military bent. Here the couple hosted a variety of important guests, and Halleck oversaw the vast mining empire. Like all the workers, he must have inhaled vapors from the smelting process, since all the mine buildings were close to the reduction works.[6]

According to a pamphlet produced in the late 1850s, the mine made $1,622,325 in 1857, had expenses of $280,000 ($80,000 of which were not directly related to mining operations,) and thus had a net profit of $1,342,325. A mid-twentieth-century report stated that New Almaden had over the years produced a million flasks of mercury worth somewhere between $50,000,000 and $75,000,000. This production equaled one third of all the quicksilver mined in the United States. Halleck was clearly involved in a very profitable business, and no doubt he received compensation beyond his $500 per month. He was too shrewd a businessman not to have made some sort of a bonus arrangement. Thus his mine management added significantly to the wealth he made as a lawyer and property owner. The danger to his health would become evident only later.[7]

In addition to supervising the mining operations, Halleck also had to deal with the dispute over New Almaden's land title, an enormously complicated litigation. The New Almaden Company—the Andrés Castillero/English bank claim—argued before the Land Commission in September 1852 that it had followed Mexican law in gaining control of the mine. However, Jose de los Reves Berreyesa had received a Mexican government grant in 1842 covering part of the same acreage, and that very year Justo Lários took possession of nearby land that itself included a valuable mine. Baron and Forbes, the British banking company that held the lease from Castillero, had bought out Berreyesa, and thus it claimed control over the New Almaden, citing both the Castillero and the Berreyesa grants. The competing Lários (later Fossat) grant had come into the hands of the Quicksilver Mining Company, whose owners were American businessmen and politicians.[8]

Given the complicated nature of the laws, the uncertain quality of Mexican documentation, and the deep pockets and political connections of the claimants, the Land Commission did not render its New Almaden decision until January 8, 1856. By a two-to-one vote, it upheld Castillero's right to the mine and decided that Berreyesa had a correct claim to the land on which the mine was located. Thus Halleck's employers, the British banking company, won a solid victory. On March 26, 1856, however, the losing claimants, supported by the U.S. government, filed an appeal before the U.S. District Court in San Francisco. The complications increased. Edmund Randolph was attorney both for the Fossat and the U.S. government sides. As the Fossat lawyer, he had the task of showing that the mine lay on the Fossat grant, and as U.S. counsel he had to show that Castillero's claim was invalid and that the mine lay on public land. In 1858, J. S. Black, the Attorney General of the United States, sent a leading attorney (and later Secretary of War), Edwin M. Stanton, to California to try to unravel another land litigation. He did so successfully and then stayed on to aid the government in the Almaden case. He acted under the supposition that the New Almaden Mine claim (Castillero and Berreyesa) was fraudulent.[9] This put Stanton in direct opposition to Halleck, an ironic situation considering their later relationship during the Civil War.

While the case was proceeding through the federal district court, Stanton asked for an injunction to close the mine, arguing that Baron and Forbes's title had been gained through fraud. The company, he argued, should not be allowed to continue mining quicksilver until the court issued its ruling. The court granted the injunction on October 30, 1858, closing the mine. The price of mercury jumped enormously, and rumors flew throughout the gold-mining district that the government was going to treat all mining claims similarly. The California legislature passed a resolution in 1860 calling for an end to the quicksilver suit because of the damage the New Almaden closing was doing to the entire gold-mining industry.[10]

The case dragged on nonetheless. Whereas the printing of the Land Commission proceedings filled only 130 pages, those before the District Court took up 3,454. Those arguing against the New Almaden Company insisted that it had obtained its title through fraud, by using antedated documents that had subsequently been tampered with. As in most California land cases, the argument was over the legality of the "expediente," the documents issued that supported the New Almaden Company's ownership of the mine and surrounding land. Opposing attorneys produced an 1848 letter in which a principal in the New Almaden Company admitted wrongdoing in producing these documents. Counter-accusations came from the New Almaden side insisting that this damaging letter had been forged.[11]

The New Almaden Company then proposed sending a delegation to Mexico to investigate the records there and take testimony from those with knowledge of the Castillero grant. The court refused, arguing that the Land Commission Act allowed no such travel. The litigants then appealed to Lewis Cass, the U.S. Secretary of State, for permission to travel to Mexico, and when he ignored the request, they appealed directly to President James Buchanan, who bucked the matter to Attorney General Jeremiah Black, the man who had sent Stanton to California in the first place. Black issued a statement using information he had gained from Stanton supporting the government case. When the claimants announced that they would go to Mexico to take testimony before the U.S. consul there, the State Department forbade that official to cooperate. The litigants now tried to get Congress to amend the original act, but J. A. Bayard, the chair of the Senate Judiciary Committee, was an attorney for the Fossat claim, and he helped block such action. Undeterred, Halleck, Peachy, and Billings sent Frederick Billings by boat to Mexico, at a cost of $200,000, to bring back to San Francisco nine witnesses who could support the validity of the documents in the Castillero claim.[12]

The U.S. District Court did not issue a ruling until January 1861, on the eve of the Civil War. It held that although there were some questions about procedure and form, the Castillero grant had been made according to appropriate Spanish and Mexican practice and thus was valid. Limiting this victory for Halleck's side, the court gave the company the minimum amount of land possible around the mine. The New Almaden Company then appealed the decision to the U.S. Supreme Court, which showed itself most impressed with the allegations of forgery brought against the company. In 1863, it ruled by a five-to-three vote, with Chief Justice Roger B. Taney not participating, that the procedure in the Castillero grant had been improper. Other litigation on the Fossat and the Berryesa claims continued meanwhile, and in separate actions the Supreme Court validated the Fossat boundaries, which included the mine, and the Berryesa boundaries, which included the smelting works and the mine office. In sum, the court divided the baby in half, ruling that each contesting grant had a legal right to a part of the New Almaden operation. In fact, however, the New Almaden Company still had actual physical control over all the property. It was not until 1864 that the tangle was finally resolved, but not without further confusion and even greater controversy.[13]

Throughout all this litigation, Halleck, Peachy, and Billings represented the New Almaden, or Castillero, claim, and the firm added to its legal team Judah P. Benjamin (later a member of the Confederate cabinet), U.S. Senator Reverdy Johnson, and several other leading Washington lawyers. A modern historian has estimated that attorney fees cost the New Almaden Company over $500,000.[14] Since Halleck was the manager of the New Almaden Mine, a member of the law firm, the gatherer of the archives that contained Mexican land documents central to the case, the author of an 1849 land report to Congress, and the compiler of the 1859 book *A Collection of the Mining Laws of Spain and Mexico,* he played a major role in this case. But he tried to keep his participation away from public scrutiny. He continued to manage the mine until the injunction closed it in 1858, and he did a great deal of behind-the-scenes research.

He was a key witness in the district court proceedings, and his performance as witness in October and November of 1857 provides insight into his role in the company and in the litigation. Peachy and Billings were already lawyers for New Almaden when he joined the firm, so he "never . . .

received any part of their fees as counsel in this case," he insisted. He admitted helping Peachy and Billings prepare the briefs, but he said that he did so without pay. When asked what he was paid to superintend mine operations, he reported a monthly salary, then added sharply: "What the amount was is my own business, and I decline to answer it." Later, however, he admitted that he earned $500 a month; he said he owned no company shares.

Over nine days, Halleck answered questions about his familiarity with the Castillero legal documents, where he had first seen them, and what he remembered about them. During his entire time on the stand, Halleck's irritable impatience was barely suppressed. He gave sharp responses and sometimes answered questions sarcastically. During a discussion of the exact area of the Castillero claim, for example, the opposing attorney said: "A square of 6,000 varas [a vara is two feet, nine inches] contains 36,000,000 square varas. A pertenencia or appurtenance 200 varas square contains exactly 40,000 square varas. Are not 40,000 contained exactly 900 times in 36,000,000?" Halleck answered: "I have not made the calculation, but presume the counsel is a sufficiently good mathematician to divide one quantity by another, and to deduce a correct result, provided the quantities are not too large."[15]

Halleck's testimony was hardly conclusive, but it did no harm to his side either. Even though Edwin Stanton long suspected him of perjury, Halleck, like the good lawyer he was, answered only what was asked of him. He demonstrated a good knowledge of the issues under consideration, but he volunteered nothing. Even in the U.S. Supreme Court hearings, lawyers for both sides were still debating the worth of Halleck's district court testimony. Perhaps the greatest irony of all was that the lead district court judge, H. Hall McAllister, limited New Almaden's rights by citing Halleck's 1859 book on mining laws. A modern historian is correct in surmising that "one can imagine that back at the [Halleck, Peachy, Billings law offices in] Montgomery Block, Halleck came in for a little ribbing by his partners." He might have taken even more direct criticism when he and Mrs. Halleck held a grand ball for the attorneys in the case and this same Judge McAllister and his large family were among the guests.[16]

The New Almaden Mining Company case, what the *New York Times* called "one of the most remarkable civil trials in this or any other country," dragged on through the courts during the 1850s, and Halleck remained involved in it whether he was testifying or not. During his 1854 visit to Washington, it was constantly on his mind. He was appalled when he learned that former Secretary of the Treasury Robert J. Walker was claiming ownership of the mine and expected "very soon to *recover* the possession." When Halleck's former convention colleague and now U.S. Senator William Gwin predicted his own appointment as a receiver for the mine, Halleck could only exclaim: "This looks decidedly bad!! Bad!!" And when the case was still dragging on in the fall of 1860, he optimistically wrote Pablo de la Guerra that "we have every hope of success."[17]

As complicated and time-consuming as this case was, it did not consume Halleck's life. When John Young took six months off in 1855 to visit relatives in England, Halleck hired his brother-in-law, Schuyler Hamilton, to take Young's place as manager at New Almaden, and he and Elizabeth spent a good part of that summer helping Hamilton supervise day-to-day operations. When the couple returned to the city in the fall, they lived, for a time, in San Francisco hotels. Halleck wrote his mother that his wife was "pleased with the country and quite contented, although it is a pretty hard trial for her to leave all her friends to live in this distant country among strangers." When she gave birth to a son in January 1856, the couple named him Henry, but called him Harry. Halleck proudly sent a photograph of him to his mother in Westernville, saying that the "picture, with his finger in his mouth, gives an excellent idea of him."[18]

Sometime in these early years, Halleck and his wife moved into a Victorian Gothic home at 326 Second Street, on the southwest corner of Folsom and Second streets. This was in the Rincon Hill section of San Francisco, "the site of the elegant homes of the most prosperous and influential men of property in San Francisco," "San Francisco's first Nob Hill." Here the family had an excellent view of the bay, and Halleck was close to his law office.[19]

Halleck also owned other property in California. On December 1, 1850, he became owner of 30,848 acres of land in Nicasio, Marin County, purchasing it from Pablo de la Guerra for $30,000, $15,000 down and $15,000 to be paid later. As part of the down payment, he probably used the $12,000 salary payment he had received from the constitutional convention. In 1855, determining that he legally should not have received this payment, the Treasury Department made him reimburse the government. By that time, however, he was wealthy enough to do so with little financial effort.[20]

Soon after the 1850 Nicasio purchase, Halleck built a redwood log cabin along Halleck Creek in Halleck Valley on his new property. At first, he used this plain structure as a getaway for hunting and fishing, but once he married, he rarely went there. Beginning in 1855, he began to sell pieces of this land at a profit. During the Civil War, his attorney and property manager, David B. Northrup, sold the last small sections of the 30,000 acres. Halleck made a substantial profit on this land and, no doubt, other land he owned in California.

He was, in fact, a very wealthy man. In 1854, the *San Francisco Chronicle* listed his law firm as the fourth wealthiest property holder in the city, just below the California Steam Navigation Company and above the Nicaragua Steamship Company. The city's largest landowner was J. L. Folsom, and Halleck later became the executor of his will. A contemporary magazine listed all this information under a heading that aptly described Halleck's place in his city: "The Rich Men of San Francisco."[21]

In their impressive home on Rincon Hill the Hallecks hosted dinner parties appropriate to their place in society. Over time, their neighbors included Albert Sidney Johnston, later a Confederate general, Senator William M. Gwin, the businessman John Parrott, two men who later became Union generals, "Fighting Joe" Hooker and William T. Sherman, San Francisco mayors, state senators, and a host of other luminaries. Little is known about Halleck's relationship with his neighbors, although he remained a "very intimate friend" of Jeremy Gilmer, his West Point classmate. Gilmer, in fact, stayed with the Hallecks after he sold his house, just before he left California in 1861 to join the Confederate Army. Halleck was also a good friend of James B. McPherson, then army commander on Alcatraz Island and later to be a general in the Civil War.[22]

But Halleck had very poor relations with two men who were destined to become his fellow generals in the Union Army. He nursed a grudge against Joseph Hooker, in part because Hooker owed him money and more generally because he disapproved of Hooker's reputation for drinking too much and carousing with loose women. His relations with William T. Sherman also remained fractured. Sherman had left California, still a soldier, in 1850, but in 1854 he returned as a civilian banker and became a well-respected San Francisco businessman. One of his clerks was Halleck's brother-in-law, Schuyler Hamilton. Halleck and Sherman were both leaders in the city's business world, Sherman especially receiving praise for his handling of a run on his bank during a mid-1850s panic. They lived in the same neighborhood but had nothing to do with each other. Time had not assuaged the hard feelings generated in their military days together under Colonel Richard B. Mason.[23]

Sherman told Schuyler Hamilton about this mutual animosity, and Hamilton, who was then living at the New Almaden Mine with the Hallecks, tried to act as a mediator between the two men. He told Sherman that he was sure that "the difficulties" were "a source of mutual regret."

He had heard both of them speak with "a just appreciation of each other's character," but both seemed to "indicate an abiding coldness." He regretted this situation particularly on his sister's account. "I shall yet hope some accident may dispel that cloud the separates my friends," he said.[24]

Soon afterward, Hamilton wrote Sherman again to report that Halleck had recently said: "Your friend Sherman deserves a good deal of credit for the manner in which he conducted his banking affairs during the past crisis." Later, after Sherman had left California to become a real estate lawyer in Kansas, another friend told him that "Halleck & myself had a good laugh at your turning lawyer. He said you read Law many years ago & with your strong common sense would make a good one." Sherman's response to these favorable comments is unknown, but Halleck seemed to be willing to let bygones be bygones. He respected Sherman's efficiency as a banker, and they were, after all, no longer debating engineer projects in the army. Yet no reconciliation took place.[25]

In the spring of 1857, Halleck's father died, leaving a wife and several children at home and a debt on his Westernville farm. The senior Halleck's namesake, Joseph Jr., suffered great grief: "It is painful for me to think that I shall never see Father again in this life," he wrote. Henry, the oldest son, never expressed such feelings. In fact, neither Henry's mother nor his sister even wrote to tell him of his father's demise, knowing that he remained angry and unforgiving.[26]

Indeed, his family in Westernville wrote infrequently, and Halleck wanted "to hear how you are all getting along." He told these relatives that he, Elizabeth, and Harry were doing well. "Little Harry was somewhat indisposed before he went to New Almaden," Halleck reported, "but a few weeks in the country seems to have entirely cured him, for he is now fat, hearty, and as lively as a cricket." Elizabeth Halleck also wrote her mother-in-law a letter full of news about Harry's antics and Henry's "grey hairs," but again there was no mention of Joseph Halleck's death. Henry's postscript merely mentioned in passing something about a "settlement of the estate."[27]

With his father dead, Halleck took his wife and son to Westernville that fall of 1858, and, while there, he purchased from his brothers and sisters their one-eighth share each in their father's farm. Through this transaction, each sibling received an immediate monetary benefit from the father's death, and the mother and two sisters would always have a place to live.[28] Halleck had finally accomplished what he had begun trying to do since early in his life. He replaced his father as head of the family. The young boy who had run away from home had now returned in the fullest sense of the word, owner of the farm he had escaped from and victorious over the parent he had rebelled against all his life.

Establishing his preeminence in his Westernville family and visiting his in-laws, the Hamiltons, in New York City to show off three-year-old Harry, Halleck must have experienced a great sense of accomplishment. Having left the East with little certain in his life, he now had money, a family, and a solid reputation. He returned with his wife and son to their home on San Francisco's Rincon Hill, where they continued to play an important role in the city's business and society. When the city feted the Chinese emperor's delegation with a banquet, for example, Halleck was among those present. He strongly opposed the California movement to expel Chinese immigrants on the grounds that their labor was essential to the survival of the California economy, so he must have been pleased to attend this show of respect to Asian leaders. In February 1851, when a group of women had formed the San Francisco Orphan Asylum, Halleck had given them, rent-free, the use of a cottage he owned. When news of President Zachary Taylor's 1850 death reached San Francisco, a group of the pre–gold rush residents decided to march in the city's memorial funeral procession as a body, "as *pioneers*." They named Halleck the interim president of their new organization. In the first regular election, he was voted one of the twenty-five members of the board of directors. From this point on, he remained a part of the Society of California Pioneers, an organization that continues to exist in San Francisco.[29]

When the California State Agricultural Society organized itself in 1854 and held its first convention in San Francisco that year, Halleck composed four speeches on agriculture that he delivered some time during the decade. In these presentations, which are preserved in his own handwriting, he offered a historical overview of agriculture's significant role in the history of the world and then gave two speeches on California crop farming and one speech on California stock raising. This soldier, lawyer, and businessman pointed out that "in all great nations, both ancient and modern, agriculture has proceeded the other arts. When man gives up the chase and resorts to tillage, he takes the first great step in human civilization." He then added that "the real wealth of the farmer is not in the *money* he makes, but in the enjoyment of a comfortable home and its pleasant surroundings," something, of course, he had not experienced in Westernville as a boy. California, he said, had "a soil capable of producing every variety of grain & fruit & flower," but to make money he warned the state's farmers against "raising too much wheat & oats & barley," and suggested instead the growing of cash crops like "rice, tobacco, cotton, sugar, &c."

Finally, he said, "experience has shown that the climate of California is peculiarly adapted to the raising of domestic animals."[30]

Halleck also wrote four books in the four years between 1859 and 1861. The first two dealt with land-title issues. In the preface of the first one, he announced that it "furnish[ed] a compilation and translation of the Mining laws of Spain, from the earliest period to the independence of Mexico, and those of the general government of Mexico from the independence of that country to the year 1853." The second book was a translation that compared French and Belgium mining codes with those of Spain and Mexico. In the 153-page introduction he wrote for this translation, he said that in order for California to write appropriate laws for the mines, "it must necessarily refer to others, and especially to the commentaries of learned jurisconsults who have discussed fundamental principles." Dennis Hart Mahan's insistence on the crucial influence of history on contemporary affairs continued to affect Halleck, even in his legal writing.[31]

The third publication was a revised edition of his book on military theory, including new information on the Mexican and the Crimean wars. The fourth and the most ambitious volume was Halleck's study of international relations, a thorough investigation of how nations dealt with one another. Having frequently been required to state opinions on this topic while California's secretary of state, "he [had] commenced a series of note and extracts," he said, "which were arranged under different heads, convenient for use." These he augmented over the years, and they formed the basis for the book. According to a leading twentieth-century historian, Halleck, along with Emmerich de Vattel and Henry Wheaton, "were perhaps the three authorities on international law most frequently cited at the time of the Civil War."[32] All these books expanded Halleck's reputation as one of the nation's leading thinkers. And he wrote them all while he was fulfilling his professional, social, and family obligations—an amazing feat..

Yet Halleck's literary success did not prevent him from being as caustic in this arena as he had been in the military and the law. In a book review, he harshly evaluated another author's work: "We most sincerely regret this chapter was ever written or published. It is so replete with errors." As for the author, Halleck said that he had "not a single characteristic as qualification of a historian." As always, Halleck had no patience with any kind of sloppiness. He expected things to be done correctly, and he spared no one's feelings in saying so.[33]

Halleck also maintained his interest in a variety of other economic pursuits. When the former army officer and leading San Francisco businessman Joseph L. Folsom died in 1853, Halleck became one of the executors of his estate, and he held this position into the 1860s. He also managed money for friends. For example, he invested funds in California for the army officer George W. Cullum and the chief clerk of the State Department, Robert S. Chew. When the Chew investment failed, Halleck made good the loss, much to his friend's amazement. Halleck felt personal responsibility for the money entrusted to him, even though he had no legal obligation to repay Chew. Along with his law partners, Halleck also investigated the possibility of investing in borax, a crystalline salt used in manufacturing. Peachy and Billings did; Halleck did not.[34] All three did, however, become deeply involved in a railroad venture, grandly entitled the Pacific and Atlantic Railroad Company.

This railroad had a checkered existence. It was actually to run only the forty-eight miles from San Francisco to San Jose. As manager of the New Almaden mine, Halleck indicated that such a road would receive a majority of the $37,000 the mine spent for sending mercury to market. In early 1855, Halleck, Peachy, and Billings became associated with the venture. Both Billings and Halleck were named to the board of directors and in January 1856 Halleck became president. He held the post for a year, but the company went into a downward spiral that not even the California legislature's political support could reverse.[35]

Halleck's railroad company passed out of existence. A new one with the more modest name of San Francisco and San Jose Railroad Company was incorporated on April 17, 1860, only to dissolve within two months. The company then reorganized itself in 1861 and finally built a road that eventually became part of a transcontinental railroad. Halleck had no connection with that effort, however, his brief board membership and presidency of a defunct earlier company being his only connection with the railroad business.[36]

All was not well in the law firm either. Earlier, in 1858, a disgruntled client had taken the firm to court "to recover damage for injuries alleged to have resulted from their negligent and unskillful management of a cause in which they were retained by plaintiff." The accuser, John Hastings, alleged that he had hired Halleck, Peachy, and Billings to represent him in a dispute with his property agents. He insisted that these agents had overstepped the authority he had delegated to them, and that Halleck, Peachy, and Billings had been negligent in not making that accusation on his behalf in court. The state supreme court threw out the case, the first malpractice suit in the history of California's legal profession. This litigation, however baseless, must have been embarrassing for the firm and deleterious to its reputation. Halleck's perfectionist personality must have been particularly affronted.[37]

Throughout the turbulent 1850s, Halleck was also caught up in the state's and the nation's politics. He remained a staunch Democrat, but it worried him to witness the divisions in the California party. There was a southern faction, called the Chivalry, which looked favorably upon slavery and had Senator William M. Gwin as its leader. The northern wing, Tammany or Free Soil (or, as Halleck called its members, the shoulder strikers) was led by state Senator David Broderick, an Irish-born immigrant from New York City. These two factions disagreed on a variety of issues, but their opposing positions on slavery were the determining factors in their animosity. The Chivalry wanted a state fugitive slave law to help enforce the national law. It also wanted another state constitutional convention, the unspoken agenda being to split the state into two, one slave and one free. The Tammany, on the other hand, pushed for a pro-squatter policy, making land as open as possible to the landless migrants to the state. This group vigorously opposed slavery in California. The animosity between these factions was so great that during the 1854 state convention each side elected its own presiding officials, then split to hold separate gatherings. Those who could not abide either of these factions came to be called the Conservative Democrats or National Democrats. These included many of the state's prominent figures, Halleck among them. In addition, there were Whigs and briefly Know-Nothings, but it was the Democratic factionalism that dominated the state's politics.[38]

Despite his long-held interest in politics, Halleck ran for office on only two occasions. As noted above, he lost to Frémont and Gwin in the 1850 California election for the state's first two U.S. senators. In 1857, he gained the Democratic party nomination for the state senate, but then he showed little enthusiasm for it. "As far as I am individually concerned, I had rather be defeated than elected," he said to Pablo de la Guerra. He got his wish; he never served in the legislative body. Rumors spread that he was going to be appointed governor of the Oregon territory, but this too never came to pass.[39]

Strait-laced as he was, Halleck expressed disgust at the widespread disorder in California in the early 1850s. When a vigilante movement sprang up in response, he offered his tacit support but did not join. Then as law and order took hold in the new state, he began to see the vigilantes as the real threat to an orderly society and considered taking arms to suppress them. "If things are going on in this way, I shall have to shoulder my musket," he warned. When William T. Sherman, militia head in the city, recommended Halleck as his successor, despite their continued enmity, Halleck did not step forward. Halleck had his opinions, but he could not bring himself to enforce them through decisive action. In response to the candidacy of the Tammany leader Broderick for the U.S. Senate in 1852, for example, Halleck said: "He is the squatter candidate, & besides, has neither the talent or moral character to fit him for that place." When his partner Peachy, an avowed Chivalry man, was elected to the statehouse, he was pleased but he opposed Peachy's recommendation to split California into two states. "California will rue the day she ever seriously enters into this question, or I am no prophet," he warned. The only reason for wanting such a convention, he said, was "to make California a slave state, and failing in that, to divide it and force negro [sic] slavery on the southern portion." Halleck even signed a petition calling for repeal of a law that prevented blacks from testifying in any legal case concerning whites. His position was more pro-California than it was pro-black. He opposed dividing California not so much because he opposed slavery as because he believed it was not in the state's interest. Once again, however, while he was a business leader and clearly unhappy with conditions in the state, he was not willing to enter the political fray as a candidate.[40]

In 1852 he verbally lashed out at both the Whigs and the Democrats. He insisted that "neither party could scarcely have selected *worse* men. But so it is, and so it will be until the land titles are settled and people acquire a permanent interest in the welfare of the country." In part, his concern was a product of self-interest. He equated his legal work with the survival of California. He could not agree with either faction of his party. "I dislike the aims & principles of the one, and the character and conduct of the other. I feel something like the woman who witnessed the fight between her husband & the Bear: 'no particular interest in the result.'"[41]

Not willing to give his support to either of the major factions, Halleck stayed out of state politics completely except to express his criticism. He had similar disdain for national politics. He had a tremendous dislike of Franklin Pierce because that Democratic President had "made such rascally appointments in California." When former California senator John C. Frémont, another rascal in Halleck's view, became the Republican party candidate in the 1856 presidential election, he thought the old Pathfinder would get few votes in California. Democratic party candidate James Buchanan was "pretty certain to get elected," he said. When that indeed happened, Halleck's friend Cullum told him that he ought to be Secretary of War in the new administration. Once again, however, public office passed him by. Halleck made no attempt to gain it and expressed no disappointment at his failure to do so.[42]

In his law office, however, Halleck found himself in the thick of the 1860 election. "All the office-holders go with the nigger party [Chivalry] headed by old Gwin. Peachy at first was for [Stephen A.] Douglas, but I am sorry to say he has gone over to the Gwin party. This kills all his hopes for the

Senate. Billings & myself will now both oppose him." As a staunch supporter of Douglas, Halleck could not have been happy, therefore, when Lincoln carried California with only a plurality, but he was not surprised that the state Democratic party split had allowed this to happen.[43] Such political differences among the three men in the law firm were not new. The Whig Billings and the Democrat Halleck had always opposed Peachy's Chivalry pro-slavery leanings, but they still supported him when he sought state office because they hoped his influence would be beneficial to their law firm. As politics became ever more slavery driven in the late 1850s, however, their political differences became a divisive problem.

The powerful law firm of Halleck, Peachy, and Billings succumbed to these political antagonisms and dissolved, although precisely how it happened is unknown. In July of 1860, Halleck wrote his friend and the firm's business colleague Pablo de la Guerra that Billings had decided to withdraw from the partnership, and that Peachy had decided to maintain only a couple of his old cases. Halleck said that he planned to "continue on as heretofore till I can form a new partnership. I hope my old friends will continue to give me their patronage." In the meantime, however, Halleck and Billings opposed Peachy's run for state senator, and in April 1861, the firm put the three thousand volumes in its law library and even the bookcases and office furniture up for auction. Halleck's days as a lawyer were over, the firm's willingness to sell all its books demonstrating that the dissolution was permanent and that Halleck had no plans to stay in practice on his own.[44]

The life that Halleck had built for himself in California was suddenly breaking apart. With the law firm dissolved, the New Almaden Mine closed under injunction, land-title cases declining, himself disgusted with politics, and even one of his trusted partners openly speaking of secession, Halleck was all but cast adrift. In California, various newspapers called either for continued Union or southern secession; a few even advocated an independent nation along the Pacific Coast. In fact, however, there was no real chance of California's seceding. For his part, Halleck was solidly for the Union and spoke out in its defense.[45]

Once more, he used history to drive home his point. He asked his listeners to recall the great success that California had experienced during the past twelve years. "Let us remember that our wonderful progress & material prosperity are due, less to the mineral wealth and agricultural capacity of our country, than to our political institutions and the character of our government." And who was responsible for the chaos the state was presently experiencing he asked? "These destroyers of [the constitution and the flag] are not from foreign lands; they have sprung up in our very midst, from the dragon teeth of party animosity & political corruption. This is the work of scheming, selfish, corrupt politicians,—of men whom we elected to office, but who have proved faithless to their trust!" Neither disunion nor a new Pacific republic could be tolerated. Corrupt politicians deserved a sound repulse; otherwise, the nation was doomed.[46]

In this time of uncertainty, a group of concerned businessmen, Halleck no doubt among them, met after the November 1860 election to evaluate California's militia. What they found was not reassuring. As of January of that year, there were forty-nine militia companies, but only seven new ones had organized during 1860 and early 1861 and the legislature had taken no action to pass any laws beneficial to the military arm. Even more alarming, the adjutant general had prepared no annual report for the year, a state Senate committee noting that his office was in shambles, with record-keeping practically nonexistent.[47]

Such disarray within the context of southern secession threats affronted Halleck's bureaucratic sense of precision. Here was an issue powerful enough to impel him into the public arena. He would return to the organization that had nurtured him during the early years of his life, and at the same time he would be able to deal with the political chaos he saw developing in the state and nation. He would rejoin the army—actually the state militia.

On December 14, 1860, the governor appointed him a major general, to command the militia's second division, his brother-in-law Captain Schuyler Hamilton being named a drillmaster. That winter, Halleck and other militia leaders lectured the assembled troops on military art and science, no doubt dusting off copies of Halleck's famous book. Halleck was appalled at the absence of structure and order. There were no records of any kind, and the militia lacked basic military necessities. He took swift action to remedy the situation, drawing up the draft of an order for the governor to issue; appointing his division staff; sending the draft of a new militia law to the legislature; and asking for and receiving the governor's permission to act in concert with the U.S. Army against any attempt to seize government installations and declare a Pacific republic. He took quick, bold administrative action to try to prepare the state's military forces for the crisis that he feared was coming. He was no longer simply complaining; he was acting.[48]

News that South Carolina had fired on Fort Sumter in Charleston harbor in April 1861 made matters even more tense in California. "Civil War seems now to be inevitable," Halleck declared, and he worried about its outcome. Once again slavery was a major part of his thoughts, and he still viewed it only in the context of its effect on the nation's future. He showed no concern for the slaves themselves. "I really hope that Maryland may not secede. . . . If no slave States remain in the Union, the North will become ultra anti-slavery, and I fear, in the course of the war will declare for emancipation and thus add the horrors of a servile to that of a civil war." He also believed the rumors that Jefferson Davis had sent emissaries to the Pacific Coast to consult with leading southern sympathizers and with General Albert Sidney Johnston, the commander of U.S. Army troops in California. Johnston had recently resigned to join the Confederacy, but he was "to remain . . . for the present upon this coast, and it is asked, for what purpose? Time alone can answer," Halleck concluded warily. "It is possible that I may have to put on the old uniform," he said.[49]

Just that thought brought Halleck's mind back to the old arguments and beliefs from his time in the U.S. Army between 1839 and 1855. He wished he was participating in the war "to make use of whatever military knowledge I may have acquired by long years of military study." He saw little hope for himself, considering that "all high Federal appointments are given to politicians or for political considerations." He was also appalled at the way the Federal Army was being recruited. "Five full regiments of artillery and one single Engrs [Engineers] troops! Is the Gov't crazy? What an absurd army organization. How is it to cross rivers, build and destroy bridges, construct, defend, and attack fortifications. Have they forgotten Napoleon's campaign of 1813–14 and the operations of Wellington in the Peninsula? It certainly seems so."[50]

Even before the first shot of the Civil War, therefore, the national crisis had disrupted Halleck's comfortable life in California. He gave up the law, quicksilver, railroads, even his family, and returned to military matters. His perception of the conflict, as he watched it unfold from California, was based on the ideas he had expressed in his mid-1840s Lowell Institute lectures and in his famous book. The man who was considered one of America's leading land-title and international law experts now reached back to his first fame, military theory. He was determined to get into the war raging in the East. If he did, he would bring with him not only his long-held expertise, his disdain for politicians, his intolerance of incompetence, but also a self that tended to be strongly opinionated, inflexible, abrasive, and intolerant. He would enter the Civil War a successful individual willing to act in a variety of areas, but one who carried inside him deeply ingrained faults and weaknesses that impelled him toward hesitancy rather than decisive action.

6

Commander of the Western Theater

WHAT HALLECK feared had happened. The United States was torn asunder. Opposing troops were set to battle. California seemed more ready to remain in the Union each day, but nothing could be certain in the confused world of 1861. Halleck kept busy with the state's militia, but he yearned for a role in the wider war going on in the East. On July 21, 1861, Union and Confederate forces clashed on the banks of Bull Run in Virginia, with victory ominously going to the secessionists. Halleck believed he had something to offer the U.S. Army in its time of peril, but there he was in California, far from the action.

Meanwhile, his friend George W. Cullum was in the middle of it all. On April 9, 1861, Cullum left army engineer work to become an aide to Commanding General Winfield Scott. Very likely, he reminded his superior of Halleck's qualifications, though Winfield Scott knew all about Halleck himself from the Californian's writings, and because the two had met years before in Washington. At some point, Scott decided Halleck was the man to succeed him as commanding general, and he so advised the new President, Abraham Lincoln. At the same time, Halleck's former West Point professor Dennis Hart Mahan thought Halleck was, of all his former students, the perfect man to fill a new chief-of staff position that Mahan believed was essential to the war effort. In mid-August, however, the President was not ready to commit himself to either recommendation. But he did order Secretary of War Simon Cameron to name Halleck a major general in the regular army, the highest possible rank at the time.[1]

A telegram arrived in California from the adjutant general "directing

Major Halleck to report at Washington." Halleck was insulted at the form of address, considering the rank of major below his proper station. He almost responded with a letter of refusal. If he had, he later shuddered, Washington might very well have thought he was declining "the appt of Major *Genl.*" Fortunately Cullum had written him privately, and then the official letter of appointment with the correct rank arrived. Halleck quickly accepted.

"This whole matter of the appt takes me so much by surprise, that I am entirely unprepared to leave," he told Cullum, but he planned to "immediately close up my business, rent my house, and before you receive this, I expect to be on my way to New York with my family. It is hard to break up a happy home and . . . [it] is a great pecuniary sacrifice to leave my business at this juncture; but," he concluded, "I regard the call as one of duty & honor, to which all else must be sacrificed." "I have been quite unwell for several days, but I think this news will make me all right very soon."[2]

A message from the Secretary of War in jumbled grammar called upon him to "report, *by letter,* for orders, to the General-in-chief." He was sure that it was intended to mean "to report *in person,*" and he responded that "as soon as such orders are received I shall repair to Washington with the least possible delay." Eager as he was to participate in the war, he nevertheless delayed his departure because of this error, which almost anyone else would have ignored. Not Halleck. The order had to be precise; he would not move until it was. Meanwhile, Winfield Scott was impatiently awaiting his arrival. When Secretary of the Treasury Salmon P. Chase complained about the huge sums of money General George B. McClellan was spending as army commander in the East, Scott urged the Secretary "to be patient. He assured Chase that "General Halleck was daily expected from California, and . . . he understood the value of money and finance, and would relieve McClellan." The old commanding general clearly wanted Halleck to replace him, but the recently appointed major general was back in California debating the precise meaning of his orders.[3]

In mid-September, Halleck demonstrated another characteristic that would continue to haunt him. When he resigned his generalship in the state militia, he refused to offer "any suggestion or recommendation respecting the appointment of my successor," leaving the decision up to the governor. Although he pointed out how important it was "to have cool & discreet officers in command" because it was such men who would determine "peace or civil war in California," Halleck refused to make any recommendations.[4]

Meanwhile, he continued to delay his departure for Washington, this time because his clerk was ill and, perhaps too, because he was waiting for clients like his friend Pablo de la Guerra to pay what they owed him. "My army pay is so small that it will not meet current expenses," he complained. In the East, Winfield Scott, ill and feeble, looked for Halleck's arrival so he could resign. "I shall try to hold out till the arrival of Maj. Genl Halleck," Scott told Secretary of War Cameron, "as his presence will give increased confidence to the safety of the Union." Halleck, however, continued to delay. Lincoln promoted another impressive general already on the scene, George B. McClellan.[5]

Scott was not alone in his high regard for Halleck. The Californian's very name was a major public boost to the Union war effort. A San Francisco newspaper said: "California will lose one of her most patriotic and useful citizens in the departure of H. W. Halleck," while the famous British reporter William "Bull Run" Russell, after listening to Winfield Scott and George W. Cullum sing Halleck's praises, decided that Robert E. Lee, Joseph E. Johnston, and P. G. T. Beauregard taken "together . . . [were] not equal to Halleck."[6]

Halleck was, after all, no ordinary man. He was one of the most famous American military men of his time. He was the author of major writings on the martial craft, and his performance in combat during the Mexican War had been exemplary. He was an acknowledged expert on land law, and to add to his already high intellectual reputation, his book on international law was leaving the presses as the Civil War began. His legal and business ventures had been outstandingly successful, making him one of the richest men in the nation. His family life was satisfying, and he appeared content with his life. He was in his late forties, at the height of his physical powers. No wonder that Scott, Cullum, Russell, and even Abraham Lincoln considered Henry Wager Halleck one of America's great men, ready to apply his enormous talents to help preserve the Union.

Halleck was finally ready to leave on October 11, and his departure proved to be a festive occasion. With his wife, son, and two servants, he boarded the S.S. St. Louis, while a delegation of his fellow Society of California Pioneers stood along the pier in full uniform, two horse-drawn artillery pieces at their side. As the ship eased its way into San Francisco Bay, the cannons boomed out salute after salute, while Halleck bared his head in acknowledgment and the steamship whistle joined in the celebration. One of the founding fathers of California was going East to help preserve the Union, and his state gave him a rousing send-off.[7]

Upon arrival on the East Coast, Halleck left his wife and son with her family in New York City, then traveled to Washington in early November.

He had to be sad at leaving his family behind, and Elizabeth must have suffered from anxiety and fear. Her husband was leaving her to go to war. Would he bear up under the dangers and stress of combat or would a musket round kill him on some distant battlefield? Would she have to raise their son alone? How would the child deal with the absence of his father? Like so many other families throughout the nation, the Hallecks looked to the future with foreboding.

Whatever his inner feelings, Halleck uncharacteristically made a good impression on the men of Lincoln's Republican administration, most of whom had never seen this California Democrat before. "He is a handsome and quiet gentleman, who dresses well and talks well," reported John Hay, one of Lincoln's two secretaries. The administration had no definite plans for Halleck at this point, Hay said, but they were "silently taking his measure, that they may cut out a piece of work for him to do." Halleck met with Lincoln and his cabinet, and he was "in frequent consultation" with McClellan, the army's commanding general. Halleck's late arrival had militated against his selection for command in the East, but rumors began circulating that the Californian was going to command in the West, apparently in Missouri.[8]

This border state remained in the Union, but it was torn during the secession crisis and afterward. Politicians of various political persuasions vied for dominance.[9] Governor Claiborne Jackson cooperated with the newly formed Confederate government of Jefferson Davis, while Francis Preston Blair Jr., of the politically powerful Blair family, worked with Captain, later Brigadier General, Nathaniel Lyon to keep Missouri in the Union. Matters came to a head in early May 1861, when the Union Home Guards, under Blair's and Lyon's leadership, marched on the pro-Confederate Camp Jackson in St. Louis. The ensuing violence resulted in the death of nearly thirty people and injuries to many more.

Throughout the state, violence between unionists and secessionists grew increasingly more prevalent. Lyon bluntly drove the secessionist governor and his supporters out of the state capital, Jefferson City, and these pro-Confederates fled to the southwest corner of the state. Blair hurried to Washington for help, and the result was the appointment of John C. Frémont as military leader of a new Department of the West. For the next hundred days, Frémont tried to bring some order out of the Missouri chaos, but he had little success. Unhappy with Frémont's lack of quick action, Lyon attacked the Confederates at Wilson's Creek on August 10, 1861, where he died in action while his forces were routed. Meanwhile, a state convention deposed Claiborne Jackson and his administration and made pro-slavery unionist Hamilton R. Gamble governor.

Frémont ran a corrupt and inefficient military regime and his heavy-handedness made matters even worse. On August 30, 1861, Frémont instituted martial law, which called for the court martial and summary execution of anyone caught armed within Union lines. He also emancipated the slaves of several pro-Confederates at a time when Lincoln was battling to keep the slave border states in the Union. Lincoln immediately quashed these pronouncements. Meanwhile, Frémont seemed to have no plan to counter Confederate General Sterling Price, who was threatening wider military operations. Unhappy with the direction of events, Lincoln sent Secretary of War Simon Cameron to Missouri with orders to fire Frémont, but the general talked his way into another chance. A congressional subcommittee then found the corruption charges against him to be warranted, so Lincoln once again ordered Frémont's removal, unless he had either won a battle, was in the midst of one, or was about to begin one. Since none of these conditions obtained, Frémont lost his command.

On November 9, Halleck replaced Frémont and became commander of the Department of the Missouri, covering "the States of Missouri, Iowa, Minnesota, Wisconsin, Illinois, Arkansas, and that portion of Kentucky west of the Cumberland River." The reaction to Halleck's appointment was almost universally positive, especially and importantly among Missourians. Those in Washington who had met him sent good reports back home. State agent Charles Gibson told Missouri Governor Hamilton R. Gamble that he "was well pleased" with Halleck because "his views about Missouri accord entirely with my own. I doubt not you will get along with him agreeably." Lincoln's Attorney General, Edward Bates, a brother-in-law to the governor, received a visit from Halleck and wrote friends in Missouri that "you'll find him accessible & frank & I think really anxious to do good & be on the best of terms with the true men of the state." Favorable press reports ensued. *Harper's Weekly* announced: "The country expects great things of General Halleck. His past record and his physiognomy encourage the belief that these expectations will not be disappointed."[10]

In St. Louis, Halleck faced a difficult task, Commanding General McClellan making it abundantly clear just how formidable it was. In his first order to Halleck, McClellan wrote with characteristic hyperbole: "You have not merely the ordinary duties of a military commander to perform, but the far more difficult task of reducing chaos to order, of changing probably the majority of the *personnel* of the staff of the department, and of reducing to a point of economy consistent with the interests and necessities of the State a system of reckless expenditure and fraud perhaps unheard of before in the history of the world." He told Halleck to make a thorough inspection, take action, and keep him informed.[11]

Missouri was a task made to order for a man of Halleck's disposition and ability. If there was anything he could not abide, that was bureaucratic disorder, and Missouri was a prime example. After arriving in St. Louis, he established himself with his brother-in-law, Schuyler Hamilton, in a suite at the Planters House Hotel, the city's best, rolled up his sleeves, and went to work. "He was forty six years old, in the prime of life, in perfect health, and full of vigor," a contemporary noted. "As he peered at us out of his large black eyes underneath dark heavy eyebrows, and a high massive forehead, he looked wondrous wise." His eyes were such as "to make all rogues tremble and even honest men look about them to be sure they have not been up to some mischief."[12]

Even usually cynical newsmen were impressed. Unlike Frémont, who had kept himself cloistered in his office, Halleck met with newspapermen soon after he arrived in St. Louis and smilingly listened to what they had to say. The newsmen left the meeting satisfied that he had been forthright with them, but they quickly realized that in reality he had told them nothing. They were to learn that they could expect nothing better in the future.[13]

Halleck made immediate progress in solving Missouri's many problems. "With a masterful hand he reduced to system what, at first blush, seemed an inextricable mass of antagonistic interests," one observer noted. "Fraudulent contracts were annulled; useless stipendiaries were dismissed; a colossal staff hierarchy with more title than brains or military capacity were disbanded; composite organizations were pruned to simple uniformity; the construction of fantastic fortifications were suspended," a friend remembered. Under the threat of arrest, Halleck ordered the city's mayor to require everyone, from ordinary voters to city and court officials, to take the loyalty oath. Any wagon displaying a Confederate flag was confiscated, and anyone, man or woman, found displaying that flag was arrested. He banished Confederate sympathizers, and he clamped down on the press. Any people destroying railroad tracks or depots or any public property became subject to arrest and execution and their slaves were impressed to make necessary repairs. To pay for the cost of caring for refugees who came to St. Louis to escape Confederate attacks, Halleck assessed wealthy secession supporters in St. Louis $10,000 each. One such individual angrily called the levy a "species of Yankee robery [sic]," but Halleck ignored all such criticism and maintained his anti-Confederate activity.[14]

He even demonstrated a sense of humor when dealing with recalcitrant women. Pro-Confederate females had begun wearing red and white rosettes to demonstrate their secessionist loyalties. Halleck said nothing and instead gave similar rosettes to the city's prostitutes and then planted a newspaper article which pointed out that the city's painted women were wearing such flowers. Confederate sympathizers stopped their protest immediately.[15]

Although he agreed with Frémont that the state needed martial law, Halleck was much more careful than his predecessor about establishing it. Experienced lawyer that he was, he petitioned Lincoln for "written authority." The President immediately granted this request, but McClellan delayed its implementation until December 2, when Lincoln personally sent Halleck written authorization.[16]

As before, slavery proved a problem for him. Recognizing the stir that Frémont's emancipation order had created among slave-holding unionists like Attorney General Bates and the Blair family, Halleck issued an order that he hoped would be more appealing to them and that reflected the kind of proposal he had presented to the California constitutional convention. On November 20, just a day after he took formal command in Missouri, Halleck issued General Orders No. 3, stating that because fugitive slaves coming into Union lines were giving "important information" to the enemy, he directed that "no such Persons be hereafter permitted to enter the lines of any camp, or of any forces on the march and that any now within such lines be immediately excluded therefrom."[17]

Halleck's exclusion order created a national uproar that would dog him throughout the war. In Virginia, Union General Benjamin Butler had been freeing slaves who entered Union camps by calling them contraband of war, and Congress's July 1861 First Confiscation Act had supported this action. In contrast, Halleck was refusing escaped slaves the safe haven of the Union Army, condemning them to remain with their masters. As a military man and a lawyer, he was adhering to the letter of the law, but in doing so he demonstrated his long-held lack of concern for enslaved people and his customary disdain for political repercussions. A Cincinnati reporter said that many army officers were upset at this order and protested against "peering into tents and wagons . . . or playing 'nigger hunter.'" Senator Charles Sumner called Halleck's order "irrational and inhuman on its face." Antislavery congressmen were so outraged that they debated the matter on the floor of the House of Representatives. Leading the attack on Halleck was the prewar abolitionist Owen Lovejoy, aided by radical Republican George Washington Julian. Missouri's Frank Blair and Illinois's Phillip Fouke defended the general. Julian argued in his later memoirs that Halleck's General Orders No. 3 and his later return of a young slave girl to her master helped provide the impetus for the creation of the powerful congressional Joint Committee on the Conduct of the War "for a more vigorous prosecution of the war, and less tenderness toward slavery."[18]

Despite all the criticism Halleck once more stood his ground. He told Frank Blair in a public letter that he would obey any law concerning fugitive slaves that Congress passed, "but I can not make law, and will not violate it." Even later in the war, after passions had cooled and the important role of runaway slaves in providing information to Union armies had become evident, Halleck still did not change his mind. He had never returned one person into slavery, he insisted, but he believed the military had no authority to free slaves either. "The ground which I have always taken on this negro question is that the military has nothing to do with it, except to carry out earnestly & faithfully the laws of congress & the orders of the President."[19] In short, Halleck would do only what the law allowed, nothing more, nothing less. The pressures of the conflict had not tempered his bureaucratic precision. He had worried in California about the war's turning into a battle over slavery, and he was not going to allow that to happen in his command.

Halleck was appalled at everything he saw in Missouri. "Affairs here a complete chaos," he wrote McClellan, the lack of good officers making it difficult to know anything for certain. He had five divisions in the field, but sickness was rampant among all of them. "Many of the troops at different points are reported to be without arms and suffering for the want of clothing and blankets," but he could not be sure that such was indeed the case. He worried that the Confederates had more troops than he had, and he knew that they were moving northward in the state, encouraging anti-Union insurrection everywhere. The civilian and military problems seemed so overwhelming that he began to believe he could not solve them and would soon be discharged from his command. He promised his cousin Minnesota Bishop H. B. Whipple to be "the instrument of no political faction, having no political aspirations. I shall do my duty faithfully, as I understand it, let the consequences be what they may."[20]

As he made some progress, he felt much better about himself. "I believe I can say it without vanity that I have talent for command and administration," he bragged to his wife. "At least I have seen no one here who can accomplish half so much in twenty-four hours as I do." He lived the same kind of regimented life he had lived as a young officer and then as a lawyer in San Francisco. He breakfasted at 7:30 A.M., walked to his office a few blocks away, and worked until 3 P.M. He had dinner at 3:30 and then went back to his office between 6:00 and 7:00 P.M., not to go to bed until around midnight. His office was always jammed with people, so he had his staff allow only those individuals with major business to see him. Even these he handled with time-saving brusqueness. One observer commented favorably that Halleck was doing "a Herculean amount of work."[21]

Halleck also had to deal with Sherman, his one-time friend and long-time California antagonist. Sherman had recently arrived in Missouri after a sensation-filled tour as commander in Kentucky.[22] Sherman had insisted that the Blue Grass State was on the verge of a Confederate takeover and had demanded enormous reinforcements, even writing directly to the President. Lincoln and McClellan had ignored him, so he had asked to be relieved, and Don Carlos Buell was sent to take his place. All kinds of rumors swirled about Sherman's alleged mental instability, such whisperings reaching the highest levels in Washington. When Sherman arrived in Halleck's jurisdiction, therefore, he was a man under suspicion.

Considering their many years of animosity in California, the first meeting between these two antagonists must have been extremely uncomfortable. Unfortunately no record exists of their conversation. Halleck sent Sherman on an inspection tour of the state, but when Sherman spoke nervously of an impending Confederate attack that Halleck believed unlikely, Halleck recalled him to St. Louis and gave him a twenty-day leave to get some rest. Sherman went home, and reporters, angry at his harsh treatment of them in Kentucky, labeled him insane. Halleck believed that there was indeed something wrong with Sherman and wrote McClellan that "it would be dangerous to give him a command" because "labors and cares" had "completely broken" his "physical and mental system." Halleck was repeating what others believed, but he clearly had doubts about Sherman's ability to lead.

When Sherman returned after his leave, Halleck slowly brought him back into command, carefully justifying his every action to Sherman's father-in-law, the powerful Ohio politician Thomas Ewing. Showing a seldom-seen side of his personality, Halleck used humor to defuse a tense situation. He told Sherman's wife, Ellen, that he "would willingly take" everything that newspapers said about her husband, "if he would take all they said against me, for I was certain to gain by the exchange!"[23] Halleck helped save Sherman for the Union, and at the same time he avoided a major political pitfall in the person of Thomas Ewing, who had the power to shorten Halleck's career. This time Halleck kept his perfectionist impatience in check to his and the Union's benefit.

As he dealt with military men like Sherman and civilians like Frank Blair, Halleck knew that reorganization efforts could not go on forever. His own book on military theory insisted that generals should go on the offensive once they had prepared their troops carefully. The leading American theorist of strategy knew what had to be done, and one late December 1861 evening over dinner in his room at St. Louis's Planters House Hotel, he explained it all to Sherman and Cullum. The three men were discussing future military operations in the West, and Halleck, the former West Point professor, stood up, pencil in hand, and pointed to a map on the table. "Where is the rebel line?" Halleck asked, so Cullum drew a line from Bowling Green, Kentucky, through Forts Henry and Donelson, to Columbus, Kentucky, on the Mississippi River, the defensive line that Confederate General Albert Sidney Johnston had established in that area. "That is their line," Halleck agreed. "Now, where is the proper place to break it?" Like a good West Pointer used to oral examinations, either Sherman or Cullum responded: "*Naturally* the centre." Halleck then took the blue pencil and drew a line in response, and it fell almost entirely on the Tennessee River. "That's the true line of operations," he concluded, signaling where Union troops should go on the offensive.[24]

It was one thing to know where to move, but it was another to have the authority to do it. While Halleck commanded the region west of the Cumberland River, Don Carlos Buell had authority in the area east of it, the Department of the Ohio, headquartered in Louisville, Kentucky. Like most military leaders in the Civil War, Buell was a West Pointer. Unlike many, however, he had remained in the army all the years after his 1841 graduation. He and Halleck overlapped at the military academy for two years, and they had both lived in San Francisco during the spring and summer of 1861, when Buell was stationed there. There is no evidence, however, of any previous close relationship between the two men. When they were thrown together west of the Appalachian Mountains in the fall of 1861, they did not know each other very well.

In some ways, they were similar. Both were conservative Democrats, Buell a slaveholder and Halleck certainly no abolitionist. Halleck was much more intellectual than Buell, but the latter had significantly more field experience. Both were administrators more than they were battlefield commanders. Each believed in well-prepared maneuver rather than direct assault in a war that they both thought would be a limited one.[25]

Above both men were George B. McClellan, the army's commanding general, Edwin M. Stanton, Secretary of War, and the nation's President, Abraham Lincoln. Like Halleck and Buell, McClellan put a great deal of emphasis on precise preparation of masses of soldiers to be maneuvered against fractions of the enemy. Neither McClellan, Buell, nor Halleck believed in jumping headlong into combat. Stanton and Lincoln, unlike these three generals, had no military experience. Lincoln frequently joked that in the 1830s Black Hawk War, mosquito bites had caused the only spilling of his blood. Still, with Stanton's hard-headed advice, Lincoln had an innate sense of strategy. He wanted action, not preparation. He felt frustrated as he watched McClellan procrastinate in the East and Halleck and Buell show no indication of movement in the West. He and Stanton became so upset that Lincoln issued the President's General War Order Number 1 on January 27, 1862, demanding that Union forces move against the Confederates no later than February 22, 1862, Washington's Birthday.[26]

Lincoln had previously written to Halleck and Buell telling them to "communicate and act in concert," but the responses he had received were disconcerting. "I am not ready to cooperate with him," Halleck told Lincoln. "Hope to do so in a few weeks." Writing again a few days later, Halleck was even more negative. "I am satisfied that the authorities at Washington do not appreciate the difficulties with which we have to contend here." Listing every problem he had encountered in Missouri and complaining about the quality of his troops, Halleck concluded: "I assure you, Mr. President, it is very difficult to accomplish much with such means. I am in the condition of a carpenter who is required to build a bridge with a dull ax, a broken saw, and rotten timber. It is true that I have some very good green timber, which will answer the purpose as soon as I can get it into shape and season it a little." As for cooperating with Buell, "I know nothing of General Buell's intended operations." The kind of joint action Lincoln apparently intended, Halleck said, would "be a repetition of the same strategic error which produced the disaster at Bull Run. To operate on exterior lines against an enemy occupying a central position will fail, as it always has failed, in ninety-nine cases out of a hundred. It is condemned by every military authority I have ever read," he concluded, aware that Lincoln knew that there was no greater authority than Halleck himself. When Lincoln saw this long complaint, he could only respond that it was "exceedingly discouraging. As everywhere else, nothing can be done." He offered Halleck and Buell more ideas on how they might cooperate, but once again neither man showed any interest in listening.[27]

Halleck was still tied to the ideas he had written about in the 1840s. He said that politicians, not generals, were responsible for the war's failures, and he insisted on the need for the concentration of well-prepared forces. As he had told Sherman and Cullum, the proper plan was to use the Ohio River as a base and then "move up the Cumberland and Tennessee making Nashville the first objective point. This would turn Columbus [on the Mississippi River] and force the abandonment of Bowling Green [in central Kentucky]." A smaller force would, meanwhile, drive Sterling Price out of Missouri as a way of ensuring a solid base of attack support. In short, massing Union troops in the West and then moving along the central line to pierce the long Confederate defense line was the only way to defeat the enemy in that theater of the war.[28]

Confident about what he was convinced he should do, Halleck still delayed. As early as December 11, 1861, one of his subordinate commanders, John Pope, had begun calling for "a rapid movement" against Sterling Price, who in early August and September 1861 had won victories at Wilson's Creek and Lexington. As late as January 27, 1862, however, Halleck was still demonstrating his adherence to the traditional principle of war and counseling delay in order to "get time to concentrate and organize our forces."[29]

One subordinate, Ulysses S. Grant, twice asked Halleck for permission to visit him in St. Louis to discuss future military movements. Finally he received a reluctant nod. Grant did not know Halleck well, though he probably had met him at West Point. Grant wanted to discuss his idea of moving up the Tennessee and Cumberland rivers, exactly the plan Halleck already had in mind, yet the visit was a disaster. "I was received with so little cordiality that I perhaps stated the object of my visit with less clearness than I might have done, and I had not uttered many sentences before I was cut short as if my plan was preposterous," Grant said. "I returned to Cairo very much crestfallen." Since Grant was only suggesting what Halleck himself was already thinking, such rudeness was difficult to understand, even considering Halleck's incomplete recovery from a mid-January bout with measles. Halleck was, in fact, reacting not to Grant's plan, but to Grant himself. Halleck knew all about Grant's reputation for having had a prewar drinking problem in California, and unfounded rumors had reached Washington that Grant had recently fallen off the wagon. Grant's unkempt appearance did not help either. Halleck had begun to suspect that Grant was not his kind of precise soldier. In mid-December Grant returned some prisoners to St. Louis because a telegram had arrived informing him that they were imposters. It turned out that the telegram was a hoax, and Halleck blasted Grant for falling for it. "It is most extraordinary that you should have obeyed a telegram sent by an unknown person and not even purporting to have been given by authority." Grant tried to defend himself, but Halleck would have none of it.[30] Feeling even more irritable because of the measles, he looked askance at this apparently gullible and careless subordinate, and thus treated him disrespectfully.

Though shaken by Halleck's rudeness, Grant did not give up on his idea of moving against Fort Henry on the Tennessee River. He persuaded the navy Flag Officer Andrew Foote to join in the pressure on Halleck, and the two were finally successful. Spurred no doubt by Lincoln's impatience, Halleck gave Grant permission to move, even though he still had reservations about his subordinate's qualities as a soldier. Meanwhile, Halleck and Buell were doing a careful dance around each other, neither willing to support the other's needs or plans. Halleck repeatedly called on Buell to bring his army to him and lamented that he could "not make Buell understand the importance of strategic points till it is too late."[31]

Not only did Grant and Foote capture the Tennessee River's Fort Henry on February 7, 1862, but then Grant moved successfully against nearby Fort Donelson, on the Cumberland River. He captured it on February 16, electrifying the nation when he demanded "unconditional surrender" from the Confederates there. Albert Sidney Johnston's long Confederate defense line was in shambles. Columbus, Kentucky, quickly fell, and Buell marched unopposed into Nashville. Confederate troops began retreating south, massing at Corinth, Mississippi, where east-west and north-south railroads crossed. At the same time, Brigadier General Samuel R. Curtis, whom Halleck had put in command of the army of Southwest Missouri despite protests from the supporters of the controversial German general Franz Sigel, drove Sterling Price out of Missouri and then ensured the state's safety with a major victory in early March 1862 at Pea Ridge, Arkansas. In mid-March, John Pope took New Madrid, Missouri, on the Mississippi River.[32]

Halleck won none of these battlefield victories himself, but he was masterly in the way he organized and supported them. He had carefully coordinated his command's logistics and made sure that supplies and men moved forward to his generals in the field. The combination of Grant's, Curtis's and Pope's aggressiveness and Halleck's careful preparation and logistical support resulted in victory. More important, Halleck was the only commanding general with troops on the move. In the East, McClellan still delayed, while Halleck boldly announced: "Fort Henry is ours. The flag of the Union is re-established on the soil of Tennessee. It will never be removed." Pro-Union people in St. Louis were so excited at the news of this victory that they marched en masse to Halleck's headquarters and cheered his name until he came out to address them. "I promised you when I came here that with your aid I would drive the enemies of our flag from your state. This has been done, and they are virtually out of Kentucky and soon will be out of Tennessee."[33] Halleck was ready to accept congratulations for this string of victories, giving no public credit to the subordinates who had pushed him into action and actually carried out the assaults.

Washington politicians were appropriately impressed. Halleck's New Almaden nemesis, now the Secretary of War, gushed with praise. "Your energy and ability receive the strongest commendation of this Department," Edwin M. Stanton said. "You have my perfect confidence," a most happy comment for Halleck, who was worried that his poor relationship with the Secretary of War in California would result in Stanton's taking "the first opportunity he can to injure me." Secretary of the Treasury Salmon P. Chase expansively spoke of the "genius of Halleck." Thirty-five leading citizens of St. Louis, including the governor and mayor, offered Halleck a "public dinner" in honor of his outstanding work, which made him happy even though he did not have the time to accept.[34]

Halleck was pleased with the praise, but grew increasingly frustrated at Buell's refusal to cooperate, and at McClellan's lack of support. Even after the success at Fort Donelson, Halleck worried that Confederate General P. G. T. Beauregard would retake either Paducah, Kentucky, or Fort Henry, Tennessee, calling the threat "the crisis of the war in the West." He repeatedly called on McClellan for help, and, the day before Grant took Fort Donelson, Halleck told Buell: "Unless I have more assistance the attack will fail."[35]

Despite his success, therefore, Halleck displayed a nervous instability. He was pessimistic and frustrated when events should have made him optimistic. He insisted that if only Buell, McClellan, and the civilian authorities in Washington would listen to him, military victory would follow.[36] It also had to bother him that Grant, a sloppy soldier in his eyes, had been so successful. That made no sense to his bureaucratic mind.

On March 2, 1862, his chief of staff, George W. Cullum, then at Cairo, where he had been logistically supporting Grant's campaign, sent a message that caused Halleck to air his dislike of Grant openly. Cullum told him that Grant had just returned from Nashville, where he had gone to see Buell. Recalling that he had not heard from Grant for a week, Halleck exploded. He wrote McClellan that Grant had gone to Nashville without authorization, that his army was "demoralized" after the Fort Donelson victory, and that Grant seemed so "satisfied that he had no thought of what he should do next." "I can get no returns, no reports, no information of any kind from him. . . . I am worn-out and tired with this neglect and inefficiency." "It is hard to censure a successful general immediately after a victory, but I think he richly deserves it," Halleck concluded. It is telling that Halleck considered Grant's continued administrative sloppiness to be more significant than his recent victories.[37]

Halleck's explosion might have been the end of it, but McClellan escalated matters with his response. The commanding general suggested that since Grant obviously needed discipline, Halleck should "not hesitate to arrest him at once if the good of the service requires it." Halleck then repeated the rumor about Grant's drinking, citing drunkenness as the probable cause of Grant's problems. He did not plan to arrest Grant, he said, but he would put General C. F. Smith in his place as field commander. "Why do you not obey my order to report strength and position in your command?" he demanded of Grant.[38]

Writing from Fort Henry, Grant calmly responded that he had been sending regular reports to Cullum, and perhaps "many of them were not thought of sufficient importance to forward more than a telegraphic synopsis of." (In fact, Halleck never got Grant's reports because the telegrapher was a Confederate sympathizer who simply failed to send them.) This response seemed to anger Halleck even more. "The want of order and discipline and the numerous irregularities in your command since the capture of Fort Donelson are matters of general notoriety, and have attracted the serious attention of the authorities at Washington. Unless these things are immediately corrected, I am directed to relieve you of the command." Grant denied all the accusations: "I have done my very best to obey orders and to carry out the interests of the service. If my course is not satisfactory, remove me at once." Back and forth the letters flew: McClellan advised arrest; Grant demanded to be fired; Halleck continued to accost Grant for not filing reports as ordered. He was not jealous of Grant's success as much as he was angry about his administrative failings. Lincoln and Stanton quickly stepped in, demanding of Halleck the exact reasons for this disagreement, obviously wanting to end the turmoil that might destroy a winning general.[39]

At the same time, Halleck was involved in a more restrained disagreement with George McClellan himself. The day after Grant took Fort Donelson, Halleck wrote a terse telegram to McClellan. "Make Buell, Grant, and Pope major generals of volunteers, and give me command in the West. I ask this in return for Forts Henry and Donelson." Two days later, he pledged "to split secession in twain in one month" if he received

Before Shiloh

overall command. McClellan responded that Buell, being in Bowling Green, knew more about the overall situation than Halleck did in St. Louis. Besides, Lincoln, who would make the final decision, was still mourning the recent death of his son, Willie, and could not deal with the matter just then. Frustrated, Halleck fired back to Stanton: "Give me authority, and I will be responsible for results." Then, realizing that he was pushing too hard, he backed off, but his continued pique was evident. He told McClellan: "You will regret your decision against me on this point."[40]

His frustration with Grant's alleged sloppiness and his failure to receive overall western command now came to a head. On March 11, 1862, the day after Lincoln had demanded to know exactly why Halleck had shelved Grant, the President promoted Halleck to overall command in the west, and at the same time limited McClellan's command to the Army of the Potomac. Halleck would now report directly to the President and the Secretary of War, who would act together as commanding general. Halleck had received the power he had been demanding, yet he told Buell that this order changed nothing. "You will continue in command of the same army & district of country as heretofore, so far as I am concerned," he said. That same day Halleck, feeling chastened yet happy with his new power, told Grant not only that he would not relieve him, but that "I wish you as soon as your new army is in the field to assume the immediate command and lead it to new victories." Grant was mollified, and Buell was shocked.[41]

In truth, Halleck no longer had to debate Buell; he could now order him. Halleck could coordinate all the armies in the western theater to complete the job of destroying the region's Confederate defense, and he would try to make a soldier out of Grant. His next military objective was clear. Move up the Tennessee River and capture Corinth, Mississippi, the important railroad center, where the Confederates were massing. With that city in Union hands, Memphis would fall and the way would be open to Vicksburg and other areas of the Deep South Confederacy. Halleck had become the dominant military figure not only in the western theater but also in the entire war. McClellan still commanded the Army of the Potomac, which protected Washington and would eventually move on Richmond, but Halleck was now his equal. And in one way he was his superior: He had produced victory; McClellan had produced delay and was now a lesser figure because of his demotion from commanding general. As for Grant, he might be "Unconditional Surrender" Grant to the nation, but he was still Halleck's subordinate.

Just a week before his promotion, Halleck wrote his wife complaining about the lack of public appreciation for the victories his command had achieved. "The newspapers give the credit of these things to Stanton, McClellan, and Buell, but fortunately I have the recorded evidence that they even failed to approve them after I had planned them." Significantly, he did not include Grant among those men he saw as his rivals. Despite Grant's successes at Forts Henry and Donelson, Halleck still did not consider him a threat and certainly not an equal. He was dismissive of Grant, not because he envied his success but because he did not respect his bearing and personal conduct. Like his father and Dennis Hart Mahan, Halleck demanded a purposeful approach that he did not believe Grant was providing in his generalship.[42]   *Before failure at Shiloh*

Halleck now decided he would personally take field command of a force composed of Grant's and Buell's armies, scheduled to mass at Pittsburg Landing on the Tennessee River in early April. If he could take Corinth, Mississippi, with this army, he was confident "the enemy must evacuate or surrender" all along the Mississippi River. His confidence increased when he received a letter from a Washington acquaintance telling him that a leading senator, during an executive session, had said that Halleck had "made the greatest showing of military genius of all the Generals in the country." A common soldier put it less grandly but no less enthusiastically: "Halleck's a perfect 'Critter,'" which, a friend said, was "his definition of a Great Man."[43]   *geog / focus*

Despite his new optimism and authority, Halleck continued to exhibit the obsession with detail that was now habitual. He twice lambasted Don Carlos Buell for not sending strength reports as Halleck had requested and for not moving troops as ordered. "Don't fail to carry out my instructions. I know that I am right," he insisted. He also continued to criticize Grant for his troops' alleged plundering at Fort Donelson, threatening to "arrest every officer in command of the troops engaged in it." Then he castigated Grant for having a civilian as his medical director and for the "gross irregularities" in his army "in regard to the disposition of the sick and wounded." Buell and Grant defended themselves, but Halleck was not interested in their denials. He would not tolerate any failure to fight the war properly, and he would make sure that his subordinates understood that.[44]

Suddenly, Halleck suffered a severe setback, and, once again, he could blame Grant. On April 6, 1862, Grant's five divisions were camped between Pittsburg Landing and Shiloh Church on the Tennessee River, to await the arrival of Buell's Army of the Ohio. Confederate General Albert Sidney Johnston launched a surprise attack and, that first day, drove the Federals back against the river. Grant's grit, Sherman's stellar battlefield performance, and the bravery of the common soldier allowed the Union troops to survive that first assault, and the next day they regained the ground they had lost and compelled the Confederates to retreat. Casualties were staggering, nearly 24,000 killed, wounded, and missing for the two sides, with Johnston among the fatalities. It was the bloodiest battle of the war so far.

Accusations of Grant's incompetence and drunkenness sprang up to explain the near Union defeat. The President and the Secretary of War, now jointly coordinating the war in the absence of a commanding general, wanted to know from Halleck "whether any neglect or misconduct of General Grant or any other officer contributed to the sad casualties that befell our forces." Halleck refused to say until he saw the official battle reports. He reminded Lincoln and Stanton, however, that "a great battle can not be fought or a victory gained without many casualties," a lukewarm defense of Grant's generalship. After the battle, when Grant, busy rebuilding his bruised army, did not send Halleck an immediate report on his troop's positions, Halleck took the opportunity to berate him again. "My orders to you are not obeyed with the promptness of the commanders of the other Army Corps."[45] Bureaucracy not battles remained primary to Halleck.

If he had needed any more persuading, Shiloh convinced Halleck that Grant was a complete military disaster, not because he would not fight, but because he was insufficiently temperate and organized. "I never saw a man more deficient in the business of organization," he said. "Brave & able in the field, he has no idea of how to regulate & organize his forces before a battle," and to Halleck that was the crucial matter. He thought better of John Pope, who kept him informed on a regular basis and, besides, Pope had completed an ingenious capture of Island #10 just two days after Grant's near defeat in the controversial Shiloh battle. Halleck predicted that Pope's "splendid achievement" would "be memorable in military history" and would "be admired by future generations." He never said anything remotely as positive about a Grant victory.[46]

Halleck arrived at Pittsburg Landing on April 11 and made an indelible impression on James Grant Wilson, an army officer and later a historian. He was "about five nine inches tall, and weighing perhaps one hundred seventy or eighty pounds," Wilson remembered. "He was carefully dressed in a new uniform, wearing his sword, and carrying himself erect, with a distant and somewhat austere manner . . . as he walked down the steamer's gangplank." What Halleck saw upon his disembarkation was ghastly. The constant heavy rain had unearthed recently buried men in the muddy soil. "*Skulls* and *toes* are sticking from beneath the clay all around and the heavy wagons *crush* the bodies turning up the bones of the buried," one soldier reported in disbelief. Flooding destroyed bridges, mud was everywhere, and sickness was rampant. What bothered Halleck even more, however, was his immediate impression that "this army is undisciplined and very much disorganized, the officers being utterly incapable of maintaining order." Halleck, in fact, gave Grant an earful of criticism; another officer remembered him dressed in a black civilian suit "pacing back and forth [on his headquarters ship] hands in his trousers' pockets, and scolding [Grant] in a loud and haughty manner." At first he lived aboard a ship tied up at the landing, but then he moved into a tent because he found "it always agrees with my health" and it had "a good effect upon the soldiers to camp with them."[47]

He was in no hurry to begin the fight against the Confederate Army in Corinth, now under the command of P. G. T. Beauregard. As in all his military efforts, he believed it was first necessary to bring order to what he considered military chaos. One of his subordinates, John A. Logan, a politician turned general, said that the battle for Corinth would be a "terrible" "slaughter." Halleck wanted to make sure he was completely prepared before he moved ahead.[48] Not until April 30 was his huge army of over 100,000 men in what he considered proper order, and only then did Halleck send them forward against the 66,000 Confederates in Corinth. It turned out to be one of the strangest campaigns of the war, yet considering the recently fought battle of Shiloh and Halleck's 1840s perception of military strategy and tactics, it made absolute sense. Halleck believed in the necessity of a commander's massing troops in the face of the enemy and overwhelming his opposition with numbers. As a student of Mahan and French engineering principles, he also believed in the value of field works, especially for inexperienced units like the ones he had in his army. Besides, he was not going to allow himself to be surprised, as Grant had been at Shiloh.

Halleck organized his massive Corinth army into three wings under George H. Thomas, Don Carlos Buell, and John Pope. Demonstrating his disdain for Grant yet again, he denied him command of any one of these segments. He named him second in overall command, on the surface the appropriate position given Grant's rank. He also told Grant to move his headquarters closer to his. In effect, this army reorganization, all according to proper rank, put Grant on the shelf, Halleck giving him no real power. "I was little more than an observer," Grant later said, and Halleck let it be known that he wanted no military advice from him. By keeping Grant close by, Halleck was no doubt hoping to demonstrate to him how an army should be run. When Grant protested, Halleck once again turned the tables on him. "For the last three months I have done everything in my power to ward off the attacks which were made upon you," Halleck wrote disingenuously. "If you believe me your friend you will not require explanations; if not, explanations on my part would be of no avail."[49]

Having put Grant in his place, Halleck conducted a campaign of excruciatingly slow movement and constant entrenchment. Some variation on the word "caution" appeared repeatedly in his military correspondence. He explained everything to Edwin Stanton in phrases that could have been written by his eastern counterpart, George McClellan: "As the enemy is strongly intrenched and his number equal if not superior to ours, it is necessary to move with great caution. Most of the country passed over is a thick forest, with numerous streams and deep marshes, which require corduroys and bridges. Our progress is necessarily slow." As a future Secretary of State, Walter Q. Gresham, explained it further: "We can't afford to be whipped down here. We teach the men it is victory or death, for we could never retreat." Even when Halleck learned of a Confederate telegram to Jefferson Davis admitting the southern army's weakness in Corinth, he still maintained his cautiousness.[50]

Skirmishing regularly but fighting no set battles, Halleck inched forward, digging in all the time. Sherman reported later that his division had "constructed seven distinct intrenched camps" after leaving Shiloh behind. The newsman Albert D. Richardson described the entire pageant graphically: "Halleck's line was ten miles in length. The grand army was like a huge serpent, with its head pinned on our left, and its tail sweeping slowly around toward Corinth. Its majestic march was so slow that the Rebels had ample warning. It was large enough to eat up Beauregard at one mouthful; but Halleck crept forward at the rate of about three-quarters of a mile per day." One time, John Pope enthusiastically pushed his unit ahead of the rest of the army, and Halleck immediately reined him back into line. It was not until May 18 that Halleck had his troops within two miles of Corinth's fortifications. Like an eighteenth-century army, about which Halleck had written, his enormous force conducted a gigantic siege by the book—Halleck's book. When General William S. Rosecrans arrived to become a senior officer in Pope's army, he was enormously impressed by what he saw. He exclaimed: "Halleck is a great man."[51]

Reporters who accompanied the army disagreed. They wrote critical reports about Halleck's slowness. In retaliation, he included them among the "unauthorized hangers-on" he ordered expelled from his command on May 13, allegedly to prevent spying. When a committee of reporters protested, he "turned his back" on them and refused to change his mind; the newsmen found his attitude "unmistakably rude and insulting." He told them they would get all the news they needed about the Corinth campaign by reading a bulletin board at Pittsburg Landing. Sherman, no slouch himself when it came to battling reporters, said approvingly that "correspondents . . . [have met] their match in him."[52]

Nearly a month passed, and the Union soldiers began to hear trains entering and leaving Corinth, Pope noting that there were few troops left in the trenches before him. After a visit from Halleck, however, Pope came to the opposite conclusion. "The cars are running constantly, and the cheering is immense, every time they unload in front of me. I have no doubt, from all appearances, that I shall be attacked in heavy force at daylight." Within hours, however, Pope changed his mind again. Now he was sure that the explosions he heard meant that the Confederates were leaving Corinth. Halleck could not decide and remained irresolute. It was, he said, "difficult to fix definitely now our plans." In fact, Confederate General Beauregard had duped Halleck. The trains and the cheering had signaled the exit of troops not the infusion of new ones. That same day, Halleck's huge army walked into Corinth uncontested. When Halleck rode in himself, his horse symbolically tripped over a low-hanging telegraph wire.[53]

In his book, Halleck had stressed the importance of capturing strategic places rather than defeating an opposing army. He sent Pope in pursuit of Beauregard and told his subordinate to "press him vigorously," but his true motive quickly became evident. On June 4, he told Pope: "The chief object now is to get the enemy far enough south to relieve our railroads from danger of an immediate attack. . . . I think by showing a bold front for a day or two the enemy will continue his retreat, which is all I desire." Corinth, not Beauregard's army, had been Halleck's true objective all along.[54]

The army's reaction to Corinth's capture ran an emotional gauntlet. An effigy hanging from a small tree with a sign proclaiming "Halleck outwitted–what will Old Abe say?" greeted the general when he entered the Confederate fortifications. A Union soldier said that "it is generally thought Halleck had been out generalled by Beauregard, but I know we have gained a great strategical point and our army is in a condition to take advantage of it." Another soldier admitted that everyone had known "more than a week ago that they [the Confederates] were going to retreat because we could hear the cars running day & night." Yet he concluded: "for one I am glad they are gone and they have my permission to keep agoing." Frustrated in his subordinate role, Grant was at first satisfied with the victory, but much later, in his memoirs, he was more judgmental: "The possession of Corinth by National troops was of strategic importance, but the victory was barren in every other particular."[55]

Had he lived to read Grant's memoirs, Halleck could not have disagreed more. Grant simply did not understand strategy, he would have thought. Halleck expressed pride in his achievement. He had caused the enemy to flee, he told his wife; he now possessed "a most important military point." Moreover, he had done it all "with very little loss of life. This to me is the great merit of the whole, although the public will be greatly disappointed that thousands were not killed in a great battle! I have won the victory without the battle! Military history will do me justice." He was particularly pleased that his officers recognized his great achievement and "even the common soldiers now understand what they could not before comprehend & have nick named me 'Old Brains.' A rather coarse title, but I am satisfied with it."[56] Not only had Halleck won an important bloodless victory, but he had also gained a nickname that could not have been more complimentary.

Ironically it was the contrast with McClellan's lack of progress in Virginia that impressed Halleck's Washington superior, Edwin Stanton. "Your brilliant and successful achievement gives great joy over the whole land," Stanton said. Abraham Lincoln was similarly elated, although he immediately wondered what Halleck planned to do next. When Halleck talked about sending Buell to East Tennessee, an area that Lincoln had long wanted to liberate, Lincoln was satisfied. Halleck had given the President another reason to view him as Old Brains, too.[57]

After he consolidated Corinth, Halleck did something that violated the very military rules that he had so long espoused. Although he was a consistent proponent of massing troops to move against the center of an enemy's strategic defenses, Halleck now did just the opposite. He broke his huge army back into its previously distinct organizations. Grant got back his Army of the Tennessee, Buell the Army of the Ohio, and Pope the Army of the Mississippi. Having done that, Halleck sent these armies off in all directions to repair railroads and resupply themselves. Disease continued to plague the troops, Halleck himself being forced to remain in his tent with severe diarrhea that he facetiously referred to as the "Evacuation of Corinth." As late as early July, he was still complaining that he was "somewhat broken in health and wearied out by long months of labor and care." Such health problems further intensified his tendency to brusqueness and rigidity.[58]

Feeling ill, unhappy when Lincoln ordered John Pope to the East to head a new Army of Virginia, and flabbergasted when Lincoln kept asking him to send troops to help McClellan on the Virginia peninsula, Halleck again displayed his chronic testiness. He lashed out at Buell for his slowness in repairing the railroad between Corinth and Decatur, Alabama; he castigated Samuel Curtis in Arkansas for not sending regular reports; and, of course, he once again found something wrong with his favorite target. He accused Grant of being taken in by unfounded rumors of an attack on Memphis: "It looks very much like a mere stampede," he thundered. "Floating rumors must never be received as facts." When Grant responded defensively, Halleck denied any intention of criticizing him and once again made Grant the villain. "I must confess," he said, "that I was very much surprised at the tone of your dispatch and the ill-feeling manifested in it, so contrary to your usual style, and especially toward one who has so often befriended you when you were attacked by others."[59] It was all Grant's fault, Halleck insisted.

Lincoln's insistence that Old Brains send troops to McClellan further fueled Halleck's frustration. He told the President: "I must earnestly protest against surrendering what has cost us so much blood and treasure, and which, in a military point of view, is worth three Richmonds." Writing to his wife that same day, he complained: "I have been so much troubled and annoyed," afraid that sending troops east would "ruin all I had gained here . . . [and I] felt utterly broken-hearted. My first impulse was to resign and go home to California. But this my duty to the country forbade. . . . I am afraid [however] that McClellan and Pope will work upon the President until he gives them a part of my army. If so it will be almost fatal."[60]

It was only when he spoke of his young son and his wife that he expressed warmth and affection. He was pleased that the boy had enjoyed the Fourth of July. Perhaps remembering how he had celebrated that holiday at West Point, he said: "I think all children should be taught to consider it a great gala day." He was also happy that his wife and son had enjoyed their visit to his home town of Westernville. "Country people differ so much than those of the city that I feared the time would be irksome to you." With his father gone, Halleck viewed his home more positively and wanted his wife and son to experience the good feelings there that he himself had never felt during his childhood.[61]

On July 2, 1862, Halleck received a telegram from Lincoln asking him to come to Washington. He had to suspect what this request meant because this was the exact procedure Lincoln had recently followed in appointing Pope to a command in the East. Halleck responded that because Braxton Bragg, who had replaced Beauregard as the Confederate commander, was getting ready to make an attack, he could not leave his army at that time.[62]

Events were moving rapidly in Washington, however. Rumors spread that Halleck was going to become Secretary of War. Then Rhode Island Governor and Senator-Elect William Sprague, future son-in-law of Secretary of the Treasury Salmon Chase, decided to go to Corinth, with Lincoln's blessing, to convince Halleck to come east with 50,000 troops for McClellan. Halleck responded bluntly: "Governor Sprague is here. If I were to go to Washington I could advise but one thing: to place all the forces in North Carolina, Virginia, and Washington under one head and hold that head responsible for the result." In short, if made commander, Halleck would mass Union troops under one leader, as he had done in the West. The next day, Lincoln, having consulted with the now retired Winfield Scott and with his Springfield, Illinois, acquaintance, John Pope, ignored Edwin Stanton's opposition, and appointed Halleck "to command the whole land forces of the United States, as General-in-Chief." He was to leave for Washington as soon as he could.[63]

The California businessman had sailed from San Francisco only nine months previously, and he was now at the top of the military profession he had rejoined. Halleck had exhibited the belief that precise military preparation was more critical to victory than rapid forward progress, yet Lincoln was still calling him to Washington to produce quick military success. It made sense, of course; no other general had a better record in the field. Lincoln did not yet know that, beneath the facade of decisive success, was a demanding administrator who made precise preparations but shunned hard military decisions.

7

Supreme Commander

H. W. HALLECK had previously insisted on becoming commanding general of the entire western theater because he was frustrated with Don Carlos Buell's uncooperativeness and because he was convinced that having complete control of the war was the only way to bring success there. His new assignment as commanding general of the entire Union Army made him one of the nation's military triumvirate, along with Abraham Lincoln and Secretary of War Edwin M. Stanton, and gave him the power to order cooperation among army units in every theater of the war. He could mass troops as he saw fit and send resources where he thought they best belonged. The President and the Secretary of War, weary of trying to do the job themselves after their demotion of McClellan, were more than willing to give him complete responsibility. He was, after all, the nation's most important military theorist and its most successful general at that point in the war. Lincoln's administration and the nation as a whole looked to him for answers, for leadership, for decisiveness, for results. There was widespread public belief that he was up to the difficult task. He would prove otherwise.

After Corinth, Mississippi, which he had captured almost bloodlessly, he had allowed the Confederate Army to escape by his delays. Soon, the Confederate departure seemed to have become inconsequential as he focused on infrastructure and preparations. His troops were busily fanning out from the Mississippi city, repairing railroads and getting ready for the next big push. Halleck continued to press his commanders to be exemplary soldiers, convinced that victory came only from strict attention to military detail and order. It was not clear just what he had in mind for the West, however; he told Stanton that he could not "at present" support the attempts of Commodore David Farragut to capture the Gibraltar of the Mississippi River, Vicksburg, an obvious target in that theater of war. He was instead "sending reenforcements to Curtis in Arkansas and Buell in Tennessee and Kentucky."[1] But he was continuing to violate his own principles—dispersing rather than massing troops. He was organizing and resupplying rather than pushing forward, a strategy that left many scratching their heads.

Before he could leave Mississippi, Halleck told Lincoln that he had to confer with Grant, the next highest ranking officer. Halleck began to exhibit the indecisiveness that would plague him. He wondered whether it was up to him to give command in the West to Grant or whether Lincoln wanted to make that decision himself. Eventually Halleck decided that neither Grant nor Buell had the ability needed for overall command. He told his wife that he realized that George B. McClellan's brilliantly conceived but poorly managed peninsular campaign against Richmond was "a failure" and that it had "greatly complicated the events of the war." Consequently, it was now a "quarrel between Stanton and McClellan," and "he did not want to get in the middle" of such "cabinet quarrels." Since Lincoln had ordered him to Washington to assume his new command, and that was "certainly a very high compliment," he would obey the President's orders. Still, he was conflicted. It bothered him that he might be seen as anti-McClellan because of his willingness to replace him even though "everybody who knows me, knows that I have uniformly supported him."[2] Halleck was already having second thoughts as he prepared to take command of the Union Army. He was not sure he could handle his new post, and was particularly worried about angering McClellan, a man whom he clearly admired and whose approval he badly wanted.

Nor did Lincoln help to speed Halleck up when he told him to have a meeting with Andrew Johnson, the military governor of Tennessee, before he left the region. Johnson was insisting on more military power than the President was willing to give him, so Lincoln wanted Halleck to convince Johnson to be less demanding. Then Lincoln told Halleck to stop Confederate cavalry raider John Hunt Morgan, who was cutting a swath of destruction across Kentucky. Taking on Morgan meant getting Buell moving, and, as always, Buell was making excuses about why he was moving so slowly toward Chattanooga. Reluctantly, Halleck told him "to put down the Morgan raid even if the Chattanooga expedition should be delayed."[3]

Meanwhile Lincoln's mind was becoming "perfectly complexed" over

McClellan's stalemate on the Virginia peninsula just a few miles from Richmond and how it could be broken. Lincoln wanted to get Halleck to Washington as quickly as he could so Old Brains could solve the problem. "I am very anxious to have you here," the President wrote. "Having due regard to what you leave behind, when can you reach here?" Despite the President's alarm, Halleck continued his methodical pace. He told Lincoln he would leave on July 17, 1862, but he did not begin his trip to Washington until the twentieth. It was not laziness or reluctance to leave that delayed him but his determination to make sure he left everything perfectly organized.[4]

As he rode the train east, Halleck continued to make sure that he did nothing to complicate his relationship with George McClellan, his former commander and now his major subordinate. He told J. N. Alsop, a friend of that general who happened to be traveling with him, that he believed that "McClellan was the ablest military man in the world." He did not, however, have the same positive attitude about the Secretary of War. Such negative feeling was mutual since it was rumored that Halleck was coming east to replace Stanton. Halleck had nothing but disdain for politicians who made military decisions—a stance that implied a certain ambivalence toward the President's powers as well.[5]

Before boarding the train for Washington, Halleck had bade a heartfelt farewell to his troops. "Soldiers, you have accomplished much toward crushing out this wicked rebellion," he said, "and if you continue to exhibit the same vigilance, courage, and perseverance, it is believed that under the providence of God you will soon bring the war to a close and be able to return in peace to your families and homes." He wrote a similarly encouraging letter to Sherman, their former animosity now gone: "Goodby, and may God bless you. I am more than satisfied with everything you have done. You have always had my respect, but recently you have won my highest admiration. I deeply regret to part from you." When he wrote Buell, however, all he said was that he was "very sorry [to be going], for I can be of more use here than there." He promised, however, to make sure that Buell's "movements" were properly explained to the President. As for Grant, he was even more terse: "You will immediately repair to this place and report to these headquarters."[6]

Sherman wrote an emotional letter in response to Halleck's warm words. "I cannot express my heartfelt pain at hearing of your orders and intended departure," he said. Stay in the West, Sherman advised, because that was where the war was going to be decided, where the major figures would emerge. Sherman profusely praised Halleck for saving the nation from "Mexican anarchy" with his imposition of "order, system, firmness and success." Conversely, Buell coldly said he was "sorry" Halleck was leaving, but "I don't know what you can do for us, except to represent the importance of matters out here and urge an increase of our cavalry force." Despite his months of castigation by Halleck, Grant still wrote glowing words about him to his Illinois congressman friend, Elihu B. Washburne. "He is a man of gigantic intellect and well studied in the profession of arms," Grant said. "He and I had several little spats but I like and respect him nevertheless." Grant admired Halleck's learning so much he was willing to ignore his brusqueness.[7]

In the minds of many others, however, Halleck was still unproven. With remarkable insight, the *Chicago Tribune* called him "a closet general who in his library will be able to give celerity and potency to military movements which in the field he would be powerless to direct." Other newspapers, however, were "blowing his trumpet and looking to him for leadership."[8]

When Halleck arrived in Washington on July 23, 1862, he found "a military camp, a city of barracks and hospitals." "Long lines of army wagons and artillery were continually rumbling through the streets; at all hours of the day and night . . . [there was] the clatter of galloping squads of cavalry; and the clank of sabers, and the measured beat of marching infantry were ever present to the ear." The 1860 census listed the District of Columbia's population as 75,080, but the influx of soldiers, families, businessmen, and a wide variety of other people, including prostitutes, catapulted the number beyond that, and the overcrowding did nothing to enhance the city's look. It was a dusty place in the summer, and mud was everywhere in the winter. The capitol building, still under construction, stood as a graphic reminder of the uncompleted nature of the capital city of the United States and of the Union itself.[9]

Upon his arrival, Halleck attended a meeting with the President, the Secretary of War, and Generals John Pope and Ambrose Burnside, the latter having recently arrived from his former station on the North Carolina coast. Lincoln openly expressed his disdain for McClellan's generalship and for the second time offered command of the Army of the Potomac to Burnside. Burnside again declined, speaking in support of McClellan. Some of Lincoln's cabinet members, when they met Halleck in the following days, urged him strongly to take the initiative and fire McClellan.[10]

As he met the powerful men in Washington and settled into his office on G Street near the War Department, Halleck came under rigorous inspection. A newsman characterized him as "a short countrified person . . . who picked his teeth walking up and down the halls at Willard's [Hotel], and argued through a white, bilious eye and a huge mouth." Lincoln's secretary, John Hay, put the best slant on what people like the reporter saw when they met Halleck. Quoting "a Western friend," who sounded a lot like Lincoln, Hay said of Halleck that he was "'like a singed cat—better than he looks.'" His uniform was "a little white at the seams, and seedy at the button-holes," and he had "a stooped and downward glance." But he had a "great head . . . [with] vast stores of learning which have drifted in from the assiduous reading of a quarter of a century." Halleck also had, according to Hay, "wide and varied impressions of human nature, gained by the laborious practice of law in the sharp and busy Pacific world. . . . He is a cool, mature man, who understands himself. Let us be glad we have got him."[11]

As he was being inspected, Halleck peered back intently at the intriguing array of people who were now part of his new life. The President, like Halleck himself, was not a physically attractive man, but his six-foot, four-inch frame allowed him to tower over most people. "His eyes were almost deathly in their gloomy depths," a reporter noted in 1862. "His face was almost colorless and drawn, and newly grown whiskers added to the agedness of his appearance." The burdens of war were clearly etched on Abraham Lincoln's face, and there is no indication that Halleck was much impressed with what he saw. Lincoln, after all, was a politician, the very kind of man whom Halleck saw as a threat to the Union's military success.[12]

Then there was Stanton, whom Halleck had known in California and had never liked. There was a "terrific earnestness" about the man. He was a "tireless worker" who stood most of the time at a high office desk. He had "tremendous energy" and an "impetuous temper" with an "opinionated, almost immovable" nature. He was a man who was not easily fooled or cowed, and people realized it as soon as they met him. He had been a harsh critic of Lincoln before he joined the cabinet, and several of the other ministers mistrusted him from the start. He and General McClellan had once been very close, but had grown increasingly distant the more they had worked together. Most important, however, Abraham Lincoln liked what he saw in his Secretary of War, and the two men grew closer as the war progressed. But there was a "brusque rudeness" about the man, resulting from his earnestness for the cause or his love of power, and this made him difficult to like.[13]

Secretary of the Navy Gideon Welles, who seemed to write everything he thought into his opinionated and later influential diary, was another hard-driving man. He kept a low public profile, however, one senator saying of him that he "did not have a tangible shape, and that one's arm could sweep through his form." Attorney General Edward Bates, a man Halleck already knew from his time in Missouri, could also be acerbic in his diary; but in person he had the reputation of being a "gentleman of the old school, short in stature, gray-haired, rather shy and reserved in manner." Secretary of the Treasury Salmon P. Chase was just the opposite. Famous as the lawyer for fugitive slaves and one of the founders of the Republican party, he believed himself superior to all those around him, especially the President, and he raised a loud voice in the cabinet on behalf of the downtrodden slaves. He always had something to say about the conduct of the war and about a lot of other things, too.[14]

These were the men with whom Halleck would have the closest official relationships in Washington, although he brought his staff with him from Corinth, headed as before by George W. Cullum, the close friend with whom he felt free to laugh and joke. Other than Cullum, Halleck had no close friends. He remained, as he had been most of his life, severely limited in his relationships. Since he looked down on politicians, as he did on Grant and anyone whose conduct he disapproved of, there was no reason to expect him to make any effort to draw close to the Washington politicians.

The city's civilian and military officials were not sure what to make of Halleck when he first arrived. Lincoln, as always, played his cards close to his vest, but others were outspoken. Ominously for Halleck, despite Stanton's praise for his capture of Corinth, the Secretary of War had not changed the negative opinions he had formed about the new commander from their time together in California. He had opposed Halleck's selection as commanding general, and now he bluntly told McClellan that on the basis of his legal investigations in California before the war he considered Halleck "probably the greatest scoundrel and most barefaced villain in America." He was, said Stanton, "totally destitute of principle," a perjurer in the New Almaden case. When Halleck conversed with McClellan, he allegedly made similarly derogatory comments about Stanton. Halleck knew that Stanton did not "like" him and believed he would "take the first opportunity . . . to injure" him. As matters developed, however, Stanton and Halleck apparently never referred to their California disagreements. On the surface, at least, they worked together during the war without obvious rancor.[15]

Others were not sure what to expect of the new general. Secretary of the Treasury Chase said he had admired Halleck until the general had taken personal command of the army in the Corinth campaign. Since that time, he said, "inaction has been its most marked characteristic." Perhaps Halleck would "come & act vigorously," but, he said, "my apprehensions . . . exceed my hopes." Attorney General Bates felt just the opposite. "We have great hopes of Halleck. . . . In fact we need nothing but activity & enterprise to crush out the power of the enemy in Virginia—and Halleck can if he will have that glory." Halleck's alma mater, Union College, voted him an honorary doctorate of humane letters, while Columbia University Professor Francis Lieber summed up most northerners' feelings: "May our army profit under you and may victory once more return to us."[16]

Halleck engendered such hope because Union troops had done exceptionally well in the West under his command, especially in contrast to McClellan's failure to take Richmond. McClellan had begun his peninsular campaign with great early success, but then he had hesitated and permitted the Confederates to take the initiative. The entire Union war effort had not been well organized, the ninety-day enlistments Lincoln had originally summoned having proved inadequate. There was need for more men for longer terms of service if the war was to be prosecuted fully. Lincoln called for 300,000 more men under a three-year enlistment and at the same time Congress passed the Second Confiscation Law on July 17, 1862, authorizing freedom for slaves of owners declared by a court to be in rebellion against the United States. Ratcheting up the pressure on the Confederacy, Grant settled into command in Mississippi, with Sherman, his chief assistant, acting as military governor of Memphis. On July 18, John Pope announced that his Army of Virginia would live off the land and punish guerrillas who destroyed public property, thus signaling that a more intense, more destructive conflict was replacing the restrained war of the early days. Publicly unknown at the time, but most significant of all, was the fact that Lincoln presented a draft of the Emancipation Proclamation to his cabinet on July 22, thus making abolition a national policy. Halleck's call to Washington to become commanding general can be seen as one part of a general movement to intensify the war. The nation looked to the successful western general to coordinate all this political and military activity into victory.

Lincoln had indeed appointed Halleck to take whatever military action he thought necessary to win the war. Halleck, however, viewed his task from a different point of view, as being primarily administrative. As he had shown in his dealings with Grant, he believed that the only successful general was one who organized thoroughly. Union arms would only be victorious if paperwork flowed efficiently. He had demonstrated his greatest anger with subordinates not when they failed on the battlefield but when they violated some rule or regulation. He reigned with an iron fist when it came to army administration; military movements themselves were up to each general without Halleck's or anyone else's distant interference. He was not prepared to tell a subordinate general in the field that he should do or not do anything. It was up to that general to decide and then make sure Halleck knew what was happening.

This was not what Lincoln had in mind. The President was under intense pressure from his cabinet to resolve the situation in Virginia. Chase, for example, called for "an immediate change in the command of the Army of the Potomac . . . [and the appointment of] a General in that command who would cordially and efficiently" be cooperative. Consequently, the President told Halleck to see what he could do to solve the McClellan problem in Virginia. On the afternoon of July 24, therefore, accompanied by Ambrose Burnside, Halleck stepped aboard a steamship for the overnight trip to McClellan's camp at Harrison's Landing on Virginia's James River. His physical bearing made a negative impression on at least one of those who saw him land. "I was greatly disappointed in his appearance," this man noted. "Small and farmer-like he gives a rude shock to one's preconceived notions of a great soldier." Unlike McClellan, Halleck simply did not look like a man destined to lead men to victory on the battlefield.[17] And he did not see that as his job anyway.

In sending Halleck to Virginia, Lincoln made it clear that his new commanding general had "supreme command" over the entire Union Army. Where previously he and Stanton had tried to run the war, now Lincoln turned briefly away from Stanton and looked to Halleck for military guidance. He told Halleck he could fire McClellan or maintain him; he should do what he thought best. The President wanted Halleck to know, however, that he was convinced that no matter how many reinforcements McClellan received he would still refuse to move until he received even more. Lincoln tried to steel Halleck for the problems he would face in dealing with McClellan.[18]

Halleck handled the Army of the Potomac's commanding officer gingerly, leaving it up to Burnside to quiz McClellan's staff and subordinate officers. McClellan had been Halleck's commander just a few short months before, and Halleck was clearly in awe of him. Little Mac, as he was known to his troops, was a handsome man with immense charisma who mesmerized his soldiers with his striking personal appearance and military dash. He had a "pleasant and winning" smile, and most people were taken by "the attractiveness of his face and manner," a contemporary newsman noted. He looked every part the soldier, and he made those who served under him feel proud to be a part of his army. McClellan was not happy to have Halleck or anyone else in command over him. In fact, he told a friend that he considered Halleck's promotion a "slap in the face." For his part, Halleck wanted only to convince the impressive McClellan to be cooperative for the good of the cause.[19]

The meeting of the charismatic, disgruntled, and outwardly confident McClellan and the plain-looking, plainly dressed, and uncomfortable Halleck was, therefore, a study in marked contrasts. At first, Halleck was tentative; indeed he later admitted that he felt the whole meeting was "somewhat embarrassing" and "unpleasant, considering their previous relationship." Instead of forthrightly speaking his mind, as he always seemed to have done with Grant, Buell, and other previous subordinates, Halleck began hesitatingly. He told McClellan that he was there "to ascertain from him his views and wishes in regard to future operations." When McClellan proposed to swing south of Richmond to cut off Confederate communications rather than attack the city itself, Halleck quickly found his tongue. He said it was "a military necessity" for McClellan to mass with John Pope's new Army of Virginia, located in northern Virginia, and then attack Richmond, keeping the concentrated Union army between the Confederates and Washington. The only other possibility was for McClellan to make an attack on his own, aided by 20,000 reinforcements that the President was able to send. Halleck never thought of or mentioned the possibility of taking command himself from McClellan. He could not imagine firing such an impressive man. He saw his role as coordinator rather than commander, administrator not fighter.

McClellan listened to his new commanding general and said that he needed at least 30,000 more men for an attack on Richmond. Halleck said no; such a large reinforcement was impossible. McClellan's only choice, Halleck insisted, was to withdraw from the peninsula and concentrate his 90,000-man Army of the Potomac with Pope's 40,000-man Army of Virginia at Aquia Creek, closer to Washington. McClellan told Halleck that such a move would demoralize his men; he wanted to stay where he was until sufficient reinforcements reached him. Halleck said he "had no authority to consider that proposition." He gave McClellan until morning to meet with his officers and make up his mind either to attack or to leave. McClellan reluctantly decided that he would attack on his own, even though he contended that the enemy force before him was much larger than his; he erroneously believed that General Robert E. Lee had 200,000 men in his army when he really had only 75,000.[20]

Halleck later heard from Burnside that McClellan's officers were even more intransigent. They were threatening a march on Washington to clear out what they considered interfering civilian officials. This information was sobering. Upon his arrival at the White House, Halleck met behind closed doors with the President, no doubt trying to make sense of it all. He had left Harrison's Landing thinking that McClellan would attack Richmond, only to receive a telegram from Little Mac that same day asking for every available soldier in the East and 20,000 from the West besides. Two days later McClellan even increased this demand to "all available troops to enable me to advance." Lincoln could only tell Halleck that he was not surprised.[21]

Halleck did not react to McClellan's foot-dragging by asserting his authority. Hoping persuasion would be more effective, he wrote a letter of petition. He confided in McClellan that he was in Washington under presidential order, much preferring to be in the West. He begged for McClellan's cooperation. "In whatever has occurred heretofore," he said, "you have had my full approbation and cordial support. There was no one in the army under whom I could serve with greater pleasure. And now I ask you that same support and co-operation and that same free interchange of opinion, as in former days." Reading such words, McClellan could only have been emboldened in his stubbornness. Halleck sounded as though he were a child, begging his father to follow his wishes, much as he had done with his own father in his early years.[22]

Halleck was much more straightforward with his wife, then still in New York City. "Gen. McClellan is in many respects a most excellent and valuable man, but he does not understand strategy and should never plan a campaign," he said. Besides, "his friends have excited his jealousy." Halleck worried that McClellan would probably not be cooperative. "I did sustain him, and in justice to me and to the country he ought now to sustain me. I hope he will, but I doubt it." Halleck was in awe of his chief subordinate when facing him, but when not in his presence he was critical. Thus he sent mixed signals to McClellan. He wanted him to cooperate but he could not bring himself to force that result for fear of injuring their relationship.[23]

McClellan's response to Halleck was similarly contradictory. He called for more reinforcements, but he also sent a long letter of reassurance. He said he was pleased with Halleck's appointment but commiserated with him at having to do the job. "I believe that together we can save this unhappy country . . . [if] selfish politicians will allow us to do so," he told Halleck. He was unhappy about some aspects of the war, however, such as the Confiscation Act, believing that "the people of the South should understand that we are not making war upon the institution of slavery, but that if they submit to the Constitution and laws of the Union they will be protected in their constitutional rights of every nature." Just as he agreed with Halleck about minimizing slavery's role in the war, he similarly agreed completely, he said, with the necessity of "concentration of forces." Yet he admitted that he continued to be opposed to "the idea of withdrawing this army from its present position." One of his subordinates was more forthright, suggesting how McClellan's entourage felt about Halleck and Washington's civilian authorities. "All we want is reinforcements that are within reach, and we will advance. . . . It is sad to see the country ruined by the imbecility in Washington."[24]

Halleck and McClellan thus pledged their mutual support, but in fact they totally disagreed over what should be done about Richmond and Robert E. Lee. McClellan wanted more reinforcements, and then he promised he would attack. Taking his cue from Lincoln, Halleck demanded an immediate attack on Richmond or withdrawal of the army from the peninsula and a concentration with John Pope's Army of Virginia at Aquia Creek. The impasse persisted, but Halleck's ordering of Ambrose Burnside's newly organized IX Army Corps to reinforce Pope should have told McClellan that the commanding general was going to order the Army of the Potomac off the peninsula if McClellan did not attack. Halleck clearly did not get that message across to McClellan, however.[25]

Worried as they were about the peninsula, Lincoln's cabinet also summoned Halleck to discuss the possibility of a new offensive in the West. They asked him about raising a "special force" to take Vicksburg and thus open the Mississippi River, a move for which the Illinois politician turned general John McClernand was lobbying. Halleck listened, but he diplomatically warned the secretaries that newly recruited soldiers could not handle such a major undertaking. He suggested, instead, that new enlistees, brought in under Lincoln's recent call, replace some veteran units and the veterans then be sent against Vicksburg. Halleck made such a good argument about the shortage of troops in the West that the cabinet stopped discussing the possibility of an immediate move on Vicksburg. When Halleck demanded a speeding up of the President's recruitment order and condemned the political practice of naming incompetent politicians to be generals, he made a good impression on the usually critical Salmon P. Chase. "The General commanded my sincere respect by the great intelligence and manliness he displayed, and excited great hopes by his obvious purpose to allow no lagging and by his evident mastery of the business he has taken in hand." Chase, however, disagreed with Halleck about leaving McClellan in command, and he was taken aback when Halleck said: "I confess, I do not think much of the negro," a shocking position considering Lincoln's still secret plan to issue the Emancipation Proclamation and Stanton's hopes to utilize black soldiers.[26] Like McClellan, Buell, and many other Union generals and reflecting his long-held views, Halleck opposed making the obviously escalating war into a conflict over freeing the slaves. Increasingly, however, political officials were doing just that.

Halleck remained focused on the Army of the Potomac. After giving McClellan every chance to move, he ordered the withdrawal of McClellan's army from the peninsula and its concentration with Pope at Aquia Creek. This massed force was to move on Richmond frontally by the overland route. The order shocked Little Mac, who never thought Halleck would issue it. "I must confess that it has caused me the greatest pain I ever experienced. . . . [It] will prove disastrous in the extreme to our cause. I feel it will be a fatal blow." "I entreat that this order may be rescinded." He did promise, however, to obey Halleck even though he was convinced that withdrawing his army would produce "disaster."[27]

The next day, after pledging once again to move "as promptly as possible," McClellan began dragging his feet, complaining that he could not move his sick and injured as quickly as Halleck desired. Halleck may have thought that having made his decision he had solved the McClellan problem, but he was quickly learning that such was not the case.[28]

Old Brains tried, once again, to use persuasion on Little Mac, to get him to move without causing him to become angry. "You, general," he began, "certainly could not have been more pained at receiving my order than I was at the necessity of issuing it." He had delayed as long as he could, he said, but he had no real choice. Lee had 200,000 men, McClellan had told him, and this Confederate force was located between the Army of the Potomac and Pope's Army of Virginia. Lee was thus capable of attacking one force and then the other, without the two Union armies being able to concentrate in response. Besides, if the Army of the Potomac stayed where it was, waiting for the increasing number of reinforcements that McClellan demanded, it would melt away from sickness "in that climate." Halleck did not blame McClellan for this situation; "I have not inquired and do not desire to know by whose advice or for what reasons the Army of the Potomac was separated into two parts, with the enemy between them. I must take things as I find them, I find the forces divided and I wish to unite them." In short, Halleck made it clear that he had made his decision according to the precepts of his military writings, and he was going to stick by it. As at the cabinet meeting, Halleck appeared here as a man of knowledge and decisiveness, just what Lincoln had hoped for when he had appointed him.[29]

Unfortunately, Halleck softened his tone. He told McClellan that he agreed with his August 1 letter about "the manner in which the war should be conducted." It should indeed be a war for the Union between armies not a war against slavery and the populace. "I must beg of you, general, to hurry along this movement," he entreated; "your reputation as well as mine may be involved in its rapid execution. I cannot regard Pope and Burnside as safe until you reinforce them. Moreover, I wish them to be under your immediate command." Merge with Pope and Burnside, Halleck told McClellan, and the result would be command of a larger force than he now had, with the reinforcements he had been asking for. There was no reason not to act quickly, Halleck concluded, confident that his logic would overcome McClellan's stubbornness.[30]

McClellan was not convinced and did not act. The pressure grew on Halleck, as he worried that Lee would attack Pope and Burnside before McClellan moved. He simultaneously had the problem of Buell's inactivity in the West and warned that general of Washington's unhappiness "at the slow movement of your army toward Chattanooga." At the same time, Grant was expressing concern about guerrilla activity in West Tennessee and North Mississippi, to which Halleck harshly responded: "Handle that class without gloves, and take their property for public use." Then, to make sure he was right, he asked Columbia University's Francis Lieber, a man he was drawing closer to, to publish a legal opinion on the matter. As for Sherman's concern about the sale of Confederate cotton for gold, it should be allowed, he ordered. Meanwhile in Kansas, Jim Lane, waging merciless warfare, had also established a recruiting officer to add blacks to the Union Army. Halleck responded that the Second Confiscation Act of July 17 allowed for the army's acceptance of black soldiers, but it did not authorize recruiting them. Then Halleck learned from General Samuel Curtis in Arkansas that Farragut's Union fleet had given up trying to take Vicksburg because of a "sad want of unity" between the army and the navy. Everywhere he turned, Halleck had a serious problem to solve. Even his chief of staff and old friend, George W. Cullum, was upset with him because his temporary brigadier generalship had expired, and he was but a mere major again. He wanted Halleck to do something about that. Lincoln and the Washington politicians similarly looked to Halleck to do something, something to bring victory in the war.[31]

Halleck felt overwhelming stress and lacked the comfort of his wife, who was spending the summer in the coolness of Newport, Rhode Island.

He confessed to her: "I feel almost broken down every night with the heat, labor, and responsibility. I have felt so uneasy for some days about Gen. Pope's army that I could hardly sleep. I can't get Gen. McClellan to do what I wish." And Lincoln and his cabinet were pushing him to fire McClellan. Ominously, he expressed a feeling that anticipated even greater heartache in the future: "The President and Cabinet have thus far approved everything I have proposed. This is kind and complimentary, but it only increases my responsibility, for if any disaster happens they can say 'We did for you all you asked.'" Halleck, who had wanted command in the West in order to be able to act efficiently, now worried about having overall command in the East because of the repercussions failure might bring. Instead of eagerly seeking opportunities for success in his new position, Halleck was dominated by fear. This trepidation about issuing orders was enervating and when added to his already existing administrative philosophy of command precluded decisive action. Halleck worried rather than acted.[32]

In all fairness to Halleck, there was plenty to be worried about. The Confederates were increasing their pressure on Pope, and McClellan was multiplying the reasons for his delay. "If Washington is in danger now[,] this Army can scarcely arrive in time to save it," Little Mac warned, insisting yet again that "it is in much better position to do so from here than from Aquia." Within two days, he insisted, he would be ready to attack the Confederate Army, weakened by its movement against Pope. "Under existing orders I do not feel authorized to make the movement," he then added. McClellan continued to thwart Halleck's order for concentration of forces. The commanding general cajoled but did not order compliance.[33]

When Pope reported that he had defeated Stonewall Jackson's force at Cedar Mountain, on the northern side of the Rapidan River, on August 9, 1862, Halleck felt greatly relieved and sent effusive praise. "Cedar Mountain," he said, "will be known in History as one of the great Battle fields of the war." Unfortunately, other problems continued to escalate. The recruitment process to add the 300,000 new men to the Union Army was proving to be an administrative disaster. The squabbles over the war effort that Union General John Schofield was facing in Missouri with the political leaders there seemed to grow worse every day, and as a veteran of that state's military and civilian wars, Halleck knew what trouble that meant. In addition, Buell's continued inaction, and his threat to quit if he was subjected to more criticism, weighed heavily on Halleck while Grant and Sherman continued to have problems with guerrillas in Tennessee and

Mississippi. "It is the strangest thing in the world to me," Halleck complained to his wife, "that this war has developed so little talent in our generals. There is not a single one in the West fit for a great command." Halleck saw himself as the only man able to provide the Union Army with the leadership it needed. Yet he did not assert that leadership or seize the opportunities for aggressive action. Instead, he worried and fretted precious time away waiting for his subordinates to move.[34]

Political pressure continued to increase. Chase, who just a few days previously had praised Halleck, now condemned him for not being able to provide informed answers about the war effort. Secretary of the Navy Gideon Welles was even more provoked. He visited Halleck and noticed the obvious strain on the man. Welles noted that during their conversation Halleck nervously "began to rub his elbows." He vaguely spoke of many things, Welles noted, but he made no effort to thank the navy for its help during the peninsular campaign. Welles was disgusted at the sight of a crumbling commanding general.[35]

Others experienced ill-treatment at Halleck's hands. General Oliver O. Howard, who had been severely wounded at Fair Oaks during the peninsular campaign, went to Halleck's house on the afternoon of August 23, to inquire about a return to his command. Halleck kept the one-armed veteran waiting for half an hour while he napped. When he finally came to the doorway of his reception room, he greeted Howard coldly. "Do you want to see me, officially, sir?" Halleck said sharply. "Partly officially and partly not," Howard replied. So what was it Howard wanted, Halleck asked. Howard said he wanted to see about rejoining his unit. Halleck, offering no commiseration about Howard's wound, simply said that the adjutant general "will tell you that" and abruptly ended the interview. Howard left the house shaking his head in disbelief.[36] Halleck had always dealt with any job he had to do in a no-nonsense manner, keeping people at arm's length. Still his lack of compassion for Howard was more marked than usual and demonstrated the effects of the stress he now found himself under.

Other discouraging actions began to cast a shadow on Halleck's once shining public reputation. Displaying the same anti-spy concern he had demonstrated in Missouri when he banned fugitive slaves and newspaper correspondents from his military camps, he ordered Pope to exclude reporters from his army. He also stopped the flow of soldiers' mail because he believed this too was a source of information for the enemy. When he discovered, the following day, that a newspaper had published this order, he was furious at Pope and what he called his "decidedly leaky" staff. John

Hay believed that the anti-press order made no sense. After Pope's victory at Cedar Mountain had lessened the concern about Lee's movements in Virginia, why, Hay asked, did Halleck not "authorize a statement that all is well?" especially since "a pall of panic terror hung over New York, and Government stocks went down with a run." Amazingly obtuse about the importance of mail to the common soldier and with no proof that it provided intelligence to the enemy, Halleck became the butt of Billy Yank's disdain. "It is hard enough to be a soldier," one man complained, "but to be compelled to give up these dear rights, which the meanest lowest citizen can enjoy, & be treated like a slave, or hireling, is a little more than I wish to or intend to stand. I will leave the army at my earliest opportunity." More and more people were beginning to wonder about the capacities of their commanding general.[37]

Inexorably, although not always noticeably, matters were continuing to deteriorate for Union arms in Virginia. Like Halleck, Pope seemed to be growing increasingly unsure of himself. In the face of a Confederate advance, Pope asked Halleck whether he should fall back or attack. Once he and McClellan had joined forces, Halleck would take overall command, would he not? Halleck, who had been encouraging caution until the concentration with McClellan was completed, now switched to encouraging an attack. But the next day he remembered his philosophy of command and backed off: "Of course in all this, these matters of detail, you, from your local knowledge, are the best judge, and what I say is only in the way of suggestion." Halleck surprisingly considered the momentous decision facing Pope to be simply a "detail." He refused to issue a direct order. Pope retreated behind the Rappahannock River, McClellan was still not there, and Halleck seemed both unsure and unable to do anything about it.[38]

While Pope and Halleck displayed such tentativeness, McClellan became more aggressive. He asked Halleck for "a kind word to my army" that he could pass on to them in gratitude for their service on the peninsula, and then he demanded to know precisely where Pope was and whether Halleck intended to keep his word and have McClellan become overall commander of the concentrated forces. When Halleck responded that he was in the dark about Pope's and even Robert E. Lee's whereabouts and "all day [had] been most anxious to ascertain" them, McClellan expressed understanding, but in a letter to his wife he lashed out at what he called the "perfect imbecility [he had] to correct." He kept telling Halleck and Stanton what they should do, but they refused to listen, he wrote home. McClellan clearly did not understand that Lincoln's cabinet was furious at him for his slowness in merging with Pope. When he told Lincoln that one of his thoughts was "to leave Pope to get out of his scrape," this jolting comment only intensified the President's animosity toward him. Astonishingly, Halleck continued to do nothing to deal with McClellan's insubordinate behavior. He could not confront Little Mac directly.[39]

Only McClellan seemed to be thriving on all this Union uncertainty. Curtly, he wrote Halleck demanding authority to direct troops as he saw fit. Halleck revealingly responded that he was busy with recruiting troops and with the western theater, and McClellan, therefore, as ranking general in the field, should "direct as you deem best." This comment further emboldened McClellan. He demanded to know if Halleck had really been critical of him in front of another general, as he had heard. Halleck insisted that it was all a misunderstanding. Little Mac inundated Halleck with ever more telegrams, and one day he came to Washington and conferred with Old Brains far into the morning hours. McClellan went back to his army satisfied, but the next day he sent even more advice to Halleck.[40]

Conversely, Halleck had not heard from Pope for four days. As had been the case with Grant after Fort Donelson, Halleck grew increasingly upset at the lack of communication, telling McClellan that he was worried about "a raid upon Washington." He wanted to know exactly where the enemy was, asserting his administrative authority forthrightly. "I am tired of guesses," he exclaimed in exasperation. Little Mac, not used to Halleck speaking to him this sharply, felt hurt. "He is not a refined person at all," he said of Old Brains, "and probably says rough things when he doesn't mean them." McClellan was acting with such apparent vigor that a rumor spread that he was actually commanding the army while Halleck was his mere advisor. When McClellan stopped a corps that Halleck had ordered to march to Pope, however, Halleck angrily protested, only to have McClellan say that Halleck should not be castigating him when he "simply exercised the discretion you committed to me." McClellan had clearly gained the upper hand in the relationship between the two men.[41]

Then Halleck received an optimistic assessment from Pope about an August twenty-eighth battle at Groveton, Virginia. Excitedly, the commanding general tried to regain his authority over McClellan, demanding, yet again, that Little Mac send troops to Pope, now arguing that "if re-enforcements reach him in time, we shall have a glorious victory." "You have done nobly," he telegraphed Pope, "God bless you" and "your noble army." In such euphoria, Halleck was not emotionally prepared for two shocking telegrams that arrived next. "I should like to know whether you feel secure about Washington should this army be destroyed," Pope wrote. Meanwhile, McClellan passed along the news that "our army is badly beaten. Our losses very heavy." The Confederates had indeed beaten Pope's army decisively on August 29 and 30, at the battle that came to be known as Second Bull Run. Under the strain of this heart-breaking news and the events of the past month, Halleck collapsed. He blamed McClellan's delays for Pope's defeat and later said so before Congress's Joint Committee on the Conduct of the War. At the time, however, he pleaded with his subordinate. "I beg of you to assist me in this crisis with your ability and experience. I am utterly tired out." Sensing victory in his struggle with his commanding general, McClellan moved more rapidly than he ever had on the battlefield to pour salt into Halleck's wounds. He said to Old Brains: "to speak frankly & the occasion requires it, there appears to be a total absence of brains & I fear the total destruction of the Army."[42]

Just a few nights earlier Abraham Lincoln had characterized McClellan as "a little crazy" with "envy, jealousy and spite," while Halleck had no such "prejudices" and did not "care who succeeds or who fails" as long as "the service is benefitted." Now he had to swallow these words. Meeting with McClellan and Halleck on September 1 and 2, the President asked Little Mac to save the Union from disaster. He also requested him to write a letter to his former officers now serving under Pope, urging them to cooperate with their new commander. Lincoln had hired Halleck to lead Union armies to victory despite McClellan; now Lincoln had to ask McClellan to prevent the loss of Washington and perhaps the war itself because of Halleck's inability to lead. Secretary of War Stanton was not consulted, and he was crushed when he learned the news of McClellan's reinstatement. He and Treasury Secretary Chase had organized a cabinet protest against McClellan, but Lincoln's decision undercut these efforts. An outraged Chase put it succinctly: "Halleck considered himself relieved [sic] from responsibility." Even when Pope called upon Halleck to visit his troops to help deal with their "demoralization," Halleck responded that it was "impossible" for him "to leave Washington." Halleck seemed to have taken his hands off the reins of military power completely. McClellan controlled the defense of Washington and added Pope's battered army to his Army of the Potomac. He had finally received the reinforcements he had been demanding. If anyone noted the irony, nothing was said, but Stanton for one was openly depressed at the developments.[43]

As he capitulated to McClellan, Halleck was worried about his wife, then ill in New York, and one of her brothers, who was suffering from recently received combat wounds. His physical health and mental well-being plummeted. He went four straight nights without sleep, and he developed a case of "very severe" hemorrhoids. He just wanted to get out from under it all, growing even more upset because he could not get McClellan to Washington fast enough. "At what hour will he be here?" he telegraphed McClellan's staff. "I am very anxious to see him."[44]

Halleck, ill and agitated, surrendered responsibility to McClellan completely, but rumors flew that Halleck had gained new powers. General Ben Butler's wife wrote her husband in New Orleans that Halleck was the new Secretary of War, over McClellan, who was back as commanding general, a possibility that the abolitionist William Lloyd Garrison thought proved that Lincoln was "near lunacy." An army surgeon reported what he called the "curious rumor" that Halleck had "declared himself 'Dictator' and that the army at Washington was satisfied that it should be so." The leading businessman George Templeton Strong even wrote in his diary that Halleck had "formally demanded" that Mrs. Lincoln be sent out of Washington for giving away in gossip secret information that had aided the Confederate cause.[45] The public continued to believe that Halleck had the power and ability to bring victory, so his growing failures caused the populace to reach such bizarre contradictory conclusions.

Yet Halleck's power was illusory and he had truly lost his way. He tried to soothe his psyche. "Everybody now admits that if I had not brought McClellan's army here when I did we should have been lost. As it is we have every hope." Rationalizing his defeat, Halleck saw himself not as one who had capitulated to McClellan's pressure but as the savior of the Union's capital city and its cause.[46] He would have yet another chance to prove himself.

Word filtered into Washington that Lee and his army were on their way to Maryland, the Confederates going on the offensive after their victory at Second Bull Run. Lincoln immediately ordered Halleck to prepare a field army, but not to weaken the troops needed to defend Washington. Furthermore, on September 5, Lincoln decided that Pope and McClellan could not get along, so one of them had to go. He fired Pope. Eventually that unfortunate general went to Minnesota because the serious Sioux Indian uprising there required an effective Union response. Once there, he began adding to Halleck's problems by demanding men and supplies. Halleck had to refuse him because his request could not "be filled without taking supplies from other troops now in the field."[47]

Halleck continued to express confidence in his own work for the Union, writing his wife: "I hope and believe I have saved the capital from the terrible crisis brought upon us by the stupidity of others." Having been under terrible stress for the previous month, he said, "I hardly know myself how

I am able to keep up amidst the excitement and labor of my office." Obviously, he believed he had functioned well enough to save Washington from a Confederate takeover. In his own mind, he was doing well.[48]

In fact, he was out of touch with reality. He remained ill, his hemorrhoids continuing to torment him. As late as September 9 he was still "obliged most of the time to lie upon the couch" in his residence on High Street in Georgetown, some medicines from a physician having only "partially relieved" him. Since an opium suppository was frequently prescribed for such a condition, that drug's effect on him may also have played a role in his lassitude. On September 23 he was still so sick that he could not answer McClellan's telegrams. The stress of command had broken down his physical health and with it his will, long under siege by the psychological pressures of his earlier life.[49]

Matters did not improve during the fall. Lee's army moved into Maryland, and despite his foot-dragging on the peninsula McClellan commanded the Union army facing it. Lincoln had no one else to turn to; once again he did not consider Halleck as a possibility for field command, and Halleck never considered making the offer. McClellan continually demanded more troops, of course, and he shadowed Lee very cautiously. Halleck, meanwhile, forcefully warned him about the continued Confederate threat to Washington, which Halleck said McClellan was not taking seriously. At the same time, the Union commander at Harper's Ferry surrendered the garrison without a fight, so infuriating Halleck that he ordered him and his subordinates arrested.[50]

Matters took a favorable turn when McClellan had the good fortune to come into possession of a copy of one of Lee's Maryland invasion orders wrapped around some cigars. These orders helped enable him to repulse Lee's army at South Mountain on September 14, 1862. Unfortunately, discovery of this order convinced him to be even more cautious in the face of the Confederates. When he clashed with Lee on the battlefield along Antietam Creek near Sharpsburg, Maryland, in what he called "the most terrible battle of the war—perhaps of history"—the two armies inflicted horrendous losses on each other, over 22,000 in all. McClellan did not put in his whole force, however, and two days later Lee slipped away. Instead of pursuing him vigorously, McClellan complained about the decimated army he had inherited from Pope, the terrible losses in the Maryland fighting, and the lack of appropriate transportation. All he could think of was a reorganization of the Army of the Potomac. The striking similarity between his preoccupations and Halleck's after Corinth is remarkable.[51]

In the West, Don Carlos Buell continued his inactivity, so upsetting Lincoln, Stanton, and even Halleck that the commanding general castigated him for "the immobility of your army." Not receiving a positive response, Halleck, following Lincoln's order, sent an aide to fire Buell and replace him with George H. Thomas. After five days of confused correspondence, however, Thomas refused the order, saying that he was not "as well informed as I should be" to become the new commander. Halleck immediately suspended the order, and Buell remained in charge of the Army of the Cumberland. Once again Halleck had backed down before a subordinate and stood by impassively while Lincoln made decisions.[52]

The only good news came from Mississippi, where troops in Grant's area won a victory over Confederate General Sterling Price at Iuka on September 19, continuing Grant's successful generalship in that region. Grant took command of the Army of the Tennessee, widening the scope of his military jurisdiction. Halleck once again gained solace from the man he had long thought so little of. The allegedly imprecise Grant continued to win victories.[53]

In the face of all these problems, criticism of Halleck grew in intensity. Chase summarized the almost hysterical attitudes of the commanding general's critics: "Defeat before Washington poorly compensated by the expulsion of the rebels from Maryland; Ohio & Indiana menaced; military stagnation throughout the South, with danger of expulsion from the points gained on the Atlantic Coast; Tennessee nearly lost, & Kentucky nearly overrun. Was there ever anything like it?" At the same time, Gideon Welles exclaimed, "Great Heavens! what a General-in-chief!" when Halleck told Lincoln that he would need "two days more to make up his mind what to do" about McClellan's lack of pursuit of Lee. A McClellan supporter even composed a sarcastic rhyme that he entitled "A Question Which Major-Gen. Halleck Won't Answer":

> If, before Corinth, you laid ninety days,
> Pleasing the foe with *masterly delays,*
> Failing, at last, to beat 'em;
> How long should you have given "Little Mac,"
> To make all ready for a grand attack,
> From the day he won "Antietam?"[54]

Halleck heard the generals' excuses, the Washington criticism, and he may even have seen the poem, and this time he did not keep his reactions to himself. He wrote forthrightly to General John Schofield, commander in Missouri. Because of the political problems Schofield continued to have there, Halleck saw him as a soulmate. Old Brains complained about the lack of substantial success in the West, which caused political leaders there to press Lincoln and the Washington leadership to do something about it. They demanded more and more military departments, and it infuriated Halleck that they insisted that political favorites and abolitionist and pro-secession Democrats have those commands. "I have done everything in my power here to separate military appointments and commands from poli-tics, but really the task is hopeless. The waste of money and demoraliza-tion of the Army by having incompetent and corrupt politicians in nearly all military offices, high and low, are working out terrible results. It is ut-terly disheartening." Politicians, he thought, were at the crux of all the Union's military problems, he, Buell, and McClellan bearing little or no re-sponsibility. Halleck did not understand the trade-offs that Lincoln and his administration had to make to maintain public support. In the 1840s he had written that professional soldiers alone should implement war. He saw that this was not happening now, and he blamed it for the military mess.[55]

Stress continued to overwhelm Halleck, and this time he demonstrated its effects before a committee of Philadelphians who had come to Washing-ton to make sure that Pennsylvania would receive adequate protection in case of another Confederate invasion. In an interview with Halleck the men found him to be "weak, shallow, commonplace, vulgar" despite the fact that he seemed sympathetic to their cause. "His silly talk was conclu-sive as to his incapacity, unless he was a little flustered with wine, an inadmissable apology for a commander-in-chief at a crisis like this." The men left the interview "in dismal silence and consternation." Halleck was losing support everywhere he turned. Now he was even suspected of drunkenness, an ironic turn considering his earlier treatment of Grant for the same alleged offense. Was he indeed using alcohol to deal with his in-ner turmoil or was he using it to buttress himself against withdrawal from the opium he had no doubt used to try to heal his hemorrhoids? Whatever it was, alcohol or not, it was affecting him noticeably.[56]

McClellan, with Antietam notched into his ego, now demanded inde-pendence from Halleck. "I feel that I have done all that can be asked in twice saving the country. . . . I have at least the right to demand a guaran-tee that I shall not be interfered with," he wrote his wife. With Stanton and Halleck holding their positions, however, he knew that was an impossibil-ity. After all, McClellan complained to Halleck, the commanding general had "couch[ed]" every communication he sent him "in a spirit of fault finding" and had not said even "one word in commendation of the recent achievements of this Army" or even "allude[d] to them." Halleck, waiting another ten days, finally sent his commendations. "A grateful country, while mourning the lamented dead, will not be unmindful of the honors due the living," he told McClellan.[57]

Perhaps not. But in McClellan's view, Washington was not equally grateful. Officials were frustrated with McClellan because he had not mounted an aggressive pursuit after forcing Lee to retreat from Antietam Creek, but kept badgering them for more troops instead. "This army is not now in condition to undertake another campaign nor bring on another battle," he insisted to Halleck. He simply could not move south of the Potomac River until his soldiers had received needed clothes, shoes, and horses. Halleck consulted with the quartermaster general, who told him that he had filled every clothes and shoe requisition he had received from McClellan. As for horses, Halleck said that McClellan's "present proportion of cavalry and of animals is much larger than that of any other of our armies." Lincoln became so exasperated with McClellan's complaints about "sore-tongued and fatigued horses" that he asked him point-blank: "Will you pardon me for asking what the horses of your army have done since the battle of Antietam that fatigues anything?" McClellan resented the jibe and also let it be known that Lincoln's promulgation of the Emancipation Proclamation immediately after Antietam and his retention of Stanton and Halleck "render[ed] it almost impossible . . . to retain my commission and self respect at the same time." McClellan was arrogant enough to threaten to quit at the very time his superiors were thinking of firing him for incompetence.[58]

Yet Halleck remained immobile. Lincoln went to see McClellan himself, and soon after he told Halleck to telegraph Little Mac and order him to "cross the Potomac and give battle to the enemy or drive him south" and to do so immediately. Halleck did so but McClellan maddeningly did not move and instead asked for clarification of that plain order. Two weeks later, he had still not moved. Now he asked Halleck "whether the President desires me to march on the enemy at once, or to await the reception of the new horses." And so it went: Washington wanted action, McClellan kept finding ways to delay. To make matters even more disconcerting, between October 9 and 12, 1862, Lee's cavalry leader, J. E. B. Stuart, and his troops rode completely around McClellan's army, repeating a feat he had accomplished the previous June. There seemed no Union military hope in the East, and the situation was getting increasingly embarrassing.[59]

McClellan was not the only general who was insubordinate and frustratingly inactive. Halleck once again had to tell Buell in the West to move immediately "for many reasons—some of them personal to yourself." A week later, Buell had still not budged, so Halleck said menacingly: "I am directed to again urge upon you the importance of prompt action." When Braxton Bragg began a movement against Louisville, Buell had no choice but to race him for that city and fortunately he arrived first, on September 25. Later, on October 8, he defeated Bragg at Perryville in Kentucky. Instead of building upon this victory, however, he complained that the desolate nature of the countryside made further offensive movement impossible. He would not occupy East Tennessee, as Lincoln had long hoped; he planned instead to go to Nashville, where he would spend the winter. If this was not satisfactory, he told Halleck, he thought the time was as good as any to bring in a new commander to replace him. This made a second Union general who was threatening Halleck with resignation if he did not get his way.[60]

Meanwhile in New Orleans, Ben Butler's controversial military administration was also creating difficulties for the Lincoln administration, while William S. Rosecrans, serving under U.S. Grant in Mississippi, was upset that he had not received a promotion befitting his military achievements. He wanted an assignment to a different department. At the same time, John Pope, fighting the Indians in Minnesota, wrote several letters of protest about his treatment while commanding the Army of Virginia, asking, on October 30, that Old Brains evaluate the "vindictive and unfriendly critiques" and "crude criticism" of "certain officers." "By yielding to and advancing McClellan, you have only put into the hands of an enemy a club to beat your own brains out with," Pope said insultingly.[61]

Yet, another problem hit even closer to home. One of Halleck's aides, Major John J. Key, said in public that the reason for all the delay on the part of the Union military was to exhaust both armies and then "make a compromise and save slavery." Although Lincoln fired him on the spot, the rumor spread that Halleck was part of such a conspiracy, aiding and abetting Buell and McClellan. If all this was not enough, Halleck remained ill and anxious, now no longer blaming his hemorrhoids but "the swamps of Miss . . . at the most unhealthy season." He had gone from constipation to diarrhea, and now was probably using opium as a paregoric, suffering continued debilitation of his body and a continued stress on his being.[62]

With all the mounting discontent and disorder, it was McClellan, whom Halleck continued to hold in such awe, who plagued him the most. "I cannot persuade him to advance an inch. It puts me out of all patience," he complained, but he could not bring himself to act decisively in response. McClellan overwhelmed Halleck and made him feel powerless through his determined stubbornness and his disdain for Halleck's suggestions. He treated Halleck not as the superior he was but as an inferior who just did not understand his place. With his stubborn brusqueness he intimidated Halleck, as had earlier unbending authorities in Old Brains' life. Halleck was unable to gather up his resources to command or even protest loudly. He submitted to the force of McClellan's arrogance and capitulated to him completely.[63]

Halleck refused to "consider himself responsible" and when Attorney General Edward Bates "quietly suggested that Halleck should take command of the army in person," Lincoln and the rest of his cabinet "concurred in the opinion that H. would be an indifferent general in the field." "He shirked responsibility in his present position," Gideon Welles said, and then added his own evaluation: "He, in short, is a moral coward, worth but little except as a critic and director of operations, though intelligent and educated." As if to prove such merciless criticism correct, Halleck wrote McClellan about this time that "since you left Washington I have advised and suggested in relation to your movements, but I have given you no orders. I do not give you any now." Halleck did not want to take the field or give orders to a subordinate general. Ill and broken in spirit, he had placed himself in command limbo.[64]

With the fall 1862 congressional elections on the horizon, Abraham Lincoln had had enough. He ordered sweeping changes in the Union Army leadership. He did not, however, fire Halleck, although rumor had it that he was angry at him about an "act of personal indignity," a refusal to discuss the military situation. On October 24, the President agreed with Halleck that W. S. Rosecrans should replace Don Carlos Buell as commander of the Army of the Cumberland. On November 5, he ordered Halleck to fire McClellan and replace him with Ambrose Burnside (who this time took the post). Fitz-John Porter, a corps commander accused of not properly aiding Pope at Second Bull Run, was also cashiered, replaced by Joseph Hooker. Finally on November 9, Halleck replaced Ben Butler with Nathaniel Banks as commander of the Department of the South, headquartered in New Orleans. He told Banks that "the opening of the Mississippi River is now the great and primary object." Significantly, U.S. Grant kept his post, forces under his command having repulsed the Confederate attack on Iuka on September 19 and on Corinth on October 4, actions showing again that he was a successful fighting general. It was during these two battles, too, that William S. Rosecrans gained the stature which earned him his army command.[65]

Halleck remained depressed through it all and wanted to be elsewhere. "I am sick, tired, and disgusted with the condition of military affairs here in the East and wish myself back in the Western army." But he still had it in him to master administrative detail. He composed the required commanding general's annual report for 1862, and it received an excellent reception particularly because of its clear explanation of the McClellan firing. The military theorist who in the 1840s had written about the primacy of capturing geographical locations rather than crushing enemy armies, and who had followed that principle at Corinth earlier in the year, now took a different position. "A victorious army," he said with all the certitude of his earlier writings, "is supposed to be in condition to pursue its defeated foe with advantage, and during such pursuit to do him serious if not fatal injury. This result has usually been attained in other countries. Is there any reason why it should not be expected in this?"[66] Halleck did not say so, of course, but a major answer to his question was that, as commanding general, he had not forced it to happen, either by fiat or by personally taking field command. Lincoln had not given up on him, but how long would the President be willing to allow Halleck's lassitude to be a political liability? Lincoln could see no one ready to take Halleck's place, so he hoped Halleck would rise to meet the high expectations that had accompanied his arrival in Washington.

Behind everything was a combination of problems that literally drained Halleck's body and psyche. He could not bring himself to be decisive because his administrative philosophy, his lack of confidence, his physical pains, and perhaps the opium he used to deal with his hemorrhoids and the alcohol he may have imbibed to deal with the drug's effects, prevented him from doing so. All the issues from his youth converged with the pressures of war, and the result was a shell of a once successful leader. His physical health would surely improve, but could he overcome the long-existing problems rooted deep in his psyche?

1. Joseph Halleck, the father from whom Halleck ran away to go to college. The two men never spoke again.

2. Catherine Wager Halleck, the mother whose large family prevented her from giving Halleck, her first-born son, the attention he needed.

3. Theodore Miller, a fellow classmate of Halleck's at Hudson Academy, New York, and his closest friend during his youth.

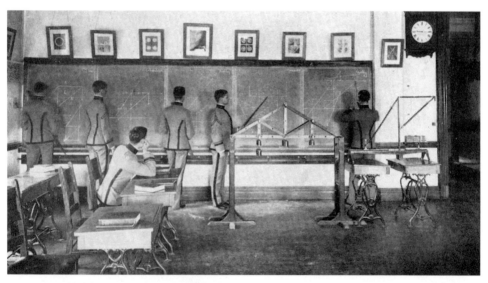

4. A classroom recitation in mechanics at West Point some time between 1858 and 1862. It was in such a class section, at an earlier time, that Halleck gained his high U.S. Military Academy cadet standing and later served as an instructor himself.

5. Etching of New York harbor, where Halleck developed the skills and the reputation that made him one of the most famous army officers of his time.

6. Army Headquarters, Monterey, California, during the late 1840s. There Halleck and William T. Sherman worked and argued during the Mexican War.

7. Richard B. Mason, Halleck's California commander, who though stern himself found Halleck's unbending nature hard to comprehend.

8. Bennet Riley, the second of Halleck's Pacific Coast commanders and the convener of the 1850 state constitutional convention.

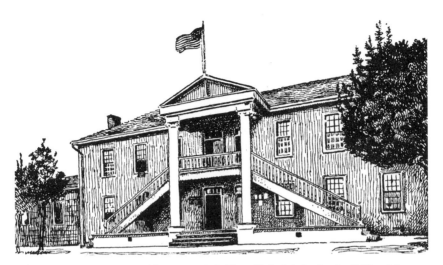

9. Colton Hall, Monterey, California, in 1850. There Halleck helped write California's first state constitution.

10. An 1851 etching of San Francisco, the rowdy, unkempt city where Halleck became a wealthy entrepreneur.

11. Henry W. Halleck (left) and
Frederick Billings (right), two of
the partners in the influential
San Francisco land-law firm of
Halleck, Peachy, and Billings.

12. A twentieth-century photograph of Casa Grande at New Almaden, California, built by
Halleck when he was manager of the New Almaden Quicksilver Mine during the 1850s.

13. Elizabeth Halleck, granddaughter of Alexander Hamilton and Halleck's beloved wife.

14. Henry and Elizabeth Halleck with their son, Henry Jr. (Harry), in the late 1850s.

15. The campaign for Corinth, Mississippi. On May 30, 1862, after Grant's April 6–7 victory at Shiloh, Halleck's grand army of over 100,000 Union soldiers captured Corinth, the key railroad center in Mississippi, a move that solidified Halleck's position as one of the Union's leading generals.

16. Henry W. Halleck in an undated photograph showing what he looked like when he came to Washington in July 1862 to become commanding general of all the Union armies.

17. *Major Genl Henry W. Halleck*. This quickly fabricated 1862 engraving expresses the excitement the nation felt at the arrival of its new commanding general.

18. *The First Reading of the Emancipation Proclamation before the Cabinet.* From left to right: Secretary of War Benjamin Stanton, Secretary of the Treasury Salmon P. Chase, Abraham Lincoln, Secretary of the Navy Gideon T. Welles, Secretary of the Interior Caleb Smith, Postmaster General Montgomery Blair, and Attorney General Edward Bates. Seated in front is Secretary of State William Henry Seward.

19. *Breaking That "Backbone."* A contemporary artist depicted Halleck's military skill as one of the reasons he believed the rebellion would be crushed.

20. George B. McClellan, the charismatic Union general who awed Halleck so much that he could not bring himself to give direct orders.

21. Francis Lieber. This Columbia University professor was Halleck's intimate during the Civil War.

INVENTED OBLIVION

UNIVERSAL ADVICE TO ABRAHAM.
DROP 'EM!

22. A January 1863 cartoon demonstrating the growing northern frustration with the direction of the war and placing the blame on Halleck and Secretary of War Edwin Stanton.

23. Henry W. Halleck in a late Civil War photograph showing the effects of the strain he underwent as commanding general.

24. Ulysses S. Grant, the Union general who, over the course of the war, went from incompetence to brilliant success in Halleck's eyes.

25. Burned-out buildings in Richmond, April 1865; much of the city was torched by fleeing Confederate soldiers and civilians.

26. An early Civil War picture of George W. Cullum, Halleck's best friend from his days as an engineer in New York harbor to his last days in Louisville, Kentucky. After Halleck's death, Cullum married Halleck's widow.

27. A statue of Henry W. Halleck in San Francisco's Golden Gate Park, erected by his friend George W. Cullum, and today hardly noticed.

War by Washington Telegraph

H. W. HALLECK came to Washington as commanding general with high hopes, not only his own but also those of the nation. Both he and the public soon learned that his performance would not live up to expectations. From late 1862 through the summer of 1863, the country experienced one military disappointment after another, and Halleck's style of command became the focus of criticism. He would defend his field generals from interference by "vulgar politicians," and he would send them advice, encouragement, even criticism, but he refused to send them orders. He never ventured into the field himself. Afflicted with physical and mental difficulties, the commanding general conducted the war only from a distance; he refused to command.

In late 1862, however, there was a resurgence of hope as a new command team settled into place. Ambrose Burnside replaced George B. McClellan in Virginia and William S. Rosecrans replaced Don Carlos Buell in Tennessee-Kentucky. But the ever aggressive U. S. Grant retained his command along the Mississippi River and Old Brains Halleck retained his post in Washington. The reorganization of the Union military high command promised a fresh start for the Federal war effort. The new generals knew that Halleck, speaking for Abraham Lincoln, wanted action; the President had sacked the previous command team because those generals had made excuses instead of advances. The new commanders knew what was expected of them: forward movement.

Lincoln was not happy with Halleck, his commanding general, but he was willing to give him the opportunity to shape these new generals into leaders of an efficient fighting machine. The President may have run out of patience with others, but he continued to respect Halleck's knowledge and wanted to give Old Brains the chance to put his talents to use for the benefit of the Union.

Halleck understood what he had to do, and he tried to get it done—in his own way. He found a willing associate, it seemed, in Ambrose Burnside. The new leader of the Army of the Potomac was a man who felt uncomfortable in high command because he did not consider himself up to the task, but he was "a man of great personal charm and character," as one historian put it. As soon as Burnside took command, Halleck told him that he should immediately send his battle plans, and within four days Burnside did. He reported that after reorganizing the army into three Grand Divisions he planned to attack Richmond by way of Fredericksburg. Within five days Lincoln approved the plan. All looked very efficient and hopeful.[1]

As Burnside prepared his offensive in early November 1862, he depended on Halleck for the logistical support Halleck was so good at providing; in particular Burnside looked to Halleck for the necessary pontoons to cross the Rappahannock River. To coordinate matters, Halleck took Quartermaster General Montgomery Meigs and the Federal railroad coordinator, Herman Haupt, to meet with Burnside; but as of November 23, the pontoons had not yet arrived owing to a lack of command coordination throughout the logistical chain reaching even to Halleck.[2]

At the same time, the more Lincoln thought about Burnside's plan, the more worried he became. When he met with Burnside, he was upset to learn that the new Army of the Potomac commander himself believed his cross-river movement was "somewhat risky." Even if Burnside was able to drive Lee's army back toward Richmond, Lincoln worried that the Confederates would gain strength as they fell back into that city's fortifications. Lincoln suggested, instead, that Burnside's massive army of over 100,000 men not attack in a straightforward manner. He recommended the establishment of two auxiliary forces first, so that when the main attack came they could prevent Lee from falling back safely into Richmond or else catch and destroy him.

Halleck and Burnside considered the President's suggestion, and both agreed that it would take too long to implement. The President backed off, so Burnside's "somewhat risky" plan became the blueprint for the advance of the army. At last, Lincoln and Halleck had a Union general in Virginia who was not procrastinating but actually planning an attack. Halleck and Lincoln had wanted someone who acted differently from McClellan, and they seemed to have found him in Burnside.[3] He made his plans and he seemed ready to press forward.

Halleck consulted regularly with Burnside and the President, but he offered mostly technical advice. He told Burnside that for security reasons he should not send his plans over the telegraph, and he "suggest[ed]" that Burnside push all his reinforcements across the Rappahannock River the first night in order to be ready for a possible Confederate counterattack the next day. This was hardly important strategic or even tactical advice. In a more substantial move, Halleck urged General John A. Dix at Fort Monroe, seventy-five miles southeast of Richmond, to create a diversionary movement to aid Burnside, but Dix insisted that it was impossible. Characteristically Halleck accepted his judgment and let the matter drop.[4]

On December 13, despairing about the arrival of the tardy pontoons, Burnside made his attack against the entrenched and alerted Confederates on Mayre's Heights, just beyond the town of Fredericksburg. He experienced a massive repulse, his army suffering 13,000 casualties compared to only 5,000 for the Confederates. Halleck's responsibility for the slow arrival of the pontoons immediately became a key factor in the fault-finding after the battle. It was complicated by conflicting claims, and even when the Joint Committee on the Conduct of the War investigated, it reached no definitive conclusion. Everyone seemed to share in the blame: the Quartermaster Department, the engineer brigade commander, Daniel Woodbury, Burnside himself, and even the weather. Burnside grudgingly accepted his share of the blame, while Quartermaster General Montgomery Meigs said his men had done their job. Woodbury said that no one had told him how important the pontoons were to the operation, and Halleck said it was all Woodbury's fault that the pontoons were so late in arriving. In truth, the blame rested with Halleck. His failure in this incident demonstrated the lack of effective communication between him and Burnside, a key subordinate only a few miles away. For a man who had always emphasized knowing exactly what was happening and expediting logistical matters, this breakdown was surprising. Halleck's administrative skills had failed him, and this lapse had hurt the Union army significantly.[5]

The defeat at Fredericksburg caused a devastated Lincoln to have to put down a Republican senatorial caucus calling for the dismissal of his cabinet and his commanding general at the same time he worried about the welfare of Burnside's troops, concerned that their location between the river and the Confederate entrenched heights was dangerous. On December 14, Lincoln paid a lightning visit to Halleck, who was then living on

Washington's I Street between 15th and 16th Streets. He was worried about the fate of the defeated army and told Halleck to order Burnside to move his army back across the Rappahannock to its northern side. Halleck refused, insisting that such an order was not his to give. As the general on the spot, Burnside alone could make that decision. A stunned Lincoln did not press the matter, and the next day Burnside made the move on his own. Nonetheless, the President had to worry about a commanding general who refused to exert his authority in a crucial situation. He was coming to realize that this was indeed Halleck's command philosophy. Secretary of the Navy Gideon Welles minced no words in his condemnation. "Halleck is General-in-Chief," he bluntly said, "but no one appears to have any confidence in his military management, or thinks him able to advise Burnside." Halleck was, Welles added later, "heavy-handed; wants sagacity, readiness, courage, and heart."[6]

Halleck simply refused to command. When he spoke to Burnside directly, he expressed this position openly: "In regard to movements[,] we can not judge here; you are the best judge. Anything you want will be supplied as soon as possible." Halleck told Burnside to take whatever action he wished because he, the commanding general, simply did not believe he could give advice at a distance. However, he never considered visiting Burnside in the field to gather information at first hand and advise Burnside in person. He stayed in Washington instead and left all decision-making to Burnside. Halleck would not seize the reins of operational authority. He had become commanding general in name only.[7]

The public perception of Halleck was exactly the opposite of the reality. Newspapers like the antislavery *New York Tribune,* blamed him and the Secretary of War for meddling too much in military affairs and personally ordering Burnside to make the bloody attack at Fredericksburg. The Senate called upon the Joint Committee on the Conduct of the War to determine who was responsible for the debacle. On December 19, 1862, the committee members traveled to Falmouth, Virginia, where the Army of the Potomac was in its winter quarters, and interviewed Burnside and his subordinate officers. Burnside did not attempt to evade responsibility, but he did intimate that the late arrival of the pontoons had delayed his attack and had given the Confederates crucial time to prepare. He refused, however, to blame Lincoln, or Stanton, or Halleck for forcing him to move. He said he had made his own command decisions, and he had.[8]

The December 23 committee report called the Union high command confused. Halleck's failure to forward the pontoons came to symbolize the overall Union failure in the battle. Halleck remained unbowed. To his cousin, the Minnesota Bishop H. B. Whipple, he wrote: "The fault was not in Genl Burnside nor in the soldiers." It was the northern press that falsely "poured their viols [sic] on my head because I had *ordered* Burnside to cross the river at that place. When it was ascertained that I had given Burnside *no orders* and *had advised* him against crossing at Fredericksburg, then I was abused because I had *not* given him orders!" In fact, Halleck said, it all came down to "corrupt politicians." "While the nation is thus drifting upon the very brink of ruin, there is not a single great and patriotic statesman to be found in the cabinet or in the halls of congress. . . . There is no help but in God. I do not despair of that help, but it may not come in our time." Halleck even wondered: "is there not some great political plot . . . to prolong the war by preventing any decisive result? I sometimes almost think so." As commanding general, Halleck acknowledged no responsibility for the Fredericksburg military disaster. It was the fault of the press and the politicians, who damned him if he did and damned him if he did not.[9] Since he could see no personal fault in himself, the hope for a change in his command style was slim.

In addition to the Fredericksburg debacle in the East, Halleck had problems in the western theater. There, William S. Rosecrans, Don Carlos Buell's replacement, telegraphed a steady litany of complaints about his lack of horses, cavalry, and officers, sounding a good deal like McClellan. Halleck efficiently provided him with what supplies and manpower he could, and then warned him about slowing his army down with too much impedimenta. Get moving against Braxton Bragg's Confederate army, Halleck said. "If you remain long at Nashville you will disappoint the wishes of the Government." A week later, his frustration was evident as he threatened Rosecrans with the loss of his position. "As I wrote you when you took the command, the Government demands action, and if you cannot respond to that demand, someone else will be tried."[10]

Rosecrans dug in his heels. He insisted that he was preparing "as rapidly as possible," but that his army was simply not ready to move. "To threats of removal or the like I must be permitted to say that I am insensible." Rosecrans bluntly refused to put his army into motion, and as with Burnside, Halleck displayed a noticeable lack of firm response. He told Rosecrans that Lincoln was "greatly dissatisfied" with his procrastination and had called Halleck in several times to make his feelings clear. "He has repeated to me time and again that there were imperative reasons why the enemy should be driven across the Tennessee River at the earliest possible moment." But then Halleck undermined the warning by telling Rosecrans that Lincoln "has never told me what those reasons were. But I imagine them to be diplomatic, and of the most serious character." Cabinet members, Halleck continued, were also "inquiring almost daily, 'Why don't [*sic*] he move?' 'Can't you make him move?' No one doubted," he concluded, "that General Buell would eventually have succeeded [had he remained in command], but he was too slow. . . . It was believed that you would move more rapidly. Hence the change."[11]

As with Burnside, however, Halleck did not issue a direct order. He told Rosecrans that Lincoln and his cabinet were upset at his lack of movement, and he was simply trying to warn him. He did not order an immediate move himself and merely kept urging such an action. The commanding general continued refusing to command; he was merely suggesting.

It was another three weeks before Rosecrans felt prepared enough to initiate action. On Christmas Eve 1862, he telegraphed Halleck to tell him that since Bragg's army was "committed to stand at Murfreesborough . . . and, having now the essentials of ammunition and twenty days' rations in Nashville, [I] shall move on them to-morrow at daylight." The result was the hard-fought battle of Stones River (Murfreesboro, Tennessee), running from December 31, 1862, to January 2, 1863. Rosecrans's forces held their ground and forced Bragg to retreat to Chattanooga. Rosecrans lost around 13,000 men (31 percent of his army) while Bragg lost around 12,000 (34 percent). The Union Army won a victory, but it was an extremely bloody one.[12]

Halleck was ecstatic, nonetheless, calling the Union success "one of the most brilliant of the war. You and your brave army," he wrote Rosecrans, "have won the gratitude of your country and the admiration of the world." Yet, with the battle over, Rosecrans once more brought his army to a halt. As before, he went back to resupplying, thus demonstrating no intent to move and press Bragg's defeated army. Halleck had to warn him that pressures were mounting to send parts of his army to the Mississippi River to aid Grant in his campaign against Vicksburg. "Should the enemy succeed in holding your army in check with an inferior force while he sends troops to the Mississippi River, it is greatly to be feared that the time of many of our troops will expire without our having accomplished any important results." Halleck was clearly upset with Rosecrans's procrastination, but, once again, he suggested, he hinted, but he did not order.[13]

It was only with U. S. Grant in the Mississippi Valley that things were different. Halleck had a rare light moment when he opened a package from Grant containing "a pair of unmentionables" of enormous size, that his soldiers had discovered in a southern house. It provided Halleck with a brief respite from his woes. Grant was not only winning victories for

Halleck, but he was also providing him with relief from his stress. Halleck began viewing the determined Grant much more positively.[14]

But there were other problems brewing in the West. John A. McClernand, a Republican congressman from Springfield, Illinois, had convinced his old friend Abraham Lincoln and Secretary of War Stanton, too, that if he could recruit badly needed troops in the Midwest, he should get command over an expedition against Vicksburg, Mississippi. McClernand reported to Halleck from Springfield of his recruiting progress at the same time that Grant, in western Tennessee, was planning his own Vicksburg campaign and receiving Halleck's support and encouragement. McClernand was, after all, a politician turned general, one of those men that Halleck viewed so negatively. Consequently, Halleck wanted to be sure that McClernand did not gain a command. Halleck told Grant: "You have command of all troops sent to your department, and have permission to fight the enemy where you please," thus authorizing Grant to use McClernand's recruits before the Illinois general arrived. When McClernand reported in mid-December that his recruiting was complete and he was ready to take command of the Vicksburg expedition, Halleck told Grant officially that Lincoln wanted McClernand to "have the immediate command under your direction." In fact, Halleck was actually trying to dump McClernand. Grant gave Sherman command of the Vicksburg expedition, and Sherman quickly led transports full of McClernand recruits down the Mississippi River. Grant's plan called for Sherman to land north of Vicksburg, while Grant marched his troops overland through Mississippi and attacked Vicksburg from the east. All this was to take place before McClernand could arrive and assume command.[15]

The plan failed. Confederate General Earl Van Dorn destroyed the Union supply base at Holly Springs, Mississippi, thus preventing Grant from taking part in the Vicksburg attack. When Sherman assaulted Confederate positions on the Walnut Hills, north of Vicksburg, he suffered a resounding defeat at Chickasaw Bayou. Halleck called on Nathaniel Banks, commanding in New Orleans, to come merge with Sherman, but then as always, he did not do so forcefully. "The condition of affairs on the Mississippi River will have so changed before this reaches you that it is useless to attempt to advise from this place. The reopening of that river, however, must be the main object of all our operations." He similarly corresponded with Samuel Curtis in Arkansas about the importance of the river, but never pressed the matter with him either. As in the East, so in the West, Halleck gave no definitive orders.[16]

Halleck had succeeded in bypassing McClernand, however. The Illinois politician arrived in Mississippi to find that his troops had already fought (and lost) under Sherman, and he wrote an angry letter to Lincoln, castigating Halleck for being "without genius, justice, generosity or policy." More important, McClernand immediately took over Sherman's army. He commanded an expedition to Arkansas Post but at the insistence of Admiral David D. Porter (who also disliked McClernand) Sherman commanded the field army. Arkansas Post was some fifty miles from where the Arkansas River emptied into the Mississippi River. The assault there, unlike the one under Sherman at Chickasaw Bayou, was a success, but a short-lived one for McClernand. Despite McClernand's complaining letter to the President, Halleck won out. Halleck gave Grant permission to "relieve General McClernand from command of the expedition against Vicksburg, giving it to the next in rank or taking it yourself." Grant took the command himself. Halleck had won a bureaucratic victory and had impressed Grant and Sherman. But he had also gained determined enemies who resented his maneuverings and had garnered little public support from the incident.[17]

These several months in late 1862 and early 1863 saw Halleck's reputation continue to decline. The year-end defeats at Fredericksburg and Vicksburg were distressing, while Rosecrans's victory at Stones River was shockingly bloody and his pre- and post-battle inertia discouraging. Halleck was commanding general, responsible for the entire Union Army, so he bore the brunt of the public anger over the lack of Federal military progress.

The criticism took various forms. As early as mid-November, a rumor spread that George B. McClellan's earlier dismissal from the Army of the Potomac had taken place so that he could replace Halleck as commanding general of all Union armies. In mid-December, people whispered that this change would take place on January 1, 1863. As the battlefield failures mounted in late December, such speculation increased. The well-known Pennsylvania senator David Wilmot thundered in the lobby at Willard's, Washington's leading hotel, that both Halleck and Stanton "must be driven out of Washington."[18]

Not content to demand Halleck's removal for his military failures, opponents also attacked him for personal inadequacies. The *New York Herald* called him "a thick headed and conceited martinet." A supporter told Halleck that "a very good friend (really such) asked me, with much solicitude, if it was true that you were habitually tight, every day after dinner. He 'had heard it from such good authority.'" Then rumors spread that Halleck and Stanton had come to blows, that Halleck had slapped Stanton's face when the Secretary of War had called him a liar. By the time this story reached the Confederates, it included the President: "Lincoln's two chief men had a fist fight the other day in Old Abe's presence, in which Halleck knocked Stanton down like a beef." Halleck was now being called an incompetent, a drunkard, and a brawler. The fact that none of these charges had any factual basis did not matter. Halleck's reputation, which had earlier been so high, was now plummeting.[19]

The man who emerged as the most caustic critic of Halleck was an 1849 Polish émigré, Count Adam Gurowski. A member of the editorial staff of the *New York Tribune,* a writer, a minor State Department official, and a radical Republican supporter, Gurowski became famous when he published his acerbic diary later in the war. He thought that Halleck was a complete incompetent on the basis of the stumbling quality of the Union war effort. He spared no energy in criticizing him. After Burnside's disaster at Fredericksburg, for example, Gurowski said that "Hell itself, would be too good a place for Halleck; imbeciles are not admitted there!"[20]

The longer there was no military progress, the more such odium fell on Halleck's shoulders. Rosecrans procrastinated in Tennessee, while Grant now seemed stymied before Vicksburg, attempting, unsuccessfully, to dig a canal that would cause the Mississippi River to bypass the river city. But it was in Virginia that Halleck still had his biggest problem, and once more, Ambrose Burnside could not seem to get it right. The Fredericksburg debacle weighed on Burnside, and he aggressively began planning another campaign to make up for it. Several of his senior officers were upset at his leadership, some still pining for the return of George B. McClellan. They complained directly to Lincoln. Halleck visited Burnside on December 18, 1862, but nothing seemed to come from the meeting. The President then called Burnside to Washington for a conference early on January 1, 1863. He discussed the officers' complaints and heard Burnside's plan. Unsure what he should do, he called in Halleck and Secretary of War Stanton. Halleck recommended arresting or cashiering the complaining officers, but nothing was decided by the time Burnside left the meeting.[21]

Burnside continued mulling over his predicament on his way back to his hotel and, once there, he sent Lincoln a letter offering to resign and urging that Stanton and Halleck be fired, too. He insisted that none of them had the public's confidence. Lincoln and Halleck must certainly have discussed these matters further, and the conversation must not have gone to Lincoln's satisfaction because he immediately wrote Halleck a letter. He reminded the commanding general that Burnside wanted to cross the Rappahannock River again, but that his three Grand Division commanders were all opposed. Lincoln wanted Halleck to study the ground, question Burnside, speak to his subordinates, and, in short, "gather all the elements for forming a judgment of your own; and then tell Gen. Burnside that you *do* approve, or that you do *not* approve his plan." All this was routine. What followed in Lincoln's January 1, 1863, letter was not. The President told Halleck: "Your military skill is useless to me, if you will not do this." Lincoln was finally dressing down his commanding general for his repeated refusals to command.[22]

All this transpired on the traditional day in Washington for receptions and visiting, January 1. Halleck and his wife, who had recently arrived in Washington from New York City, held a reception in their home, and then Halleck attended those of other administration officials before leading some eight hundred army and navy officers to Lincoln's reception at the White House. At Stanton's home, he received the President's letter and, some time during that busy day, he penned a response. "I am led to believe that there is a very important difference of opinion in regard to my relations toward generals commanding armies in the field, and that I cannot perform the duties of my present office satisfactorily at the same time to the President and to myself. I therefore respectfully request that I may be relieved from further duties as General-in-chief." Rather than command, Halleck would resign.[23] He was coming under increasing criticism for his command philosophy of allowing subordinate generals to do as they saw fit, and his life's experiences would not allow him to change. He had now reached the point that he would not even criticize a subordinate's plan. His psyche could not bear that stress, so he decided to resign.

Lincoln was also extremely busy that January 1, 1863, with helping his wife host a massive reception and signing the final Emancipation Proclamation. When he saw Halleck's response, the President wrote, in exasperation, across his own letter: "Withdrawn because considered harsh by Gen. Halleck." For once, the commanding general had taken a firm stand, and he had won. His stand, however, was not to instigate action against the enemy but to avoid issuing commands to generals in the field. He twice refused to advise Burnside and he did it a third time when that general specifically asked for help on January 5 and offered to take full responsibility for any action that resulted from the advice. Halleck would tell Burnside only what he and Lincoln now realized: that Lee's army, not Richmond, was Burnside's main objective. "It will not do to keep your large army inactive," Halleck said. "As you yourself admit, it devolved on you to decide upon the time, place, and character of the crossing which you may attempt. I can only advise that an attempt be made, and as early as possible." Lincoln was stuck with a military leader who refused to lead, and a subordinate who "entertained profound contempt for his [Lincoln's] military knowledge," and showed it regularly. Lincoln discouragingly referred to "General Halleck's habitual attitude of demur." He did not like it, but he still could see no one better to put in his reluctant commanding general's place.[24]

Burnside's new plan, which Halleck and Lincoln accepted by default, once again led to disaster. His attempt to outflank the Confederates in January bogged down in the rain-soaked Virginia countryside and became known derisively as the Mud March. Burnside's subordinate generals, particularly Joseph Hooker and William B. Franklin, openly criticized him, and Burnside once again appealed to Halleck for help. Halleck responded: "You must judge for yourself as to the propriety of your coming up [to Washington]."[25]

Frustrated, Burnside bypassed Halleck and went directly to see the President late on January 24. Lincoln asked Halleck and Stanton to join them the next morning. When they were all together, Lincoln told his Secretary of War and commanding general that Burnside wanted to fire his subordinates who were criticizing him, and if not allowed to do so, he would resign himself. Without asking for Halleck's or Stanton's opinion, Lincoln said he had decided to relieve Burnside and replace him with Joseph Hooker, one of the very officers Burnside had hoped to cashier. Halleck was unhappy with Lincoln's choice of Hooker, but he simply acquiesced in the decision. His silence once more served Lincoln poorly.[26]

Fighting Joe Hooker, as he was known, was, according to a contemporary, "a strikingly handsome man, [had] a clean-shaven, comely face, with somewhat florid complexion, keen blue eyes, well-built, tall figure, and erect soldierly bearing. Anybody would feel like cheering when he rode by at the head of his staff." Hooker, however, was also arrogant and stubborn, more than willing to work behind the scenes to advance himself, and reputed to have a headquarters that Charles Francis Adams Jr. described as "a combination of barroom and brothel." Lincoln reluctantly appointed Hooker to command the Army of the Potomac, because he could think of no one else to take the position. Both William B. Franklin and Edwin V. Sumner, that army's two other Grand Division commanders, had deficiencies. Franklin had come out of Fredericksburg with a sullied reputation for his poor performance, and the soon-to-be deceased Edwin V. Sumner was simply too infirm at sixty-six to command. Halleck and Stanton favored George G. Meade, a corps commander, but Hooker outranked Meade, and he also had widespread support among the more radical elements in the national government. Lincoln was always one to consider the political ramifications of any decision, so, on his own, despite the contrary sentiments of Halleck and Stanton, Lincoln settled on Joseph Hooker as the new leader of the Army of the Potomac.[27]

Lincoln was not, however, sanguine about his choice, and he let Hooker know it. The President wrote his new commander a letter that expressed, as only Lincoln could, exactly how he felt. He told Hooker that he had appointed him to command the Army of the Potomac despite "some things in regard to which, I am not quite satisfied with you." He praised Hooker as a "brave and skilful [sic] soldier," but he criticized him as a man who had done all he could to unseat Burnside. Lincoln had also heard about Hooker's allegedly saying that "both the Army and Government needed a Dictator." Lincoln said that "only those generals who gain successes, can set up dictators. What I now ask of you is military success, and I will risk the dictatorship."[28]

Hooker and Halleck had been at West Point at the same time, but their "relations" had "not [been] particularly intimate," as Hooker later phrased it. In California in the late 1840s and early 1850s, Hooker was an assistant adjutant general when Halleck was territorial secretary of state and a practicing lawyer. According to Hooker, Halleck had asked him to drum up land business for the law firm and then overcharged several of the people that Hooker had recommended. Hooker said he had written Halleck a strong letter of protest, "and trusted that hereafter he would never again make use of me in the execution of his schemes of avarice and plunder." "Ever after," Hooker remembered in the 1870s, "our intercourse was still more formal and constrained than it had been." For his part, Halleck said he had information about Hooker's unsavory behavior during their days together in California. To try to mitigate this problem, Lincoln accepted a key part of Hooker's terms. The new commander could bypass the commanding general entirely and report directly to the President. This was a situation fraught with danger, one that demonstrated how disappointed Lincoln was with Halleck over his refusal to help him sort out the Burnside problem. If Halleck would not issue orders, Lincoln would take him out of the chain of command, in fact out of the very flow of information. Lincoln believed that he now needed Hooker more than he needed Halleck, so he yielded to Hooker's demand.[29]

Because of his obsession with administration, Halleck was unhappy with Lincoln's decision about Hooker. He did not believe he should tell subordinate generals on the spot what to do, but he wanted to know exactly what was going on. In this vein he worried about the lack of definitive regulations for fighting a civil war. Earlier in his life, he had produced a famous book on military theory, but this publication dealt with international conflict and only touched on internal war in the briefest fashion. He now felt the need for well-thought-out regulations for the American war but he was too busy to produce them himself. He noted with interest a series of eight lectures in late 1861 and early 1862 given by Francis Lieber, a Columbia University professor who from 1835 to 1857 had been on the faculty at South Carolina College. Lieber, an 1827 German émigré, was already corresponding with Halleck, the two men having dined together in New York City when Halleck was an engineer there in the 1840s. It was Lieber, in fact, who during one of these dinner conversations had inspired Halleck to write what became the first chapter of his military theory book. The two men had later renewed their acquaintance during Lieber's visit to his wounded son after the battle at Fort Donelson. Lieber was ecstatic when Halleck became commanding general, pleased that such an intellectual was now heading the Union war effort. Their friendship flowered. When Lieber mentioned that he was researching the role of guerrillas in warfare, Halleck, who was trying to produce appropriate advice for field officers on this topic, encouraged Lieber to write an essay. "It has now become an important question in this country and should be thoroughly investigated," he said. "I know of no one who can do it as well as yourself," he told Lieber. When the paper was completed in the late summer of 1862, Halleck immediately had five thousand copies printed and distributed throughout the army. Lieber made what Halleck considered appropriate distinctions between the various kind of partisans, and Halleck agreed with Lieber's conclusion that the law of war sanctioned punishment for such people, ranging from prisoner-of-war status to the death penalty.[30]

Encouraged by Halleck's enthusiastic support, Lieber now began pushing for a more generalized set of regulations, exactly what Halleck knew the Union war effort needed. On November 13, 1862, Lieber suggested to Halleck that Lincoln establish a committee to draw up a general war code with appropriate punishment for its violation. "I should propose that you, both as General-in-chief and as a prominent writer on the Law of Nations, ought to be chairman of this important Committee, to supervise the general laying out of the plan and for the ultimate revising of the whole. I know full well how much your time is occupied, but this business seems to me as important as any other that can now occupy the minds of men in highest positions." Halleck could not have agreed more, but he was indeed busy with Burnside, Rosecrans, Grant, and many other issues. He had unfortunately "no time at present to consider" Lieber's proposal.[31]

It never strayed far from his mind, however. When he received complaints that General Horatio G. Wright was "pursuing 'too milk and water a policy toward the rebels in Kentucky,'" he as usual refused to intervene but did offer some strong advice, demonstrating that his attitude toward warfare was changing. "Domestic traitors, who seek the overthrow of our Government, are not entitled to its protection and should be made to feel its power. . . . Make them suffer in their persons and property for their crimes and the sufferings they have caused to others. . . . Let the guilty feel that you have an iron hand; that you know how to apply it when necessary. Don't be influenced by those old political grannies," he told Wright. Halleck recognized that the days of chivalric war were over, and the need for a general war code was therefore even more urgent.[32]

Letters passed between Halleck and Lieber, even as the former continued to insist that he was too busy to take up a war code. Lieber said he understood, but he hoped his friend would "take the suggestion out of the pigeon hole of your mind." In the meantime, Halleck said, he himself would continue working on aspects of his own war policy. He issued his November 1862 end-of-the year report as commanding general and reproved McClellan for his slowness in aiding Pope before Second Bull Run, causing Lieber to express thanks "in the name of all right-minded citizens." Two days later, Halleck called Lieber to Washington. The professor made the necessary arrangements to obtain a leave from Columbia and prepared to come, even though he did not know, he said, "for what my presence is wanted." Halleck had made up his mind to set up a commission in Washington to work on their mutual desire, a war code. Lieber hurried to the nation's capital. On December 17, 1862, along with four generals, Lieber "constitute[d] a board to propose amendments or changes in the Rules and Articles of War, and a code of regulations for the government of armies in the field, as authorized by the laws and usages of war."[33] In early January 1863, Lieber and his board went to work, and Halleck was pleased. He had reveled in this kind of intellectual labor before the war, and in 1863 he considered it absolutely essential to the war effort.

At the same time the commission began its task, Halleck was again discussing his own publication possibilities. A New York publisher wanted to print the battle plans and reports of his early war activity in the western theater. Another New York company informed him that the U.S. Navy was planning to purchase copies of his book on international law. (Lieber provided a blurb for this book, calling Halleck "at one and the same time a jurist and a high military commander.") This publisher was also ready to put on sale the translation of Jomini's four-volume *Life of Napoleon* that Halleck had labored on during his 1846 voyage to California. He had only to give them an estimate of the length of the proposed introduction, the company said, and the printing would begin. Count Gurowski was furious when he heard about Halleck's translation. "What an inimitable narrow-minded pedant. If Halleck had brains, he would have realized that, during war, he could not have an hour leisure for translation."[34]

In truth, Halleck could spare little time for his writing. He had too many generals to deal with, even if Hooker reported directly to the President. Rosecrans was still delaying in eastern Tennessee, continuing to demand cavalry, arms, and equipment of all sorts. Every general believed he needed men or materials of some sort but successful ones like Grant did not let that stop them from action. Those like Rosecrans, and McClellan before him, used it as an excuse for inaction. Halleck impatiently snapped at Rosecrans that his "complaints" were "without reason." In the Carolinas, Generals David Hunter and J. G. Foster were carrying on a nasty dispute over who had control over a detachment of Foster's army corps then located in Hunter's jurisdiction. In Missouri, General John M. Schofield wanted to quit his command because Department of the Missouri commander Samuel Curtis refused to allow him to go on the offensive. Curtis himself protested having a segment of his troops sent to aid Grant in his battle for Vicksburg. Similarly, the favorite of German immigrants, Franz Sigel, wanted to resign his commission because Hooker had so drastically reduced his army corps. Only Grant uncomplainingly pressed forward. His troops were continuing to dig at his canal, and he was preparing his Yazoo Pass expedition, trying to find some way to bypass Vicksburg. Grant remained positive, in early March 1863, promising: "I will have Vicksburg this month, or fall in the attempt."[35]

Halleck found such turmoil discouraging, and once more he lashed out at the "political power," which, he said, "over-rules all military considerations." "How long the president will submit to this dictation is uncertain. He must either put it down, or it will sink him so low that the last trump of Gabriel will never reach his ears!" Halleck continued to blame politicians for military problems. If only they would let West Point–educated professional soldiers fight the war, all would be well. He again began thinking of resigning. When Lieber pointed out that such a resignation would result in someone like Butler or McClellan disastrously gaining the post, Halleck quickly settled down. He was dissatisfied, talked of running away, but he could not make that important decision either.[36]

His frustration especially focused on Hooker, ironically a West Pointer. Although he did not like Hooker personally and worried about his military ability, and although he had to deal with him through the President rather than directly, Halleck still tried to cooperate with the new commander. He carefully explained the military situation to Hooker when Fighting Joe assumed command in late January 1863. The Ninth Corps was going to Fort Monroe to be under the command of John A. Dix, while Harper's Ferry and the Shenandoah Valley were the jurisdiction of Robert C. Schenck, commander of the Middle Department, headquartered in Baltimore. Benjamin F. Kelley commanded on site in Harper's Ferry, and Samuel P. Heintzelman was in charge of Washington's defense. These "forces, however," Halleck pointed out, were "not sufficient to resist a strong attack from the main army of the rebels, and . . . [thus] the Army of the Potomac [had] to either cover these places or to succor them in case they should be seriously threatened by the enemy."

In keeping with the philosophy demonstrated so graphically in the Burnside dispute with Lincoln, Halleck told Hooker: "In regard to the operations of your own army, you can best judge when and where it can move to the greatest advantage, keeping in view always the importance of covering Washington and Harper's Ferry either directly or by so operating as to be able to punish any force of the enemy sent against them." Then, to make sure Hooker understood clearly what he was saying, Halleck included his January 7 letter to Burnside. In that communication, Halleck had told Burnside that Lee's army, not Richmond, was his primary object and that how he dealt with it was strictly up to him. Halleck once again gave advice but left the decision-making to a subordinate general.[37]

Hooker began his tenure with resoluteness, quickly scrapping Burnside's grand-division concept and restoring the Army of the Potomac to its more usual corps organization. For that , he gained Halleck's praise. Morale improved as Hooker made sure the men were properly fed and sheltered and received generous furloughs. Throughout this process, Hooker ignored Halleck and spoke directly to Lincoln about his battle plans. But he still had to deal with Halleck on a variety of administrative matters, and, as always, Halleck demonstrated his no-nonsense insistence on the regulations. Hooker tried to establish his own system of granting officers leaves, for example, and Halleck responded forcefully: "All leaves to officers to visit Washington without the consent of the War Department are deemed null and void, and hereafter all general officers who come here on leave not properly granted will be dismissed."[38]

Despite Hooker's refusal to deal with him, Halleck sent Hooker regular advice, which was never well received. In mid-March 1863, for example, the two men had a disagreement over whether or not Hooker should send a relief column to Harper's Ferry, and in late March Halleck told Hooker that since it was obvious that Lee's army was "now scattered for supplies and for operations elsewhere," it was "advisable that a blow be struck." In mid-April, Halleck joined Lincoln and Stanton in visiting Hooker in Virginia, and allegedly Hooker refused to move immediately and warned his three superiors that "he would not submit to being interfered with."[39]

Halleck was clearly unhappy with this situation and on April 30 he complained bitterly to Francis Lieber: "The great difficulty we have to contend with is *poor, poorer,* and *worthless* officers. Many of them have neither judgement, sense, or courage. And I almost despair of any improvement." On May 1, 1863, as Hooker began a movement against Lee's army, Halleck complained that he had no clear idea as to what was going on. He asked Samuel P. Heintzelman, the commander of Washington's defenses, what he had heard from Hooker because he himself knew nothing. "The President has taken the direction and General Halleck is not consulted," Heintzelman commented incredulously.[40]

Hooker had indeed put his army into motion against Lee, and at first his giant envelopment against the Confederate left at Chancellorsville went well. Then Hooker lost his nerve and instead of pressing forward ordered his flanking force to dig in. Seeing what was happening, Lee split his army in the face of Hooker's superior numbers and had Stonewall Jackson outflank the dug-in Union soldiers on the Federal right. He sent them reeling. Hooker passed up opportunities to fight back and ordered a retreat that appalled his subordinate commanders. Lee lost 21 percent of his army (13,000) to Hooker's 15 percent (17,000), and the Confederacy also lost Stonewall Jackson. But still the Confederates won an important tactical and psychological victory.[41]

Halleck's immediate response to Hooker's defeat at Chancellorsville was to join Lincoln in another visit to Fighting Joe's headquarters. General George Meade, one of the corps commanders, found the meeting strange. Lincoln and Halleck had lunch and consulted with only a few army people. Lincoln let it be known that he blamed no one for the defeat, and this comment seemed to revive Hooker's spirits. Halleck remained behind for a day to see what else he could find out about Hooker's army, and on his return to the capital he told Lincoln that Hooker was to blame for the defeat and the precipitous retreat. He also reported that Hooker was so dispirited that he was ready to resign his command. Not surprisingly, Halleck thought Lincoln should accept the resignation, but the President disagreed. He wanted to give Hooker another chance to show his mettle.[42]

Despite his obvious animosity toward Hooker, Halleck did not use the defeat at Chancellorsville to undercut his California rival. He defended him whenever he could. He told Francis Lieber, for example, that "Genl Hooker's army has met with no disaster. It simply *failed* to accomplish its object, but inflicted a loss upon the enemy much greater than our own." He repeated the same message to General J. G. Foster in North Carolina. He also indicated what was becoming ever clearer in his mind. He believed that the war would be won not in the East, but in the western theater. He repeated to Nathaniel Banks in New Orleans something he had said before, but now emphasized more forthrightly. "The Mississippi River is the all-important object of the present campaign. It is worth to us forty Richmonds."[43]

Many other military leaders and the public in general did not agree. The success or failure of the Army of the Potomac in the East, where the nation's population and its leading newspapers were concentrated, was essential to Union morale. Hooker's defeat at Chancellorsville, therefore, was crucial to the public perception of how the war was going, and that perception was negative.

As a result of Union setbacks, Halleck had to endure another round of criticism. A close friend of the President told Lincoln that "the office of General in Chief should either be abolished or filled by a person other than General Halleck." Organizations throughout the nation called for Halleck's dismissal. The Chicago branch of the German Loyal Citizens of the West, at a mass meeting in late May, called for Halleck's firing, even listing, much to his anger, Francis Lieber as a vice president of the organization. The famous diplomat Caleb Cushing reported that Halleck wanted Hooker's command, and a pro-Halleck newspaper insisted that he indeed had to become more active: "He should take the field and endeavor, at least, to win his spurs. There is no other way of silencing his assailants—no other road to the confidence of the country. . . . [N]o office General, with a fame purely factitious [*sic*] ought to be any longer tolerated in attempts to conduct campaigns by telegraph." The abolitionist Wendell Phillips agreed in a New York City speech: "Lincoln and Halleck,—they sit in Washington, commanders in chief, exercising that disastrous influence which even a Bonaparte would exercise on a battle, if he tried to fight it by telegraph, a hundred miles distant."[44]

The criticism grew increasingly louder. A small boy shouted out a catechism question-and-answer criticism of Halleck at a Boston mass meeting of Union Leagues. He ended with: "Quest. No. 17. Who is hated by soldiers and honest men, and must be, at all hazards, disposed of, if the country is to be saved? Ans. *Halleck*." Most ominously of all, one of Halleck's former supporters, Attorney General Edward Bates, now reported in his diary a rumor that Halleck "was a confirmed *opium-eater* . . . That he is sometimes bloated, and with watery eyes, is apparent, but whether from brandy or opium I cannot tell." Halleck indeed looked tired and worn, the stress of his office apparent in his face and frame for all to see. His medicinal use of opium to deal with his hemorrhoids or diarrhea may have caught up with him, or he may have been overusing alcohol to compensate for drug withdrawal or mental anxiety. He also smoked incessantly and the habitual scratching of his elbow continued. The physical and psychological stress on Halleck was becoming all too obvious. He did not look healthy or alert.[45]

Meanwhile, Hooker continued to ignore Halleck and report directly to Lincoln. In early June 1863, after Lee began the movement that would culminate in the momentous battle at Gettysburg in July, Hooker sent a new battle plan to the President proposing that the major part of his army attack Lee's weakened troops at Fredericksburg and move on Richmond, while a smaller force shadowed Lee's invasion. Lincoln said no: "In one word, I would not take any risk of being entangled upon the river, like an ox jumped half over a fence and liable to be torn by dogs front and rear, without a fair chance to gore one way or kick the other. If Lee would come to my side of the river, I would keep on the same side and fight him or act on the defense."[46]

Lincoln then sent Hooker's plan to Halleck for his evaluation. The commanding general once again refused to take a stand, immediately reminding Hooker that his January 31 telegram had left such matters in Hooker's hands. He said, however, that he thought it made more sense to counter Lee's invasion before attacking the entrenched Confederates. Hooker, in short, could do what he wished, despite any advice. Halleck again urged John A. Dix to move his 33,000 men at Fort Monroe and Norfolk up the peninsula toward Richmond, but when Dix once more responded with a variety of excuses, Halleck backed down, as he had before.[47] Halleck continued giving general recommendations, but he would not give definitive orders.

Matters between Halleck and Hooker grew increasingly tense, so Hooker unburdened himself to the president in a 11:00 A.M. telegram on June 16. "You have long been aware, Mr. President, that I have not enjoyed the confidence of the major-general commanding the army, and I can assure you so long as this continues we may look in vain for success." There followed a series of telegrams between the three men that demonstrated the desperateness of the situation. At 3:50 P.M. Halleck warned Hooker about the threat to Harper's Ferry and wondered what Hooker was going to do about it. At 4:00 P.M., Hooker asked for more information, and at 7:50 P.M. he said he would relieve the 10,000-man garrison there, only to have Halleck respond at 8:20 P.M. that he had no definitive information. Lincoln then told Hooker at 10:00 P.M. that he was "in the strict military relation to General Halleck of a commander of one of the armies to the general-in-chief of all the armies. . . . I shall direct him to give you orders and you to obey them." The President thereby handed Halleck the victory in this jurisdictional conflict, but Halleck surrendered it just fifteen minutes later. "You are in command of the Army of the Potomac," he told Hooker, "and will make the particular dispositions as you deem proper." Halleck refused to make Hooker a real subordinate even after Lincoln ordered him to do so. The President could only shake his head in disbelief. The only apparent reason Lincoln did not fire Halleck on the spot was that he did not know whom to put in his place. Even though Halleck would not command, he still gave good advice and perhaps that had to suffice for Lincoln for the time being.[48]

Hooker did not wait long to shift the blame for the disagreement back to Halleck. Having received the commanding general's 10:00 P.M. telegram at 1:00 A.M., he complained about the contradictory information coming "from Washington" (read, from Halleck) about Harper's Ferry. Halleck said he "regret[ed]" the situation, but "so-far, we have had only the wild rumors of panic-stricken people." Obviously Hooker could not blame him for that. Hooker then put forth a stunning scenario. "Has it ever suggested itself to you," he asked Halleck, "that this cavalry raid [Lee's movement toward Gettysburg] may be a cover to Lee's re-enforcing Bragg [in Tennessee] or moving troops to the West?" Halleck replied pointedly that it was up to Hooker to know what Lee was doing. "Officers and citizens are on a big stampede. They are asking me why does not General Hooker tell where Lee's army is: he is nearest to it." Hooker then complained to Halleck that Generals Schenck and Heintzelman were not obeying him and that they needed to be reminded by Halleck to do so. He also complained about press leaks exposing his army's movements. Halleck threw this back in his face, telling him that he saw "no way of preventing it as long as reporters are permitted in our camps."[49]

Back and forth the telegrams flew, the two men making little progress toward solving the Army of the Potomac's problem of countering Lee's continuing advance into Pennsylvania. Hooker protested that "I don't know whether I am standing on my head or feet." The conflict between the men finally came down to Halleck's insistence that Hooker maintain control of

Harper's Ferry and Hooker's determination to give it up as unimportant and incorporate the 10,000-man garrison into his Army of the Potomac. Hooker became so angry that he told Herman Haupt during the railroad coordinator's visit that he would do nothing to oppose Lee's invasion without specific orders. He also continued to tell Halleck, Stanton, and Lincoln that he wanted to let Lee go north so he could go after Richmond. The Union triumvirate was appalled, Halleck later telling Haupt that Lincoln, to put it mildly, thought "it would be a very poor exchange to give Washington for Richmond."[50]

Not getting anywhere with his demands, Hooker wired Halleck an ultimatum: "My original instructions require me to cover Harper's Ferry and Washington. I have now imposed upon me, in addition, an enemy in my front of more than my number. I beg to be understood, respectfully, but firmly, that I am unable to comply with this condition with the means at my disposal, and earnestly request that I may at once be relieved from the position I occupy." That was it. Halleck went to Stanton, who showed the letter to Lincoln. The President did not delay in replacing Hooker and, to add to the insult, Halleck had Hooker arrested when he came to the capital without a proper pass. A furious Hooker later unfairly blamed everything on Halleck, telling the Committee on the Conduct of the War: "If the general-in-chief had been in the rebel interest, it would have been impossible for him . . . to have added to the embarrassment he caused me from the moment I took command of the army of the Potomac to the time I surrendered it." Even in separating, Halleck and Hooker demonstrated their animosity toward each other. As late as December 1863, Hooker continued to lash out at Halleck. He told Senator William P. Fessenden that Halleck "never fought a battle & I doubt if he ever heard a shot whistle." He sat "on his backsides lifeless within the hearing of the artillery of our enemies. A woman would not do that." Even long after the war, Hooker could not forgive Halleck. He believed that "the impartial student of history will find Genl. Halleck to have been the *evil genius* of the War."[51]

The new commander of the Army of the Potomac, Halleck's and Stanton's choice, was George G. Meade, whom a later historian said "was a curious blend of diffidence and authoritarianism." His relationship with fellow officers was always edgy, and his soldiers looked upon him with trust but little affection. One soldier once referred to him as "a damned goggle-eyed snapping turtle," while another said he was "conservative and cautious to the last degree, good qualities in a defensive battle, but liable to degenerate into timidity when an aggressive or bold offensive becomes imperative." Reporters became so outraged at his disdainful treatment of them that they conspired to keep his name out of print. The result was that most northerners knew little about him.[52]

Halleck thought he was the best man for the job, but, as he had done with Burnside and Hooker, he refused to command him. "You will not be hampered by any minute instructions from these headquarters," he told the new general. "Your army is free to act as you may deem proper under the circumstances as they arise." The only caveat he gave Meade was that the Army of the Potomac had to protect Washington and Baltimore "as far as circumstances will admit." When Meade asked Halleck about taking some troops from Harper's Ferry, the issue Halleck and Hooker had tangled over, Halleck surprisingly responded: "The garrison at Harper's Ferry is under your orders. You can diminish or increase it as you think the circumstances justify." Halleck had insisted that Hooker continue holding Harper's Ferry to the point of forcing Fighting Joe's resignation, but he gave Meade complete freedom over the same garrison. It seems that Halleck was acting on a personal more than on a professional basis. In doing so, he revealed his petty and unprofessional side. His dislike for Hooker caused him to deny Fighting Joe what he had no compunction granting Meade.[53]

Meade had little time to prepare before he faced Lee's legions in the battle of Gettysburg on July 1, 2, and 3, 1863. The Army of the Potomac achieved victory at Gettysburg despite having three commanders in less than a year. Lee lost 28,000 men, an astonishing 33 percent of his army. Meade lost 23,000 soldiers, fewer in number than Lee and, more significant, "only" 20 percent of his force. George G. Meade produced a major victory in the East over Robert E. Lee just a week after assuming command of the Army of the Potomac. Had Lincoln and Halleck finally found the right general in the East?

In Mississippi, meanwhile, Grant was winning an even more significant victory. In mid-April 1863, after numerous failed attempts to reach the city, Admiral David D. Porter, at Grant's request, sent the navy steaming past Vicksburg's cannons while Grant's army marched down the opposite side of the Mississippi River to a position below the city. Halleck had been pressuring Grant and Nathaniel Banks in New Orleans to cooperate, as late as April 2 telling Grant that he had to concentrate forces to be successful and asking: "If he [Banks] cannot get up to co-operate with you on Vicksburg, cannot you get troops down to help him on Port Hudson?" He repeated that same injunction on May 11, so once Grant had his troops and navy vessels below Vicksburg, he had a crucial decision to make.[54]

Should he conquer Port Hudson first and then march up with Banks's troops against Vicksburg? He made the momentous decision to ignore Halleck's order and instead move on Vicksburg alone. (After all, Halleck repeatedly told his generals that since they were on the battlefield, they had the final say.) The result was a spectacular campaign resulting in the July 4 surrender of the city and the fall of Port Hudson the following week.

It was, of course, not that quick and easy. There was a great deal of concern in Washington about Grant's daring to place himself between Confederate armies in Vicksburg and Jackson. Grant planned to capture Jackson first, chasing that army away, and then turn on Vicksburg and the other Confederate force. Jackson proved no problem, but on May 19 and 22, when Grant made direct assaults on the Vicksburg fortifications, he failed and had to settle into what Halleck and Lincoln had repeatedly told Hooker to avoid: a siege. Halleck was extremely displeased with both Grant and Banks. "If these eccentric movements," he lectured in his most pedantic voice, "do not lead to some serious disaster, it would be because the enemy does not take full advantage of his opportunity. I assure you," he concluded in a letter to Banks, that "the government is exceedingly disappointed that you and Genl Grant are not acting in conjunction." And, in an echo of the days of Forts Henry and Donelson, Halleck scolded Grant (though mildly this time) for not keeping him sufficiently informed of his activities. He said nothing negative, however, when Grant fired John McClernand for insubordination.[55]

Halleck also remained unhappy with William S. Rosecrans in Tennessee. Not only had this general made no movement since his victory at Stones River in late December, but he was also inundating Halleck with telegrams demanding more of everything. Halleck wanted Rosecrans to work in concert with Grant—at least create a diversion so that troops from Braxton Bragg's army could not be sent against Grant in Mississippi. In early June 1863, Halleck became so concerned that he began a telegraphic campaign to get reinforcements to Mississippi. Using this technological marvel in a way that no one had before, Halleck was able to hear from his subordinates and instruct them at lightning speed by nineteenth-century standards. In this instance he sent troops to Grant from Burnside, now in command of the Army of the Ohio in Cincinnati, from Schofield, now in command of the Department of the Missouri, from Banks, yet again in New Orleans, and especially from Rosecrans. "All accounts concur that [Joe] Johnston is collecting a large force against General Grant, a part of which comes from Bragg's army. If you can do nothing yourself, a portion of our troops must be sent to Grant's relief." Rosecrans, of course, said that was impossible. The same day that Halleck had spent so much time telegraphing back and forth with Hooker, he also telegraphed Rosecrans: "Is it your intention to make an immediate movement forward? A definite answer, yes or no, is required."[56]

Fortunately, Grant's brilliance at Vicksburg and Meade's bloody repulse of Lee at Gettysburg produced Union victories that deflected attention from Rosecrans. That general continued to be immobile, but he maintained his command. When in March 1863 Halleck wrote to Hooker, Grant, and Rosecrans that whoever "first" won "an important and decisive victory" would receive the vacant major generalship, Rosecrans was outraged. "As an officer and a citizen, I feel degraded to such auctioneering of honor." Halleck responded that "before receiving your letter, I had not supposed that a Government which offered and bestowed its highest offices for military success either deprecated patriotism, encouraged baseness, or bartered away honor." Halleck won that war of words, but Rosecrans still refused to move.[57]

Besides being happy about Vicksburg and Gettysburg, Halleck could take special personal credit for one other achievement during this period: the appearance in May 1863 of General Orders 100, "Instructions for the Government of Armies of the United States in the Field." The product of the commission Halleck had organized, these orders were the handiwork, primarily, of Francis Lieber, who called them "a contribution by the U.S. to the stock of common civilization." The document was a reasonable statement of how armies and governments should behave toward each other in this civil war. It did not uphold the concept of a chivalrous war, but it did call for limitations on excessive or brutal behavior such as torture, poisoning, or pointless destruction. Yet in a case of military necessity or retaliation, the destruction of property and the withholding of food, for example, were within the rules. Sherman's destructive war, to cite a specific approach, was admissible. Slavery was one form of property that received no protection in Lieber's rules, and disloyal citizens, not loyal ones, were to suffer the consequences of the conflict.

In essence, however, despite Halleck's and Lieber's pride of authorship, most northerners never heard of General Orders No. 100, and southern reaction was thoroughly negative. Jefferson Davis cited the military necessity exception as demonstrating that General Orders No. 100 merely proved again the barbarity of the Union side.[58]

Pleased with this document that spelled out rules and regulations for warfare, Halleck told Grant that the old rules no longer held. "The character of the war has very much changed within the last year. There now is no possible hope of reconciliation with the rebels. The Union party in the South is virtually destroyed. There can be no peace but that which is forced by the sword. We must conquer the rebels or be conquered by them." In a public letter to the Union League, he was just as forthright. "This rebellion can not be put down by peaceful measures. Those who pretend to think so are either madmen or traitors in disguise."[59]

Alas, Halleck's much sterner view of the Union war effort did not cause a corresponding increase in his own decisiveness. Gideon Welles was sure that Halleck had no interest in annihilating Lee's army after Gettysburg; he only wanted it "driven back." The military coordinator of railroads, Herman Haupt, thought the same thing about Meade. Lincoln was so concerned when he read Meade's order to his army to "drive the invaders from our soil," and so worried that Meade had no plans to destroy the opposition military force, that he wrote Halleck to "please look to it." When Halleck told Meade to "push forward, and fight Lee before he can cross the Potomac," Meade wondered what he should do in case Lee did cross that river. Back and forth the letters and telegrams flew, Meade hesitating, and Halleck pushing him to go after Lee without specifying when or how.[60]

In fact Old Brains seemed to Lincoln to show little enthusiasm for pressing Meade, so "I drop the subject," the President told Gideon Welles. "This is the President's error," the Secretary of the Navy said in grief. He believed that Lincoln had better military instincts than Halleck, but the President always seemed to give in to the commanding general. "It being strictly a military question," Lincoln would say, "it is proper I should defer to Halleck, whom I have called here to counsel, advise, and direct in these matters where he is an expert." In truth, both Lincoln and Halleck, as well as Stanton, wanted Meade to go after Lee; they sent him repeated telegrams with that message. As always, however, Halleck regularly gave Meade a way out. "Do not be influenced by any dispatch from here against your own judgment. Regard them as suggestions only," he said characteristically.[61]

When Meade called a counsel of war with his officers that voted not to attack Lee's army, Halleck responded forcefully that Meade was "strong enough" to defeat Lee before he crossed the Potomac. "Act upon your own judgment and make your generals execute your orders. Call no council of war. It is proverbial that councils of war never fight." Meanwhile, Welles viewed Halleck just as harshly in his diary: "The army is still at rest. Halleck stays here in Washington within four hours of the army, smoking his cigar, doing as little as the army. . . . Why does he not remove to headquarters in the field?" In truth, Halleck could not bring himself into the field because then he would gain the direct information whose lack, he said, prevented him from making decisions. He preferred advising from a distance to ordering on the spot.[62]

Lincoln became nearly mad with exasperation when Lee made it back across the Potomac River without Meade attacking him. "What does it mean, Mr. Welles? Great God! What does it mean?" Lincoln lamented. Welles asked the President what kind of orders had been sent to Meade, and the subject quickly turned to Halleck. "Why he is within four hours of Meade," Welles pointed out. "Is it not strange that he has not been up there to advise and encourage him?" Halleck was inept as commanding general, Welles said. Lincoln immediately grew quieter. "Halleck knows better than I what to do. He is a military man, he has had a military education. I brought him here to give me military advice. His views and mine are widely different. It is better that I, who am not a military man, should defer to him, rather than he to me." Welles disagreed. Halleck "was, as now, all the time waiting to hear from Meade or whoever was in command," but he did not act. Lincoln still held Halleck in high esteem despite the repeated disappointments, but Welles, like most others, had long since lost all patience.[63]

For his part, Halleck continued to pass along Lincoln's frustration to Meade. "I need hardly say to you that the escape of Lee's army without another battle has created great dissatisfaction in the mind of the President, and it will require an active and energetic pursuit on your part to remove the impression that it has not been sufficiently active heretofore." Meade angrily responded that he had done the best he could and believed that the president's feeling was "undeserved." "I feel compelled most respectfully to ask to be immediately relieved from command of this army." Halleck responded soothingly that his telegram had been intended not "as a censure, but as a stimulus to an active pursuit." He refused Meade's resignation, and nothing changed. Lincoln was "distressed immeasurably," but he never sent the letter he composed to Meade expressing his feelings.[64] Only Grant, in the West, seemed ready and determined to fulfill the President's and the commanding general's hopes for victory. Halleck left it up to those commanding in the field to decide how to wage the war. He knew what was needed, but he could not bring himself to order it. In Grant's case alone, he did not have to.

9

The Western Generals Bring Success

THOUGH he refused to take decisive action himself, Halleck, like the rest of the nation, was frustrated with the war in the East. George B. McClellan, Ambrose Burnside, Joseph Hooker, and George G. Meade had all begun their tenures as leaders of the Army of the Potomac with great hope, and all had failed in one way or another. McClellan had won at Antietam, and Meade had thrown Lee back at Gettysburg, but then neither had taken advantage of their victories. Instead, they had demanded more men, more horses, more of everything, insisting that it was shortages that prevented them from pursuing the Confederates. Burnside and Hooker were willing to attack the Army of Northern Virginia, but their inept handling of troops resulted in shocking defeats at Fredericksburg and Chancellorsville. Lincoln grew more haggard each day from frustration, regularly urging his generals to be more aggressive or trying to get Halleck, his commanding general, to compel them to get moving. But Halleck insisted that he could only make suggestions to his subordinate generals; he could not give them direct orders because they knew best their fields of operations. Lincoln regularly fired generals to try to improve Union war fortunes in the East, but he did not fire Halleck. Misfortunes piled one upon another and although Halleck provided no answers to the problems Lincoln could not bring himself to dismiss his commanding general.

Things were not much better with the western armies. Don Carlos Buell and Williams S. Rosecrans were also slow to take decisive action, and General Benjamin F. Butler, a former politician, was so disliked in New Orleans that Lincoln had to replace him with a less controversial political general, Nathaniel Banks. Halleck shared Lincoln's frustrations, and his appreciation of Grant's actions in the West increased proportionately. Grant was one ray of military hope. The general that Halleck had found so sloppy and unprofessional in his personal conduct early in the war (despite his victories at Forts Henry and Donelson) had since that time demonstrated a self-reliant boldness that was refreshingly reassuring. William T. Sherman, the general accused of insanity in early wartime Kentucky and during Halleck's tenure in Missouri, was demonstrating similar qualities as Grant's subordinate. He may have lost at Chickasaw Bayou, but he showed a no-nonsense style that, like Grant's, presaged future success. Halleck increasingly looked to these two western generals for relief from the recurring disappointments everywhere else. To his pleasure, he even found them intellectually sound and satisfying.

Gratifying as these western generals were, Halleck and Lincoln both recognized the importance to Union morale of the war in the East. Lee had suffered serious losses at Antietam and Gettysburg, but the memories of Fredericksburg and Chancellorsville gave him an aura of invincibility in spite of those defeats. In reality, the eastern war was a stalemate; the years of military leadership shifts and horrendous battlefield casualties provided no measurable military progress. The loud cry of "On to Richmond" that had opened the war in 1861 was still being heard by late 1863.

Moreover, military and political leaders in the East also had to deal with the shocking Draft Riots in New York City that July. Angered over the March 1863 Enrollment Act, particularly its $300 military service exemption fee, which enabled men to buy their way out of service, eligible draftees believed that they were being asked to fight for black freedom only to lose their jobs to freed black men. New York City workers (notably the Irish) went on a rampage. They attacked white men who looked as if they could afford the $300 exemption, and they beat or murdered any black person they encountered. The well-known animosity of New York Governor Horatio Seymour toward the Lincoln administration, due to his belief that it overstepped its constitutional authority in waging the war, did not help calm matters.[1]

When news of the city violence reached Halleck, he demanded that Seymour call out the militia to restore order. But not expecting quick action from the uncooperative governor, Halleck, with Stanton's full support, ordered Federal troops from Meade's and other nearby armies to hurry to New York. He sent General John A. Dix from Fort Monroe to take charge of the troops being sent to the rescue, encouraging an iron-fisted response to the rioters. His friend Francis Lieber, whose house was located "between the worst points of the riotous days," reported to Halleck that "negro children were killed in the street, like rats with clubs."[2]

It was less the thuggery that angered Halleck than the disloyalty. Halleck ignored the horror and cried out instead against what he called "traitors." "There is abundant evidence," he said, "of an understanding between the Peace Men of the North & the Secesh of the South." He especially blamed Governor Seymour. "He acts a man stark mad," Halleck said. "May not the Governor have inherited his father's insanity? This is the most charitable view I can take of his recent conduct." Halleck promised that Federal troops would remain in New York until the riot was completely suppressed, but he said it was really up to people on the scene to quell it. "The loyal men at the north, who have not been called into the field, must take care of these traitors & assassins. If they do not, the traitors & assassins will take care of them and their property." Such anarchy was a boon to southern forces because it forced Union troops from the field to the city and thwarted the draft. Halleck here acted more decisively than he did in waging the war because he saw affairs in New York more clearly and mob control was easier to direct than battlefield combat.[3]

Halleck was so concerned about New York's violence spreading to other cities that he told Meade, "it would be best to hold for the present the upper line of the Rappahannock without farther pursuit of Lee." Meade, who was not showing any signs of movement anyway, did not argue. His inactivity now seemed to have gained military legitimacy. Secretary of the Navy Gideon Welles grew furious, blaming the stalemate in Virginia and most of the Union's other military difficulties on Halleck. He "originates nothing, anticipates nothing, . . . takes no responsibility, plans nothing, suggests nothing, is good for nothing" Welles thundered.[4]

The news was better in the western theater. Thanks mainly to Grant, Union troops had taken control of the Mississippi River and garrisoned major cities such as New Orleans, Memphis, and Nashville. Even the slow-moving Rosecrans had won a victory at Stones River, opening the way to Chattanooga and the vast interior of the Confederacy. There, too, the combat had become more destructive, the war affecting civilians and their property more than ever. In the West, Halleck, the author of the major American book on military theory and the patron of General Orders No. 100, supported carrying the war directly to recalcitrant Confederate civilians.

As in the East, however, Halleck did not give specific orders to his western commanders. He presented overall strategic goals and left it up to his subordinates to meet them. The difference in the West was that Grant and later Sherman did not require direct supervision. They had the same short-ages and needs all the other generals had, but these deficiencies did not stop them from moving forward. Unlike Meade in the East, Grant in the West knew what had to be done and went about doing it. For Halleck, who did not want to make decisions for the generals in the field, Grant was proving to be his best subordinate, his favorite general. Grant listened to Halleck's advice, he made up his mind, he kept Halleck informed, and he acted. In Halleck's eyes, the undisciplined general of 1862 had become his and the President's best hope in 1863.

Grant's victory at Vicksburg, the most spectacular military campaign in American history, gained him an unaccustomed level of respect in Halleck's eyes. Old Brains gave Grant his ultimate compliment; he compared him to the soldier he most admired. "In boldness of plan, rapidity of execution, and brilliancy of results," Halleck said of the Vicksburg campaign, "these operations will compare most favorably with those of Napoleon about Ulm." Perhaps even more important in Halleck's mind, Grant also deserved praise for his administrative accomplishments. "Your narrative of this campaign, like the operations themselves, is brief, soldierly, and in every respect creditable and satisfactory." Halleck, who had castigated Grant for his administrative lapses after Shiloh, now showered him with praise for the overall quality of his military activities.[5]

What was even more encouraging was that Grant did not rest on his laurels. Even before he completed his Vicksburg report, he called on Halleck to authorize a move against Mobile, Alabama. Grant said that he could not make the campaign himself, because during the summer months there were water shortages between Vicksburg and Mobile. The best route of attack was from the New Orleans area, although "I have not studied this matter, . . . it being out of my department." Grant was thinking broadly, and he was not adverse to suggesting a military action that might bring glory to a fellow general, in this case Nathaniel Banks. Banks expressed enthusiasm for the project, but Lincoln and Halleck had other ideas. Instead of mounting a campaign against Mobile, they wanted Grant to help Banks move into Texas. The Lincoln administration wanted to make sure that France understood U.S. disapproval of Ferdinand Maximilian, Napoleon III's puppet in Mexico. Grant believed that placing a garrison at Brownsville on the Rio Grande River would make the same point, but he accepted his commanding general's orders, earning ever more approval from Halleck.[6]

Despite his new respect for Grant, Halleck still kept his aggressive subordinate under control. Lincoln told Halleck what to do and he followed orders. Halleck ordered some units to go to Banks in Louisiana for the excursion into Texas and later sent others to fend off Sterling Price's raid in Missouri. Grant was frustrated at the loss of men, but once again he obeyed without complaint. He simply kept planning his next move, and Halleck continued to be impressed.[7]

Halleck's experiences with William S. Rosecrans were a very different matter. Although he compared Grant to Napoleon, Halleck wrote to Rosecrans: "There is great disappointment felt here at the slowness of your advance. Unless you can move more rapidly, your whole campaign will prove a failure, and you will have [Braxton] Bragg and [Joseph E.] Johnston against you." Not only did Rosecrans continue to stall, but he also took it upon himself to lecture his commanding general: "Any disappointment that may be felt at the apparent slowness of our movements would be readily removed by a knowledge of the obstacles and a true military appreciation of the advantages of not moving prematurely." Provoked, Halleck responded sharply: "In other words, general, while I am blamed here for not urging you forward more rapidly, you are displeased at my doing so." By contrast with Rosecrans, Grant's behavior became even more admirable.[8]

Rosecrans finally got his army moving on August 28, 1863, and maneuvered it efficiently into Chattanooga on September 9 "without a struggle" being mounted by Braxton Bragg, as he correctly phrased it. Ambrose Burnside, after delays of his own, captured Knoxville on September 2. These were both splendid achievements, but Halleck did not have much time to express his admiration. Word leaked out that the Confederates in Virginia were sending James Longstreet's corps to aid Braxton Bragg in Tennessee. Halleck immediately told Burnside to link up with Rosecrans and ordered Grant and Sherman in Vicksburg, and Stephen Hurlbut in Memphis, to send all available troops to Chattanooga. He also made it clear to Meade that the Union's main effort now lay in the West, and his job in the East was to keep Lee from sending any more troops to Bragg. The West had become more important than the East in Halleck's eyes, and that was largely because of Grant.[9]

On September 19 and 20, 1863, Braxton Bragg, reinforced by James Longstreet, launched an attack on Rosecrans at Chickamauga Creek, across the Georgia line from Chattanooga. On the second day of the fierce battle, Rosecrans mistakenly ordered one of his divisions to move to another position, thus opening a hole in the Union defense line. Longstreet's charging Confederates, by chance, attacked just at that spot and went pouring through, forcing the Federal right flank back against its left. Rosecrans and several other generals fled in the belief that their army was routed. Fortunately for the Union cause, George H. Thomas rallied his units on Snodgrass Hill and stymied the charging Confederates, gaining the nickname "the Rock of Chickamauga." Rosecrans and his army fell back into the Chattanooga fortifications, and Bragg had to establish a siege. The Confederate Army had won the battle, but the Federals maintained control of the strategically important Tennessee city. The casualties on both sides were horrendous, 28 percent each, the Confederates losing 18,500 men out of 66,000 and the Federals 16,000 out of 58,000. According to Adam Gurowski, that was all Halleck's fault because he did not support his subordinate properly. "Rosecrans is worsted. Hurrah for Lincoln, who believes in Halleck."[10]

In response to this disaster, Secretary of War Stanton called an emergency midnight meeting of the cabinet and told the shocked secretaries of the bloody defeat. The discussion immediately revolved around reinforcements for the besieged Union forces in Chattanooga: Should Burnside be sent from Knoxville or would it be better to send Sherman from Vicksburg? Stanton, saying that there was no way any of these forces could arrive quickly enough, called for Hooker to travel west with 20,000 men from the Army of the Potomac. He thought it would take only a few days to make that transfer by rail. Halleck and Lincoln immediately disagreed, Halleck arguing that it would take at least forty days. Besides, the President and the commanding general opposed taking any troops from Meade. Stanton called General D. C. McCallum, the head of military railroads, to the meeting and asked him how long it would take to get Hooker's troops from Virginia to Chattanooga. McCallum's answer: seven days. Stanton was ecstatic: "Good! I told you so! I knew it could be done. Forty days! Forty days, indeed, when the life of the nation is at stake!" Stanton shouted, ridiculing Halleck's estimate. Stanton's argument carried the day. Hooker with three divisions departed on September 25, and the first of these troops reached Rosecrans's army exactly seven days later. For the first time during the war, Stanton and Halleck publicly disagreed.[11]

The Chickamauga debacle and the Chattanooga siege occasioned new criticism of Halleck. Gideon Welles remarked with great disdain: "General Halleck has earnestly and constantly smoked cigars and rubbed his elbows, while the Rebels have been vigorously concentrating their forces to overwhelm Rosecrans." Salmon P. Chase, once a supporter of Halleck, now said the commanding general "was good for nothing, and everybody knew it but the President." Undeterred by such criticism, Halleck continued rushing troops to Rosecrans's support. Sherman moved up to Memphis from Vicksburg and then led four divisions along the Charleston and Memphis Railroad, across three hundred miles of Tennessee toward Chattanooga. In mid-October, Halleck signaled further significant action. On Lincoln's order, the commanding general appointed Grant commander of all the military departments between the Appalachian Mountains and the Mississippi River: the Departments of the Ohio, the Cumberland, and the Tennessee. The new western leader quickly named Sherman to replace him as commander of the Army of the Tennessee and moved to relieve the siege at Chattanooga. Halleck told him he could also replace Rosecrans with George H. Thomas if he saw fit, words that Grant took under advisement. The aggressive Grant was back on the move, his Halleck-imposed post-Vicksburg inactivity over.[12]

These promotions proved to be among the most significant of the war. In Grant and in Sherman, Halleck had generals who would not sit idly by, gathering supplies; they would push ahead. He also had two generals who still respected him and his military knowledge. When Sherman gained promotion to brigadier general in the regular army, his thanks to Halleck were effusive: "I will endeavor in the future to merit your good opinion, which I value above all others. I have abundant faith that you & you alone can grasp the mighty questions of government that are now in issue in America, & only aspire to be one of the instruments to be used in their solution." Grant felt the same way, long believing Halleck to be "one of the greatest men of the age." For the first time in the war, Halleck was working with subordinates who admired him, and whom he similarly respected. He had never had such good fortune in the East.[13]

Grant and Sherman did not disappoint Halleck. After meeting with Stanton in Louisville, where the secretary had rushed to discuss matters, Grant quickly relieved Rosecrans and made George H. Thomas the commander of the Army of the Cumberland. He hastened troops to Chattanooga, and, together with Hooker, Sherman, and Thomas, put together a battle plan. Then, in late November 1863, he watched as his army carried the day. Hooker took Lookout Mountain, and though Sherman was stymied in his attack against the north end of Missionary Ridge, Thomas's men in the middle of the line dashed all the way up Missionary Ridge in a frontal attack that sent Bragg's Confederates fleeing. Grant had relieved the siege of Chattanooga and placed the important city firmly in Union hands. Halleck was ecstatic: "I congratulate you and your army on the victories of Chattanooga," he wired Grant. "This is truly a day of thanksgiving."[14]

Halleck still had problems, however. Ambrose Burnside remained under siege at Knoxville, and this time it was Sherman who came to the rescue. Burnside needed quick relief, all accounts indicating that he was in a life-and-death situation, surrounded by Longstreet's forces. Sherman and his men were exhausted from their long march from Memphis and their participation in the Chattanooga battle itself. The route to Knoxville was mountainous and the weather frigid. Although Sherman was unhappy with the order he received from Grant to go to Burnside's relief, unlike other generals who would have delayed or even refused to move, he immediately marched his troops six long, hard days to the outskirts of the city. There, to his amazement, he found Burnside sitting down with linen and silverware to eat a turkey dinner. Burnside sheepishly admitted that he had never been in as difficult straits as rumor had suggested. No matter, he said, Sherman's approach had frightened Longstreet enough to cause him to return to Virginia, where Lee wanted him anyway.[15]

The Union Army had gained another success in the West, and it was clearly due to the decisive actions of Grant and Sherman. Meanwhile, Halleck told Grant that in the East Meade continued to be a disappointment. "Nothing has been done, and it does not appear that anything is likely to be done by the Army of the Potomac in this campaign." Meade and other eastern generals remained idle and did nothing to ease the pressure on Halleck, while in the West Grant and Sherman were making him look good.[16]

On the Pacific Coast, Halleck's name remained important enough for a group of investors to incorporate a new Sonoma County California mining venture in his honor, the Halleck Gold & Silver Mining Company. Halleck had no connection with this group, but it was obviously named after him, a welcome respite from the usual criticism he faced.[17]

It was not this mine, however, but a more familiar one in California that now impinged on Halleck's life in a way that he could never have imagined. When Halleck had departed from San Francisco in 1861, the litigation surrounding the New Almaden Mine was still pending. He had severed all his ties with the company, and his law firm, Halleck, Peachy, and Billings, no longer existed, so he had no connection with the continuing litigation over the mine's ownership. He probably remained curious about the cases making their way to the U.S. Supreme Court, but, if he did, he never mentioned the litigation in his Civil War correspondence. Consequently, New Almaden's reappearance in his life in 1863 must have come as a major shock.[18]

It all began on May 8, 1863, when Lincoln, distracted with war issues, signed a writ calling on the Federal marshal in California, with military help, to seize the quicksilver mine. Both Halleck and Secretary of War Stanton had been involved in the 1850s California litigation, though on different sides of the issue, but Lincoln, a talented attorney himself, issued the writ without consulting them. He based his action instead on the advice of Interior Secretary John P. Usher and Attorney General Edward Bates, neither of whom knew the various still-pending cases except through documents. They seemed to base their advice on the Supreme Court decision in only one of these cases. Lincoln sent a friend, Leonard Swett, to California, peculiarly accompanied by the president of the Quicksilver Mining Company, one of the litigants in the case and the organization that would lease the land once it was in government hands. Ominously, this was the company Stanton had represented in court during the early litigation. Swett did not arrive in San Francisco until July, and it was not until the ninth that he and the Federal marshal served the writ on the mine's superintendent. Matters then quickly escalated. Fear spread that no mining company was safe from government takeover if the wealthy and important New Almaden Company lost its land and quicksilver operation. The gold and silver mining companies in both California and Nevada were particularly frightened, and talk circulated of violent opposition to a government occupation of New Almaden. At the mine, officials refused to honor the writ, and 170 armed men backed up their refusal. Violence seemed imminent.

Realizing how volatile the situation was, the U.S. marshal had already contacted U.S. Army General George Wright in San Francisco. Wishing to avoid bloodshed, Wright telegraphed Halleck in Washington to advise Lincoln that his order should "be deferred for the present." By that time, Lincoln had already counseled California officials and Swett to avoid violence. Secretary of the Treasury Salmon P. Chase, upset at what he was hearing, suspected that Halleck was somehow behind this takeover and told him he should suspend the writ. Obviously upset at being placed under such suspicion, Halleck insisted, "I have no interest in this matter of this Almaden. As I have given no orders and have no information of any orders issued by the Govt in relation to this matter, I cannot either suspend them or countermand them. Those who instigated or issued them must take responsibility of their suspension or execution," he insisted angrily.[19]

Halleck did not escape from the controversy that easily. Two former California business partners implored him to intervene. John Parrott asked him to have the President rescind the writ "at least until the rights of conflicting claimants shall be determined by the courts." Frederick Billings warned that there was "great excitement, and unless the mandate is revoked, the State is in danger of being lost [to] the Union. . . . The people will not stand it. . . . See the President and answer." The whole matter was fraught with uncertainty. Lincoln could not have imagined that this issue would escalate into such a major controversy. In California, however, mine ownership and operation were of major concern to the public at large.[20]

Halleck responded quickly to these appeals of his friends, but he only made matters worse. He told both General Wright and his former law partner and friend Billings that Lincoln's order had been "surreptitiously obtained." He specifically told Wright that the Secretary of War had "no information of any military order to take possession of New Almaden Mine." Therefore, Wright was to do nothing further, and he was to "withdraw and restore everything to the condition" it was in before he received the order. Fortunately, Wright had kept the marshal and the army from taking any action, so matters had calmed down. Lincoln now backed off and wrote several conciliatory letters to California officials. Violence was averted.[21]

The controversy continued in Washington, however. Halleck's letter to Billings appeared in the San Francisco press, and Lincoln and his cabinet heard about it in mid-August. Attorney General Bates and Interior Secretary Usher were furious at Halleck's slur, and during a cabinet meeting, with Halleck not present, Bates said Halleck's "surreptitiously obtained statement" "did not exhibit a pure mind, right intentions, or high integrity." Lincoln tried to calm everyone down by saying that he thought Halleck "had been hasty and indiscreet but he *hoped nothing worse.*" Bates was not appeased. Not satisfied with blasting Halleck in the cabinet meeting, Bates, that same evening, wrote Halleck a personal letter in which he told him that, in the cabinet, he had "denounce[d] the telegram as unfounded in fact, & eminently wrong, coming from any source, and peculiarly objectionable, as coming from you."[22] Halleck wisely remained silent. In California, the Quicksilver Mining Company bought out the assets of the New Almaden Company, and the press praised Lincoln for quickly rescinding his writ. Halleck's comments caused no permanent damage, except perhaps to his reputation in California. Fortunately, Edwin Stanton remained silent throughout the controversy, and it did not cause a rift between him and Halleck.

Halleck's frustrations with his job seemed in direct contrast to the contentment of his personal life. He remained happily married, although his wife and son were frequently away, visiting relatives in New York City and elsewhere. He leased a house in Georgetown some time after arriving in Washington to become commanding general, but as late as November

1862 he was writing his wife in New York City that it would take a "great deal of work to make it habitable." Precisely when the family moved in is unclear, but apparently Elizabeth Halleck and Harry stayed in Georgetown during the summer of 1863, where they suffered from the excessive heat of late August. Halleck never discussed his wife in any of his correspondence, and Francis Lieber mentioned her only in passing. After the newsman and writer Charles G. Halpine had tea with Halleck one day, he said nothing about Mrs. Halleck except that her "strong tea sent me home sleepless and tossing uneasily in a bed." Halleck's wife remained a shadowy figure in her husband's life.[23]

Halleck was very proud of his only child, who in 1863 was seven years old and called either Henry or Harry. Lieber always referred to him as the "big-eyed boy." Halleck rarely gave any details about the child, but he did mention near the end of 1863 that "Master Henry is all excitement in expectation of a visit from Santa Claus tonight." Halleck also maintained contact with his family in Westernville, New York. He regularly sent money home to his mother and sisters, living on the farm he had purchased for them from his father's estate. His wife and son visited these relatives early in the war, but Halleck's duties kept him in Washington. Uncle David Wager wrote him once during these years to ask for his help in obtaining an army discharge for a friend's wounded son, but no other family correspondence has survived.[24]

Halleck had to spend much of his time away from his home and family in the War Department or the White House. A favorite haunt for him near these places was Lafayette Park. People frequently saw him in this green area pacing up and down or sometimes walking with another officer, discussing war matters. One evening, he became so absorbed in his thoughts that he let the ten o'clock curfew pass and found himself locked in the park. He was in no physical shape to scale the high fence and calling out to the empty streets or sleeping until morning on one of the benches was not appealing. Fortunately, Halleck found an army private in the same predicament. Doing a reconnaissance, the two men decided to have the private get on Halleck's back and from that higher point climb over the fence to find the gatekeeper. "Halleck took care of this young soldier ever afterwards," the private's supervisor later reported.[25]

Unfortunately, Halleck did not always react this cordially to strangers. One day, as Halleck was going up the capitol stairs, he passed an Englishman walking in the opposite direction. This Britisher, complete with monocle, stopped Halleck and asked: "Ah! Beg pardon, what's this building just behind." Halleck responded "rather harshly and contemptuously" that it was "the bakeshop of the army!" (the capitol basement at one time had been a bakery for the military). The Englishman did not appreciate Halleck's tone and manner, and it looked as though there might be a fistfight. The Britisher then tried to smoothe things over by handing Halleck his card, but the general contemptuously tossed it to the ground. Fortunately, the confrontation ended there, but what Sherman called Halleck's "abrupt, brusque style, even to members of Congress," had almost caused a fight.[26]

Halleck was frequently rude to army personnel. On one occasion he excoriated a messenger from General Meade who was bringing information on the Army of the Potomac, then in pursuit of Lee after Gettysburg. The officer who was escorting the body of General Hiram G. Berry, killed at Chancellorsville, had gone to have Berry's body embalmed before reporting. He then received a tongue lashing from Halleck for his delay. In response to the verbal assault, the shocked officer said he knew the penalty for an alleged disobedience to orders, and, turning to walk away, said he was willing to accept his punishment and be dismissed from the army. President Lincoln, who had observed the exchange in silence, now intervened. He quieted Halleck and softly explained to the irate officer that he and the general had received no news from the battlefield and were eager to hear what he had to say. The lieutenant then told the two men what he knew and left quietly. Halleck's administrative impatience might have resulted in the court martial of a good officer had not Lincoln spoken up. The young man, no doubt, told anyone who would listen about the kind President and the difficult commanding general. Halleck's reputation for abrasiveness was widespread.[27]

As always, Halleck's long-standing physical and psychological problems manifested themselves in his ill-temper. He may have had a bad day at his desk, a sleepless night because of health problems, anxiety about supporting his extended family on his military salary, or continued tension generated by the war. He admitted to his friend and staff member G. W. Cullum, one day in October, that "I was up all night last night in the War Dept., and feel today a little *mean*." His finances were an ongoing concern. His California property was not providing income, and the last reference he made to income from legal fees was in early 1862. "My pay does not suffice to support my family including what I have to contribute for my mother's family in Western. I am now actually borrowing money for current expenses."[28]

He loved literary work, and there was always the chance that one or more of his books would provide additional income. He just did not have much opportunity to work on their revisions, however, and this, too, was provoking. He could not find time to complete his translation of Jomini's life of Napoleon that a New York company wanted to publish. When he heard that a new book on international law cited him, he excitedly asked the State Department to send over a copy if it had one. His passion for his books and intellectual pursuits persisted even as he fought a major war. As always, he was torn between public purpose and private pleasures. Since he could not spend time on his writing, he seemed to find enjoyment corresponding with Francis Lieber on a variety of intellectual and contemporary topics. He could speak his mind to Lieber and say things that in his official position he could not say to many others. For example, when Congress came back in session in December 1863, he told Lieber that he expected "the usual intrigues and wire-pulling." He also lamented that he was "to be made a special subject of attack by a certain class of politicians," the radical antislavery men, who increasingly insisted that he remained too tolerant of slavery. Halleck told Lieber defiantly: "They are welcome to turn me out as soon as they please—they cannot do me a greater favor."[29]

He seemed to get even more enjoyment from discussing military affairs with Grant and Sherman. Here he could combine his job with his pleasure. When he wrote to most of his other generals, he found himself thinking of new ways to urge them to move their armies or explaining why he did not have the men, horses, or supplies that they were demanding of him. Halleck's letters to his two western generals concerned substance, a give and take of possibilities rather than delays. When Grant arrived in Chattanooga, for example, he immediately gave Halleck a full report on what he found there and promised "to get the troops in a state of readiness for a forward movement at the earliest possible day." Halleck eagerly responded with suggestions for such an undertaking. After Grant telegraphed news of the Union victory at Chattanooga, Halleck was effusive about the importance of this victory. He told the Secretary of War: "Not only did the officers and men exhibit great skill and daring in their operations on the field, but the highest praise is also due to the commanding general for his admirable dispositions for dislodging the enemy from a position apparently impregnable."[30]

At Halleck's urging, Grant discussed his strategic ideas with him. He suggested that instead of continuing direct assaults against Richmond, as Burnside and Hooker had attempted, a 60,000-man Union army out of southeastern Virginia should move against Raleigh, North Carolina, destroying railroads along the march, thus isolating Richmond and Lee's army from the south. He concluded humbly: "From your better opportunities of studying the country, and the Armies, that would be involved in this plan, you will be better able to judge of the practicability of it than I possibly can." Halleck then responded with several letters, including one in which he went into great detail about the various Union military possibilities. The tone of the letter was that of one strategist carrying on a discussion with another, concluding that the North Carolina plan was not feasible, but assuring Grant that it deserved serious attention. Halleck's prose in places was even graphic, as when he wrote that "we have given too much attention to cutting the toe nails of our enemy instead of grasping his throat." Halleck obviously enjoyed such talk with another soldier he had come to respect. "As an interchange of views on the present condition of affairs and the coming campaign will be advantageous," Halleck wrote Grant in early 1864, "I hope you will write me freely and fully your opinions on these matters."[31]

Halleck's correspondence with Sherman was even fuller and more personal. When Halleck asked Sherman's advice about reconstruction in Louisiana, Mississippi, and Arkansas so that he could pass it on to the President, Sherman responded with a long, detailed letter calling on Lincoln's administration to continue the war in earnest until "*all* the organized armies of the South are dispersed, conquered, and subjugated." Only then should reunion be discussed, he said. Grant did not agree with Sherman and thought the Union should offer the South "terms" that included "the protection of our laws." Halleck thought Sherman was correct about the necessity of continuing the war until total victory was won. Back and forth the letters and telegrams flew, Halleck disagreeing about the validity of Sherman's Meridian, Mississippi, campaign but expressing a willingness to accept it as long as Grant did. As he had done with other generals, Halleck gave Grant the right of "final decision," but he did it after a more thorough discussion of the possibilities and within a context of mutual respect. Halleck seemed to sense that in Grant and Sherman he had subordinate generals who would take his advice into account and would then act with decisiveness.[32]

Halleck was not the only person looking favorably upon Grant. Secretary of War Edwin Stanton sent his assistant, the newsman Charles A. Dana, to Grant's army to evaluate, at first hand, this successful general. The rumors about Grant's alleged drunkenness had never been put to rest, and Stanton wanted to know how much validity there was in them. Was Grant as good as he looked from a distance? Dana thought he was, so the Secretary of War began thinking about having Grant come East to take command of the Army of the Potomac. Dana and Halleck both opposed such a move at that time, and Grant said they were "right in supposing that it would cause me more sadness than satisfaction to be ordered to the command of the Army of the Potomac." Grant showed no desire for command advancement, and that only made him more appealing.[33]

Lincoln kept a close watch on Grant, too, comparing him favorably to his other generals. The night that Sherman, on Grant's order, reached Knoxville and relieved Burnside, Lincoln mused out loud about having Grant command in the East. "Can anybody doubt, if Grant were in command, that he would catch" Longstreet, then moving away from Knoxville back to Lee's army? Lincoln believed so, but he too did not want Grant to come East. Halleck agreed with the President, lamenting, however, Meade's continued inactivity. "You know, Mr. President, how hard we have tried to get this army to move toward the enemy, and we cannot succeed." Still, it was not time for Grant to be traveling East. Lincoln and Halleck believed Grant was still needed in the West, where the Union Army was inexorably moving forward.[34]

Sherman, who came close to idolizing Grant, also opposed the idea of making him commanding general. He told his brother that "Halleck is yet the best man as Genl in Chief." Grant, he continued, "has not the qualities for that place. . . . No man can do anything so near Washington as the Army of the Potomac. That army can do nothing till the Closing Scenes. It would be cruel & inhuman to take Grant or any western officer there. I told Halleck so at Corinth but he obeyed orders though he found he was going to the slaughter. He still remains the only man who could keep the peace six months."[35]

By February 1864, however, the pressure had increased on the administration to bring Grant east. The House of Representatives called for him to be made a lieutenant general, a new rank that would place him above every other general in the Union Army, even Halleck. Only George Washington and Winfield Scott had ever held this rank before in American history, and there was even talk of running Grant for President. The rumors mills began their inexorable grinding, and Halleck was said to be ready to resign if the House bill passed the Senate. The possibility seemed so strong that one of Halleck's aides became very "anxious," fearing that Halleck's resignation would put him "in a devil of a fix." In fact, congressional feelings were so anti-Halleck that a fellow Democrat, Reverdy Johnson of Maryland, insisted that any vote for Grant's promotion was not to be interpreted as a vote against anyone else (read Halleck). The Senate passed the bill, and after Lincoln was satisfied that Grant posed no political threat to him, he signed it. U.S. Grant became a lieutenant general, and Stanton had Halleck order him to Washington.[36]

The California newsman Noah Brooks was convinced that Grant would never have received this promotion had it not been for congressional unhappiness with Halleck. "I doubt if the most outspoken and malignant copperhead [antiwar Democrat] in Congress was so disliked, so riled against, and so reviled by the more radical members as [was] this unfortunate general-in-chief." Antislavery congressmen saw Halleck as an opponent of abolition, and thus responsible for failing to support antislavery generals like Ben Butler, Franz Sigel, and others. Certainly, Halleck was no abolitionist, but his opposition to Sigel and Butler had little to do with slavery. He simply thought them incompetent—politicians not military men.[37]

Halleck realized that some people were trying to drive a wedge between him and Grant over this promotion, but he said he would not allow it to happen. He would be "glad to be relieved from so thankless and disagreeable a position," he said. The public did not understand that "I am simply a military adviser of the Secretary of War and the President, and must obey and carry out what they decide upon, whether I concur in their decisions or not." That was not the role that Lincoln and Stanton had envisioned for Halleck when they brought him east, but it was the role that he had defined for himself. "As a good soldier, I obey the orders of my superiors." Halleck saw himself as a subordinate, not a decision maker, a follower not a leader. This was a deeply felt sentiment, long present in his character, but made conspicuous under the stress of war.[38]

On March 5, Halleck telegraphed Nathaniel Banks in New Orleans that Grant was "expected in Washington about the tenth," and Halleck "presume[d]," that he would take his (Halleck's) place and "assume the command of the Army as General-in-Chief." He "sincerely congratulate[d]" Grant on "this recognition of . . . [his] distinguished and meritorious service" and then expressed his fuller feelings to a friend. He told Francis Lieber that "the newspapers will, as usual, misrepresent whatever I may do in regard to the matter of command," but he really was happy to see Grant replacing him. It was nothing but a matter of rank anyway, Halleck said, writing in his most pedantic administrative style. Grant had to become commanding general, because his rank was higher than anyone else's, including his own. He had no doubt that "it will be said that I throw up my office in dudgeon, because Genl Grant has been promoted over my head," but "there is no possible ground for such an accusation. Genl Grant is my personal friend, and I heartily rejoice at his promotion. The honor was fully due to him," Halleck said, adding significantly, "and with the honor, he must take the responsibilities which belong to his office." As for himself, Halleck concluded, I "shall go wherever ordered by my superiors. I shall ask for nothing. I shall not even intimate a preference. If the government has no command for me," he concluded with resignation, "I am ready for the *shelf*." Lieber disagreed. "Shelving? Bah! Don't talk of it."[39]

Lieber was right. Halleck was not fired. In fact, little changed for him in his usual work day. Grant decided to be commanding general in the field, accompanying the Army of the Potomac but keeping George G. Meade as its day-to-day commander. Sherman took Grant's former slot as commander of the western armies, and James B. McPherson gained Sherman's old command. As for Halleck, he readily stepped aside in favor of Grant. "By order of the President," Stanton announced, "Maj. Gen. Henry W. Halleck is, at his own request, relieved from duty as General-in-chief, commanding the Armies of the United States."[40]

Two days later on March 12, 1864, General Orders No. 98 officially established the new military order. It relieved Halleck, placed Grant legally in command, appointed Sherman and McPherson, and provided insight into Halleck's new, yet familiar, role. "The headquarters of the army will be in Washington, and also with Lieutenant-General Grant in the field," the order ran. Halleck was "assigned to duty in Washington as Chief of Staff of the Army, under the direction of the Secretary of War and the lieutenant-general commanding. His orders will be obeyed and respected accordingly." Whether Grant, Lincoln, or Stanton came up with this new position is unclear, but it did keep Halleck in the forefront of the war effort and it set a precedent for modern army organization. Halleck became the link between the President and his generals, providing ideas and suggestions to both, explaining one side to the other, and freeing Grant from having to deal with administrative details that Halleck had mastered and enjoyed handling. Halleck could now administer without commanding, which is essentially what he had been doing since his arrival in Washington in July 1862.[41]

Lincoln did not let Halleck go without offering some kind words about him. "The President desires to express his approbation and thanks," the General Orders stated, "for the able and zealous manner in which the arduous and responsible duties of that position have been performed." This was a most kind statement, but in private Lincoln was much more critical of his long-time general-in-chief. Once before, when asked why he kept Halleck in command, despite all the opposition to him, Lincoln lamely replied that "he was Halleck's friend because nobody else was." Now he said that Halleck had acted as a true general-in-chief only up to the time of John Pope's defeat at Second Bull Run in August 1862. After that, Lincoln lamented, "he . . . shrunk from responsibility wherever it was possible."

Lincoln saw Halleck's collapse better than anyone because he was there when it happened. Still, he kept him in command until he could find someone who could effectively replace him. Lincoln was happy to see the decisive Grant supplant the tentative Halleck.[42]

Private and public reaction to Halleck's new position was mixed. As always, Adam Gurowski was critical. "Mr. Lincoln cannot spare his pet, who has wound himself around Lincoln's heart," he said. Despite assurances that "Halleck will do no more mischief," Gurowski predicted that "he will find an outlet, and in some way or other repeat his former accursed tricks. I am certain." The New York businessman George Templeton Strong thought the change was "judicious," while the *New York Times* said there was "no officer in the army . . . who is less ambitious, and more ready to serve in any capacity, so that he can serve his country." One of Halleck's military aides agreed: "My chief is to be '*Chief of Staff of the Army*,' or in other words to remain the scapegoat for other people's blunders and interference. People may abuse him as they like, but his whole course has shown a disregard of self interest and devotion to the cause." Most amazing of all, the Mexican minister to Washington wrote his home government about "a vague rumor that Major General Halleck would be proposed as a candidate for the Democratic nomination."[43]

Halleck himself was pleased with the new military hierarchy. "Although I would have preferred my old army in the west, both for my own reputation and from personal feeling, I am perfectly willing to labor wherever the Prest, Secty of War & Genl Grant decide I can be most useful," he wrote. Since Grant was going to be out in the field, "someone must be here to attend to the vast amount of military administrative duty." And then, in an absolutely candid declaration of his long-held attitude, he said: "Although I am to perform the same duties as before, the responsibility of *deciding* upon plans of campaigns & movements of armies must hereafter rest on the shoulders of others. It will be my business to advise, and *theirs* to decide." In making this statement, Halleck's sense of relief was palpable. Members of Grant's staff, worried about Halleck's undercutting his former subordinate, were pleasantly surprised to see that he "manifested complete subordination to his new commander." Adam Badeau later remembered that Halleck "indeed seemed glad to be relieved from the cares and responsibilities of supreme command." Joseph Hooker ridiculed him for this attitude. He said Halleck now became like the man who got married but did not sleep with his wife.[44]

Indeed, Halleck had finally found the military position that he was best suited for, and that his former West Point professor Dennis Hart Mahan had recommended him for early in the war. As chief of staff, he would continue to handle the administration that he believed was essential for any army's success. He would also continue to look at the war from a broad strategic point of view. He would make suggestions, as he always had, but he no longer had to worry about giving orders. That was now in Grant's hands, and Halleck could properly avoid issuing them. In the East, Grant would directly order Meade and his Army of the Potomac, while in the West, Sherman needed little guidance. Grant, Sherman, and Halleck, three as unlikely compatriots as one could imagine, became the new Union Army leadership team. In their hands they held Lincoln's hopes for victory.

10

Chief of Staff under Grant

THE FORMER commanding general of the U.S. Army and now its first chief of staff did not have to move from his office or even experience a change in routine. He remained in Washington as an intermediary between the administration and the army's other generals. He continued to handle the military's administrative details, he kept the supplies and men flowing, and he provided explanations to generals about what the politicians were saying, while telling the political leaders what the military leaders were doing. As one historian has phrased it, his office "became a grand clearing house in the final year of the war."[1]

Halleck assumed his new title, convinced that he had done well as commanding general. In his final report to the Secretary of War, he argued that under his tenure, the successes of the Union had outweighed its failures. He insisted that the nation had made great progress in the war, implying that his leadership was responsible. "We have repelled every attempt of the enemy to invade the loyal States, and have rescued from his domination Kentucky and Tennessee, a portion of Alabama and Mississippi, and the greater part of Arkansas and Louisiana and restored the free navigation of the Mississippi River. . . . The extent of country thus recaptured and occupied by our armies is as large as France or Austria, or the entire peninsula of Spain and Portugal, and twice as large as Great Britain, or Prussia, or Italy." His report elicited varied responses. The *New York Times* thought he was too hard on his subordinates, without admitting his own mistakes. The legal scholar John C. Gray considered the report to be the mark of "a man of ability and of sense" but not of "military genius." A foreign publication, the *Military Zeitung* of Vienna, on the other hand, praised him and suggested that the victories in the West were the result of his leadership while the failures in the East were due to Fighting Joe Hooker's ignoring him.[2]

Echoing the optimism of his formal report, Halleck privately believed that 1864 would be another successful year for him and the Union cause, if the nation could only avoid "the interference of political combinations & political intrigues." "I sometimes feel sick, almost to dispair [*sic*] at what I see & hear daily," he said. "Patriotism seems to be swallowed up in personal ambition & selfishness." Politicians were appointing other politicians to key military posts, and these blunderers were hurting the war effort. If only professionals like him were given free rein, he insisted, Union success would be ensured.[3]

Halleck praised only two generals. He viewed Grant as an effective leader, no doubt, he thought, because of his own guidance. He felt the same way about Sherman; after all he had nursed his former California antagonist during the time of Sherman's depression early in the war, and Sherman was now a successful general. If the politicians would allow Grant and Sherman (with Halleck's advice) to run this war, all would be well. Halleck had to realize that his relationship with Grant was crucial to the war effort. Lincoln, Stanton, and the other political leaders were ready to hand over the reins of military leadership to Grant, but the conqueror from the western theater had to prove his mettle as commander of all the Union armies. His task was not only to defeat Robert E. Lee in Virginia, but also to coordinate the rest of the war effort and bring the entire conflict to a successful conclusion. Since Grant had decided to make his headquarters with George G. Meade's Army of the Potomac, he had to depend on Halleck back in Washington to take care of all the administrative details that he and the Secretary of War had no time for. He also had to be sure that Halleck was his defender in Washington's political circles. Grant had to trust Halleck to follow his orders implicitly, provide good advice where necessary, and be his faithful alter ego in the seat of Union power.

For this arrangement to work, Grant had to be certain that Halleck understood who was in charge; he dealt with this issue quickly. As soon as he took over, he told Halleck he "desire[d]" the specific movement of a number of troops in the Deep South, and he let it be known that he would not tolerate it if Rosecrans got any more soldiers since he already had more than enough. He sent a steady stream of such letters, telling Halleck what he wanted. He received, in return, messages indicating that these orders would be carried out "as you direct." Halleck also let other commanders know that it was not he but "General Grant [who] determines where their commands are to go." Halleck showed immediately that he felt unburdened and eager to allow Grant to give the orders, thus quickly putting Grant's mind at ease.[4]

Halleck always felt free to offer Grant advice, but he did so carefully. For example, he recommended the timing for certain troop movements and also urged Grant "to prevent officers from corresponding" with politicians "on military affairs, without going through the proper military channels." Grant reacted well to Halleck's suggestions, not always agreeing with them but always replying courteously. He frequently asked Halleck's advice too, as when he sought Halleck's views about who would make a good commander for a new military division Grant proposed to establish in the Trans-Mississippi West. The two men recognized their distinct roles, and they acted accordingly. The relationship was militarily efficient from the start.[5]

Despite that, rumors began to circulate, in the newspapers and elsewhere, that Grant, Stanton, and Halleck were actually at each other's throats. Perhaps the story got out that Grant had suggested that Old Brains go to Louisiana to replace Nathaniel Banks, though only temporarily. A comment Lincoln made about Halleck must certainly have gotten out, too, and helped fuel the gossip. The President told his secretary that Halleck was "little more . . . than a first-rate clerk." Halleck heard all the rumors about his alleged problems with Grant and Stanton, and he may have heard about Lincoln's comment too. He told Sherman and Lieber, both of whom admired him, that the talk about supposed problems with the commanding general and Secretary of War was "all bosh!" "Not the slightest foundation for such malicious statements. There has not been the slightest disagreement upon any point whatever." His relations with Grant, he said, were "not only friendly and pleasant, but cordial." One of Halleck's aides supported his boss. "They are earnestly working together to carry on the war," Robert N. Scott said. Grant had "all the honor and power of being General in Chief," while "the administrative responsibilities of that position remain[ed] on the shoulders of 'Old Brains.'" Halleck and his staff were pleased with this arrangement.[6]

Halleck proved his loyalty to Grant, a novice in the capital's politics, by sharing his knowledge of Washington. Like Halleck, Grant did not think much of Nathaniel Banks, then commanding in New Orleans, and wanted to fire him. Halleck agreed but pointed out to Grant some major political problems with sacking him. "General Banks is a personal friend of the President, and has strong political supporters in and out of Congress."

These attachments would keep Lincoln from acting, unless Grant made "a definite request" that Banks be removed "as a military necessity." Then Lincoln, if he was convinced, would "have something in a definite shape to fall back upon as his justification." Grant appreciated this advice and pulled back. He regularly recognized Halleck's political insights and respected them.[7]

When it came to fighting the war, however, Grant showed little such deference. On his way to Washington, Grant had conferred with Sherman, and the two men had coordinated their plans for the coming year, not asking for any input from Halleck. Grant would move against Lee in Virginia, and Sherman would simultaneously go after Joseph E. Johnston in Georgia, thus preventing the two major Confederate armies from reinforcing each other. At the same time, Grant wanted other Union armies to be on the move too. He understood that the best way to utilize the Union's manpower superiority was to keep the Confederates under pressure everywhere. Lincoln was thrilled with the plan because he saw in it his "old suggestion so constantly made and as constantly neglected, to Buell & Halleck, et. al. [early in the war], to move at once upon the enemy's whole line so as to bring into action to our advantage our great superiority in numbers." Halleck offered no opposition now.[8]

Then, in early May 1864, Grant began fighting Lee in Virginia, while Sherman went after Joe Johnston in Georgia, both men scrupulously keeping Halleck informed of their movements, while Stanton nervously watched. Meanwhile, Nathaniel Banks's Army of the Gulf was to begin moving on Mobile, Benjamin Butler's Army of the James was to push up the peninsula toward Richmond, and Franz Sigel was to campaign in the Shenandoah Valley. Grant fought bloody battles with Lee in Virginia's Wilderness, while Sherman fought a flanking war against Johnston between Chattanooga and Atlanta, both Federal generals pushing their opponents back. Unfortunately for the Union cause, Banks, Butler, and Sigel were not nearly so successful, and all eventually had to be replaced with more aggressive and competent commanders. But in contrast to their behavior during the war's earlier years, the Union armies were now taking the fight to the Confederates rather than simply reacting to southern actions. Grant best expressed the new Union determination when he said, "I shall take no backward steps" and "propose[d] to fight it out on this line if it takes all summer."[9] The days of short bursts of intensive warfare followed by long periods of rest and resupply were over. Grant and Sherman now made the Civil War one seemingly never-ending battle.

Such constant combat put a great deal of pressure on Halleck to keep

Grant, Sherman, and all the other generals supplied. He had to "wright [*sic*] & sign all confidential official papers" regarding military movements. Day after day, he labored. "Either from over work or rheumatism my right hand has been at times for the last few weeks very sore," he complained. "To organize & send forward so many troops, with horses, forage, provisions, ammunition & transportation, & to bring away & provide for so many wounded . . . keeps me pretty busy. Moreover, while Genl Grant is in the field I have to attend to all the business of the Armies in the West & South." He had very little "leisure time," he concluded wistfully. Stanton, meanwhile, kept the public informed by sending reports to General John A. Dix in New York, but also sending them, at the same time, to the Associated Press for publication.[10]

As always, Elizabeth Halleck and Harry spent extended periods of time with her family in New York; and when George W. Cullum was away on assignment, Halleck lived alone in the house he leased in Georgetown. When the family returned home from New York in June 1864, Harry caught a bad case of the measles, causing his parents "considerable anxiety." As spring turned into summer, the heat and humidity of Washington grew unbearable. "You complain of the thermometer at 86," Halleck wrote Francis Lieber in New York: "We have had it 96° here in-doors & 118° in the sun!" None of this did anything to improve Halleck's normally acerbic public persona. Charles Francis Adams Jr., with the approval of Grant, approached Halleck one day about an idea for finding mounts for a horseless cavalry unit. The reception he received from Halleck was blunt: "In about one minute he signified an emphatic disapproval of me and of my plan," Adams said, "and of General Grant and of everything else, and concluded an emphatic statement that he wouldn't give me a horse, if he had his own way, or without a positive order, by slamming his door in my face."[11]

Despite such typical brusqueness, there were those who still found redeeming qualities in Halleck. The journalist and soldier Charles G. Halpine told Halleck's friend Cullum, who fed the *New York Herald* reporter information, that he considered Halleck to be "'the greatest man by all odds that he (the writer) has yet met in the public life of this country." Had Halleck gone back to California when Grant arrived in Washington, Halpine believed he would have gained the 1864 Democratic presidential nomination. Grant was also pleased with Halleck. "The promptness and rapidity with which you have forwarded re-enforcements have contributed largely to the feeling of confidence inspired in our men and to break down that of the enemy." Lest Halleck's head grow too big, however, his old nemesis Adam Gurowski continued to ridicule him "as utterly unfit for the duties of a chief-of-staff, or rather a general *du jour.*" Gurowski concluded that "his unfitness is intensified by his ill-will and envy."[12]

Grant and Sherman continued to press the enemy, and it became evident that both were indeed going to have to fight it out all summer; there was not going to be a swift victory. The Grant-Lee conflict in the Wilderness was a bloodbath for both sides, while Sherman seemed unable to flank Johnston successfully, no matter what he tried. Yet, Sherman pointed out, "one of my chief objects being to give full employment to Johnston, it makes but little difference where he is, so [long as] he is not on his way to Virginia."[13] Grant and Sherman were pressing forward, but they had not yet achieved the victory that the public was expecting. In Washington, Halleck remained pleased with Sherman's progress, but he was growing increasingly worried about Grant.

As early as the third week of the Union campaign in Virginia that May of 1864, Halleck reminded Grant that "every man we can collect should be hurled against Lee, wherever he may be, as his army, not Richmond, is the true objective of this campaign. . . . I therefore propose to send to you everything I can get without regard to the calls of others, until you direct otherwise." Echoing words he had spoken during the days of the McClellan-Pope controversy in 1862, Halleck told Grant that Butler's army was part of Grant's immediate command. "I do not like these divided commands, with the enemy intervening," he said. Grant agreed and ordered all of Butler's troops except those needed to defend City Point, Virginia, to march to him.[14]

Halleck grew more apprehensive when Grant crossed the James River in June and moved toward Petersburg, worried that Lee was now between Grant and Washington. "I cannot write just now on military matters," he told Lieber with obvious worry, "for I don't like the appearance of things." This time, Halleck's comments did not budge Grant. The commanding general told his staffers decisively: "We can defend Washington best by keeping Lee so occupied that he cannot detach enough troops to capture it." His siege of Petersburg, however, forced him to have to concentrate the Union effort on the war in Virginia and Georgia. He put a halt to all other movements that were "not directly in co-operation with these moves." Halleck obediently passed this order along to other commanders, pleased that, at least, Grant was concentrating his effort. Halleck had not given up on his 1840s core belief.[15]

In June 1864, Confederates Jubal Early and John C. Breckinridge defeated Union General David Hunter at Lynchburg, Virginia, surprising the

Union's forces. Then Early and his 14,000-man corps followed Hunter north and chased Franz Sigel and his 5,000 men into Maryland, arriving at Frederick, only forty miles from Washington, on July 9. This movement confused the Union leadership. Halleck at first thought that Early was Confederate raider John Mosby, while Grant received reports from a deserter that Early's group was Richard Ewell's corps. Grant did not believe the Confederate activity posed a major problem, however, and Halleck agreed. "I think your operations should not be interfered with by sending troops here," he wrote Grant. But if Grant wanted to send some dismounted cavalry to Washington, that would be fine because "most of our troops are not of a character suitable for the field (invalids and militia)." Most veterans of the city's defenses had earlier been sent to Grant for his offensive. Two and a half hours later, Halleck sent a more worried telegram. He did want troops from Grant's army to defend Washington and Baltimore. Grant immediately sent to Washington some 3,000 dismounted cavalry and to Baltimore James Ricketts's 6,000-man infantry division from Horatio Wright's VI Corps, "followed by the balance of the corps, if necessary . . . to crush out and destroy any force the enemy have sent north."[16]

Grant expected similar promptness from the military men and civilians in Washington and Baltimore. He demanded the destruction of Early's force and called for another Union raid up the Shenandoah Valley to destroy supplies and communications. Halleck, meanwhile, blamed David Hunter and Franz Sigel for their incompetence in allowing this mess to develop, as usual assessing no blame to himself. He asked the chief engineer in Washington to provide him with a report on the capital's defenses and learned, to his dismay, that the fortifications were in horrible shape, and there were not enough soldiers to man them properly. There was also a dire need for heavy artillery units because the militia manning the guns in Washington "scarcely know how to load or fire the guns." Halleck had by now convinced himself that both Early and Breckinridge were coming, the raid probably being "larger than we first supposed."[17]

At this juncture, Halleck pointed to Grant. He believed he was wrong to cross the James River and thus allow Lee to be positioned between the Union Army and Washington. He told Francis Lieber: "I predicted this [raid] to Genl Grant before he crossed the James River, and that Lee would play the same game of shuttle-cock between him & Washington that he did with McClellan."[18] Halleck, who had demonstrated such loyalty to and admiration for Grant, now compared him to the discredited McClellan. Grant, like McClellan, was violating the traditional rules of warfare that Halleck's writings had long supported, and he was thus committing a cardinal military error. Old Brains knew that warfare had changed in this conflict, and he had long been calling on his armies to live off the land and punish secessionists, but he did not believe that other basic military principles could be ignored except at a commander's peril. Again Halleck was beginning to have doubts about U. S. Grant as a strategist and a commander.

Then Halleck received some good news. Lew Wallace, the general whose reputation had never recovered from his marching the wrong way during the Shiloh battle in 1862, telegraphed Halleck on July 7 that at Monocacy, Maryland, he had "handsomely repulsed" the raiders. Just a few hours later, however, Wallace was not so sure and said that he would "endeavor to hold this place until the force of the enemy is fully developed." Indeed, the real battle of Monocacy did not take place until July 9, and it resulted in a victory for the Confederates. Yet Wallace had delayed the Confederate horsemen long enough to give Halleck the time to prepare Washington.[19]

At first, Halleck had ridiculed the reports of Wallace's defeat, telling Grant to consider "the character of the source," the newspapers. Later on the night of July 9, however, Wallace admitted his defeat and reported that he was "retreating with a foot-sore and battered and half demoralized column." Within seventeen minutes of receiving this telegram, Halleck consulted with the President, who instructed him to order Wallace to "rally" his "forces and make every possible effort to retard the enemy's march on Baltimore." Meanwhile Halleck called on Grant to send the rest of VI Corps to Washington, and Grant immediately gave that order and even expressed willingness to come there himself if Lincoln thought "it advisable."[20]

Everywhere Halleck looked, he found reason to worry. The telegraph went silent, and trains stopped running into and out of the capital. Unionists from Maryland were rushing into the capital's protective fortifications, and an unmilitary-looking collection of militia and convalescents, the city's sole defenders, just milled around. Government clerks began to bring weapons to work. The capital of the United States prepared for what seemed to be an imminent attack. Stanton even ordered Lincoln and his wife out of their summer residence at the Soldier's Home because it was dangerously close to the city's fortifications. An admiral, on his own, prepared a boat for the President's quick removal, should that become necessary. The nonrelated resignation of Secretary of the Treasury Salmon P. Chase intensified the city's panic and uncertainty, while the obvious glee of Confederate sympathizers was chilling.[21]

Halleck had his own fort at his Georgetown home, what one historian described as "a guard of invalid soldiers and nightly bugle-blowing of tattoo and taps." From there and his office near the War Department, he began organizing all the available manpower within the capital, calling on the Signal Corps, Cavalry Bureau, and Navy Department for riflemen. He also summoned convalescent personnel from Philadelphia and army troops from New York. The more he tried to mobilize the city's defense, the more pessimistic he became. "What can we do with such forces in the field against a column of 20,000 veterans?" he asked Grant.[22]

Halleck's mounting panic about what he believed was the inevitability of Jubal Early's capture of Washington increased the concern of the city's political leadership. On July 10 Lincoln telegraphed Grant: "Gen. Halleck says we have absolutely no force here fit to go to the field." Wallace's and Hunter's troops were of little use and "what we shall get in from Penn. & N.Y will scarcely [be] worth counting." Lincoln told Grant to hold on to the territory he had gained in Virginia and then come to Washington. If he moved promptly, Lincoln thought (no doubt on the basis of Halleck's advice) that Grant could completely dispose of the Confederate raiders. Halleck and the President clearly believed that only Grant could save the day.[23]

Washingtonians recognized Halleck's inadequacy, and criticism was rampant. Gideon Welles said the chief of staff was "in a perfect maze, bewildered, without intelligent decision or self-reliance." Adam Gurowski agreed. "All the incapacity, all the blunderings are exclusively Halleck's work." He was nothing but Lincoln's "military clown." Lew Wallace reported a similar concern in Baltimore. "The panic here is heavy and increasing," he said. Already worried about Washington, Halleck did not appreciate the added burden of Baltimore. When a unit-less brigadier general telegraphed him from New York offering his services, Halleck vented his frustration: "We have five times as many generals here as we want, but are greatly in need of privates. Anyone volunteering in that capacity will be thankfully received."[24]

Halleck scurried around posting whatever troops he could muster and waited for the reinforcements from Grant to arrive. On July 11, Jubal Early closed in on lightly manned Fort Stevens, part of the thirty-seven miles of fortifications encircling Washington. Early's men, having fought at Monocacy on July 9, were exhausted, and found the terrible heat and dusty roads hard to bear. Instead of pressing his tired men forward and overrunning the weak defenses immediately, Early rested his soldiers and gave his sharpshooters free rein. The few Union defenders simply hunkered down. Adam Gurowski, ready as always to chastise Halleck, blamed him for the lack of Union response. Fort Stevens had become "the object of fashionable promenade" for Washington's elite, Gurowski groused, and Halleck did not seem to want to disturb this social frivolity with military action.[25]

Fortunately for the Union cause, Horatio Wright's VI Corps arrived that same afternoon and immediately entered Fort Stevens and the surrounding fortifications. Some time that afternoon of July 11 and the next day, Abraham Lincoln himself appeared, each time exposing himself to enemy fire and being warned to keep his head down. General Wright warned Lincoln with the respect due a President, but Captain Oliver Wendell Holmes, Wright's aide and a later Supreme Court justice, showed no such restraint. "Get down, you fool," he allegedly yelled at Lincoln, and this time the President obeyed.[26] There is no evidence that Halleck joined Lincoln at Fort Stevens or visited any of the other forts encircling Washington. He apparently remained behind his desk near a telegraph ticker, ever the administrative general even when the enemy was at the gates.

Early planned to make his attack on the morning of July 12, but he noted at dawn the presence of veteran reinforcements in the Union forts. He hesitated, and the Federals then attacked him instead. By dawn of the next day, he was retreating back to Virginia. "Washington is now pretty safe," Halleck told Grant, "unless the forces in some part of the entrenchments, and they are by no means reliable, being made up of all kind of fragments, should give away before they can be re-enforced from other points." Halleck remained worried and pessimistic even as Early withdrew.[27]

There was general unhappiness throughout the city about the military response to the Early raid, and the lack of an effective pursuit of the enemy increased the anger. Secretary of War Edwin Stanton became so upset at the lack of command coordination that he had Charles A. Dana, one of his assistants, write Grant insisting that he become more deeply involved in the capital's defense. David Hunter was commanding troops in the Shenandoah Valley; C. C. Augur was in charge of Washington's defenses; Horatio Wright commanded his VI Corps, which had come to the rescue; Quincy A. Gillmore had temporary command of some other recently arrived troops; and Lew Wallace was in command in Baltimore. "But there was no head to the whole," Dana concluded. In his letter to Grant, Dana said: Mere "advice or suggestions from you will not be sufficient. General Halleck will not give orders except as he receives them; the President will give none, and until you direct positively and explicitly what is to be done, everything will go on in the deplorable and fatal way in which it has gone on for the last week." "History has not on record military conduct so below any honor or manhood as that of Halleck in this campaign," Gurowski wrote in his diary.[28]

Early's departure thus brought Halleck no immediate relief from criticism. Indeed, he and the Secretary of the Navy got into an argument over what had happened. Viewing a map together and discussing the Confederate retreat, Welles pointed out to Halleck that he did not think the Confederate leader had ever concentrated his forces. "Halleck asked by what authority I said that. There was harshness and spite in his tone," Welles reported. "He said he did not think I had heard so from any military man who knows anything about it." As always, Halleck grew petulant when someone tried to tell him how he had performed his duties. Civilians did not understand military matters, he believed, and they had no right to air their opinions about them. As he had reprimanded Sherman in California with similar words, so he now reproved Welles. He could see no validity in the Secretary of the Navy's comments and considered them insulting.[29]

The major criticism of Halleck, however, came from another member of Lincoln's cabinet, Postmaster General Montgomery Blair. Blair was enraged because the Confederate raiders had burned his house in Silver Spring, Maryland, just outside Washington. According to an equally furious Halleck, Blair said that "the officers in command about Washington are poltroons; that there were not more than 500 rebels on the Silver Spring road, and we had 1,000,000 of men in arms; that it was a disgrace; that General Wallace was in comparison with them far better, as he would at least fight." Halleck demanded to know whether Lincoln agreed with this statement, and said that if he did, he should dismiss the guilty officers from the army; if not, then "the slanderer should be dismissed from the Cabinet." Lincoln was not impressed. Of course, he did not agree with Blair's statement, he said, but he thought it was "said in a moment of vexation at so severe a loss." Besides, he reminded his chief of staff: "I propose continuing to be myself the judge as to when a member of the Cabinet shall be dismissed."[30]

To add to Halleck's problems, newspapers were trumpeting the publication of his translation of the four volumes of Jomini's biography of Napoleon. The timing allowed people to agree with Adam Gurowski that Halleck had been so busy with the translation that he had not paid sufficient attention to the Confederates, thus making the raid on Washington possible. General Benjamin Butler, angry at Halleck's treatment of him, put it most harshly of all: "At a moment when every true man is laboring to his utmost, when the days ought to be forty hours long, General Halleck is translating French books at nine cents a page; and, sir, if you should put those nine cents in a box and shake them up, you would form a clear idea of General Halleck's soul."[31]

The most significant, though most indirect, criticism of Halleck came from Grant himself. When rumors of yet another Confederate raid on Washington surfaced, Grant called for a more united response. "It is absolutely necessary that some one in Washington should give orders and make dispositions of all the forces within reach of the line of the Potomac." He did not suggest Halleck for the job, however, nor did Halleck offer his services. It was Lincoln who made that decision. Although Stanton now believed that Halleck should be replaced, Lincoln had the Secretary of War put Halleck in command of Washington's defenses. The public expressed no great boost in confidence as a result, Congressman Ben Wade insultingly expressing the widespread attitude in the nation's capital when he said: *"Put Halleck in the command of 20,000 men and he will not scare three setting geese from their nests."*[32]

Halleck continued to believe that the raid was all Grant's fault. He told Sherman: *"Entre nous,* I fear Grant has made a fatal mistake in putting himself south of James River. . . . south of Richmond he opens the capital and the whole North to rebel raids. Lee can at any time detach 30,000 or 40,000 men without our knowing it till we are actually threatened." To his credit, Halleck repeated the same criticism to Grant directly: "While your army is south of the James River and Lee's between you and Washington," Lee will be able to send raid upon raid against Washington, West Virginia, Pennsylvania, and Maryland. It was therefore necessary to keep Wright's VI Corps in Washington as a defense force. "In my opinion raids will be renewed as soon as he [Wright] leaves." As always, however, Halleck left it up to Grant. "You are the judge whether or not a large enough movable force shall be kept here to prevent them." True to his character, Halleck refused to press Grant to agree. He would leave the decision up to him, thus avoiding any responsibility for what might ensue. Halleck would do what he was told to do, but he would not take any initiative.[33]

A string of unfortunate events followed soon after. A Rebel cavalry force under John McCausland, part of Early's valley army, entered Chambersburg, Pennsylvania, demanding $500,000 in cash, allegedly in compensation for David Hunter's destructive campaign in the Shenandoah Valley. When the city refused, the Confederates torched it. Meanwhile, Grant's troops dug a tunnel under Confederate lines at Petersburg and detonated a huge pile of explosives, creating a crater into which Union troops charged, only to be repulsed with huge losses. "It was the saddest affair I have witnessed in the war," Grant reported. During this same period, Sherman made a disastrous attack on Joe Johnston's Confederates at Kenesaw Mountain, and Union General James B. McPherson, Grant's and Sherman's favorite general officer, died during an unsuccessful Confederate attack in Atlanta. When Sherman declined to give McPherson's former command to Joseph Hooker, Fighting Joe became so upset that he resigned command of the XX Army Corps.[34] What looked so promising for the Union in the spring seemed to be unraveling completely in the summer. Grant and Sherman seemed to be going the way of McClellan and other unsuccessful Union generals, and Halleck was once more doing little except complaining in private.

In the face of setbacks, Grant did not remain as passive as Halleck and other generals once had. Upset with the way Jubal Early's corps had chased David Hunter's and Franz Sigel's forces out of the Shenandoah Valley to the gates of Washington, Grant ordered a change in command. With Lincoln's support, he sent Philip Sheridan to the valley, telling Halleck to order him to "put himself south of the enemy and follow him to the death." Halleck hesitated because of uncertainty about Hunter's and Sheridan's command responsibilities in the valley, but then he suddenly remembered that he did not make decisions; as chief of staff, he only implemented them. He wrote Grant: "I must beg to be excused from deciding questions which lawfully and properly belong to your office. . . . I await your orders, and shall strictly carry them out, whatever they may be." Grant once again ordered Sheridan to take over from Hunter, and this time it was done.[35]

Grant was clearly unhappy with Halleck's reluctance to remove Hunter, as he was with the way Old Brains had dealt with the challenge of Jubal Early. He was similarly distressed when Halleck warned him that there was going to be "a forcible resistance to the draft" in the northern states, and this might "require the withdrawal of a very considerable [number] of troops from the field." Grant brushed aside this suggestion. If such danger really existed, "our loyal Governors ought to organize the militia at once to resist it." Grant was quickly reaching the end of the road with Halleck, or so it seemed. He wrote Stanton, who earlier wanted to fire Halleck, that Old Brains might be just the person to fill a vacant post on the Pacific Coast. Grant tried to put the best face on the suggestion by saying that this region needed "a commanding officer of firmness enough to do his duty in spite of opposition, but without interference with civil rights and without trying to enforce his own peculiar opinions upon the community." He knew from experience that Halleck was just such a man, good at nonintrusive administration, but not capable of independent forceful thinking. Against all odds, then, Halleck stayed on as chief of staff. Obviously neither Lincoln, nor Stanton, nor Grant thought much of his military behavior, but they did not believe the time was ripe for such a momentous change.[36]

Grant was frustrated with the stalemate around Petersburg, and Sherman seemed equally stymied before Atlanta. The two major Union armies were going nowhere that summer of 1864, and Union patience was wearing thin. This would have been bad enough in normal times, but the nation was undergoing a presidential election. Abraham Lincoln was seeking reelection, running against the Democratic candidate, former General George B. McClellan, who was running on a peace, or Copperhead, platform with which he himself disagreed. Halleck's friend Francis Lieber was "very, very gloomy" about what he called "the shameless, disgraceful and treasonable proclamation of the McClellan convention." There were only two things that might salvage the situation now, Lieber concluded, "a telling [military] victory, or rather the taking of Richmond, and Mr. Lincoln's withdrawal." Halleck hoped things were not that bad, but then he proceeded to agree with Lieber about the danger of an antiwar candidate. "Although Mr Lincoln has not the qualities suited to times like the present," he said, "it seems to me that no man having the interest of the country at heart should hesitate between him & the copperhead candidate." Halleck concluded "that McClellan's election would lose us all we have fought for." Although he had been a Democrat all his life, Halleck vowed that he could not support McClellan. Halleck was so worried about the effect of McClellan's candidacy, in fact, that he sent the commander of the Northern Department, Samuel P. Heintzelman, to Chicago to confer with Democratic party luminaries there. Heintzelman reported that these leaders told him that there would "be no organized resistance to the [military] draft," a statement that Halleck found somewhat reassuring.[37]

Halleck was greatly relieved to learn that Admiral David Farragut had won an important naval victory in Mobile Bay on August 23, 1864. This was soon followed by Sherman's news on September 3 that "Atlanta is ours, and fairly won."[38] Sherman's army had forced John Bell Hood to abandon the city, producing a victory that was a beacon of good news in a time of dark discouragement. The war would not have to be a stalemate forever; the Union Army was capable of winning important victories and ending the war. The antiwar message of the peace Democrats suddenly rang hollow.

Halleck was ecstatic at the triumphal news and at Sherman's effusive thanks: "I confess I owe you all I now enjoy of fame." Halleck had saved him from "a perfect 'slough of despond'" back in 1861 and opened the way for his future success. Halleck responded that he did not "hesitate to say that your campaign has been the most brilliant of the war." He also came to believe that "McClellan would have swallowed the Chicago platform entire, had it not been for our success at Atlanta and Mobile." Then he rejoiced at "another splendid victory announced from Sheridan at Fishers Hill!" When he, Stanton, and Lincoln discussed Grant's latest moves against Lee, Halleck became optimistic about Grant. "He would not be surprised," he said, "if he [Grant] got either Richmond or Petersburg by the maneuver. . . . Nearly all the western Generals that I selected & put forward," he told his friend Cullum, "have turned out Trumps," he said exuberantly. "I don't give myself so much credit for the selection as I do for impressing all with the idea that if the[y] earned promotion, and if they did not earn it, they would get no assistance from me. This is the only principle which can make good generals & good officers." As ever, Halleck complimented himself on inaction.[39]

Halleck was now so confident of Lincoln's success in the election that he opposed the use of field troops to prevent violence at the polls. He now agreed with Grant that "local authorities [could] settle their own local troubles." The recent military successes meant that "Mr Lincoln will surely be reelected," that is, he added, "if he will only hold still, & not meddle in diplomacy & military matters till after the election." Halleck was thrilled when Lincoln's election became certain. "What do you think of McClellan's chances now?" he jokingly asked Cullum. "Its quite safe to guess who'll be president, after [the] election. I understand the price of *copper* has fallen very much within the last two days." Even amidst this good news, however, he managed to find a reason for self-pity. "As election news is getting stale, I suppose every body will soon be impatient for something from the army."[40]

People did not have to wait long for exciting war news. On November 16, Sherman and an army of 60,000 men left Atlanta and began the fabled march to the sea with its war of property destruction. Halleck supported Sherman's policy of sending away Atlanta's populace and turning the city into a military post. He also encouraged Sherman's destructive war by complimenting him that "your mode of conducting war is just the thing we now want. We have tried the kid-glove policy long enough." He had "endeavored," he said, "to impress these views upon our commanders for the last two years. You are almost the only one who has properly applied them." He disapproved of destroying private property, but "approve[d] of taking or destroying whatever may serve as supplies to us or to the enemy's army."[41]

Meanwhile, George H. Thomas and John M. Schofield prepared to face the Confederate army of John Bell Hood that Sherman left behind when he marched to the sea. As Sherman continued his destructive march through Georgia, Schofield defeated Hood severely at Franklin, Tennessee, on November 30, 1864, gaining a three-to-one advantage in casualties and then falling back to join Thomas at Nashville. Sherman had so completely cut himself off from the newspaper correspondents he despised that no one knew where he was and how he was doing. Unlike some, Halleck was not worried, and once again he gave himself credit. "I have no fears of him. He has my old army of the west, which was taught to move mud or no mud, & with or without baggage." When Sherman arrived at the gates of Savannah, Halleck was once again ecstatic. "I congratulate you on your splendid success. . . . Your march will stand out prominently as the great one of this great war."[42]

The news from the rest of the West, however, was not as good. George H. Thomas's campaign against John Bell Hood's Army of Tennessee at the gates of Nashville was still in doubt. Thomas was a Virginian who had maintained his loyalty to the Union when secession came, as a result becoming pariah in his own family. His war record had been admirable, highlighted by his stand near Chattanooga, which had gained him the nickname the Rock of Chickamauga. His men had then made a spectacular frontal attack, routing the Confederates at Chattanooga, and he had also played a major role in Sherman's Atlanta campaign. Thomas had the reputation of being a solid general on defense, but he often exasperated Sherman and Grant because of his deliberate movement, which gained him another nickname, Slow Trot. He did move slowly, but it could also be said that when he did move he moved well. Sherman was convinced that Thomas could more than handle Hood, and, after the war, he would even call Thomas one of the greatest generals of the Civil War.[43]

Considering his reputation, therefore, it was not surprising that Thomas did not undertake an immediate offensive. On November 9, 1864, a week before Sherman began his march to the sea, Thomas told Halleck that he would go forward only when he was sure he was ready. On November 27, after Sherman had already been marching for nearly two weeks, Thomas was still merely promising an offensive. On December 1, after Schofield's success at Franklin, Thomas worried about not having enough cavalry to match the Confederates, so he planned to delay any attack until he had all the necessary horsemen organized and ready to fight. Grant urged Halleck to send Thomas more troops, any soldiers from anywhere, because "now is the time to annihilate Hood's army." Halleck responded that "every available man" had already been sent to Thomas.[44]

Grant and Halleck impatiently communicated with each other while Thomas continued to offer excuses. "I have labored under many disadvantages since assuming the direction of affairs here," he insisted, though promising that "if I can perfect my arrangements I shall move against the advanced position of the enemy on the 7th instant." When Halleck answered his request for more horses by saying that he already had been sent a huge number, Thomas insisted that most of those animals had been lost in battle or died from disease. He could not attack until "General [James H.] Wilson can get together a sufficient cavalry force to protect my flanks." As this correspondence of delay went on between Thomas and Halleck, so reminiscent of earlier ones Halleck had had with McClellan, Buell, and Rosecrans, Grant grew increasingly irritated. He wanted action, not excuses. He ordered Halleck to send more Missouri troops to Thomas and then bluntly told his chief of staff: "If Thomas has not struck yet, he ought to be ordered to hand over his command to Schofield. There is no better man to repel an attack than Thomas, but I fear he is too cautious to ever take the initiative." Halleck would not hear it; this sounded too much like Grant hinting that he wanted Halleck to make a decision. "If you wish General Thomas relieved from [command], give the order," Halleck said. "No one here will, I think, interfere. The responsibility, however, will be yours." Grant should know, however, that no one in Washington was calling for Thomas's "removal."[45]

Once again, Grant quelled his initial impatience with Thomas and expressed willingness to give him another chance. Grant wrote Slow Trot himself and told Halleck to be sure that Thomas understood "the importance of immediate action." This was more like it. Halleck was willing to issue Grant's orders, but he was not going to take responsibility for making decisions himself. He minced no words in telling Thomas that "General Grant expresses much dissatisfaction at your delay," and if he waited for enough cavalry before he moved, he would soon find himself in the same position Rosecrans had occupied the previous year, "with so many animals that you cannot feed them." Thomas once more disagreed. He was sorry to hear of Grant's impatience, but he insisted that he was moving as fast as he could. If Grant ordered his firing, he would "submit without a murmur." And, by the way, he concluded, "A terrible storm of freezing rain has come on since daylight, which will render an attack impossible until it breaks."[46]

Before he had heard Thomas's latest excuse, Grant had decided that Slow Trot had to go and that Schofield should replace him. Halleck obediently prepared the order, and then Thomas's telegram about the ice storm arrived. Cautious as ever, Halleck wired Grant to learn if the order should still be issued. Reluctantly Grant gave in again, being "unwilling to do injustice to an officer who has done as much good service as General Thomas has." He was willing to give Thomas one more chance, so this time Halleck's intervention proved to be one of the most significant of his career. As the ice glistened in Nashville, Halleck and Thomas continued their debate over cavalry. But now, it was not horses but weather that Thomas said was keeping him immobile. "As soon as we have a thaw, I will attack Hood," he said, repeating the same promise on the next two days. Now it was Halleck who became irritated, telling Thomas how much damage he was doing to Grant's overall strategy. Thomas continued to insist that an earlier attack had been impossible "with any reasonable hope of success." In any case, the ice was disappearing, so he would attack the next day.[47]

He did. On December 15, Thomas drove Hood's army back and then shattered it the next day, forcing it to flee in disarray. Thomas began pursuing the demoralized Confederates, but as he encountered flooding rivers, he slowed down. Halleck urged "a hot pursuit." If Thomas could destroy or capture Hood's army, Sherman would be able to "entirely crush out the rebel military force in all the Southern States." With obvious irritation, Thomas reminded Halleck (and Grant, too) that Sherman had taken with him "the complete organizations of the Military Division of the Mississippi." Thomas insisted that he was doing all he could with what he had.[48]

George H. Thomas came as close to annihilating an army as any general did during the entire Civil War. The Confederate Army of Tennessee no longer existed as an effective fighting force. Yet Halleck and Grant were not satisfied. Thomas's ineffective pursuit of its tattered remnants and his desire to wait until the spring to continue his campaigning caused Halleck to recommend to Grant that he detach 20,000 men from Thomas's army for service elsewhere. "If Thomas was as active as Sherman," Halleck said, he would recommend his marching south and living off the land. "But I think Thomas entirely too slow to live on the country." Let him stay and defend that region, Halleck concluded. Grant said no. He ordered Halleck to "ready [Thomas] for active operations in the field." There was not going to be any winter quarters. Thomas agreed, but reluctantly: "I do believe that it is much the best policy to get well prepared before starting on an important campaign"; and he continued to call for new horses and to complain about the terrible winter roads as he conducted a reconnaissance of Hood's army into Mississippi.[49]

The controversy surrounding George H. Thomas at Nashville demonstrated how much the Union war effort and Halleck himself had changed during the war. Had this been 1862, Halleck would have agreed with Thomas about the need for careful preparation and would have viewed Grant's impatient insistence on quick action as an example of his lack of military knowledge. Now, instead of opposing Grant as he had at Forts Henry and Donelson in 1862, Halleck joined Grant in calling upon Thomas to stop preparing and get moving. Halleck the military theorist had thrown his book away. He was now supporting the kind of warfare that would earlier have been completely foreign to him. He supported Sherman's destructive war and Grant's war of annihilation. Nowhere to be seen were the maneuverings and entrenchments of the French theorist Antoine Henri Jomini and the West Point professor Dennis Hart Mahan. Even the recent General Orders No. 100 had faded out of view. The war experience had finally made Halleck into an aggressive warrior, willing to support the use of every means at the nation's disposal to bring the conflict to a successful conclusion. "Should you capture Charleston," he said to Sherman in mid-December 1864, "I hope that by some accident the place may be destroyed, and if a little salt should be sown upon its site it may prevent the growth of future crops of nullification and secession."[50] Yet Halleck did not want to make the decisions to put all these destructive forces into motion. That was Grant's job. His job was to shuffle telegrams and papers across his desk and transmit those decisions.

Meanwhile, Halleck tried to maintain some semblance of a personal life. With his wife and son regularly in New York City visiting family and with his close friend George W. Cullum now superintendent at West Point, he found his home in Georgetown lonely. He invited Francis Lieber to stay with him when he came to Washington, and he was extremely pleased when Lieber and his wife did so in mid-September 1864. He also tried hard to find a government position for Lieber: something in Washington, a lectureship at West Point, or a diplomatic post somewhere. When his own family returned in mid-October, the summer heat of Washington was still oppressive, and they suffered from it. So did he, as he battled his usual "attack of 'coryza' or hay cold" in September, so bad that "it affects my eyes so much that I can hardly see to write."[51]

He kept up a regular correspondence with Cullum and Lieber, nonetheless, sharing jokes and complaints and more serious intellectual discussions. He needled Cullum, a bachelor, about his alleged desire that young officers with pretty wives be assigned to West Point. This looked "very suspicious," Halleck laughed, adding later that the rumor was circulating that Cullum was especially happy to have a particular officer's wife back at West Point, "since the cold weather has set in." He expressed great pride in his son to his friend. Harry was having a wonderful time tending his pet goats and was thrilled to receive a package of books from Cullum. His "composition and hand-writing [were] decidedly improving," Halleck proudly pointed out, helped in no small degree by the fact that he was now attending school. When Cullum did not answer a thank-you note from Harry, Halleck reported that Harry "threatens to break off the correspondence in high dudgeon." Like father, like son.[52]

Halleck was obviously happy following Grant's successes. He matter-of-factly told another general who questioned one of the directives Halleck had sent: "You have the same discretion in executing orders communicated through me that I have in sending them." Yet he continued to question Grant's strategy in Virginia, astonishingly saying, once again, that Grant's "campaign is almost as great a failure as that of McClellan, so far as strategy is concerned." He believed, however, that Sherman's forthcoming movement through the Carolinas would help Grant's cause, and "Grant's bull-dog tenacity will do much to redeem his faults of strategy."[53]

Although no longer in command, Halleck remained a target of politicians who distrusted his influence. In late January 1865, the Radical Republican Representative Robert C. Schenck, a former Union army officer himself, introduced a resolution in the House of Representatives calling on the Secretary of War to inform the House precisely what Halleck's "duty or command" was and "whether he is drawing double rations." When Stanton answered that Halleck was chief of staff by Lincoln's order and that it was "the usage of the War Department to give to officers exercising command over two or more military departments the same allowances as to his subordinate who commands only a single military department," Shenck was unhappy with the answer. He had all the paperwork sent to the Committee on Military Affairs, where the possibility of censure died, but not before causing Halleck much irritation.[54]

Halleck was also summoned to appear before the Joint Committee on the Conduct of the War in mid-February 1865, to defend his role in the unsuccessful Red River campaign of General Nathaniel Banks. Former Attorney General Bates even found reason, at this distant time, to criticize

Halleck for some of his activities as commander in Missouri during the early years of the war. It seemed that Halleck had not gained any new support or stature since taking his position under U. S. Grant; he remained a target for those who disliked him personally or were critical of him professionally and of his command of the Union war effort.[55]

His excellent relationship with Sherman, however, brought him great satisfaction. Even though he refused to give orders to Sherman because that was Grant's job, he was pleased that his friend and admirer continued to ask his advice. His sincere congratulations after Sherman's victory at Atlanta and then after the completion of the march to the sea drew the men even closer together. Halleck privately criticized Sherman for letting Confederate General William Hardee's force escape from Savannah, but he conceded, "his campaign has been quite a success." He also offered some sensitive advice to Sherman in a "private and friendly way." He warned him that the Radical Republicans, unlike everyone else, who was praising his military accomplishments, were "decidedly disposed to make a point against you. I mean in regard to 'inevitable Sambo.' They say that you have manifested an almost *criminal* dislike to the negro [*sic*], and that you are not willing to carry out the wishes of the Government in regard to him, but repulse him with contempt!" Halleck said that these politicians believed that Sherman had prevented fugitive slaves from escaping, so he advised his friend to take some positive action to undercut such criticism.[56]

Sherman was most appreciative of Halleck's warning, but he vociferously denied all such accusations, insisting that the slaves would be the first to agree with him. "I do and will do the best I can for negroes, and feel sure that the problem is solving itself slowly and naturally. . . . I thank you for your kind hint and will heed it as far as appearances go." The war prevented any further discussion of this matter, Stanton's visit to Savannah and the praise for Sherman he heard from black leaders there apparently putting it all to rest.[57]

At the end of January 1865, Sherman began his march through the Carolinas, and Halleck once again gave him complete support. When Sherman asked Halleck to critique his plan before he plunged into the countryside, Halleck responded in detail that "I fully agree with you." In response to Francis Lieber's criticism of Sherman's techniques of destructive warfare, Halleck forthrightly defended him. He was "not a cruel man," Halleck said, and he was right to wage war as he did. South Carolina deserved special chastisement for starting the war. "She should be punished, & that sternly & severely," Halleck said. When in early March he admitted some concern for Sherman's safety, he quelled his anxiety by reminding himself, once again, that "I first organized that army & know it well." In his own mind, Halleck continued to share credit with Sherman for the latter's military successes.[58]

Like others, Halleck expressed concern about possible disruption of Lincoln's second inauguration in early March 1865, but he was happy to note that it "passed off well. Thanks to abundant preparations, we had no disturbance, no fires, no raids, or robberies." He spent the entire night and day on watch, so he "did not join in the proceedings," he told Lieber, his name not even being included among the many managers of the National Inaugural Ball. He did, however, attend the swearing-in, one reporter describing him as "smiling and happy, to receive greeting from his friends." During late February and early March personal loss struck. Three family members died, including his mother. The press of duties, however, kept him from the funerals, and he did not even have much time to grieve.[59]

Sherman's march through the Carolinas proved as successful as his march through Georgia and, in conjunction with Grant's increasing pressure on Lee in Richmond and Sheridan's devastation of the Shenandoah Valley, it was bringing the war to a victorious conclusion. Lee surrendered to Grant at Appomattox Courthouse in early April, and Grant provided generous terms for the Confederates, even allowing soldiers who owned a mule or horse to take it home for spring plowing. Halleck immediately wired Sherman the good news of Lee's capitulation and stated: "If Johnston [who had replaced Hood as commander of the depleted Army of Tennessee] will surrender as Lee has[,] I presume you will give him the same terms." Sherman had fought the war on a hard war–soft peace basis, so he was ready to be kind to the Confederates.[60]

Sherman, Grant, and Admiral David D. Porter met with Lincoln at City Point, Virginia, to discuss how best to conclude the long war. Sherman left the meeting convinced that the President wanted the mildest terms possible for the defeated Confederates. Significantly, Halleck was not present at this summit, a notable absence considering his long-time central role in the war at the highest levels. Lincoln clearly saw Halleck as merely a "clerk," as he had phrased it on several occasions in the past, and the generals and admiral must have agreed. No one thought it strange that Halleck was not in attendance at City Point. He had so lost any will to make decisions that even when Stanton asked him to evaluate an engineer's report on the nation's fortifications, he simply regurgitated the study's facts. "I should be very sorry to see our Engr Corps constructing fortifications so far behind recent experience & improvements," he said, but "I don't like to subject myself to the charge of impertinent meddling."[61]

With total victory now on the horizon, matters suddenly spun out of control, for Halleck and for the nation. On April 14, 1865, the Confederate supporter John Wilkes Booth assassinated Abraham Lincoln. As frightening and shocking as that was, other cabinet officials were also either attacked, as Secretary of State William H. Seward was, or rumored to be targets of a grand Confederate conspiracy. Francis Lieber called the violence the result of the "unprincipled, impudent, whiskey soaked booey-knife [sic] spirit" of the South. Halleck was at Lincoln's bedside when he died, but if he felt any emotion or said anything personal, it was never recorded. Stanton, of course, made the memorable comment that Lincoln now belonged to the ages.[62]

Uncharacteristically, Halleck acted with decisiveness in response to the assassination crisis, and the repercussions made him wish he had not. He sent orders to military commanders throughout the region to "arrest all persons who may enter your lines by land or water." He told the military to "do everything in your power to detect the murderers and assassins." Any people captured should be brought in "double irons" to the navy yard, where they would be kept "on a monitor to be anchored in the stream." He even alerted Sherman that there was an assassin named Clark on the way to murder him. He remained calm throughout, concluding that "this sad event may have the effect to open the eyes of all to the dangers of the times and the absolute necessity of a strong & firm policy but not a cruel one towards our unscrupulous enemies. But the greatest danger is that popular demagogues may take advantage of the present excitement to do things which we shall all wish undone." How prophetic he proved to be.[63]

Compounding Halleck's shock was his unexpected appointment to become commander of the Military Division of the James, headquartered in Richmond. He would have preferred to go to California, he said, but Stanton, the driving force in the new presidential administration of Andrew Johnson, would not agree to let him do that.[64] The former commanding general and present chief of staff was removed from the seat of power and given the job of policing the former Confederate capital. The new administration clearly believed that Richmond needed his strong bureaucratic hand. The times now required administrators not fighters, so he was the perfect man for the job. Clearly, his chronic unwillingness to make military decisions and the fact that Grant could now establish his headquarters in Washington influenced the change.

Meanwhile, Sherman had met with Confederate General Joe Johnston and worked out an agreement to stop the fighting between their two armies. In fact, Sherman went much beyond that. He and Johnston signed a pact that would end the entire war and establish some principles for reunion. The Confederate Army was to take its weapons for deposit to state armories, the Federal government was to recognize properly constituted state governments, political rights for all citizens were guaranteed, and there was to be a general amnesty. Conspicuously absent from their agreement was any mention of slavery. The terms that guaranteed property rights may even have allowed its continuance. Sherman had forgotten Halleck's "inevitable Sambo."[65]

As soon as the Sherman-Johnston terms arrived in Washington, the political leaders properly rejected them and sent Grant to Sherman's army with the news. Halleck, who had displayed genuine affection for Sherman throughout the war, now began to question him. He telegraphed Stanton that "respectable parties" in Richmond said that Jefferson Davis had taken a great deal of money with him on his escape from Richmond. The plan was "to make terms with General Sherman or some other Southern commander" so that Davis and his companions could escape to Europe or Mexico. "Johnston's negotiations look to this end. Would it not be well to put Sherman and all other commanding generals on their guard in this respect?"[66]

Stanton responded immediately that the government had already disapproved the Sherman-Johnston terms. Similarly, the military had negated a Sherman order that, Stanton said, would have "allow[ed] Jeff. Davis to escape with his plunder." Criticism of Sherman continued to increase, one of Halleck's subordinates in Richmond even calling him a "fool" and "crazy" and his peace negotiations "folly." The press joined in the torrent of criticism.[67]

Busy as he was with governing Richmond, Halleck kept himself involved in the Sherman affair. Unable or unwilling to resist the rising tide of animosity toward Sherman, Halleck joined in decisively. He told Generals Meade, Sheridan, and Wright "to pay no regard to any truce or orders of General Sherman suspending hostilities," and he suggested that Stanton send such a general directive to the entire army. When he heard from Grant that Johnston had surrendered again on the same basic terms as had Lee, Halleck still sent two more directives calling on army leaders to disregard Sherman's original agreement. He called it "an unfortunate mistake" and "fear[ed] there is some screw loose [in Sherman] again." He further told Cullum that he had done all he could to "counteract" the treaty "by directing Sheridan & Meade to operate without any regard to his [Sherman's] truce or orders, as he could bind no troops not in his command. I fear he has permitted Davis to escape with all his booty."[68]

When Grant first went to North Carolina to tell Sherman that his treaty had been scrapped, he had taken it all in stride. Quickly, however, news of Halleck's and Stanton's accusations made him furious. In early May 1865, he "exploded" before Admiral John A. Dahlgren. The admiral "tried to calm him," believing that "Halleck's cold blood would be more than a match for Sherman's fiery humor." Sherman ignored Dahlgren's advice, ridiculing Halleck as someone who "had not been under fire once." Dahlgren agreed: "He is a great sinner against the mass of respectable mediocrities."[69]

In Richmond, Halleck did not yet realize how angry Sherman was. He nonchalantly sent a routine telegram asking for information about conditions in North Carolina and indicating, matter-of-factly, that "everything is quiet here." Sherman's army was marching north toward Richmond and eventually to Washington, as these events unraveled, and Sherman remained angry at "Halleck's insult." Grant tried to calm him, saying that it was all "a difference of opinion, which *time* alone *will decide* who was right." Sherman did not agree. When Halleck offered him a room in his Richmond lodgings, Sherman coldly replied that he could not "have any friendly intercourse" with him. "I prefer we should not meet."[70]

Halleck was stunned. His mind must have raced back to the time in California when he and Sherman had stubbornly refused to talk to each other for several years, or he might have remembered his exchange of letters with Grant over Forts Henry and Donelson. He quickly tried to prevent a repeat of such hard feelings. "You have not had during this war, nor have you now, a warmer friend & admirer than myself," he wrote Sherman. He had only been "carrying out what he knew to be the wishes of the War Dept, in regard to your armistice" and if he "used language which has given you offence, it was unintentional & I deeply regret it." He wanted to remain Sherman's friend, he said, but "the matter" was now in his "hands."[71]

Sherman refused to be appeased. He sent Halleck a formal letter about his army's march to Washington and bluntly told him there would be no review in Richmond as Halleck had ordered. Halleck responded just as formally, and the schism between the two men was complete. Sherman remained furious. "Tomorrow I march through Richmond with colors flying and drums beating as a matter of right and not by Halleck's favor, and no notice will be taken of him personally or officially. I dare him to oppose my march." Halleck, for his part, accepted no blame for the controversy, attributing it all to "one of his [Sherman's] grand excitements, worse even than in Kentucky & St. Louis." "He accuses me of having formed a plot with the authorities to stab his reputation and to incite the north against him, and thus prevent the ending of the war!" he wrote to Cullum. "Did you ever hear of such ridiculous nonsense?" Halleck confided to Lieber that it was Sherman's problem. "He is very easily excited, and on such occasions his mind loses its balance, and he has no self control. I have seen him in this condition more than once." Writing to Stanton, Halleck said the misunderstanding was all Grant's fault. He had simply been following the commanding general's orders. As always, Halleck could find no blame in his own actions—he refused to take responsibility for what he had said and done when he was following orders.[72]

Sherman's troops knew all about the rift and supported their commander to the hilt. They were already unhappy that Halleck had issued an order keeping them from visiting Richmond, even though former rebels had free access to the city. One Missouri soldier reported that as Halleck stood on the portico of his headquarters in Richmond "we marched by . . . at a right shoulder shift, and without saluting in any manner." Two northern women who came to Richmond knew about the feud and regretted that "this personal fight deprived us and the army of what might have been a splendid sight."[73]

Sherman's snub of Halleck in Richmond did not end the dispute. When his army participated in the Grand Review of the Union armies in Washington at the end of May 1865, Sherman snubbed Stanton, whose press assault had added to his difficulties. Sherman ascended the reviewing stand as his army marched by and shook hands with the President and all the other dignitaries save one. He conspicuously refused Stanton's extended hand. Sherman felt justified, and the excitement over the end of the war ended the controversy over Sherman's generous peace terms. Halleck was in Richmond, so he missed the review in Washington. Yet a soldier called it "a magnificent spectacle," and added that "the vanity of Halleck, that prince of military humbugs . . . must have been fully gratified at such an extravaganza."[74]

In his officious pedantic style, as he had earlier done in criticizing Grant, Halleck had attacked a successful general. It would be simple to say that he did such things out of jealousy, but that was not the case. He attacked Sherman, as he had Grant, because an imprecise, incorrect military action upset him. Sherman had neither legal nor administrative right to sign a complete treaty; he went beyond his authority, and thus he jeopardized the war effort. He had to be reined in and taught the proper rules. Halleck was simply doing his job; it was Sherman's reaction that was irrational, he believed. Halleck decided Sherman had become mentally unhinged just as he had in Missouri early in the war.

Halleck thus ended his active war role in the last days of the conflict as he began it, as an exponent of rules, not as a victorious fighter. He was not an inspiring leader like Grant and Sherman, but he had the knowledge and ability to provide those leaders with the support they needed, both logistical and strategic. In his own inflexible way, he allowed the generals to develop their ideas without his interference. At the same time, when he had dealt with officers of lesser talent, he had not been able to give them the guidance and orders they needed. Yet in the administrative and logistical sphere that he enjoyed so much, he had brought order and success to Union arms. He was a chief of staff by nature and not a commanding general. His happiest days during the war and his greatest success and satisfaction came in advising Grant and implementing his orders. To the very end, Halleck could not exhibit the stuff of martial fame. He was, to the depths of his being, an administrator, not a fighter.

11

From War to Peace

THE WAR was over. Victorious Union troops marched in triumph through Washington's streets, and the soldiers planned their trips home to take up their lives where they had left them to do battle for the Union's preservation. H. W. Halleck, however, had no plans to return to his prewar legal and business profession. He would remain in military service until the day he died; indeed, the peacetime army with its reams of paperwork was more appealing to him than the army at war had ever been. His assignments took him throughout the nation: to restore order in Richmond, to maintain an efficient military presence in San Francisco and on the Pacific Coast, and to bring stability to Louisville and the Reconstruction South. As he had done during the Civil War, Halleck pushed all the proper papers, but he provided no inspirational leadership and, unlike Grant and Sherman, he inexorably faded into the national background.

On April 16, 1865, Halleck learned of his assignment to Richmond, told that he was being sent there because of dissatisfaction "with the policy of our officers in that city & state towards blatant rebels." Now that U. S. Grant was able to command in Washington, there was no further need or desire for Halleck to remain in the nation's capital. The new Andrew Johnson presidential administration believed that Halleck's firmness in Missouri early in the war was just what was needed at present in Richmond. The government hoped that Halleck would be strict on the conquered Confederates and make them toe the line in the preserved Union. Halleck agreed on the wisdom of such an approach. He believed that President Andrew Johnson would "not be as lenient toward rebels" as Lincoln would have been and "perhaps, after all, it may be better."[1]

Halleck reached Richmond on April 22, 1865, and took command of the Military Division of the James (Department of Virginia and the Army of the Potomac and that part of North Carolina not under Sherman's command). He brought his staff with him from Washington as well as General E. O. C. Ord, commanding the Army of the James, and Provost Marshal General Marsena R. Patrick, who had oversight of military police and relief agencies. Under Halleck's command, the army's job was to bring order to the chaos that reigned in the former Confederate capital city.

Richmond was a smoldering ruin. While the Confederate government was evacuating the city to escape the onrushing Federal troops on April 2 and 3, 1865, Lee's troops had exploded arsenals full of weapons and ammunition and torched tobacco and cotton warehouses. They had even left timed charges at the city's powder magazine and in Confederate ships on the James River. The numerous explosions did tremendous damage to the city and killed an unknown number of people. Several thousand others, hungry men and women, broke into the commissary depot and took the food stored there. City officials, meanwhile, tried to dispose of whiskey and other alcohol by pouring it into the gutters, but city dwellers of all classes and Confederate soldiers drank it right off the streets or scooped it up in buckets or in hats. A drunken mob then pillaged and torched businesses everywhere. All these fires roared out of control, and only the entering Union troops were able finally to beat back the spreading flames. More than twenty square blocks lay in ruins, some eight hundred to twelve hundred buildings, representing nine-tenths of the business district. And fires continued to burn under collapsed buildings for the next three months. It was a disaster of the first magnitude, for which Lincoln and his troops were unfairly blamed.[2]

The city had other problems, too. The stench from rotting garbage and human waste was overpowering, and the townspeople were plagued by persistent flies and starving dogs. The wholesale desertion of Confederate troops, the sight of weeping women and children and grim-faced men, and then the April 4 appearance of Abraham Lincoln walking amidst the rubble exacerbated the shock of Confederate defeat. Richmond was a city in ruin and turmoil.[3]

Several weeks after the evacuation fire, Halleck arrived in Richmond, and he quickly realized that he had a massive job before him. Despite appearances to the contrary, he immediately decided that Richmond was "more loyal than Washington and Baltimore" and said that "the people acknowledge that they are thoroughly conquered." "I was sent here to tame the people after the fashion of St Louis!" he told his friend Cullum, but "they require no taming, but are distressingly submissive. Talk of subjugating the south! They are abundantly *subjugated* now." Slavery was dead, and the people were furious at "the rebel-barbarians" who had torched the city, Halleck said. He urged Secretary of War Stanton to allow "free access" to Richmond in order to "prevent monopolists with special trade permits from swindling those who have anything to sell." He also asked for an ordnance officer to take charge of the Tredegar Iron Works and an aide to preserve the "rebel archives," which he said everyone was "plundering." He even called on the quartermaster general to allow the sale of condemned horses and mules so that Virginia farmers, their own horses taken from them by the Confederate troops, would be able to plant their crops. "We must either feed the poor or help them feed themselves," he argued.[4]

Despite Halleck's compassionate approach, Virginians reacted negatively to his arrival. Not all their aversion was simply automatic Confederate dislike of a Union general. One of Richmond's leading citizens who had been a West Point senior during Halleck's plebe year described him as "a cold blooded German . . . & one in whose sympathies or sentiments no rebel need hope." Black Richmonders shared the white concern, but for a different reason. Blacks worried that Halleck had not changed his attitude toward their race from the time he had issued his famous Order No. 3 in 1861 Missouri, banning fugitive slaves from entering army camps. They "are not satisfied," a black reporter said, "that his feelings have undergone a radical change in reference to the loyal blacks."[5]

The whites were wrong about Halleck. He was extremely sympathetic toward them and acted accordingly. He continued the army's rebuilding of the railroad and wagon bridges, and until a civilian government could be established, his army took up many municipal functions. Soldiers served as policemen, and he established a Court of Conciliation to deal with property matters. He even issued orders in early June mandating that Richmond citizens stop throwing garbage and other refuse into streets, alleys, or their own yards. He worked hard to get conditions back to normal as quickly as possible.[6]

When the matter of punishment for former Confederates came up, he backed gentle treatment for those who supported a return to the Union. He particularly mentioned Robert E. Lee, who, he had heard, was "considering the propriety" of taking the oath to the United States and "petitioning President Johnson for pardon." Halleck did, indeed, issue an order, the first such based on Andrew Johnson's mild presidential Reconstruction, to allow any Confederate, regardless of his position in the war, to swear allegiance to the United State and have his citizenship restored. He told General George G. Meade that "the Army of the Potomac has shown Virginians how they were to be treated as enemies. Let them now prove that they know equally well how to treat the same people as friends." Despite his clearly pro-white attitude, Halleck took action that former Confederates still found unpalatable. He prohibited the showing of Confederate flags, and he insisted that ministers offer the traditional prayer for the President of the United States. Some Episcopal priests ignored this order, so he closed their churches until they changed their minds. He also arrested two Confederate army officers for allegedly stealing money from Union prisoners of war, but when it later became clear that the men were innocent, he let them go. When any couple applied for a wedding license, he made them swear the loyalty oath, to prevent "the propagation of legitimate rebels." Those who had no job in the city, Halleck sent out to the country if they had "homes or friends to go to."[7]

Halleck was not nearly as generous with black people, who constituted about 45 percent of the approximately 50,000 inhabitants of the city. Supported by Ord and other Union military leaders, he labeled the XXV Corps, a black unit, "a very improper force for the preservation of order in this department." The corps's soldiers had committed a "number of cases of atrocious rape," he insisted, and their "influence" in general on "the colored population" was "bad." He urged Grant to order this unit to some new post. As for former slaves, he had his soldiers keep them in the same subordinate positions they had occupied under slavery and told Grant that, for order's sake, he had to keep them from coming into Richmond.[8]

Halleck's challenge was "to organize some labor system in the interior immediately as the planting season . . . [would] be over in two or three weeks." He quickly issued a general order calling upon all army units to help freedmen and former masters work out labor differences, insisting that the freedmen "must be made to understand that the Government will protect but cannot support them." "Interest as well as humanity requires that the former masters of the colored race should unite in devising the best measures for ameliorating their condition, and introducing some practical system of hired labor." Despite the end of slavery, Halleck wanted an economic system in which whites were clearly and unquestionably dominant. The army arrested thousands of rural blacks who came to Richmond looking for work, incarcerated them in the old slave pens, and then took them back to the plantations to labor.[9]

Having given whites the task of putting freed people to work, he also called upon them to improve black peoples' allegedly defective morals. Clergymen and judges, he said, should change blacks' views on matrimony. "They [blacks] must be made to understand that the laws of God as well as the laws of their country forbid their living together as man and wife without the solemnization of marriage." "It is hoped," he concluded, "that all persons interested in ameliorating the condition of the colored race, and in improving their social character, will use their influence in promoting the object in view."[10]

In sum, Halleck and the army were working hard to restore white supremacy and traditional values in the new nonslave environment. Halleck handled whites sympathetically, but he demonstrated a racially biased attitude toward blacks. A Richmond physician summarized matters accurately when he said that "perfect order was preserved" under army rule, and it was, all in all, "a very mild government." In June 1865, Halleck reported proudly that there were only about ten thousand Union soldiers in Richmond, and, of those, there was just one black cavalry regiment and a few black military musicians. Grant had taken Halleck's recommendation and ordered the XXV Corps out of the city, out of the state, all the way to the lightly populated frontier of west Texas.[11]

Anyone walking around Richmond found "heaps of papers flying about, a large number of autograph letters of distinguished rebels," one newsman reported. In late April 1865, Halleck, who had first suggested the preservation and printing of the war's military records in 1863, set aside a room in the Customs House for these documents and appointed an officer as Keeper of Public Archives. "All books, printed documents, maps, manuscripts, &C., found in any public office here, or belonging to Confederate or State authorities, will be carefully preserved," he said. Insisting to Secretary Stanton that such papers might contain "much evidence in regard to plots of assassination, incendiarism, treason, &c," he also thought that they would "prove of great value to those who may hereafter write the history of this great rebellion."[12]

He decided to have all such papers boxed as soon as they arrived in the Customs House and then quickly sent to Washington for disposition there. When Schofield captured a huge collection of Confederate War Department records, consisting of "eighty-one boxes, weighing ten tons," Halleck ordered him to send those to Washington, too. There, his friend Francis Lieber, the recently appointed head of the archives, sorted through the captured Confederate papers, many of them, as his biographer said, "intermingled with street dirt and debris." He worked at this task for several years, finding little of an incriminating nature, but providing the basis for the later publication of the official military records of the Civil War. Just as he had been a leader in preserving land records in California, Henry Halleck was clearly the father of the *Official Records* of the Union and Confederate armies and navies, a major source for the military history of the Civil War.[13]

Halleck also dealt with Richmond's major industrial complex, the Tredegar Iron Works. This factory had survived the terrible fires of early April 1865, because its owner, Joseph R. Anderson, had given rifles to his employees, enabling them to repel Confederate torches. When Halleck entered the city, he took over the complex, a move that made Anderson think the factory would be confiscated. "I gave him no encouragement," Halleck commented, noting, however, that "the machinery . . . is mostly worn out and would be of very little value to us." The works stood idle for two months, and then Halleck recommended that it be turned back to its owners and placed into operation until the courts determined its legal status. He opposed having the government run it, and he opposed turning it over to the Treasury Department as abandoned property. Stanton, however, disagreed and ordered the Tredegar Iron Works placed into the hands of treasury agents.[14]

Halleck also had to deal with the former Confederate president. "If Jeff. Davis was captured in his wife's clothes," Halleck said with obvious glee to Stanton, "I respectfully suggest that he be sent north in the same habiliments." More seriously, he suggested that Davis be sent north by sea rather than over land in order to avoid "disturbances." Stanton responded that there were no plans to send Davis to Washington; he would be tried in Virginia. He asked Halleck to prepare "bomb-proofs in Fortress Monroe, where he can be confined until tried," and then told Halleck to go there himself to "take charge." Halleck traveled to Fortress Monroe as ordered and oversaw preparations for the arrival of Davis and other Confederate officials. He gave detailed instructions to General Nelson Miles, commander at Fortress Monroe, on how to handle them in prison and how to deal with their families, who were to be returned to Savannah. Halleck opposed having Davis put in irons, but he agreed that Miles should "have fetters ready if he thinks them necessary." That was the extent of Halleck's participation in the jailing of the former Confederate president. He had nothing to do with the later controversy over Davis's shackling.[15]

As Halleck worked at maintaining order in Richmond, it was obvious that his attitude toward black people had not changed since his days in

California and Missouri. Keeping blacks suppressed was a primary goal. Particularly galling for blacks were the existence of a pass system for them and the imposition of corporal punishment for any violation of it. A group of black community leaders grew angry at Halleck and his subordinates, Ord and Patrick, and on June 7 composed a letter to the editor of the *New York Tribune* in protest. Another group gathered oral information from blacks who had suffered harassment at the hands of Union military authorities. Halleck refused to discuss these complaints with any delegation, so blacks called a mass meeting for June 10. Three thousand people packed the First African Baptist Church and approved sending a committee to complain to President Andrew Johnson in Washington. They also demanded an end to the recently established local government, headed by Joseph Mayo, the long-time prewar and wartime Richmond mayor, known for his willingness to whip blacks. Virginia Governor Francis Pierpont, in office under Johnson's presidential Reconstruction, was supportive of the black complaints, as was O. O. Howard in Washington, the head of the Freedmen's Bureau. Even Andrew Johnson, whom history knows was no supporter of freed people, promised to help. Halleck insisted that he practiced no discrimination but treated white and black "assassins & robbers" equally. Accusations that blacks were being whipped indiscriminately were "not only false but ridiculous."[16]

Even so, the black complaints brought quick results. By the end of June 1865, Provost Marshal Patrick had resigned, while Ord and Halleck had been reassigned. Black people thus gained one of their few victories of the Reconstruction period at the expense of Henry Halleck. His replacement, General Alfred H. Terry, was much more sympathetic to black needs than Old Brains had been. Halleck was not that sorry to leave Virginia, however, and his new assignment bolstered his willingness to depart.[17]

He had no desire to return to Washington, however, in part because he had vacated his house in late April, having had his wife join him in Richmond in mid-May. At Stanton's suggestion, he was more than happy to let U. S. Grant and his wife stay there in his absence. Halleck even made his furniture, bedding, and two servants available to Grant, who was pleased at his former chief of staff's generosity. Halleck may have been willing to offer his house to Grant, but he felt renewed hostility toward his former commander, and that was another reason he did not want to serve in Washington again. "The jealous influences which surround Genl Grant would render my position there unpleasant," he said. Besides, he told Cullum, Grant was "much prejudiced against the Engr Corps," and "a very narrow and jealous" opinion of engineers would soon become evident in the army. He did not want to have to deal with that, loyal engineer that he remained.[18]

On June 10 (after Halleck had spent only a few months in Richmond). Stanton advised him that, as part of "the new assignment of military commands," the President was sending him back to California, to command "the Military Division of the Pacific, embracing the Department of the Columbia and Department of California, with headquarters at San Francisco." Ord would go with him as commander of the Department of the Columbia. It took until June 27 for the change to be made officially, and it was part of a complete reorganization of the entire army command structure under Grant as commanding general. Halleck joined Meade, Sherman, Sheridan, and Thomas as commanders of the five military divisions in the nation, while eighteen other officers received department commands.[19] Halleck's mixed tenure in Richmond had not hurt his chances of gaining the command he had really wanted all along.

As one of his final official acts in Richmond, Halleck sent Stanton a report on his tour of duty. In it he boasted that he had overseen the change in Virginia from a chaotic wartime existence to a more harmonious peacetime existence. While it was true that both Union and Confederate soldiers had plundered their way home, that was understandable, he said, and was "one of the necessary evils of rebellion and war. The blame," he said, "must rest upon those who caused the war." The ending of slavery meant that both whites and blacks had to be taught their new relationship, and the military was forced to take on this "ungrateful and disagreeable" "task." "While the whites have been made fully sensible of the fact that they are no longer slave holders, their former slaves have been taught that their own well-being must depend upon their industry and good conduct." The biggest problem, he thought, was with "colored females," who, "released from the restraints imposed by their former masters and mistresses, and having thrown around them no legal restrictions and no marital obligations, naturally fall into dissolute habits." To improve this scandalous situation, the law had to enforce marriage, and all elements of society had to join in the effort. As for "a proper system of labor," he believed it could be implemented successfully, but "any abstract theory or enforced system will necessarily fail." A southern white leader could not have made the case for the old order any more favorably or emphatically than Halleck did.[20]

Reflecting on the whole Richmond experience in a letter to Lieber, Halleck noted that heading a military department was "very different" from working as he had in Washington, "with nose to the grindstone day & night, and certain to be abused, no matter how well the work was done." He believed he had had a much easier time in Richmond. "The work of reconstruction in the south will not be difficult if managed with judgement and good sense," he declared. "The great mass of the people are utterly disgusted with their former leaders and will firmly support the Union. Nor need there be any difficulty in the slave question, unless hotheaded radicals and extremists at the north make trouble." Reconstruction of the Union would be easy, Halleck believed, if only Radical politicians, whom he had regularly accused of creating difficulties during the war, cooperated. The white South, he was sure, would cause no problems at all.[21]

He would not himself have an immediate chance to test this Reconstruction certitude. Together with his wife and son, Halleck left by boat for California in late July 1865. As the *Golden City* steamed through the fog into San Francisco Bay on August 25, cannon at Fort Point fired a salute of welcome, as did the navy warship the *Saginaw.* On the wharf a welcoming committee from army headquarters awaited, "but he slipped quietly ashore," most other people not noticing his arrival until he was almost at the Occidental Hotel, where General Irvin McDowell, the man he was replacing, greeted him. There was no formal reception.[22]

Halleck brought with him to California "a great deal of unpopularity," evident both at his departure from the East and at his arrival in San Francisco. Charles A. Dana, a long-time Assistant Secretary of War under Edwin Stanton and now the editor of the *Chicago Republican,* felt constrained to write an impassioned, though unconvincing, defense of his old colleague. Halleck "never sought to ingratiate himself with any portion of the public," Dana said, but exhibited "an overweening repugnance for fools and bores." "This constitutional peculiarity," he continued, "has not been relieved by the brilliancy of military success which would have left all else in forgetfulness." He had no spectacular triumphs in the field, and as commanding general, he "did not satisfy the people, nor retain the entire confidence of Congress." But his "peculiar manners" and "the attacks of unsuccessful commanders" did "great injustice to a manly, accomplished, unobtrusive, upright, patriotic officer." His services were always "of great importance and value." He always did his duty. To insist, as some did, that "he willfully allowed other officers to be defeated in the field because of some unfriendliness" toward them was "unfounded and calumnious."[23]

The major San Francisco newspaper wrote a similarly mixed endorsement. It pointed out all Halleck's problems with other generals and concluded that "the cause of General Halleck's disagreements with the

Generals in the field arose in all probability from the conviction that campaigns could not be successfully conducted from an office in Washington. It was at one time a subject of remark that our armies were uniformly victorious only when they were outside of the telegraphic circuit of the capital." Halleck was, however, the *Alta California* concluded, Lincoln's "trusted advisor," and besides, in California he would be "among his friends and neighbors" with "a thorough knowledge" of them and his surroundings. As a result "his administration of the military affairs of the coast [would be] eminently successful and popular.[24]

Halleck recognized such criticisms, but they did not keep him from being optimistic. The voyage had been "delightful," he said. "Both oceans were as smooth as the Hudson River" and the ship itself was "a floating palace with accommodations & force equal to any first class hotel in New York." He also liked what he saw of postwar San Francisco, and he was pleased with the warm "resolutions of welcome" from the city council, particularly in light of the "most profane . . . abuse" of his wartime adversary General William S. Rosecrans and his other military and business enemies there. His house would soon be ready, and in the meantime his wife and son were staying with friends in the country. Harry was particularly excited at the gift of a "beautiful Peruvian Pony" and enjoyed riding with the host's daughter, "his old sweetheart." Halleck even praised the "most delicious" fruit he found at the market, "abundant & cheap."[25]

San Francisco was not the city Halleck had left in 1861. The population had continued to increase steadily during the war, going from 57,000 in 1860 to 150,000 in 1870, with women still in the minority. Silver production now played an important role in the city's economic life, as did the production of grain, fruit, and lumber. The increase of ship trading continued to match the increase in other aspects of economic life. Montgomery Street remained a major thoroughfare, and the Montgomery Block, which Halleck and his former law partners still owned, continued to be a sought-after address for a variety of business and professional men. Shade trees remained few in the city, but flower gardens seemed to be everywhere in the residential areas.[26]

The Civil War had obviously been good to California, and even with its strong pro-southern element the state had supported the Union throughout the conflict. It recruited 17,000 men for the army and sent many military units into the war, including the Halleck Rifles, formed in Trinity County in 1862. California soldiers had won numerous victories and tempered pro-Confederate feeling. They had also ensured a continued gold flow to the rest of the states, an important contribution to the nation's wartime economic health.[27]

Halleck soon realized that though he had been gone for four years he still had ties to his past life, and his expertise in land litigation remained particularly useful. When the famous California pioneer John A. Sutter was preparing to travel to Washington, Halleck wrote a letter of introduction for him. He told Secretary of State William H. Seward that Sutter had been "robbed" of most of his holdings "by some fifteen years of litigation by government officials to contest his right to lands given to him by the Mexican government." On the other hand, Halleck opposed the claim of John C. Frémont's wife for land in San Jose that he believed was essential for the area's defense. He was also able to savor some revenge over the earlier loss of the New Almaden Quicksilver Mine by driving off San Francisco's Presidio squatters, who, he said, were the hirelings of those individuals who "used the government money in stealing New Almaden from its rightful owners."[28]

Halleck's task in California was not to deal with the past, with the Civil War, or with Reconstruction. He had administrative duties, which was where his talent lay after all, but he also had to confront Indians, who were unhappy at the continuing white encroachment on their ancestral lands. Halleck toured his military division regularly, but he participated in no skirmishes with the Native Americans. His troops, however, had to make sure the trade routes from the East remained open, a factor that increased in importance with the building of the transcontinental railroad. He was responsible for a huge area: California, Oregon, Nevada, Arizona, Idaho, Washington, and, by 1867, Alaska, fully one-third of the United States. To guard this territory, he had assigned to him only seven regiments out of the army's 1867 total of sixty. His seven regiments were distributed by company in forts throughout the region.[29]

As soon as he arrived in California, Halleck began the flow of paperwork. No doubt unhappy with the way reports were coming in from subordinate units, he quickly issued an order detailing how official letters and reports were to be "folded and endorsed." In response to an earlier request from Washington for a breakdown of the money spent in his command fighting Indians and carrying out river and harbor maintenance, he explained to his superiors, in his usual brusque manner, that most of the money had been spent on fighting the Indians, with much less spent on coastal duty. "The expenses of these companies for the past year can be more correctly ascertained at the several Bureaus of the War Dept than at these Head Qrs," he lectured.[30]

Such orders and letters came out regularly, but, in truth, Halleck was not particularly busy. "My command is extensive," he reported to a friend, "but gives very little trouble so far. Consequently I am having a pretty good rest, which I much need, being somewhat worn out by the labors & anxieties of the last 4 years." Poor health, which had troubled him throughout the war, continued to plague him. He was spending most of his time catching up on the reading "of the publications of the past five years." He could not put the stress of the war years behind him, however; in fact, they continued to cause him more problems than his present duty. In 1867, he received a statement from the third auditor of the Treasury Department that he had been overpaid $49.90 for his 1861 trip from California to St Louis. The Treasury wanted its money back, but Halleck refused. He calculated that the government actually owed him a dollar, "which sum you are respectfully requested to credit me on the books of the Treasury."[31]

Even more stressful were the unresolved controversies left over from the war. John Pope, for example, demanded that Halleck send him a copy of the alleged report from the 1862 Corinth campaign in which Pope supposedly told Halleck (incorrectly it developed) that he had captured 10,000 prisoners. Pope could remember no such report. Halleck responded that his papers were "all boxed up for transportation to California," but he knew that he had "never reported to the Secretary of War dispatches received from you which were not so received." Pope angrily wrote again, insisting that Halleck had blamed him for a numerical inaccuracy for which he was not responsible. The disagreement remained contentious enough for Pope to refuse an assignment to a department in Halleck's Pacific command.[32]

Halleck remained interested in the captured Confederate documents that Francis Lieber was meticulously organizing. Old Brains recalled to his friend the existence of a letter in a Confederate official's papers from the 1840s Secretary of State, John C. Calhoun, admitting that Texas had been annexed to the United States to strengthen the institution of slavery. He advised Lieber where to look for this letter, seeing it as a good example of the kind of damning information about the southern war effort that the nation needed to know in order to reunite the country properly. With all the time he had for reading, he said, he had found "what terrible trash about the war is being published. . . . More than one half is utterly false. I begin to believe that 'all history is a lie.'" He thought it was important that all Union and Confederate documents be gathered to correct such falsehood.[33]

When he tried to right a historical wrong, however, he ended up making trouble for himself. During a dinner at his house for General George H. Thomas, his 1869 replacement as Pacific Division commander, Halleck discussed the near firing of Thomas during the 1864 Nashville campaign.

A *Chicago Tribune* reporter overheard these comments and published them. Halleck allegedly told Thomas that he had consciously delayed Grant's order to fire him that December and that the agreed-upon replacement would not have been John A. Logan, as Thomas had always suspected, but John M. Schofield, his trusted subordinate. The implication, which Halleck did not intend, was that Schofield had plotted with Grant to get Thomas's post. The issue remained unresolved until 1881, long after Halleck and Thomas were both dead, when Schofield asked Grant to clear up the whole matter. Grant denied ever being involved in any plot to relieve Thomas.[34]

Halleck remained interested in the history being made on the other side of the nation, in the Reconstruction of the South. Though he initially approved of President Andrew Johnson's "leniency towards Southern rebels," he noted that the South's stubbornness took away "all northern sympathy." "I hope that not a single disloyal member will be admitted to Congress. Let them understand that they are to stay out in the cold till they elect loyal men. If they have not got them, let them raise or import a new stock. The old is bad." As for the battle between Johnson and Congress, he had not seen the text of the Civil Rights Bill over which the two sides were arguing, so he had nothing to say. But, he said, he was sorry to see Johnson "in the hands of Seward & the Blairs," whom he believed to be "thoroughly unreliable" people.[35]

He was also strongly opposed to waging a war against any foreign nations, as some were urging. The French adventure of establishing a puppet regime in Mexico would end on its own, he believed, so there was no need for any incursion into that Latin American country. He hoped, too, that the legal controversy with England over the Civil War depredations of the British-built Confederate raider the *Alabama* would soon be settled. The boundary disagreement over British Columbia was another problem, he said, "as foolishly dangerous as carrying about in one's pocket a can of nitroglicerine [*sic*]." Halleck did not want to see the nation fighting another war; there was simply no need for such a conflict.[36]

He had a reconstruction issue all his own, close to home. His West Point classmate and prewar California neighbor, Jeremy F. Gilmer, had fought for the Confederacy. Now, out of friendship, Halleck endorsed his pardon application to the President. He told Gilmer he could always "rely on my old feelings of personal friendship." He thought Gilmer had been wrong to fight for the Confederacy, "but all these things are bygones and I desire to remember only what is agreeable." When Gilmer asked him if he should come back to California now that the war was over, Halleck immediately hesitated. "You know I seldom advise anyone about such matters." There still were some hard feelings about the war, but these were mainly among the "stay-at-homes." Those who had fought did not share such attitudes. Nonetheless, Gilmer might very well fare better financially by rebuilding railroads in the South than by coming back to California. But that was as far as Halleck was prepared to go.[37]

He was much more forthcoming in his attitude toward the Indians. Like most army officers, Halleck had little patience with recalcitrant Indians; he believed in the full use of force to keep them in line. "Let them fully understand," he wrote a subordinate on one occasion, that "depredations upon our people must entirely cease, or they must be exterminated." As for the Indian Bureau officials, whom he also despised, he told his officers: "As far as possible keep clear of all Indian agents & Indian agency, and have nothing to do with their treaties. As a general rule, their treaties are a fraud upon the government and the Indians." He was especially hostile to the Apaches, the tribe that was particularly troublesome in his military division. "There is no hope of peace in that country till he [the Apache] is destroyed or thoroughly conquered. His style of warfare is simply that of murder & robbery." The Apaches, Halleck concluded, had to be "hunted out as wild beasts are hunted & exterminated." The problem was, he told a complaining Nevada governor, that there were simply not enough troops to handle Indian problems there and elsewhere in his command. The Indian wars, he concluded, were "perennial. They will last till all Indian Agents and Contractors are hung."[38]

Next to the Indians, Halleck's major concern during his time on the Pacific Coast was coordinating the effort to bring Alaska under U.S. control. On April 9, 1867, Russia and the United States signed a treaty for the American purchase of the Russian territory. It then became the task of the army on the Pacific Coast to take control of the new territory. As early as February 1867, Halleck had begun preparations for new military posts in the Military District of Alaska, the entire territory to be under the command of former Union General Jefferson C. Davis (no relation to the Confederate ex-president). In May 1867, Halleck sent Washington his detailed recommendations. He called for troops to be sent to Alaska as soon as possible to prepare for the hard winter. He could spare only four companies and listed the four places where they should be sent. He presumed that a civil territorial government would soon follow, and in organizing it, special attention would have to be given to the Indians. He considered those in Alaska to be "of a character far superior" to those on the lower Pacific Coast. The Russian government, its traders, and the Hudson Bay Company had done a good job in keeping those Indians friendly, but if the United States established its system of Indian treaties and agents, "Indian wars must inevitably follow, and instead of a few *companies* for its military occupation[,] *regiments* will be called for with the resulting expenditure of many millions of dollars every year." As for what the place should be called, despite other suggestions he had seen, Halleck believed that Alaska was the most appropriate name.[39]

Preparations for the army's occupation of the new territory proceeded steadily. Grant told Halleck that Stanton wanted Halleck to go himself "to receive the formal delivery of the Territory," and that four companies were indeed sufficient as a garrison force. Gideon Welles said that both Stanton and Seward had proposed the high office of commissioner for Halleck. "I did not like it, for I do not like Halleck, but I said nothing," he complained. "Neither did the President nor any other member of the Cabinet." Halleck seemed pleased with the assignment. He "read everything" he could on Alaska, thinking "favorably of the acquisition." In the end, however, Halleck did not go to Alaska to receive it for the United States from the Russians; the former Civil War General and postwar U.S. Congressman and Senator Lovell H. Rousseau went in his place. As reward for Rousseau's political support, President Andrew Johnson had just reinstated him into the regular army as a brigadier general and had then assigned him to the Department of Louisiana. Now, to get him out of Louisiana, where he and the Military Division commander, General Philip Sheridan, were having disagreements, Johnson sent Rousseau to Alaska as the official American commissioner.[40] If Halleck was disappointed, he never said so.

Halleck gave Jefferson C. Davis, commander of the Division of Alaska, explicit directions about the army's role in the transfer, even telling him to remain aboard ship with his troops until the formal transfer was made. Once the ceremony was over, he was "to take possession of all public lots and squares, vacant lands, and all public buildings, barracks and edifices, and all public property in Sitka ceded by the treaty and transferred to the United States." Later he was to do the same throughout the rest of the territory. Halleck also called on Davis to treat both the white and the Indian people in the territory fairly. "In regard to the aboriginal and uncivilized tribes . . . you will . . . act as their general superintendent, protecting them from abuse, and regulating their trade and intercourse with our own people." If any one of them causes any problems, the entire tribe should be held accountable. "It may be well to have guns charged with grape and canister always bearing on their village, ready at an instant's warning to destroy them. Such precautions may prevent serious troubles and disasters."[41]

The more he investigated Alaska, the more intrigued Halleck became with the territory. He even contemplated writing an article on it, but never followed through, "finding myself anticipated by [Senator Charles] Sumner's published speech," which described the potential benefits of the territory to the nation. He hoped to visit Alaska in the spring and would decide what to say about it then. He was so impressed with the size of the place and the good work that Jefferson C. Davis was doing there that he urged the making of the department into a division and Davis's continuance in that expanded command.[42]

Davis indeed did a good job in Alaska, so Halleck did not have to do much more than offer advice, write reports, and ask for more governmental support for the military there. It was clear, however, that he saw himself as the overall military authority, with Davis in charge of day-to-day operations. The annexation of Alaska resulted in problems with neighboring British Columbia, and Halleck called for the American annexation of the British land. In answer to the British Columbia and Washington Territory dispute over San Juan and other nearby islands, he recommended that the only possible remedy was "to extinguish by purchase and treaty the British claim to all territory west of the Rocky Mountains." When the government did nothing, he warned Washington again that unless it acted there could be war with Britain. Echoing comments he so frequently made during the Civil War, he concluded: "Having performed my duty in pointing out the danger, the responsibility of the result must rest on others." That fall, he happily implemented the order for a joint British-American military occupation of San Juan Island.[43]

As was the case during most of his military career, Halleck spent the majority of his time dealing with routine. Keeping limited office hours, "9 AM to 3 PM, Sundays excepted," he issued orders that exemplified the administrative bureaucracy that consumed most of his time: "Post and company commanders within this Division are hereby notified that copies of post, or ordnance, and other property returns, are not required at these head Quarters." He also carried on an extended correspondence with the quartermaster general in Washington about blankets for the soldiers. "I have personally examined these blankets and I have never seen a more worthless lot of Shoddy." Later he refused to accept similarly inferior clothing and, with his refusal, enclosed ten documents to demonstrate how bad the clothes really were. His attention to detail was consistent and meticulous. Perhaps his most exciting task, though unsuccessful, was his attempt to determine who in San Francisco sent Supreme Court Justice Stephen J. Field a package bomb.[44]

Once he had all the administrative machinery working to his satisfaction, and except when he was on tour, he had plenty of time to read and complete writing an abridgement of his book on international law. Friends urged him to cut the volume down to about a fourth to a third of its original size by eliminating "all references to authorities, & all discussions and most of the historical illustrations," yet to add material about the recently completed Civil War. He began the project but then stopped to see if there was a market for such a publication. He decided there was, and by the late winter of 1866 he had a manuscript ready for Lippincott and Company in Philadelphia. The abridged book was published in 1866 and long remained a standard text on international law.[45]

For the first time since his marriage, Halleck had leisure time to spend with his wife and son. Early in his Pacific tour, he frequently mentioned how tired he was, his poor health still being a problem, so a more relaxed home life was just what he needed. The family lived comfortably in their prewar home at 326 Second Street, in the fashionable Rincon Hill section of the city. From there, they had a wonderful view of the bay, and Halleck was not far from the heart of the city's offices and businesses. Their neighbors were the city's first families. Halleck felt at ease, because he knew many of these people from his earlier business career and his continued ownership of the Montgomery Block. His old firm, although no longer practicing law, continued to be listed as one of the largest property holders in the city, Montgomery Block remaining a lucrative building.[46]

He was very proud of his son, noting, for example, that Harry was "just entering the portals of Latin grammar," but also mentioning that he was "healthy but delicate and I do not push him in his studies." In the late spring of 1867, Harry battled a case of typhoid fever, but by early July he was "about again & past all danger." Still, Halleck did not push him too hard, believing that "the formation of a good physical constitution is in every way most desirable. Hence I have him give as much attention to riding & outdoor exercises as to study." No doubt, while not reading or riding, Harry continued to tend his Japanese hen and rooster, gifts from family friends. Halleck, who had run away from farm work as a youngster, heartily encouraged it in his son.[47]

Halleck had little to say about his wife and her activities, but the few hints left in the historical record seem to indicate that they had a full social life. He belonged to the Associated Veterans of the Mexican War and was a regular mourner at members' funerals. He also retained his membership in the Society of California Pioneers. Despite his long interest in politics and his frequent private comments on the national scene, he politely refused the invitation to be one of the speakers at a political gathering. It was, he said, "improper for officers of the Army to take, under ordinary circumstance, active part in political party contests." He did, however, attend the fifteenth- anniversary celebration of California's statehood and the 1868 welcoming dinner for the diplomat Anson Burlingame.[48]

He continued to be ill at ease at social functions. One instance in 1866 no doubt amused William S. Rosecrans, with whom he had had so many disagreements during the war. Halleck and his staff were returning home from a tour of Nevada, Idaho, Oregon, and the Washington Territory, completing by steamboat the journey earlier taken on horseback, by stagecoach, and in an army ambulance. Understandably, considering his long history of health problems, Halleck had found the journey of over two thousand miles "fatiguing." He ran into Rosecrans and some other acquaintances on the steamboat during the last leg of the trip. According to Rosecrans, Halleck "sneaked out of the way into the outside of the crowd looking humiliated and uneasy. No one spoke to him or noticed him." That evening at the captain's table, Halleck "slipped into" a chair "with downcast eyes" and "during the whole meal[,] which he bolted[,] scarcely spoke."[49]

In early 1869, rumors began to circulate that George H. Thomas was going to replace Halleck, who was now fifty-five years old, as army commander on the Pacific Coast and that if that happened Halleck would resign his commission rather than leave California again. The gossip proved only partially correct. Thomas was indeed assigned to replace Halleck, but Old Brains accepted the order to command the Division of the South, headquartered in Louisville, Kentucky. San Francisco's leading newspaper praised "his just, honest and efficient administration" and said it had "secured for him the respect and esteem of all his fellow citizens." He was undertaking a very important post, the paper said, but doubted whether that would "compensate General Halleck for the sacrifice of feeling which he must make in leaving here." "Many will regret," the paper concluded, "to lose General Halleck from the various activities of this rising young State with whose history so much of his own career is identified." His own response to the change was to accept his new commission and to issue General Orders No. 21, lauding Thomas and thanking all his department commanders for their cooperation "in enforcing an economical administration of government expenditures." He praised all the officers and soldiers "who have been engaged in an harassing but successful warfare with the hostile Indians on this coast."[50]

The Associated Veterans of the Mexican War acknowledged Halleck's departure with an appropriate ceremony. As he prepared to leave in early June 1869, the Veterans "formed a line [at their meeting site] and made a ceremonial walk" to his residence on Rincon Hill. Halleck met them graciously and after they exchanged pleasantries, A. J. Marsh, the leader of the group, presented Halleck with a gold badge, the equivalent to the veterans, Marsh said, of the French Legion of Honor. He wished Halleck "God speed," in the sure belief that his "future career in the field of duty" would be "as productive of glory to our common country and of honor to your name and fame as has been your past career." Visibly touched, Halleck noted how few Mexican War veterans were left, "our number diminishing almost weekly." He was going "East to take command of the Division of the South, comprising nearly all of the Southern States." He knew that the "existing difficulties there" were "increasing and I shall remain there as long as I deem it my duty to do so." "I shall return as soon as I can after having fulfilled the obligations which I owe my country. This is my home, and I hope to return again to live and die here." Then Halleck invited the Veterans to partake of the refreshments his wife had prepared, and the group had several hours of "social enjoyment." The next day they reconvened at the pier to see Halleck and his family off for his new duty.[51]

He assumed command in Louisville on June 13, 1869, and by June 21 he was on a ten-day tour of the various department headquarters in his jurisdiction. The Military Division of the South included four departments, the Cumberland, Louisiana, Mississippi, and the South, and covered the states of Kentucky, Tennessee, West Virginia, Arkansas, Louisiana, Mississippi, Alabama, Georgia, Florida, and North and South Carolina. There were eighty-one companies in all under his supervision, with the departments commanded by P. St. George Cooke in Louisville, J. A. Mower in New Orleans, Adelbert Ames in Jackson, Mississippi, and Alfred H. Terry in Atlanta.[52] By the time Halleck arrived in Louisville, all but two of the states in his division, Mississippi and Georgia, had already been readmitted to the Union, and these two states achieved that status in 1870. The problem continued to be one of white resistance to a black role in southern society, with the Ku Klux Klan and other white-supremacy terrorist organizations using violence to try to maintain white dominance over blacks. Violence was particularly rife during elections, but terrorism as well as economic coercion of all kinds remained a constant problem at all times.

As always, Halleck was most concerned with the administrative side of his command. He created a board of inspectors for all military facilities in Louisville and kept his mail full of military detail. No matter of protocol seemed too small for his attention. For example, he wrote the adjutant general of the army the following note: "I am unaware that Aides-de-camp are required to perform the duties of Asst Adjut Genl; but the law does not say that they shall also perform those of Asst Inspectors Genl. It is therefore not 'superfluous' to announce such aides as Acting Asst Adjts Genl, if at the same time they are required to act as Asst Inspectors Genl under sec. 7 of the act of July 5th 1830." His adherence to military order and protocol was unbending. Similarly, he became angry whenever his judgment was questioned by someone whom he did not believe had the stature to challenge him. Writing to the adjutant general himself, he insisted that he was not upset with Quartermaster General Montgomery Meigs over his disagreement about some estimates he had provided. He was upset that Meigs had "called upon a subordinate to review the endorsements made at these Head Quarters."[53]

His department commanders, meanwhile, consistently expressed their concerns about the violence within their jurisdictions. P. St. George Cooke reported "a dereliction of their most important duties by State officers [in areas of Kentucky and Tennessee], and an unworthy timidity" in dealing with "murderers and outlaws." When he wrote his yearly report, Cooke noted press reports in Kentucky of "a Ku-Klux action" whereby masked men broke into houses and killed several people and "scourged most unmercifully a white man and several negroes." In Georgia, General Alfred H. Terry said, "The worst of crimes are committed, and no attempt is made to punish those who commit them. . . . The abuse in various ways of the blacks is too common to excite notice." The only answer, he believed, was "to resume military control." Adelbert Ames concluded that "the disturbances and lawlessness have their origin in political animosities, and the incapacity or unwillingness of many to recognize the change, resulting from the late war, in the condition of the freed people." Mississippians, he said, believed that those whites who found fault with the majority view should be driven out, while blacks should simply be kept out of the political process altogether.[54]

Halleck rejected all such complaints and recommendations. "After a careful examination of all the evidence" provided by those "unbiased by partizan feelings," he concluded that the amount of crime committed in his division was about the same as it had been before the Civil War. Even in those few areas where crime had increased, he believed that "very few have any partizan character or political significance. Those who murder and rob do so simply as murderers and robbers. . . . I am of the opinion that no such general organization [such as the Ku Klux Klan] now exists in the southern States." He totally opposed using military force "under the pleas of maintaining peace and good order." His units, he said, had spent a great deal of time assisting revenue officers, but if these officials would only do their job properly, "calls for military aid would be less frequent." In fact, he believed he could easily spare one or two regiments of infantry anytime they were needed elsewhere.[55] Once more, Halleck was unwilling to go out into the field and investigate these reports for himself. Thus he could not accept new phenomena or threats that did not fit into patterns familiar to him. He remained the armchair commander who saw his job as maintaining the status quo and refusing to take any risks.

He never changed his mind about these Reconstruction matters, making similar statements in later reports to the Secretary of War. In 1870, for example, he bragged about how much he had cut expenditures in his division, and called for further cutbacks in the use of the military to deal with civil problems. "Such restrictions on the use of military force in civil matters would, in my opinion, not only effect a large saving in military expenditures, but would relieve army officers from much of the responsibility which they are now obliged to incur in the performance of disagreeable duties, which can hardly be said to legitimately belong to the military service." Halleck, who had demonstrated antiblack attitudes in California, during his time in 1861–1862 Missouri, and in postwar Richmond, was now making sure that he and his army units did as little as possible for freed people during Reconstruction, despite the repeated violent attacks on them. One of Sherman's former soldiers, then living in northern Alabama, said Halleck's report "grates harshly on the nerves of loyal men," who were "indignant" at his attitude.[56] Halleck had never seen the welfare of black people as within his or the military's purview. The passage of the fourteenth amendment did not change that view.

No evidence has survived concerning Halleck's family in Louisville, other than that they lived on Second Street between Green and Walnut. His brief correspondence with George W. Cullum during these years provides no personal information, and there are no surviving letters to Francis Lieber or to anyone in California. When John M. Schofield, about to go to the Pacific Coast to replace George H. Thomas, who had died suddenly, asked about the possibility of renting Halleck's San Francisco house, Halleck indicated little knowledge of its condition. He did maintain contact with his family in Westernville, however, continuing to send money as Christmas presents.[57]

Throughout the post–Civil War years, Halleck's health continued to be problematical. He seemed to be tired frequently and he had a bout of facial neuralgia. He said nothing more specific about any symptoms until his years in Louisville. Then matters seemed to grow worse. His first year in the Kentucky city, he had facial pain and was "laid up with neuralgia on the Sciatic and adjacent nerves" of his right thigh, never having "so much pain in the same length of time" as he did then.[58] He might actually have been suffering from lumbar disc disease or from a peri-rectal abscess affecting the sciatic nerve.

His collapse came quickly. Around November 1, 1871, he had a hemorrhage in his bowels, together with what one reporter called "dropsical symptoms." He grew increasingly weaker, but in early January 1872 he seemed to rally, only to fall into a twenty-four-hour coma on January 8. His breathing was labored during part of that time, but at the end "it became easy at last. . . . He passed away apparently unconscious of his condition or anything around him, and evidently without pain." Death came swiftly according to the report General Alfred H. Terry sent to the adjutant general: "Halleck died at twenty four minutes past eight o'clock [on January 9th] . . . of softening of the brain superinducing an organic disease of the heart and liver." Although he had never talked about it, newspapers reported that he had been suffering from liver disease for a long time. Halleck clearly had developed organic diseases of the heart and liver. A stroke no doubt caused the so-called softening of his brain, while the dropsical symptoms stemmed from congestive heart disease. The rectal bleeding was probably the result of his hemorrhoids, although diverticulosis or colon cancer might have been the cause, with bleeding aggravated by poor clotting because of liver disease. His chronic fatigue might have been the result of anemia due to hemorrhoidal bleeding and/or liver disease.[59]

If we take all these symptoms together, it is conceivable that Halleck suffered from hemachromatosis, an iron-storage disease that frequently causes cirrhosis of the liver, heart disease, depression, and fatigue. It is also possible that he contracted a parasitic disease in California or during the May 1862 Civil War campaign for Corinth, Mississippi. Such a condition might have led to cirrhosis of the liver. Since the worst of his physical symptoms appeared in August 1862 and never seemed to disappear, perhaps there is some validity in suspecting the influence of a parasite. Conversely, since hemorrhoids are a common complication of ascites (the accumulation of abdominal fluid), which is frequently found in people suffering from liver disease, hemachromatosis may be a better diagnosis.

Halleck's death prompted the usual obituaries in the nation's leading newspapers but no outpouring of national grief, as was the case when Grant and Sherman died later. The columns followed a common pattern, giving brief information on the circumstances of his death and an outline of his life, with facts frequently mangled as, for example, the listing of a wife and daughter as his descendants. George W. Cullum wrote an obituary in a military newspaper extolling his civilian and military careers, but the *New York Post* evaluated the overall situation more accurately. "Nobody talked about this man Halleck['s death]—the gossips on the street and in the stages passed him and his career by as a barren theme." Only in California did people express much emotion. There flags flew at half mast in his honor.[60]

His remains were placed in a vault in Louisville's Cave Hill Cemetery for later burial with full military honors in Brooklyn's historic Green-Wood Cemetery. Internment occurred on January 25, 1872, the lot having been purchased only the day before. There was so little interest in the New York burial that the newspapers ignored it. A California newspaper mused that "he was a cold, reserved man, not likely to win much affection except from intimate associates."[61]

A young widow at forty-one, Elizabeth Halleck took her husband's death calmly and looked to the future. She wrote his sister in Westernville within the week, knowing that this relative shared her grief more than anyone else did. She told her sister-in-law that "our dear one went to his rest full of faith and hope & passed off like an infant without a moan." Halleck's brother-in-law, Schuyler Hamilton, and his cousin Bishop Whipple had been with him at the end and witnessed his accepting the Episcopal faith. Elizabeth told her sister-in-law not to worry about the financial support that Halleck had regularly provided. "I shall as soon as possible make every arrangement for your happiness." Elizabeth soon welcomed the financial advice of her husband's former California partner, Frederick Billings, now a Northern Pacific railroad magnate. She planned to keep Harry at school in Faribault, Minnesota, where Bishop Whipple lived, intending to reside there herself in a small renovated cottage.[62]

She even tried to resolve the 1865 Sherman-Johnston treaty conflict between her now deceased husband and William T. Sherman. She wrote Sherman on March 11, 1873, and he responded quickly with a long discussion of the Civil War controversy: "We both lived in turbulent times and were both strong natures," he said, "and that we should have collided was to be expected, but I have always endeavored to do him in life all possible honor, and in death to cherish in memory his better qualities." That must have been enough solace for the widow, or else she saw it as a hopeless cause. She never wrote to Sherman again, and he never wrote to her.[63]

She did not want for money. Halleck's will, dated February 20, 1868, was filed in mid-February 1872, in the city and county of San Francisco and was probated on May 30 of the same year. He left everything to Elizabeth, except for $5,000 to his mother or her heirs. He decreed that his mother could remain on the Westernville family farm as long as she lived. (She had, however, preceded him in death.) The total value of his estate was $460,000, the net worth after expenses being $430,785.19, an enormous sum by nineteenth-century standards.[64]

Some time during this period, Elizabeth began leaning on George W. Cullum, her husband's long-time bachelor friend, whose eye for women Halleck had regularly found amusing. The acquaintance turned to affection and in the fall of 1875, the two were married. They commemorated Halleck's memory, commissioning a bust of him in Italy, which Harry presented to the Society of California Pioneers in San Francisco. Elizabeth's "extravagance nearly drove" Cullum "crazy," Halleck's former business manager later said, her generosity toward the Halleck relatives and others never giving him "any delight." Yet, by all accounts, they had a happy marriage, even though Cullum was sixty-six when they married and Elizabeth was only forty-four. (Halleck had been seventeen years older than Elizabeth.)[65]

On May 19, 1882, the couple suffered a severe loss when Harry, only twenty-seven years old, died on his farm in Littleton, Halifax County, North Carolina, of an acute or chronic inflammation of the kidneys (Bright's disease). The wake was held in the Cullum home at 261 Fifth Avenue in New York City, with burial in Green-Wood Cemetery alongside his father. Harry left to his mother an estate of $200,000 that he had somehow acquired.[66]

Elizabeth Halleck Cullum had only a few more years to live herself; she died of cancer on September 15, 1884, at the age of fifty-three. Just four months previously, she and Cullum, together with John J. Astor and his wife, had founded the New York Cancer Hospital, and, among other contributions, she had endowed a bed there "in perpetuity." She served as a trustee of that institution and as vice president of the Woman's Hospital. At her death, she was buried next to her first husband and her son. In her will, she left the Cancer Hospital several pieces of New York City and San Francisco property and gave her "diamonds, laces, shawls and jewelry" to a sister and her one-ninth share in the Hamilton Building at the corner of Broadway and Barclay in New York to another sister. She left George Cullum everything else she had inherited from Halleck and Harry.[67]

Elizabeth's bequest made Cullum a very rich man indeed. He was apparently careful with his money, so when he died in 1892 at the age of eighty-three he was able to leave large sums to a variety of institutions and individuals. He left $250,000 to the U.S. Military Academy for the erection of a building, to be named Cullum Hall, to house representations in stone and paint of distinguished academy graduates, trophies of war, and "such other objects as may tend to give elevation to the military profession." He bequeathed for the new building a bust and painting of Halleck, his sword, and Cullum's own portrait. He left $20,000 as a trust fund for the later purchase of materials for Cullum Hall and another $20,000 to underwrite a revision every ten years of *General Cullum's Biographical Register of the Officers and Graduates of the United States Military Academy at West Point, N.Y.* He left $20,000 to the Metropolitan Museum in New York for the purchase of Greek, Hellenistic, and Roman period casts, and in 1895 the Medieval Department of the New Cast Collection was named the Cullum Collection, according to his wishes. He left the Westernville farm to one of Halleck's sisters.[68]

Cullum was also buried in Green-Wood Cemetery. He lies to the right of Elizabeth Halleck Cullum, while Halleck rests to her left. They each have separate tombstones: Elizabeth a simple cross, Halleck a low wide monument that is reminiscent of the fortification architecture he favored, and Cullum a pillar that overshadows both. In San Francisco, Halleck is commemorated by a monument in Golden Gate Park, a granite figure in military uniform, erected in 1886, with funds "from his 'best friend,'" Cullum.

Henry Wager Halleck was one of the most successful and influential Americans of the nineteenth century. He reached the pinnacle of achievement as an intellectual, writer, soldier, statesman, archivist, architect, attorney, and businessman. Not many men in all of American history have made such significant contributions to as many fields of endeavor as he did. Yet he is remembered most for what he did not do. Cast in the national spotlight at the time of a devastating civil war, he could not break the mold of a cautious and obsessive administrator at a time when the nation needed him to apply his many talents decisively to save the Union. He could not bring himself to take charge, to command men into battle, so his wartime career was disappointing.

There is a plausible explanation for Halleck's inability to build on the fame and success of his earlier life. He experienced a constant conflict between the purposeful disciplined life his father represented and his rebellion against it. He was precise and disdainful of men like Grant, whom he viewed as sloppy, yet he obviously enjoyed bantering suggestively with Cullum. He had strong opinions, but he did not want to force them on others. He was his father ordering him to stay on the farm, *and* he was the fourteen-year-old boy leaving the farm to experience the outside world. He projected both these sides of his personality onto others, and he reacted accordingly. The critical part of his being no doubt castigated his undisciplined side and he criticized those he found guilty of the same failing. No matter how disciplined he became, he could never resolve the conflict between the strict father and the freewheeling child, both of whom he had internalized and assimilated into his persona.

The result was stress, which produced physical problems that created more stress, which produced more ill-health, and so on in a tragic and unending spiral. His hemorrhoids and gastrointestinal difficulties no doubt stemmed from heightened pressure; and certainly heavy cigar smoking, meant to alleviate the stress he felt, led to physical problems such as heart disease. He no doubt used opium as a suppository and a paregoric, to deal with hemorrhoids and diarrhea, and he may have used alcohol to anesthetize himself against the pain of his physical ailments, to deal with any opium withdrawal symptoms, and, most important, to cope with the lack of ease within himself.

Carrying such physical and psychological burdens, Halleck at first drove himself toward success and provided financial support to his siblings because he had an unconscious desire to surpass his father. Yet his search for father figures and his purposefulness indicate that he was constantly trying to have a parental relationship. He wanted to outdo his father, but when he did so, he felt guilty about it.

During the Civil War, Halleck had power over generals such as McClellan, yet he could not issue orders to them. So he reverted to being a subordinate who did not have to make decisions. He became the dutiful son who needed nurturing and desired a parental relationship. As for Abraham Lincoln, Halleck saw him as an incompetent bungler, a weak politician who dared meddle in military matters. He felt no conflict in refusing to issue orders for Lincoln, as in the case of Ambrose Burnside. The President never became a father figure to Halleck, even though, ironically, he was "Father Abraham" to many Union soldiers.

It seems clear, therefore, that Halleck's personality and his performance as a Civil War general were largely the result of deeply ingrained psychological factors and the physical ailments that developed as a result. Henry

Wager Halleck's drive to succeed, his many accomplishments, and his eventual failure to reach his potential all stemmed from deeply embedded conscious and unconscious forces. The powerful man of success was also the tormented child, and, under the stress of war, the torment won out over the power. Indecision became his surrender to, his way of coping with, the turmoil he had felt all his life.

Today, the surrounding vegetation almost overwhelms Halleck's San Francisco monument, and his fashionable old neighborhood on Rincon Hill is part of the western approach to the San Francisco–Oakland Bay Bridge. Both these sites are fitting symbols of Old Brains's little remembered, though important place in American history.[69]

Bibliographical Essay

ALTHOUGH Henry W. Halleck was among the leading figures of the nineteenth century, historians have paid him little attention. Until the publication of this book, there has not been a full biography of this important American. The fullest account until now has been Stephen E. Ambrose, *Halleck: Lincoln's Chief of Staff* (Baton Rouge: Louisiana State University Press, 1962; paperback edition, 1990). More recently there appeared Curt Anders, *Henry Halleck's War: A Fresh Look at Lincoln's Controversial General-in-Chief* (Carmel, IN: Guild Press of Indiana, 1999). Ambrose's book is far superior to Anders's volume, but neither is a full biography. Both give almost no attention to the years before and after the Civil War.

John Y. Simon, the well-known editor of U.S. Grant's papers, has written a number of perceptive essays on Halleck. These are *Grant and Halleck: Contrasts in Command,* Frank L. Klement Lecture No. 5 (Milwaukee: Marquette University Press, 1996); "Lincoln and 'Old Brains,'" *North and South* 2 (November 1998): 38–45; "Lincoln and Halleck," in Charles M. Hubbard, ed., *Lincoln and His Contemporaries* (Macon: Mercer University Press, 1999), 69–85. These, too, deal almost exclusively with Halleck's role in the Civil War.

Over the years, there have been authors who planned a Halleck biography, but none ever published one. Some did, however, contribute essays that provide important information on him. These authors and their writings are David S. Sparks, *Henry Wager Halleck,* Union Worthies No. 17 (Schenectady: Union College, 1962); William E. Marsh, "Lincoln and Henry W. Halleck," in Allen Nevins and Irving Stone, eds., *Lincoln: A Contemporary Portrait* (Garden City, NY: Doubleday, 1962); and John D. Yates, "The Land That Halleck Called His Own," *San Rafael Independent Journal,* June 24, 1972, M7–11.

Over the years, too, there have appeared a variety of articles, of varying quality, on various aspects of Halleck's life. In chronological order these are G. W. Richards, *Lives of Generals Halleck and Pope* (Philadelphia: J. Magee, 1862); OJV, *Men of the Time: Being Biographies of Generals Halleck, Pope, Sigel, Corcoran, and Others*, Beadle's Dime Series, No. 1 (New York: Beadle, 1862); S. H. Willey, "Recollections of General Halleck as Secretary of State in Monterey, 1847–1849," *The Overland Monthly* 1 (1872): 9–17; Anonymous, *A Short History of Gen. H. W. Halleck* (Park Place, NY: Knapp, 1888); Samuel Miller Quincy, "The Character of General Halleck's Military Administration in the Summer of 1862," *Papers of the Military Historical Society of Massachusetts*, 10 vols. (Boston: Houghton Mifflin, 1895), 2:3–30; James Grant Wilson, "Types and Traditions of the Old Army. II General Halleck—A Memoir," *Journal of the Military Service Institution of the United States* 36 (1905): 537–556, and 37 (1905): 333–356; Milton H. Shutes, "Henry Wager Halleck: Lincoln's Chief of Staff," *California Historical Quarterly* 16 (1937): 195–208; Idwal Jones, "General Halleck: The Unknown," *Westways* 42 (February 1950): 18–19; W. F. Skyhawk, "John Parrot and Henry Halleck," *Pony Express* 20 (June 1953): 3–7; Stephen E. Ambrose, "Lincoln and Halleck: A Study of Personal Relations," *Journal of the Illinois State Historical Society* 52 (1959): 208–224, and "Henry Halleck and the Second Bull Run Campaign," *Civil War History* 6 (1960): 238–249, and "Halleck: The Despised 'Old Brains,'" *Civil War Times Illustrated* 1 (July 1962): 15–16, 33–34; Brian McGinty, "'Old Brains' in the Old West," *American History Illustrated* 13 (May 1978): 10–19; R. F. Snow, "Henry Wager Halleck," *American Heritage* 32 (March 1981): 42–43; Beverly E. Bastian, "'I Heartily Regret That I Ever Touched a Title in California': Henry Wager Halleck, the Californios, and the Clash of Legal Cultures," *California History* 72 (1993): 310–333. I have also published several articles on Halleck: John F. Marszalek, "Lincoln and Old Brains Halleck: An Effective Team?" in Timothy P. Townsend, ed., *The Annual Lincoln Colloquium: Papers from the Thirteen and Fourteenth Annual Lincoln Colloquia, September 26, 1998, Galesburg, Illinois, October 9, 1999, Springfield, Illinois* (Springfield, Ill.: n.p., n.d.), 131–141, and an article on Halleck's unsuccessful orders to General John A. Dix while Confederate General Robert E. Lee was moving on Gettysburg: "Second Union Misfire on the Peninsula," *America's Civil War* 14 (2001): 54–60.

Any biography depends on primary sources. In the case of H. W. Halleck, there is no one major repository of his correspondence. There are, however, both personal and professional correspondence in a variety of institutions. The most significant collections of Halleck's letters and records exist in numerous collections at the Huntington Library, San Marino, California, especially the Francis Lieber correspondence. There are also three Halleck lectures on California agriculture, a lecture on secession, a book review, a short autobiographical account, and Halleck's personally bound general orders from the Military Division of the James and the Military Division of the Pacific. Also important are the collections of Henry W. Halleck, George Washington Cullum, Jeremy F. Gilmer, and official academy ledgers at the U.S. Military Academy, West Point, New York. There are Halleck and a variety of other collections in the Manuscript Division of the Library of Congress; a number of Halleck's letters to his law partner preserved at the Frederick Billings

Farm and Museum, Woodstock, Vermont; the U.S. Army Generals' Papers (RG 94), Halleck's Personnel File (M-1395), United States Military Academy Cadet Applications (M-688), Records of the Chief of Engineers (RG 77) and other official documents in the National Archives and Records Administration, Washington, D.C.; the Halleck, Peachy, Billings Records and other collections at the Bancroft Library, University of California, Berkeley; the Pablo de la Guerra Papers at the Santa Barbara Mission Archives and Library, Santa Barbara, California; the James S. Schoff Civil War Collection, William L. Clements Library, University of Michigan; George W. Granniss scrapbooks and San Jose and San Francisco Railroad Company records at the California State Library, Sacramento; California Constitutional Convention papers, militia records, and various legal documents in the California State Archives, Sacramento; William Alexander Leidesdorff Papers (legal) and miscellaneous documents in the California Historical Society, San Francisco; Henry Benjamin Whipple Papers, Minnesota Historical Society, St. Paul; Isaac I. Stevens Papers, University of Washington, Seattle; and the William S. Rosecrans Papers, UCLA.

Family papers, which include correspondence, newspaper clippings, genealogies, and legal documents, are in the hands of Eleanor Sexton, Westernville, New York. David Sparks, William Marsh, John D. Yates, and several other researchers were aware of these papers, but no one used them as much as I did in this book. They provide important information and insights on Halleck, available nowhere else.

The greatest number of Halleck letters are found in *War of the Rebellion: Official Records of the Union and Confederate Armies,* 128 volumes (Washington, D.C.: Government Printing Office, 1880–1901). Important letters also appear in the James Grant Wilson articles listed above and in "Letters of Gen. Henry W. Halleck, 1861–1862," *Collector* 21 (1908): 29, 39–40, 52–53. There are also numerous Halleck letters in John Y. Simon et al., *Papers of Ulysses S. Grant,* 24 vols. (Carbondale: Southern Illinois University Press, 1967–). Many Halleck letters written during his army career in California have been preserved in 31st Cong., 1st Sess., Sen. Exec. Doc. 18. There is a selection of the correspondence between Halleck and Francis Lieber in Richard Shelby Hartigan, *Lieber's Code and the Law of War* (Chicago: Precedent, 1983). Two annotated editions of Halleck's commentary on his Mexican War combat experiences are John D. Yates, ed., "Insurgents on the Baja Peninsula: Henry Halleck's Journal of the War in Lower California, 1846–1848," *California Historical Quarterly* 54 (1975): 221–244, and Doyce B. Nunis Jr., ed., *The Mexican War in Baja California: The Memorandum of Captain Henry W. Halleck concerning His Expedition in Lower California, 1846–1848* (Los Angeles: Dawson's Book Store, 1977). Halleck's speeches in the California Constitutional Convention are found in J. Ross Browne, *Report of the Debates in the Convention of California on the Formation of the State Constitution in September and October, 1849* (Washington, D.C.: John T. Towers, 1850). His testimony in a New Almaden Mine court case is located in *Transcript of the [US Federal District Court in San Francisco] Proceedings, in Case No. 366, Andres Castillero, Claimant, vs. The United States, Defendant, for the Place Named New Almaden* (San Francisco: Whitton, Towne, 1858).

As well as performing his duties in the Civil War and managing his many business ventures, Halleck was a prodigious writer. Here, in chronological order, are his writings, which appeared in a wide variety of publication forms: "Congressional Report on the Militia of the United States," *New York Review* 14 (1840): 277–305; *Bitumen: Its Varieties, Properties, and Uses* (Washington: Peter Force, 1841); "A Notice of Some of the Foreign Military Periodicals," *Army and Navy Chronicle and Scientific Repository* 2 (1843): 566–570; "Army Organization," *United States Democratic Review* 16 (1845): 121–136; "Report on the Means of National Defense," 28th Cong., 2nd Sess, Sen. Doc. 85, (1845); *Elements of Military Art and Science . . .* (New York: D. Appleton, 1846, and later editions); "Report on the Laws and Regulations Relative to Grants or Sales of Public Lands in California," 31st Cong., 1st Sess., House Exec. Doc. No. 17 (1850); *A Collection of Mining Laws of Spain and Mexico* (San Francisco: O'Meara and Painter, 1859); trans. and ed., *Fundamental Principles of the Law of Mines by J. H. N. De Fooz* (San Francisco: J. B. Painter, 1860); *International Law; or Rules Regulating the Intercourse of States in Peace and War* (New York: Van Nostrand, 1861); trans., *Life of Napoleon by Baron Jomini*, 4 vols. (New York: D. Van Nostrand, 1864); *Elements of International Law, and Laws of War. Prepared for the Use of Colleges and Private Students* (Philadelphia: J. B. Lippincott, 1866).

The endnotes indicate the other primary and secondary sources I found most helpful in writing Halleck's life story.

Abbreviations Used in the Notes

Ad Gen	Adjutant General of the Army
AEB	Ambrose E. Burnside
AG	Adam Gurowski
AL	Abraham Lincoln
Basler	Roy P. Basler, ed., *The Collected Works of Abraham Lincoln,* (New Brunswick, NJ: Rutgers University Press, 1953–1955)
BL	Bancroft Library, University of California, Berkeley
CaHS	California Historical Society, San Francisco
CH	Catherine Halleck
CHS	Chicago Historical Society
CSA	California State Archives, Sacramento
CSL	California State Library, Sacramento
DCB	Don Carlos Buell
EH	Elizabeth Halleck
EMS	Edwin M. Stanton
FB	Frederick Billings
FBFM	Frederick Billings Farm and Museum Library, Woodstock, Vermont
FL	Francis Lieber
GBMc	George B. McClellan
GGM	George G. Meade
GHT	George H. Thomas
GW	Gideon Welles

GWC	George Washington Cullum
HBW	Henry B. Whipple
HL	Huntington Library, San Marino, California
HPB	Halleck, Peachy, and Billings
HWH	Henry W. Halleck
IIS	Isaac I. Stevens
JAD	John A. Dix
JaH	Jabez Halleck
JAMcC	John A. McClernand
JFG	Jeremy F. Gilmer
JGT	Joseph G. Totten
JH	Joseph Hooker
JP	John Pope
LC	Library of Congress
MHS	Minnesota Historical Society
NARA	National Archives and Records Administration, Washington, D.C.
O.R.	*War of the Rebellion . . . Officials Records of the Union and Confederate Armies,* 128 vols. (Washington, D.C.: Government Printing Office, 1880–1901)
PBP	Peachy, Billings, and Park
PdlG	Pablo de la Guerra
RBM	Richard B. Mason
RG	Record Group
Schoff	Schoff Civil War Collection, William L. Clements Library, University of Michigan, Ann Arbor, Michigan
SFP, UNDA	Sherman Family Papers, University of Notre Dame Archives, Notre Dame, Indiana
Simon	John Y. Simon, ed., *The Papers of Ulysses S. Grant,* 24 vols. (Carbondale: Southern Illinois University Press, 1967–)
SP	Eleanor Sexton Papers, Westernville, New York
SPC	Salmon P. Chase
TM	Theodore Miller
UI	University of Iowa Libraries
USG	Ulysses S. Grant
USMA	Special Collections and Archives Division, United States Military Academy Library
UW	University of Washington
WSR	William S. Rosecrans
WTS	William T. Sherman

Notes

1. Born to Gentility, Educated to Elitism

1. Henry J. Cookinham, *History of Oneida County New York from 1700 to the Present Time*, 2 vols. (Chicago: S. J. Clarke, 1912), 1:60, 457.
2. HWH, "Autobiographical Account, 1861," EG 23, HL; Samuel W. Durant, *History of Oneida County, New York* (Philadelphia: Everts and Fariss, 1878), 594; Bicentennial Book Committee, ed., *Moccasin Tracks to Ski Trails: The Story of the Town of Western* (Westernville, NY: Town of Western Bicentennial Committee, 1976), 57–59.
3. Bicentennial Book Committee, 18–19, 64–67, 69, 76; Durant, 595, 596.
4. Ellen Mills Halleck Cogswell, "Henry Wager Homestead," SP; Daniel E. Wager, ed., *Our County and Its People: A Descriptive Work on Oneida County New York* (Boston: Boston History Co., 1896), 76–77; Charles H. Whipple, comp., *Genealogy of the Whipple-Wright, Wager, Ward-Pell, McLean-Burnet Families* (n.p., 1917), 55–56.
5. Untitled, undated, handwritten genealogical sheet, SP. Most later biographical sketches such as that in the *Dictionary of American Biography* and Stephen E. Ambrose, *Halleck: Lincoln's Chief of Staff* (Baton Rouge: Louisiana State University Press, 1962), list Halleck's birth year as 1815. Family records and genealogies and his record at Union College indicate that he was born in 1814. See, for example, Ellen Cogswell to Lucius H. Hallock, December 18, 1925, SP.
6. Wager, 598; untitled, undated newspaper clipping, HWH Papers, USMA.
7. Cookinham, 1:261–265.
8. Books in SP.
9. Lucius Henry Hallock, *A Hallock Genealogy . . .* (New York: H. Lee, 1928),

428; Durant, 600; *An Appeal to the People of the State of New York, from the Inhabitants of Jefferson, Lewis, and Oneida Counties* . . . (Albany: J. F. Kittle, 1841); *Journal of the New York State Assembly,* 64th Session, 1841.

10. Frank T. Moore, ed., *The Portrait Gallery of the War, Civil, Military, and Naval: A Biographical Record* (New York: G. P. Putnam, 1865), 216.

11. David Wager to Martin Van Buren, December 7, 1833; HWH, Application Papers, USMA, Microcopy 688, NARA.

12. HWH to JaH, March 9, 1839, January 21, 1840, SP.

13. HWH to CH and Elizabeth Halleck, April 5, 1840, ibid.

14. HWH, "Autobiographical Sketch, 1861," EG 23, HL; Thomas C. O'Donnell, *Tip of the Hill* (Booneville, NY: Black River Books, 1953), 97, 105–106; *History of Columbia County, New York* (Philadelphia: J. B. Lippincott, 1878), 195, 207–209; HWH to TM, April 10, September 20, 1834, HWH Papers, USMA.

15. James Grant Wilson, "Types and Traditions of the Old Army," *Journal of Military Service Institution of the United States* 36 (May-June, 1905): 538n.

16. Moore, 216.

17. O'Donnell, 15–23, 99–100, 140.

18. HWH to TM, April 10, 1834, HWH Papers, USMA.

19. O'Donnell, 170–173; HWH to TM, April 10, 1834, HWH Papers, USMA.

20. HWH to JaH, January 21, 1840, September 22, 1839, SP; HWH to TM, August 11, 1834, HWH Papers, USMA.

21. HWH, Vertical File, Schaffer Library, Union College.

22. HWH to TM, September 20, 1834, HWH Papers, USMA.

23. C. Van Santvoord and Tayler Lewis, *Memoirs of Eliphalet Nott, D.D. LL.D., for Sixty-Two Years, President of Union College* (New York: Sheldon, 1876), 231; Andrew V. Raymond, *Union University* . . ., 3 vols. (New York: Lewis, 1907), 1:153–170.

24. Van Santvoord, 232–234.

25. HWH to TM, September 20, 1834, HWH Papers, USMA; Raymond, 155.

26. HWH, Vertical File, Schaffer Library, Union College; *Catalogue of the Officers and Students in Union College, 1836* (Schenectady, 1836); David S. Sparks, *Henry Wager Halleck,* Union Worthies No. 17 (Schenectady: Union College, 1962), 12; Sarah Weiner, Executive Assistant, the Phi Beta Kappa Society, to the author, October 20, 1999, in the author's possession.

27. Sparks, 12.

28. Raymond, 1:183.

29. Wager, 29–32; Samuel Beardsley to Louis Cass, December 31, 1832, January 3, 1833, HWH Cadet Application Papers, USMA, Microcopy No. 688, NARA.

30. David Wager to Martin Van Buren, December 7, 1833, Beardsley to Cass, February 17, 1834, January 27, February 25, 1835, Wager to Cass, March 14, 1835, Beardsley to Cass, March 20, 1835, Wager to Cass, April 3, 1835, HWH and Henry Wager to Cass, April 15, 1835, HWH Cadet Application Papers, USMA, Microcopy No. 688, NARA.

31. Wager, 32. The Democrats carried Oneida County every presidential election between 1832 and 1884 with the exception of 1872 and 1880. Cookinham, 1:183–185; HWH to TM, August 11, September 20, 1834, HWH Papers, USMA.

32. A brief description of the antebellum military academy reservation may be found in George Crockett Strong and Benson John Lossing, *Cadet Life at West Point* (Boston: T. O. H. P. Burnham, 1862), vii–xvii; *The Centennial of the United States Military Academy at West Point New York,* 2 vols. (Washington, D.C.: Government Printing Office, 1904; republished by Greenwood Press, 1969), 2:94, 97; *Regulations of the U.S. Military Academy at West Point* (New York: J. J. Harper, 1832), 7; Abner Riviere Hetzel to John Hetzel, June 17, 1823, in Sidney Forman, ed., *Cadet Life before the Mexican War,* Bulletin No. 1, The Library, USMA (West Point, 1945), 6–7. The best book on the academy before the Civil War is James L. Morrison Jr., *"The Best School in the World":
West Point, the Pre-Civil War Years, 1833–1866* (Kent: Kent State University Press, 1986). WTS to Hugh Boyle Ewing, January 25, 1844, Hugh Boyle Ewing Papers, Ohio Historical Society. This letter is available in printed form in John F. Marszalek, ed., "William T. Sherman on West Point—A Letter," *Assembly* 30 (Summer 1971): 14–15, 38, and in *Civil War Times Illustrated* 10 (January 1972): 22–23.

33. Max L. Heyman, *Prudent Soldier: A Biography of Major General E. R. S. Canby, 1817–1873 . . .* (Glendale, CA: A. H. Clark, 1959), 29; Roswell Park, *Sketch of the History and Topography of West Point* (Philadelphia: Henry Perkins, 1840), 104.

34. Wallace J. Schutz and Walter N. Trenerry, *Abandoned by Lincoln: A Military Biography of General John Pope* (Urbana: University of Illinois Press, 1990), 12.

35. Morrison, 73; HWH's description of the full summer encampment schedule is found in HWH to TM, July 16, 1838, HWH Papers, USMA.

36. Morrison, 72–74; JP to Lucretia Pope, July 7, 1838, in Forman, 8.

37. "Cadets Admitted to the U.S.M.A.," USMA.

38. Wilson, "Types and Traditions," 539. For a listing of the courses cadets took each year, the professors and assistant professors who taught them, and the texts they used, see Dorwin Wayne Newman, "West Point Graduates in the Mexican War: Internships for Generals in a Future War," Ph.D. diss., San Diego State University, 1991, 186–187.

39. Order No. 66, June 15, 1836, "Post Orders No. 6, 1832–1837"; Order No. 75, June 14, 1837, Battalion Order No. 59, June 23, 1838, Battalion Order 33, April 19, 1839, "Post Orders, No. 7, 1837–1839"; "Statement of Cadet Accounts, January 1838 to June 1841"; Order No. 131, "Post Orders No. 7, 1837–1838"; "Statement of Payments, January 1834 to December 1837, Treasurer's Office," "Statements of Cadets Accounts, January 1838 to June 1841," USMA.

40. John F. Marszalek, *Sherman: A Soldier's Passion for Order* (New York: The Free Press, 1993), 23.

41. Special Orders No. 31, "Post Orders No. 6, 1832–1837," USMA; GWC, *Biographical Register of the Officers and Graduates of the United States Military Academy* (Boston, 1891), 1:740.

42. John T. Hubbell and James W. Geary, eds., *Biographical Dictionary of the Union, Northern Leaders of the Civil War* (Westport, CT: Greenwood, 1995), 232.

43. Wilson, 538; JH to Samuel P. Bates, June 23, 1878, Samuel P. Bates Collection, Pennsylvania State Archives, Harrisburg; HWH to TM, November 28, 1837, HWH Collection, CHS.

44. "Register of Deficiencies, 1834–1839," p. 29, USMA; HWH to TM (?), January 7, 1836, Leslie Hindman Auctioneers, Chicago.

45. Morrison, 57.

46. HWH to "Dear Uncle," February 8, 1836, in the possession of Donald Winoski, Chadwick, NY.

47. HWH to TM, November 28, 1837, HWH Collection, CHS; HWH to TM, July 16, 1838, HWH Papers, USMA.

48. HWH to TM, July 16, 1838, HWH Papers, USMA.

49. HWH to TM, November 28, 1837, HWH Collection, CHS; HWH to TM, February 22, 1839, HWH Papers, USMA.

50. Thomas E. Griess, "Dennis Hart Mahan: West Point Professor and Advocate of Military Professionalism, 1830–1871," Ph.D. diss., Duke University, 1968, 190, 192, 193, 196.

51. Edward Coffman, *The Old Army: Portrait of the American Army in Peacetime, 1784–1898* (New York: Oxford University Press, 1986), 98.

52. Quoted in Samuel P. Huntington, *The Soldier and the State: The Theory and Politics of Civil-Military Relations* (Cambridge: Harvard University Press, 1957), 220–221.

53. Griess, 214–227, 248.

54. Leslie Chase, *Oration Delivered before the Corps of Cadets at West Point, July 4, 1837* (Newburgh, NY: J. D. Spalding, 1837).

55. Alan Aimone, Senior Special Collections Librarian, to the author, fax, October 22, 1999, in possession of the author; HWH, "Address to Graduating Class at West Point," EG 24, HL.

56. Edwin Wright Morgan to James Duncan, July 9, 1835, in Forman, 22.

57. HWH to TM, July 16, 1838, HWH Papers, USMA.

58. Orders No. 144, "Post Orders No. 7, 1832–1837," USMA; *Regulations*, 4, 51; Griess, 105.

59. Morrison, 52–53.

60. *Regulations*, 17–18.

61. HWH to TM, February 22, 1839, HWH Papers, USMA.

62. "Halleck Autobiographical Account, 1861," EG 23, HL.

63. HWH to S. Cooper, October 21, 1853, RG 77, NARA; Engineer Order No. 6, "Post Orders No. 7, 1837–1839," USMA.

64. Watch fob on the website EBAY.com, item number 12159, February 25, 2001; HWH to Fred A. Smith, July 16, 1839, RG 77, NARA; HWH to JaH, Septem-

ber 22, March 9, 1839, HWH to "My Dear Sister," November 3, 1839, HWH to JaH, January 21, 1840, SP.

65. *Regulations*, 11–12.
66. HWH to JaH, September 22, 1839; HWH to "My Dear Sister," November 3, 1839, SP.
67. HWH to TM, December 28, 1839, pasted in Rare Book 37810, HL.
68. HWH to JaH, January 21, April 8, 1840, SP.
69. HWH to TM, December 28, 1839, pasted in rare book 37810, HL; HWH to "Dear Brother," April 8, 1840, SP.
70. HWH to CH, September 25, 1840, SP.
71. HWH to TM, December 28, 1839, pasted in Rare Book 37810, HL.

2. Army Engineer at Home and Abroad

1. "Report of Absence of Officers and Professors, Vol. 1, December 22, 1837 to May 13, 1867," March 20, 1840, USMA.
2. HWH to CH, September 25, 1840, HWH to JaH, October 3, 1840, SP; On at least one occasion he was a groomsman for a member of the Hope Club. Robert Chew to HWH, April 9, 1855, HPB, BL.
3. HWH to TM, November 11, 1840, HWH Papers, USMA.
4. HWH to HBW, October 30, 1841, HBW Papers, MHS. For a biography of John Forsyth, see Alvin Leroy Duckett, *John Forsyth, Political Tactician* (Athens: University of Georgia Press, 1962).
5. James Grant Wilson, "Types and Traditions of the Old Army," *Journal of the Military Service Institution of the United States* 36 (1905): 543; HWH to TM, November 11, 1840, HWH Papers, USMA.
6. HWH to JaH, June 11, 1841, July 13, 1844, February 4, 1842, HWH to Joseph Halleck, February 4, 1842, November 17, 1843, HWH to CH, August 25, 1845, SP.
7. HWH to JGT, October 17, 1840, RG 77, NARA.
8. HWH to JGT, July 8, 29, September 20, 1841, RG 77, NARA.
9. HWH to JGT, September 27, 1841, ibid.; HWH to TM, October 8, 1841, in Wilson, 551–552; JGT, "Report of the Chief Engineer," *Army and Navy Chronicle and Scientific Repository*, January 11, 1844, 35. A detailed overview of coastal defenses is Russell Reed Price, "American Coastal Defense: the Third System of Fortification, 1816–1864," Ph.D. diss., Mississippi State University, 1999.
10. John Howard Williams to HWH, February 20, 1862, HWH Papers, LC; HWH to JaH, February 25, 1843, October 3, 1843, HWH to CH, August 31, 1843, November 20, 1843, SP.
11. [HWH], "Congressional Report on the Militia of the United States," *New York Review* 14 (October 1840): 277–305; HWH, *Bitumen: Its Varieties, Properties, and Uses* (Washington, D.C.: Peter Force, 1841); HWH to HBW, October 30, 1841, HBW Papers, MHS; HWH to JGT, October 16, 1842, RG 77, NARA; HWH, "A Notice of Some of the Foreign Military Periodicals,"

Army and Navy Chronicle and Scientific Repository 2 (November 2, 1843): 566–570; "Trustees Minutes Book C," July 26, 1843, Schaffer Library, Union College; HBW, *Lights and Shadows of a Long Episcopate* (New York: Macmillan, 1899), 102; HWH, "Report on the Means of National Defense," 28th Cong., 2nd Sess., Sen. Exec. Doc. 85, Serial No. 541.

12. "Report on the Means of National Defense," 2, 7, 50.

13. Ibid., 74, 76.

14. HWH to JGT, November 13, 17, 1843, RG 77, NARA.

15. Matthew Moten, *The Delafield Commission and the American Military Profession* (College Station: Texas A and M University Press, 2000), 83–85.

16. Thomas E. Griess, "Dennis Hart Mahan, West Point Professor and Advocate of Military Professionalism," Ph.D. diss., Duke University, 1968, 122–133.

17. HWH to JGT, January 3, 1844, RG 77, NARA; Harvey Levenstein, *Seductive Journey: American Tourists in France from Jefferson to the Jazz Age* (Chicago: University of Chicago Press, 1998), 13–23.

18. HWH, "Autobiographical Account, 1861," EG 23, HL; HWH to JGT, January 3, 1844, RG 77, NARA.

19. HWH to CH, January 28, 1844, SP; the candelabra and the clock are with SP; James L. Morrison Jr., *"The Best School in the World": West Point, the Pre-Civil War Years, 1833–1866* (Kent: Kent State University Press, 1986), 57; Erasmus Darwin Keyes, *Fifty Years Observation of Men and Events, Civil and Military* (New York: Charles Scribners Sons, 1884), 78–81.

20. HWH to JGT, February 4, 1844, RG 77, NARA.

21. HWH to JGT, April 1, May 19, 1844, RG 77, NARA.

22. HWH to JGT, May 19, 1844, RG 77, NARA.

23. HWH to JGT, July 25, 1845, RG 77, NARA; Dorwin Wayne Newman, "West Point Graduates in the Mexican War: Internships for Generals in a Future War," Ph.D. diss., San Diego State University, 1991; HWH to JGT, May 29, 1844, RG 77, NARA.

24. HWH to JGT, May 19, July 13, December 11, 1844, January 3, 1845, January 19, 1845, December 17, 1844, June 12, 1844, RG 77, NARA.

25. HWH to GWC, February 13, 1845, HWH Papers, USMA.

26. For a discussion of Halleck Tustenuggee and the issue of Indian names in Florida, see John K. Mahon, *History of the Second Seminole War, 1835–1842* (Gainesville: University of Florida Press, 1967), 10–11, 282–283, and J. Leitch Wright Jr., *Creeks and Seminoles: The Destruction and Regeneration of the Muscogulge People* (Lincoln: University of Nebraska Press, 1986), 29–30; Professor David Heidler queried several experts in Indian names and the conclusion was that Halleck Tustennuggee was not named after HWH. David Heidler, emails to the author, December 2, 2002, February 21, 2003, in the possession of the author. The letters in which Halleck uses the name Halleck Tustennuggee or it is applied to him are HWH to GWC, September 11, November 23, 1846, April 22, 1847, April 11, 1848, GWC Papers, USMA, and Robert Chew to HWH, December 18, 1854, August 2, 18, 1856, HPB, BL. Francis B. Heitman, *Historical Register and Dictionary of the United States*

Army, vol. 1 (Washington, D.C.: Government Printing Office, 1903), 491; HWH to JGT, December 20, 1844, March 28, 1845, RG 77, NARA.

27. [HWH], "Army Organization," *The United States Magazine and Democratic Review* 16 (February 1845), 121–136; HWH to JGT, November 29, 1845, RG 77, NARA.

28. Unless otherwise noted, the section on the Lowell Institute is based on Edward Weeks, *The Lowells and Their Institute* (Boston: Little Brown, 1966), and Harriette Smith, *The History of the Lowell Institute* (New York: Lamson, Wolffe, 1898).

29. HWH to GWC, January 20, 1846, UI.

30. Silliman quote is in Weeks, 43; HWH to GWC, January 20, 1846, UI.

31. Dennis Hart Mahan, *An Elementary Treatise on Advanced-Guard, Outpost, and Detachment Service of Troops . . .* (New York: J. Wiley, 1847).

32. Griess, 302, 302n.

33. An excellent analysis of Jominian theory is found in Thomas L. Connelly and Archer Jones, *The Politics of Command: Factions and Ideas in Confederate Strategy* (Baton Rouge: Louisiana State University Press, 1973), 3–30.

34. HWH, trans., *Life of Napoleon by Baron Jomini,* 4 vols. (Kansas City, MO: Hudson-Kimberly, 1897), 1:21, originally published in 1864.

35. Edward Hagerman, "From Jomini to Dennis Hart Mahan: The Evolution of Trench Warfare and the American Civil War," *Civil War History* 13 (September 1967): 205n. Russell L. Weigley, *The American Way of War: A History of United States Military Strategy and Policy* (New York: Macmillan, 1973), 86–87.

36. HWH, *Elements of Military Art and Science* (New York: D. Appleton, 1846), 23.

37. Ibid., 145.

38. Ibid., 40, 41–42, 51.

39. Ibid., 51, 58.

40. Grady McWhiney, "Conservatism and the Military," *Continuity* 4/5 (1982): 41–42, 44; HWH, *Elements of Military Art and Science,* 116, 124; Edward Hagerman, "The Professionalization of George B. McClellan and Early Civil War Field Command: An Institutional Perspective," *Civil War History* 21 (June 1975): 114.

41. Hagerman, "From Jomini to Dennis Hart Mahan," 205–206; George Peterson Winton, "Ante-Bellum Military Instruction of West Point Officers and Its Influence upon Confederate Military Organization and Operation," Ph.D. diss., University of South Carolina, 1996, 101; James L. Morrison Jr., "Military Education and Strategic Thought, 1846–1861," in Kenneth J. Hagan and William R. Roberts, eds., *Against All Enemies: Intrepretations of American Military History from Colonial Times to the Present* (New York: Greenwood Press, 1986), 123; Allan R. Millett and Peter Maslowski, *For the Common Defense: A Military History of the United States of America* (New York: The Free Press, 1984), 128; Russell L. Weigley, *History of the United States Army* (New York: Macmillan, 1967), 181, argued similarly four decades ago.

42. HWH to IIS, June 28, 1846, IIS Papers, UW; HWH to JGT, January 24, 1847, RG 77, NARA.

43. HWH to IIS, June 28, 1846, IIS Papers, UW.

44. HWH to JGT, July 11, 1846, RG 77, NARA; HWH to CH, July 12, 1846, SP.

45. HWH to GWC, January 20, 1846, UI.

3. War and Peace in California

1. For two other discussions of this voyage, see John F. Marszalek, *Sherman: A Soldier's Passion for Order* (New York: The Free Press, 1993), 54–61, and Bernarr Cresap, *Appomattox Commander: The Story of General E. O. C. Ord* (San Diego: A. S. Barnes, 1981), 20–25; Winfield Scott to C. Q. Tompkins, June 20, 1846, WTS Papers, LC.

2. Doyce B. Nunis Jr., ed., *The Mexican War in Baja California: The Memorandum of Captain Henry W. Halleck concerning His Expedition in Lower California, 1846–1848* (Los Angeles: Dawson's Book Store, 1977), 148; WTS to Ellen Sherman, August 3, 7, 1846, SFP, UNDA.

3. HWH to GWC, September 11, November 23, 1846, GWC Papers, USMA; WTS to Thomas Ewing, May 3, 1862; Joseph H. Ewing, ed., "WTS Bashes the Press," *American Heritage* 38 (July-August 1987): 30.

4. HWH to GWC, September 11, 1846, GWC Papers, USMA.

5. HWH to GWC, November 23, 1846, GWC Papers, USMA.

6. Journals of Henry A. Wise, October 21, 1846, RG 45, NARA.

7. HWH to GWC, September 11, November 23, 1846, GWC Papers, USMA.

8. WTS Journal, September 21, 1846, quoted in Marszalek, 59.

9. John S. Wise, *The End of an Era* (Boston: Houghton Mifflin, 1900), 1–9.

10. HWH to JGT, November 23, 1846, RG 77, NARA; HWH to GWC, November 23, 1846, GWC Papers, USMA.

11. HWH to GWC, January 15, 1847, GWC Papers, USMA.

12. WTS to Ellen Sherman, January 27, 1847, SFP, UNDA.

13. HWH to JGT, January 27, 1847, RG 77, NARA.

14. HWH to JaH, January 28, 1847, SP; Walter Colton, *Three Years in California* (New York: A. S. Barnes, 1850), 163; Theodore H. Hittell, *History of California*, 4 vols. (San Francisco: N. J. Stone, 1885), 2:630; Certificate, June 20, 1848, Sen. Exec. Doc. 18, 31st Cong., 1st Sess., Serial No. 557, 174–175. Hereafter cited as Serial No. 557.

15. Journals of Henry S. Wise, March 30, 1847, RG 45, NARA; Colton, 189.

16. HWH to GWC, April 22, 1847, GWC Papers, USMA.

17. HWH to JGT, February 13, 1847, RG 77, NARA.

18. Edwin Bryant, *What I Saw in California* (New York: D. Appleton, 1849), 429; HWH to GWC, April 22, 1847, GWC Papers, USMA.

19. HWH to JGT, May 30, 1847, April 11, 1847, RG 77, NARA.

20. HWH to GWC, April 22, 1847, GWC Papers, USMA.

21. HWH to JaH, April 26, 1847, SP; HWH to JGT, May 30, 1847, RG 77, NARA.

22. William R. Ryan, *Personal Adventures in Upper and Lower California in 1848–1849*, 2 vols. (London: Shoberl, 1850), 1:282; Hittell, 2:669.

23. HWH to GWC, October 11, 1847, GWC Papers, USMA.

24. HWH statement, [January or early February 1849], RG 94, NARA.

25. Chester S. Lyman, *Around the Horn to the Sandwich Islands and California, 1845–1850*, ed. Frederick J. Teggert (New Haven: Yale University Press, 1925), 221–223; Samuel H. Willey, *The Transitional Period of California from a Province in Mexico in 1846 to a State of the American Union in 1850* (San Francisco: Whitaker and Ray, 1901), 66–67.

26. HWH to Stephen Smith, HWH to James Black, August 16, 1847, HWH to "Occupants of the Missions of . . .," September 6, 1847, HWH to Mariano G. Vallejo, August 16, 1847, HWH (Circular) to the Receivers of Customs, August 19, 1847, HWH to R. Semple, August 23, 1847, HWH to J. L. Folsom, August 27, 1847, Serial No. 557, 356–357, 370, 357–358, 361–362, 365, 366; HWH to "Sir," September 18, 1847, HPB Papers, BL.

27. HWH to GWC, October 11, 1847, GWC Papers, USMA.; HWH to JGT, October 8, 1847, RG 77, NARA.

28. Unless otherwise noted, this account of HWH's military adventures in Lower California is based on Nunis and on John D. Yates, "Insurgents on the Baja Peninsula: Henry Halleck's Journal of the War in Lower California, 1847–1848," *California Historical Quarterly* 54 (Fall 1975): 221–244.

29. John Gallagher, "Personal Reminiscences of the War in Upper and Lower California between the America and California Troops," in Honoria Twomey, ed., *History of Sonoma County California*, 2 vols. (Chicago, S. J. Clarke, 1926), 1:280.

30. HWH, "Autobiographical Account, 1861," EG 23, HL, 3; Gallagher, 282.

31. HWH to RBM, April 12, 1848, in Nunis, 199–206, and John Frost, *Frost's Pictorial History of the State of California* (New York: Derby and Miller, 1850), 496–508.

32. James M. Merrill, *DuPont:The Making of an Admiral* (New York, 1986), 188; Samuel F. Du Pont to Benjamin Gerhard, August 2, 1862, in Samuel F. Du Pont, *A Selection from His Civil War Letters*, ed. John D. Hayes, 3 vols. (Ithaca: Cornell University Press for the Eleutherian Mills Historical Library, 1969), 2:178.

33. *Alta California*, January 25, 1849; HWH to GWC, April 11, 1848, GWC Papers, USMA; HWH to "Sir," May 6, 1848, unsigned draft, HPB Papers, BL.

34. Willey, 73; WTS to J. D. Stevenson, August 26, 1848, quoted in Donald C. Biggs, *Conquer and Colonize: Stevenson's Regiment and California* (San Rafael, CA: Presidio, 1977), 157.

35. HWH to J. L. Folsom, August 9, 1848, HWH to R. Semple, August 14, 1848, HWH to E. H. Harrison, September 25, 1848, HWH to Stephen C. Foster, August 26, 1848, Serial No. 557, 568, 570, 636–637, 536–37; *Laws for the Better Government of California, the Preservation of Order, and the Protection of the Rights of the Inhabitants, during the Military Occupation of the Country by the Forces of the United States* (San Francisco: S. Brannon, 1848);

Lindley Bynum, "Laws for the Better Government of California, 1848," *Pacific Historical Review* 2 (September 1933): 279–291; ca. July 1862 untitled newspaper clipping, HWH Papers, USMA.

36. WTS to HWH, January 25, 1849, HWH to WTS, January 25, 26, 1849, RBM to HWH, January 26, 1849, HWH to RBM, January 26, 1849, WTS to HWH, January 26, 1849, RG 94, NARA; RBM to WTS, January 26, 1849, WTS to RBM, undated, with annotation by RBM dated January 27, 1849, WTS to HWH, January 29, 1849, copies, WTS Papers, LC; WTS to HWH, HWH to WTS, January 29, 1849, HWH statement [January or early February, 1849], RG 94, NARA.

37. HWH to CH, April 4, 1849, SP; Announcement, May 1, 3, 1849, Serial No. 557, 730, 733; W. E. P. Hartwell, *Translation and Digest of Such Portions of March 20th and May 23rd, 1837 as Are Supposed to Be Still in Force and Adopted to the Present Condition of California* (San Francisco: Alta California, 1849).

38. Theodore Grivas, *Military Governments in California, 1846–1850* (Glendale, CA: Arthur H. Clark, 1963), 118, 125–126; HWH, "Autobiographical Account, 1861," EG 23, HL.

39. Augustias de la Guerra Ord, *Occurrences in Hispanic California,* ed. William Ellison (Washington, D.C.: Academy of Franciscan History, 1956), 27; "Report on the Laws and Regulations Relative to Grants or Sales of Public Lands in California, H. W. Halleck," March 1, 1849, Serial No. 557, 120–183.

40. Walter Colton to RBM, June 14, 1848, in "Report on the Laws," in Serial No. 557, Appendix 27, 170–171; Cardinal Goodwin, "The Establishment of State Government in California, 1846–1850," Ph.D. diss., University of California, Berkeley, 1916, 316n; HWH to Juan M. Marron et. al., May 15, 1849, Serial No. 557, 740–741. For a brief synopsis of HWH's argument, see W. W. Robinson, *Land in California . . .* (Berkeley: University of California Press, 1948), 97–98.

41. HWH to GWC, April 11, 1848, GWC Papers, USMA; HWH to CH, August 28, 1848, SP.

42. HWH to CH, April 4, 1849, SP.

43. Grivas, 135–137.

44. RBM to JGT, July 17, 1849, HWH to RBM, October 31, 1849, RG 77, NARA; Willey, 83.

4. From Soldier to Businessman

1. For a brief overview of the attempts to form a civilian government, see Donald C. Biggs, *Conquer and Colonize: Stevenson's Regiment and California* (San Rafael, CA: Presidio, 1977), 177–181.

2. HWH to J. D. Stevenson, June 1, 1849, LE 463, HL; Proclamation . . . June 3, 1849, Sen. Exec. Doc. 18, 31st Cong., 1st Sess., Serial No. 557, 752–756. Hereafter cited as Serial No. 557.

3. Zoeth Skinner Eldredge, ed., *History of California,* 5 vols. (New York: Century History Company, 1915), 3:288–289.
4. A detailed discussion of the major delegates appears in David Alan Johnson, *Founding the West: California, Oregon, and Nevada, 1840–1890* (Berkeley: University of California Press, 1992), 101–120; for a list of all delegates and basic information about them, see J. Ross Browne, *Report of the Debates in the Convention of California on the Formation of the State Constitution in September and October, 1849* (Washington, D.C.: John T. Towers, 1850), 478.
5. George Hamlin Fitch, "How California Came into the Union," *Century* 40 (1890): 785; James Bayard Taylor, *Adventures and Life in San Francisco,* 2 vols. (London: Richard Bentley, Parry, 1852), 1:149–150; the Colton quotation is from Eldredge, 3:285.
6. Lina Fergusson Browne, ed., *J. Ross Browne: His Letters, Journals, and Writings* (Albuquerque: University of New Mexico Press, 1969), 125, 126, 129; Samuel H. Willey, *The Transition Period of California from a Province in Mexico in 1846 to a State of the American Union in 1850* (San Francisco: Whitaker and Ray, 1901), 90–91.
7. Browne, *Report,* 7; HWH to K. H. Dimmick, September 3, 1849, serial 557; original in California Constitutional Convention, Working Papers, CSA.
8. Browne, *Report,* 7–10, 14–17, 20.
9. Ibid., 20–29.
10. Ibid., 43–44, 339.
11. Ibid., 305, 306–307, 78, 92.
12. Ibid., 98, 130, 135, 245, 351.
13. Walton Bean, *California: An Interpretive History,* 2nd ed. (New York: McGraw-Hill, 1973), 131; Browne, *Report,* 175–176; see HWH's long speech in Browne, *Report,* 433–437; for Gwin, HWH, and other delegate boundary proposals, see "Article XII, The Boundary," California Constitutional Convention, Working Papers, CSA.
14. Browne, *Report,* 441, 457, 458.
15. Ibid., 259, 75.
16. Ibid., 284.
17. Ibid., 393–394, 397, 399.
18. Biggs, 185–186; Samuel H. Willey, "Recollections of General Halleck as Secretary of State in Monterey, 1847–1849," *The Overland Monthly* 1 (1872): 16; Fitch, 787. P. G. T. Beauregard, later a Confederate general, sent HWH a letter of congratulations, Beauregard to HWH, June 14, 1850, Society of California Pioneers, San Francisco.
19. HWH, "Autobiographical Account, 1861," EG 23, HL.
20. Browne, *Report,* 477; Bayard Taylor, *Eldorado, or Adventures in the Path of Empire,* 8th ed. (New York: Richard Bentley, 1857), 165–166.
21. Willey, "Recollections," 16; Fitch, 788; Theodore H. Hittell, *History of California,* 4 vols. (San Francisco: N. J. Stone, 1885), 2:786; HWH, "Autobiographical Account, 1861," EG 23, HL; HWH to David Spence, November 20,

1849, Sen. Exec. Doc. 52, 31st Cong., 1st Sess., Serial No. 561, 26–27. Hereafter cited as Serial No. 561.

22. HWH to CH, December 4, 1849, William W. Halleck to Father and Mother, December 22, 1849, SP; Proclamation to the People of California, December 12, 20, 1849, in Peter H. Burnett, *Recollections and Opinions of an Old Pioneer* (Oakland: Biobooks, 1946), 215–216; second proclamation in Serial No. 561, p. 40.

23. HWH, proclamations, Serial No. 557, 749, 750, 783, 760.

24. Robin W. Winks, *Frederick Billings: A Life* (New York: Oxford University Press, 1991), 39–44, 44–45; Oscar T. Shuck, ed., *History of the Bench and Bar of California* (Los Angeles: Commercial Printing House, 1901), 411–412.

25. Jane Curtis, Peter Jennison, and Frank Lieberman, *Frederick Billings, Vermonter* (Woodstock, VT: Woodstock Foundation, 1986), 25–26; FB to S. H. Willey, July 10, 1883, Letters from FB to Samuel Hopkins Willey, 1883–1889, BL; Taylor, 179.

26. Erasmus Darwin Keyes quoted in Kenneth H. Johnson, *The Bar Association of San Francisco: The First Hundred Years 1872–1972* (San Francisco: The Bar Association, 1972), 73.

27. HPB to "Don," April 21, 1850, HPB Papers, BL; *Alta California*, December 31, 1849, to February 1850; certificate, October 25, 1851, HPB Papers, BL. H. Trevor Park, like FB a Vermonter, belonged to the firm from September 1852 to August 1855. He left because of pressure from Peachy, who could never get over Park's refusal to stand up to another man's insult. Winks, 47–48.

28. A graphic overview of San Francisco in the early 1850s is J. D. Borthwick, *The Gold Hunters* (Oyster Bay, NY: Doubleday, 1917), 53–98; "Arrival of American Vessels," *Hunt's Merchant Magazine,* 28 (1850): 627; Francesca, "Reminiscences of San Francisco in 1850," The *Pioneer* 1 (1854): 16; Borthwick, 62–63; J. S. Holliday, *Rush for Riches: Gold Fever and the Making of California* (Berkeley: University of California Press, 1999), 228; Malcolm E. Barker, *More San Francisco Memoirs, 1852–1899* (San Francisco: Londanborn, 1996), 27; Jonathan Frost Locke to Mary M. Locke, January 29, 1859, Locke Papers, BL.

29. HWH to CH, March 25, 1850, January 31, 1852, SP.

30. Joseph Ellison, *California and the Nation, 1850–1869 . . .,* reprint (New York: Da Capo Press, 1969), 10–12.

31. Beverly E. Bastian, "'I Heartily Regret That I Ever Touched a Title in California': Henry Wager Halleck, the Californios, and the Clash of Legal Cultures," *California History* 72 (1993): 311–312. For an overview from the squatter point of view, see Paul W. Gates, "California's Embattled Settlers," *California Historical Society Quarterly* 41 (1962): 99–130. A good overview of the land issue is Paul W. Gates, "Adjudication of Spanish-Mexican Land Claims in California," *Huntinton Library Quarterly* 21 (1958): 213–236; Milton Hall Jr. to his father, April 15, 1852, October 25, 1854, Milton Hall Papers, BL; Gates, "Adjudication," 233; HWH to Henry Huber, January 14, 1852, G. W. Bissell to HPB, April 30, 1853, HWH to Bissell, undated, HPB Papers, BL; HWH to

PdlG, FAC 667 (487), HL; HWH to FB, September 18, 1852, FBFM. For a discussion of HPB fees, see Gates, "Adjudication," 233–234.

32. HWH to FB, September 12, 27, 1852, FBFM; HWH to PdlG, January 29, 1852, FAC 667 (487), HL; Petition of Jose Antonio de la Guerra [y Noriega], no date, HM 42974, HL.

33. William Edgar to HWH, February 21, 1853, HPB Papers, BL. HWH's own precision is evident in a scrapbook of land cases he pasted together for reference, CSL, and in a "Notebook Relating to California Land Claims, San Francisco," BL; James Grant Wilson, "Types and Traditions of the Old Army II," *Journal of the Military Service Institution* 36 (1905): 543.

34. W. W. Robinson, *Land in California: The Story of Mission Lands, Ranchos, Squatters, Mining Claims, Railroad Grants, Land Scrip, Homesteads* (Berkeley: University of California Press, 1948), 102; HWH to PdlG, April 23, 1853, (?) 1853, October 26, 1853, FAC 667 (487), HL; Bastian, 312; HWH to John Young, November 27, 1853, HPB Papers, BL; HWH to PdlG, March 5, 1853, FAC 667 (487), HL.

35. General Orders No. 19, Adjutant General's Office, War Department, May 20, 1852, HPB Papers, BL; HWH to JGT, July 5, 1850, RG 77, NARA; IIS to WSR, December 31, 1851, WSR Papers, UCLA; Special Orders No. 224 in Samuel Cooper to HWH, December 21, 1852, RG 26, NARA; JGT to HWH, April 18, 1853, HPB Papers, BL; for preparation of reports, see John D. Sloat to HWH, June 24, 1852, HPB Papers, BL; see HWH to E. L. Hardcastle, November 20, 1853, RG 26, NARA, for a list of lighthouse construction; GWC, *Biographical Register of the Officers and Graduates of the U.S. Military Academy,* 3rd ed. (Boston: Houghton Mifflin, 1891), 1:733.

36. Background for the following sketch of Montgomery Block is Idwal Jones, *Ark of Empire* (Garden City, NY: Doubleday, 1951), James D. Hall, "Halleck's Majestic Folly," *Pony Express Courier* 6 (March 1940): 3–7, and Oliver Perry Stidger, *The Story of the Mongomery Block of San Francisco. Originally the Washington Block and Known as "Halleck's Folly," 1852–1853* (n.p., n.d.); HWH to Henry Coppee, April 16, 1852, HWH Papers, USMA; HWH to JGT, September 1, 1851, HPB.

37. Hubert Howe Bancroft, *The Works of Hubert Howe Bancroft,* 39 vols. (San Francisco: History Co., 1888), 35:286; William J. Eames to Thomas O. Larkin, February 15, 1853, *The Larkin Papers . . .,* 11 vols. (Berkeley: University of California Press, 1951–1955), 8:220.

38. Works Progress Administration, Writers Program, *San Francisco: The Bay and Its Cities* (New York: Hasting House, 1947), 211.

39. Kenneth H. Cardwell, *Montgomery Block,* Historic American Building Survey, CAL 1228. August 1958, 1–2, CaHS; Hall, 4; George Tays, *The Montgomery Block,* Registered Landmark # 80, California Historical Landmark Series, for the State of California, Department of Natural Resources, WPA No. 65–3–3218, 1936, 6–8, CaHS; Agnes Foster Buchanan, "Some Early Business Buildings of San Francisco," *Architectural Record* 20 (1911): 25–27.

40. *LeCount and Strong's San Francisco City Directory for the Year 1854 . . .* (San

Francisco: San Francisco Herald Office, 1854), 190–192; Cardwell, 2–3. The building survived the 1906 earthquake and fire but was torn down in 1959 to make way for a parking lot. Now the Trans America Tower stands on the site of HWH's Montgomery Block.

41. HWH to E. L. Hardcastle, October 31, 1853, RG 26, NARA; HWH to Elizabeth Halleck, November 13, 1853, SP; Special Order No. 163, War Department, December 5, 1853, HPB Papers, BL; James Guthrie to HWH, December 21, 1853, RG 26, NARA.

42. HWH to CH, February 15, 1854, SP; John D. Kurtz to WSR, March 1, 1854, WSR Papers, UCLA; James Kimmins Greer, *Colonel Jack Hays, Texas Frontier Leader and California Builder* (New York: Dutton, 1952), 291.

43. HWH to "Companieros," April 19, 1854, FBFM.

44. Ibid.; HWH to PBP, May 18, July 3, 1854, HWH to FB, May 5, June 3, 20, 1854, FBFM.

45. HWH to T. A. Jenkins, July 6, 1864, RG 26, NARA; HWH to JGT, July 17, 1854, RG 77, NARA. According to correspondence dated July 26, 1854, in RG 77, NARA, HWH's official retirement date was August 1, 1854; Robert Chew to HWH, July 18, 1854, HPB, BL; HWH to PdlG, August 29, 1854, FAC 667 (487), HL.

46. The wedding was announced in San Francisco's major newspaper, *Alta California*, on May 8, 1855, although the date listed for the nuptials was incorrect. HWH to PBP, April 4, 1855, FBFM; GWC to Mrs. Gilmer, April 28, 1855, JFG Papers, USMA; EH to CH, April 19, 1855, SP.

47. Allen C. Clark, "Abraham Lincoln in the National Capital," *Records of the Columbia Historical Society* 27 (1925): 77; Robert Chew to HWH, August 3, 1855, HPB, BL; HWH to William R. Hutton, May 31, 1855, FAC 814, HL; HWH to PBP, April 4, 1855, FBFM.

5. From Peace to War

1. Unless otherwise noted, information in this chapter on the New Almaden Mine is from Idwal Jones, *Ark of Empire* (Garden City, NY: Doubleday, 1951), a source that must be used with care; Edgar Herbert Bailey and Donald L. Everhart, *Geology and Quicksilver Deposits of the New Almaden District, Santa Clara County, California* (Washington, D.C.: Government Printing Office, 1964); Lawrence E. Bulmore, "Our First Mercury Mines," *Pony Express* 16 (August 1949): 6, 11; Bulmore, "The Human Side of New Almaden," ibid., 16 (December 1949): 3–5, 14. The qotation is from J. S. Holliday, *Rush for Riches: Gold Fever and the Making of California* (Berkeley: University of California Press, 1999), 142.

2. Contemporary descriptions of the mine come from J. Ross Browne, "Down in the Cinnabar Mines: A Visit to New Almaden in 1865," *Harper's New Monthly Magazine* 31 (1865): 545–560; T. S. Hart, "The Almaden (Quicksilver) Mine, California," *The Mining Magazine* 1 (1853): 209; William Vincent

Wells, "The Quicksilver Mines of New Almaden, California," *Harper's New Monthly Magazine* 27 (1863): 25–41.

3. The quotations are from Wells, except for "disorders of the brain," which comes from Browne, and "mercurial soot," which comes from S. B. Christy, "Quicksilver Reduction at New Almaden," *American Institute—Mining Engineering Transactions* 13 (1885): 555. The medical information on mercury poisoning is from R. Robinson Baker, M.D., to the author (with journal article enclosures), December 14, 1999, in the author's possession.

4. *Transcript of the [U.S. Federal District Court in San Francisco] Proceedings, in Case No. 366, Andrés Castillero, Claimant, vs. the United States, Defendant, for the Place Named New Almaden* (San Francisco: Whitton, Towne & Co., 1858), 328, 329, 331; 2 Black 372.

5. 2 Black 337; William Rich Hutton, *Glances at California, 1847–1853* (San Marino, CA: HL, 1942), xvi–xviii; Kenneth M. Johnson, *The New Almaden Quicksilver Mine, with an Account of the Land Claims involving the Mine and Its Role in California History* (Georgetown, CA: Talisman Press, 1963), 46, 34–35; Phyllis F. Butler, "New Almaden's Casa Grande," *California Historical Society Quarterly* 54 (1975): 315. For an example of the working relationship between Halleck and Young, see John Young to HWH, July 29, 1857, HPB, BL.

6. Jimmie Schneider, "The Famous New Almaden Mine," *Pony Express* 16 (October 1949): 4; Butler, 316–318; Christy, 556. In the 1930s, the building housed striptease shows. Now it is an attractive museum and the headquarters for the New Almaden Quicksilver County Park.

7. *Facts concerning the Quicksilver Mines in Santa Clara County, California, for Private Circulation* (New York: Anthony, 1859), 14–15, preserved in Pamphlets on New Almaden, Volume 1, BL. Bailey and Everhart, 2; Bulmore, 6; Edgar H. Bailey, *Suggestions for Exploration at New Almaden Quicksilver Mine, California*, Special Report 17 (San Francisco: Division of Mines, 1952), 3.

8. Christian G. Fritz, Michael Griffith, and Janet M. Hunter, *A Judicial Odyssey: Federal Court in Santa Clara, Santa Cruz, and Monterey Counties* (San Jose: Advisory Committee, San Jose Federal Court, 1985), 44–45; Leonard W. Ascher, "The Economic History of the New Almaden Quicksilver Mine, 1845–1863," Ph.D. diss., University of California, Berkeley, 1934, 70–72.

9. Marc W. Johnston, "Faith with Our Victims: The Litigation of Mexican Land Grants in California after the Ascension—A Case Study of the New Almaden Claims," MA thesis, Harvard University, 1974, 59–60; Ascher, 73–74.

10. Ascher, 74–78.

11. Johnson, 58; Ascher, 79–87.

12. Ascher, 87–96; Mary Billings French, ed., *Letters from Mexico, 1859, by Frederick Billings* (Woodstock, VT: Elm Tree Press, 1936), xiii–xiv, 51; Schneider, *Pony Express* 16 (December 1949): 8.

13. Ascher, 99–101, 113.

14. Johnson, 6; Milton H. Shutes, *Abraham Lincoln and the New Almaden Mine* (San Francisco: Lawton R. Kennedy, 1936), 6.

15. The quotations from Halleck's testimony are taken from *Transcript [U.S. Federal District Court],* 325, 328, 329, 331, 340, 362–363.

16. Benjamin P. Thomas and Harold M. Hyman, *Stanton: The Life and Times of Lincoln's Secretary of War* (New York: Knopf, 1962), 81; 2 Black 29–38, 119–123; Johnson, 66; Robert Douthat Meade, *Judah P. Benjamin, Confederate Statesman* (New York: Oxford University Press, 1943), 132–133.

17. *New York Times,* October 7, 1859; HWH to FB, June 3, 1854, January 2, 1856, FBFM; HWH to PdlG, October 27, 1860, FAC 667 (487), HL.

18. HWH to William R. Hutton, May 31, 1855, FAC 814, HL; HWH to GWC, December 2, 1855, USMA; HWH to CH, May 21, December 5, 1855, SP.

19. Alvin Averbach, "San Francisco's South of Market District, 1850–1950: The Emergence of Skid Row," *California Historical Quarterly* 52 (Fall 1973): 198; Malcolm E. Barker, *More San Francisco Memoirs, 1852–1899* (San Francisco: Londonborn, 1996), 39; Albert Shumate, *Rincon Hill and South Park, San Francisco's Early Fashionable Neighborhood* (Sausalito, CA: Windgate, 1988), 17. See Shumate, 89, for a photograph of Halleck's home taken from a distance.

20. J. P. Munro-Fraser, *History of Marin County* (San Francisco: Alley, Bowen, 1880), 283; Jack Mason and Helen Van Cleve Park, *Early Marin* (Petaluma, CA: Marin County Historical Society, 1971), 67; HWH to PdlG, October 31, 1850, FAC 667 (487), HL; John D. Yates, "The Land That Halleck Could Call His Own," *San Rafael Independent-Journal,* June 24, 1972, M7–11; Third Auditor, Treasury Department to HWH, July 31, 1855, HPB Papers, BL.

21. Mason and Park, 69; Yates, 9; "The Rich Men of San Francisco," *Hunt's Merchants Magazine,* 32 (1854): 619.

22. EH to Margaret and Hereford Wilson, 1856(?), WN 1327, HL; Hamilton Boner, "The House of Traung," *Pony Express* 13 (July 13, 1946): 8; Mildred Brooke Hoover, *Historic Spots in California,* rev. ed. by William Abeloe (Stanford: Stanford University Press, 1966), 364; Gary W. Gallagher, ed., *Fighting for the Confederacy: The Personal Recollections of General Edward Porter Alexander* (Chapel Hill: University of North Carolina Press, 1989), 29–30; Clarence Edward Macartney, *Grant and His Generals* (New York: McBride Company, 1953), 55.

23. Walter H. Hebert, *Fighting Joe Hooker* (Indianapolis: Bobbs Merrill, 1944); John F. Marszalek, *Sherman: A Soldier's Passion for Order* (New York: The Free Press, 1993), 77–122.

24. Schuyler Hamilton to WTS, June 2, 1855, WTS Papers, LC.

25. Charles Welch to WTS, December 12, 1856, ibid.

26. Joseph Halleck Jr. to CH, July 6, 1857, SP.

27. HWH to CH, December 4, 20, 1857, EH to CH, HWH to CH, February 14, 1858, SP.

28. HWH to GWC, August 19, 1859, USMA; three indentures dated November 1, 1859, and *Utica Observer,* 1861 clipping, SP.

29. Charles Caldwell Dobie, *San Francisco's Chinatown* (New York: D. Appleton-Century, 1936), 78–79; HWH, "Expulsion of the Chinese from California and of the Moors from Spain," EG 23, HL; Frank Soule, *The Annals of San Francisco* (New York: D. Appleton, 1855), 716; *LeCount and Strong's San Francisco City Directory for the Year 1854* . . . (San Francisco: San Francisco Herald Office, 1854), 258; Nellie Stowe, "'Tower of Strength in the City's Building': A Reminiscence of Nellie Stowe, Secretary of the San Francisco Protestant Orphanage," January 7, 1941, CaHS; Society of California Pioneers, November 14, 1850, broadside, BL; Ruth Teiser, ed., *This Sudden Empire, California: The Story of the Society of California Pioneers, 1850–1950* (San Francisco: Society of California Pioneers, 1950), 3–6. In 1853, HWH also attempted to get the state legislature to organize a state historical society. Milton H. Shutes, "Henry Wager Halleck, Lincoln's Chief of Staff," *California Historical Society* 16 (1937): 200.

30. Walton Bean, "James Warren and the Beginnings of Agricultural Institutions in California," *Pacific Historical Review* 13 (1944): 361–375; Roger W. Lotchin, *San Francisco, 1846–1856: From Hamlet to City* (New York: Oxford University Press, 1974), 80; HWH, "Agriculture," "Farming in California" (two lectures), and "Stock Raising in California," EG 23, HL.

31. HWH, *A Collection of Mining Laws of Spain and Mexico* (San Francisco: O'Meara and Painter, 1859); HWH, *Fundamental Principles of the Law of Mines by H. N. De Fooz* (San Francisco: J. B. Painter, 1860).

32. HWH, *Elements of Military Art and Science . . .*, 2nd ed. (New York: D. Appleton, 1859); HWH, *International Law; or Rules Regulating the Intercourse of States in Peace and War* (New York: D. Van Nostrand, 1861). Emmerich de Vattel was an eighteenth-century Swiss philosopher and jurist who argued, in his 1758 *Rights of Nations,* that natural law was superior to legislation. Henry Wheaton was a nineteenth-century American jurist whose 1836 *Elements of International Law* was his most important work. James G. Randall, *Constitutional Problems under Lincoln* (New York: D. Appleton, 1926), 347n. Halleck allegedly also wrote a six-hundred-page history of California that this writer has never discovered. William E. Marsh, "Lincoln and Henry W. Halleck," in Allan Nevins and Irving Stone, eds., *Lincoln: A Contemporary Portrait* (Garden City, NY: Doubleday, 1962), 62.

33. HWH, Review of *The Natural Wealth of California* by Titus Fey Cronise, EG 24, HL.

34. Will of Joseph L. Folsom, November 18, 1853, Folsom Papers, CaHS; R. E. Cowan, "The Leidesdorff-Folsom Estate," *California Historical Society Quarterly* 7 (1928): 105–111; Halleck et. al. v. Mixer (1860), Case no. 2797, Supreme Court of California, WPA 8874, CSA;. GWC to HWH, December 6, 1856, Chew to HWH, March 4, August 2, 1856, HPB, BL. Regarding borax, see, for example, Butterworth to HWH, June 20, 1857, and Henry Toomey to Peachy and Billings, November 9, 1859, HPB, BL.

35. William J. Lewis, "Route of the Pacific and Atlantic Railroad between San Francisco & San Jose . . . October & November 1851," map, BL; *Articles of*

Association and By-Laws of the Pacific and Atlantic Railroad Company with the Reports of the Chief Engineer and Secretary (San Francisco: Whitton, Towne, 1854); Louis Richard Miller, "The History of San Francisco and San Jose Railroad," MA thesis, University of California, Berkeley, 1948; Records of the San Jose and San Francisco Railroad Company Minutes, 1851–1857, CSL; California Assembly, *Report of the Committee on Federal Relations on the Pacific and Atlantic Railroad, February 15ᵗʰ, 1857* (San Francisco, James Allen, 1857).

36. *Alta California,* June 16, 1860; see Miller for information on this short-lived railroad.

37. Hastings v. Halleck et. al., 13 Cal 207; Kenneth H. Johnson, *The Bar Association of San Francisco: The First Hundred Years 1872–1972* (San Francisco: Bar Association of San Francisco, 1972), 72; Hastings v. Halleck, Case No. 2160, WPA 6560, CSA; Hastings v. Halleck, 10 Cal 31 and 12 Cal 203.

38. HWH to IIS, February 12, 1854, IISPapers, UW; David A. Williams, *David C. Broderick: A Political Portrait* (San Marino, CA: HL, 1969), 35, 41; Nicholas Cullinan, "The History of Party Politics in California, 1848–1854," MA thesis, University of California, Berkeley, 1928; HWH, "Autobiographical Account, 1861," EG 23, HL; Williams, 52–53.

39. HWH to PdlG, October 21, 1850, August 17, 1857, FAC 667 (487), HL; *Oregon Spectator,* August 26, 1853, quoted in "Not Geary, Not Halleck," *Oregon Historical Quarterly* 44 (1943): 413.

40. An excellent study of the California vigilantes is Robert Senkiewicz, *Vigilantes in Gold Rush San Francisco* (Stanford: Stanford University Press, 1985); HWH to JFG, September 30, 1851, JFG Papers, USMA; HWH to "Dear Sister," January 11, 1852, SP; Willey, 50; Robin W. Winks, *Frederick Billings: A Life* (New York: Oxford University Press, 1991), 81–82; HWH to PdlG, January 29, 1852, September 12, 1851, April 23, 1853(?), FAC 667 (487), HL; "Petition to the Honorable Senate and Assembly of the State of California (1852)," CSA.

41. HWH to PdlG, July 27, 1852, July 24, 1853, FAC 667 (487), HL; HWH to IIS, February 12, 1854, IIS Papers, UW.

42. HWH to GWC, March 12, 1856, attached to HWH to GWC, February 20, 1870, GWC Papers, USMA; HWH to PdlG, September 9, 1856, FAC 667 (487), HL; GWC to HWH, December 6, 1856, HPB, BL.

43. HWH to PdlG, September 2, October 18, 1860, FAC 667 (487); Jane F. Carson, "California: Gold to Help Finance the War," *Journal of the West* 14 (1975): 27.

44. HWH to PdlG, July (?) 1860, September 2, 1860, FAC 667 (487), HL; HPB, *Catalogue of Law Library, 1861,* CaHS, and Pamphlets of San Francisco Libraries, BL.

45. Steven M. Avella, "California," in David S. Heidler and Jeanne T. Heidler, eds., *Encyclopedia of the American Civil War,* 5 vols. (Santa Barbara, ABC-CLIO, 2000), 1:340.

46. "Halleck Politico-Historical Argument against Disunion," EG 23, HL.

47. Dello Grimmett Dayton, "The California Militia, 1850–1866," Ph.D. diss., University of California, Berkeley, 1951, 142–147.

48. Certificate of appointment, December 14, 1860, EG 23, HL; HWH to J. G. Downey, December 17, 1860, photostatic copy, CSL; *Alta California,* December 18, 1860; DeWitt Thompson, *California in the Rebellion; A Paper Prepared and Read before California Commandery of the Military Order of the Loyal Legion of the United States, July 1891* (San Francisco: Bacus, 1891), 130–131; HWH to J. G. Downey, January 21, February 9, 11, 1861, Downey to HWH, February 12, 1861, Military Department, Adjutant General, CSA; HWH to H. A. Cobb, February 25, 1861, HWH to F. G. E. Little, February 26, 28, 1861, EG 23, HL.

49. HWH to Reverdy Johnson, April 30, 1861, James Grant Wilson, "Types and Traditions of the Old Army," *Journal of the Military Service Institution of the United States* 36 (1905): 553.

50. HWH to GWC, July 18, 1861, GWC Papers, USMA; HWH wrote a sharp letter to his old boss, the chief engineer, regarding the need to increase the number of engineer units. HWH to JGT, July 18, 1861, O.R., III, I, 336–337.

6. Commander of the Western Theater

1. Undated, unnamed newspaper clippings, GWC Papers, USMA; Thomas E. Griess, "Dennis Hart Mahan: West Point Professor and Advocate of Military Professionalism, 1830–1871," Ph.D. diss., Duke University, 1968, 334–335; James Grant Wilson, "Types and Traditions of the Old Army," *Journal of the Military Sevice Institution of the United States* 36 (1905): 544; AL to Simon Cameron, August 17, 1861, Basler, 4:489.

2. HWH to GWC, September 17, 1861, GWC Papers, USMA.

3. HWH to E. D. Townsend, September 11, 1861, letterpress copy, EG 23, HL. HWH made the same point in HWH to Lorenzo Thomas, September 17, 1861, ibid.; Schuyler Hamilton to James Grant Wilson, August 21, 1902, Wilson, 544; Charles Winslow Elliott, *Winfield Scott: The Soldier and the Man* (New York: Macmillan, 1937), 732–733.

4. HWH to John G. Downey, September 18, 19, 1861, CSL.

5. HWH to HBW, September 26, 1861, HBW Papers, MHS; HWH to PdlG, October 8, 1861, FAC 667 (487), HL; Winfield Scott to Simon Cameron, quoted in H. J. Eckenrode and Bryan Conrad, *George B. McClellan: The Man Who Saved the Union* (Chapel Hill: University of North Carolina Press, 1942), 35.

6. *Alta California,* September 18, 1861; William H Russell, *My Diary North and South,* ed. Fletcher Pratt (Gloucester, MA: P. Smith, 1969), September 6, 1861, 309–310.

7. *Alta California,* October 11, 1861; Milton H. Shutes, "Henry Wager Halleck, Lincoln's Chief of Staff," *California Historical Quarterly* 16 (1937): 200–201.

8. Michael Burlingame, ed., *Lincoln's Journalist: John Hay's Anonymous Writ-*

ings for the Press, 1860–1864 (Carbondale: Southern Illinois University Press, 1998), November 7, 1861, 136; Kenneth P. Williams, *Lincoln Finds a General,* 5 vols. (New York: Macmillan, 1949), 5:105.

9. For an excellent insight into Missouri during this period, see William E. Parrish, *Turbulent Partnership: Missouri and the Union, 1861–1865* (Columbia: University of Missouri Press, 1963) and Parrish, *Frank Blair, Lincoln's Conservative* (Columbia: University of Missouri Press, 1998). Unless noted, what follows is based on these two books. For the standard biography of Frémont, see Allan Nevins, *Frémont, Pathfinder of the West* (New York: D Appleton-Century, 1955).

10. General Order No. 97, Headquarters of the Army, November 9, 1861, O.R., I, 3, 567: Charles Gibson to H. R. Gamble, November 10, 1861, Gamble Papers, Missouri Historical Society; Edward Bates to James O. Brodhead and L. L. Glover, November 12, 1861, James O. Brodhead Papers, Missouri Historical Society; Howard R. Beale, ed., *Diary of Edward Bates, 1859–1866,* in *Annual Report of the American Historical Association, 1930* (Washington, D.C.: Government Printing Office, 1933), November 15, 1861, 4:201; *Harper's Weekly,* November 30, 1861, 754.

11. GBMc to HWH, November 11, 1861, O.R., I, 3, 568.

12. For a thorough study of St. Louis during the Civil War, see Louis S. Gerteis, *Civil War St. Louis* (Lawrence: University Press of Kansas, 2001); HWH to EH, December 14, 1862, Schoff; Galusha Anderson, *The Story of a Border City during the Civil War* (Boston: Little, Brown, 1908), 234; O. J. V, *Men of the Time: Being Biographies of Generals Halleck, Pope, Sigel, Corcoran, and Others,* Beadles Dime Series No. 1 (New York: Beadle, 1862), 19; *Seventh Brigade Journal* [Columbia, Tennessee], May 2, 1862.

13. J. Cutler Andrews, *The North Reports the Civil War* (Pittsburgh: University of Pittsburgh Press, 1955), 159.

14. Anderson, 235, 236–240, 242–243; Wilson, 545–546; *New York Times,* December 9, 1861; William M. McPheeters to Thomas C. Reynolds, January 9, 1863, EG 38, HL.

15. Bruce Catton, *Grant Moves South* (Boston: Little Brown, 1960), 127.

16. HWH to GBMc, November 20, 1861, AL endorsement, November 21, 1861, HWH to GBMc, November 30, 1861, AL to HWH, December 2, 1861, O.R., II, 1, 230, 232, 233.

17. General Order No. 3, Headquarters Department of Missouri, November 20, 1861, John A. Logan, *The Great Conspiracy, Its Origin and History* (New York: A. R. Hart, 1886), 372. In December 1861, however, HWH freed sixteen slaves from the St. Louis jail, on the basis of the July Confiscation Act. He said that state courts would have to decide if he had acted properly. Gerteis, 267.

18. The Cincinnati reporter's quote is in Bernard Weisberger, *Reporters for the Union* (Boston: Little Brown, 1953), 243; *Charles Sumner: His Complete Works,* 20 vols. (New York: Negro Universities Press, 1969; orig. published in 1900), 7:359; *Congressional Globe,* 37th Cong., 2nd Sess., December 9, 11,

1861, 33–34, 57–60; George Washington Julian, *Political Recollections, 1840–1872* (Chicago: Jansen, Mc Clurg, 1884), 200–201.

19. HWH to Frank Blair, December 8, 1861, *Congressional Globe,* 37th Cong., 2nd Sess., December 12, 1861, 76; HWH to FL, June 9, 1863, LI 1670, HL.

20. HWH to GBMc, November 27, 28, 30, 1861, O.R., I, 8, 382, 389–390, 395; HWH to HBW, November 29, 1861, Wilson, 553–554.

21. HWH to EH, December 14, 1861, Schoff; Charles G. Halpine to Mary G. Halpine, December 17, 1862 [1], HP 68, HL.

22. Unless noted, the following account of Sherman is based on John F. Marszalek, *Sherman: A Soldier's Passion for Order* (New York: The Free Press, 1993), and Marszalek, *Sherman's Other War: The General and the Civil War Press,* rev. ed. (Kent: Kent State University Press, 1999).

23. HWH to GBMc, December 2, 1861, O.R., I, 7, 2, 198; HWH to EH, December 14, 1861, Schoff.

24. WTS, *Memoirs of General W. T. Sherman* (New York: The Library of America, 1990), 238; GWC, *Biographical Register of the Officers and Graduates of the U.S. Military Academy,* 3rd ed., 3 vols. (Boston: Houghton, Mifflin, 1891), 1:34.

25. Stephen D. Engle, *Don Carlos Buell, Most Promising of All* (Chapel Hill: University of North Carolina Press, 1999), 79–80. This is the best biography of Buell.

26. David Herbert Donald, *Lincoln* (New York: Simon and Schuster, 1995), 45 (this is the definitive biography); President's General War Order Number 1, January 27, 1862, Basler, 5:111–112; The standard biography of EMS is Benjamin P. Thomas and Harold M. Hyman, *Stanton: The Life and Times of Lincoln's Secretary of State* (New York: Knopf, 1962).

27. AL to HWH, January 1, 1862, Basler 5:87; HWH to AL, January 1, 6, 1862, O.R., I, 7, 526, 532–533; AL to Simon Cameron, January 10, 1862, AL to DCB, January 13, 1862, Basler, 5:95, 98–99. According to Basler, the AL letter to HWH is lost.

28. HWH to GBMc, January 20, 1861, O.R., I, 8, 508–511.

29. JP to HWH, December 11, 1861, HWH to JP, January 27, 1862, O.R., I, 8, 426, 528. A thorough study is William Garrett Piston and Richard W. Hatcher, *Wilson's Creek: The Second Battle of the Civil War and the Men Who Fought It* (Chapel Hill: University of North Carolina Press, 2000).

30. USG to J. C. Kelton, January 6, 25, 1862, O.R., I, 7, 534, 565–566; USG, *Ulysses S. Grant: Memoirs and Selected Letters* (New York: The Library of America, 1990), 190. The two most recent biographies of USG are Brooks D. Simpson, *Ulysses S. Grant: Triumph over Adversity, 1822–1865* (Boston: Houghton Mifflin, 2000), and Jean Edward Smith, *Grant* (New York: Simon and Schuster, 2001); HWH to Samuel R. Curtis, January 13, 1862, HWH to GBMc, January 20, 1862, O.R., I, 8, 498, 511; Simpson, 107–108; USG to Kelton, December 17, 1862, HWH to USG, December 19, 1862, USG to HWH and HWH to USG, December 20, 1861, O.R., II, 1, 120, 121–122.

31. Simpson, 110; HWH to USG, January 30, 1862, O.R., I, 7, 121–122; HWH to

Thomas A. Scott, March 6, 1862, O.R., I, 10, 2, 10. For more information, see Kendall D. Gott, *Where the South Lost the War: An Analysis of the Fort Henry–Fort Donelson Campaign, February 1862* (Mechanicsburg, PA: Stackpole, 2003).

32. For a contemporary's discussion of Halleck's alleged treatment of Sigel and his supporters, see Thomas J. McCormack, ed., *Memoirs of Gustave P. Koerner, 1809 to 1896*, 2 vols. (Cedar Rapids, IA: Torch, 1909), 2:196–204. The standard biography of Sigel is Stephen D. Engle, *Yankee Dutchman: The Life of Franz Sigel* (Fayetteville: University of Arkansas Press, 1993). The best book on Pea Ridge is William L. Shea and Earl J. Hess, *Pea Ridge: Civil War Campaign in the West* (Chapel Hill: University of North Carolina Press, 1992).

33. HWH to GBMc, February 7, 1862, O.R., I, 7, 590; Catton, 179.

34. EMS to HWH, February 8, 1862, O.R., I, 8, 547; HWH to EH, January 15, 1862, HWH, "Letters of Gen. HWH, 1861–1862," *Collector* 21 (January 1908): 29; SPC to M. D. Potter, February 17, 1862, in John Niven, ed., *The SPC Papers*, 5 vols. (Kent: Kent State University Press, 1993–1998), 3:135; Thirty-Five Citizens of St. Louis to HWH, February 28, 1862, HWH Papers, USMA; HWH to Willard P. Hale and Daniel Taylor et. al., March 3, 1862, HWH Papers, Missouri Historical Society.

35. HWH to GBMc, February 10[17], 1862, HWH to DCB, February 15, 1862, O.R., I, 7, 599, 621.

36. See, for example, HWH to GBMc, February 14, 17, 1862, O.R.. I, 7, 612, 627–628.

37. GWC to HWH, March 2, 1862, HWH to GBMc, March 3, 1862, O.R., I, 7, 676, 679–680.

38. GBMc to HWH, March 3, 1862, HWH to GBMc, March 4, 1862, O.R., I, 7, 680, 682; HWH to USG, O.R., I, 10, 2, 3.

39. USG to HWH, March 5, 1862, in Simon, 4:317–319; HWH to USG, March 6, 1862, USG to HWH, March 7, 1862, O.R., I, 10, 2, 13, 15; HWH to USG, March 9, 1862, USG to HWH, March 11, 1862, O.R., I, 10, 2, 22, 30; Lorenzo Thomas to HWH, March 10, 1862, O.R., I, 7, 688.

40. HWH to GBMc, February 17, 19, 1862, GBMc to HWH, February 21, 1862, EMS to HWH, February 21, 1862, HWH to EMS, February 23, 24[21], 1862, O.R., I, 7, 628, 636, 645, 648, 655, 660; HWH to GBMc, March 10, 1862, O.R., I, 10, 2, 24–25.

41. President's War Order No. 3, March 11, 1862, HWH to DCB, March 13, 1862, HWH to USG, March 13, 1862, USG to HWH, March 14, 1862, O.R., I, 10, 2, 155, 33, 32, 36; Engle, *Buell*, 205–208.

42. HWH to EH, March 5, 1862, HWH, *Collector* 21 (January, 1908): 29.

43. HWH to DCB, March 26, 29, 1862, O.R., I, 10, 2, 66, 77; HWH to Andrew Foote, March 21, 1862, O.R., I, 8, 631; Milton S. Latham to HWH, March 21, 1862, HWH Papers, LC; Gunter Barth, ed., *All Quiet on the Yamhill: The Civil War in Oregon—the Journal of Corporal Royal A. Bensell, Company D., Fourth California Infantry* (Eugene: University of Oregon Books, 1959), April 3, 1862, 10.

44. HWH to DCB, March 19, 24, 17, 1862, O.R., I, 52, 1, 126, O.R., I, 10, 2, 64, 44, HWH to USG, March 17, 24, 1862, O.R., I, 10, 2, 42, 63.

45. The three most important books on Shiloh are Larry J. Daniel, *Shiloh: The Battle That Changed the Civil War* (New York: Simon and Schuster, 1998); James Lee McDonough, *Shiloh: In Hell before Night* (Knoxville: University of Tennessee Press, 1976); and Wiley Sword, *Shiloh, Bloody April* (New York: Morrow, 1974). The long-time standard biography of Johnston is Charles P. Roland, *Albert Sidney Johnston: Soldier of Three Republics* (Austin: University of Texas Press, 1964). EMS to HWH, April 23, 1862, HWH to EMS, April 24, 1862, O.R., I, 10, 1, 98–99; HWH to USG, April 28, 1862, Simon, 5:89n.

46. HWH to E. A. Hitchcock, April 18, 1862, Hitchcock Papers, LC; HWH to JP, April 8, 1862, O.R., I, 8, 675. A thorough account of this battle is Larry J. Daniel, *Island No. 10: Struggle for the Mississippi Valley* (Tuscaloosa: University of Alabama Press, 1996).

47. Wilson, 549; Mildred Thorne, ed., *The Civil War Diary of Cyrus F. Boyd, Fifteenth Iowa Infantry* (Millwood, NY: Kraus, 1977), April 21, 1862, 44; HWH to EMS, April 29, 1862, O.R., I, 10, 1, 664; William Hemstrett, "Little Things about Big Generals," *Personal Recollections of the War of the Rebellion: Addresses Delivered before the Commandery of the State of New York, Military Order of the Loyal Legion of the United States*, 3rd ser. (New York: G. P. Putnam's, 1907), 557, reprinted (Wilmington, NC: Broadfoot, 1992), 22:157; HWH to EH, April 14, 1862, Wilson, 556.

48. John A. Logan to Mary Logan, April 17, 1862, John A. Logan Family Papers, LC.

49. Special Field Orders No. 35, Headquarters, Department of the Mississippi, April 30, 1862, O.R., I, 10, 2, 144–145; HWH to USG, April 30, 1862, O.R., I, 52, 1, 245; USG, *Memoirs,* 251, 252; HWH to USG, May 12, 1862, O.R., I, 10, 2, 183. T. W. Freelon, in a handwritten biographical sketch of HWH, argues that HWH protected Grant throughout and "to save him from being absolutely shelved, General Halleck placed him second in command to himself, it being impossible to continue him at that time of popular prejudice in command of one of the armies." EG 23, HL.

50. HWH to EMS, May 14, 1862, O.R., I, 10, 1, 166; Matilda Gresham, *Life of Walter Quinton Gresham,* 2 vols. (Chicago: Rand McNally, 1919), 1:189; Edwin C. Fishel, *The Secret War for the Union: The Untold Story of Military Intelligence in the Civil War* (Boston: Houghton Mifflin, 1996), 184.

51. WTS to George E. Flynt, May 30, 1862, O.R., I, 10, 1, 740; the Richardson quotation is in Otto Eisenschiml and Ralph Newman, *The American Iliad: The Epic Story of the Civil War . . .* (New York: Grosset and Dunlap, 1956), 276; D. S. Stanley, "The Battle of Corinth," *Personal Recollections of the Civil War . . . Commandery of the State of New York Military Order of the Loyal Legion of the United States* (New York: G. P. Putnam, 1897), 269; HWH to EMS, May 18, 1862, O.R., I, 10, 1, 666; WSR to wife, May 25, 1862, WSR Papers, UCLA.

52. James G. Smart, ed., *A Radical View: The "Agate" Despatches of Whitelaw*

Reid, 1861–1865, 2 vols. (Memphis: Memphis State University Press, 1976), 1:192–197; Philip Kinsley, *The Chicago Tribune,* 3 vols. (Chicago: Chicago Tribune, 1943), 1:238; WTS to Ellen Sherman, June 6, 1862, SFP, UNDA.

53. WTS to HWH, May 27, 1862, JP to HWH, May 27, 30, 1862, HWH to DCB, May 30, 1862, JP to HWH, May 30, 1862, HWH to JP, May 30, 1862, O.R., I, 10, 2, 215–216, 225, 228, 225, 227; Chicago *Tribune,* June 2, 1862, in Stephen E. Ambrose, *Halleck: Lincoln's Chief of Staff* (Baton Rouge: Louisiana State University, 1990), 55.

54. HWH to JP, June 1, 1862, O.R., I, 10, 2, 237.

55. The effigy quotation is in Engle, *Buell,* 251; Mary Ann Anderson, ed., *The Civil War Diary of Allen Morgan Greer, Twentieth Regiment Illinois Volunteers* (Denver: R. C. Appleman, 1977), May 30, 1862, 34–35; Thorne, May 30, 1862, 53; USG, *Memoirs,* 255.

56. HWH to EH, May 31, 1862, Schoff.

57. EMS to HWH, June 2, 1862, O.R., I, 10, 2, 242; AL to HWH, June 4, 1862, O.R., I, 10, 1, 671; EMS to HWH, June 11, 1862, O.R., I, 16, 2, 8.

58. Special Field Orders No. 90, Headquarters, Department of the Mississippi, June 10, 1862, O.R., I, 17, 2, 3; HWH to DCB, June 4, 1862, O.R., I, 10, 2, 254; HWH to JP, June 14, 1862, HWH to AL, July 2, 1862, O.R., I, 17, 2, 9, 89.

59. HWH to EMS, June 30, July 1, 1862, O.R. I, 17, 2, 52, 59; HWH to DCB, June 21, 1862, O.R., I, 16, 2, 44; HWH to Samuel R. Curtis, June 23, 1862, O.R., I, 13, 117; HWH to USG, June 29, 1862, USG to HWH, June 29, 1862, HWH to USG, July 3, 1862, O.R., I, 17, 2, 46, 46–47, 67–68.

60. EMS to AL, June 30, 1862, O.R., I, 17, 2, 52–53; HWH to AL, July 5, 1862, O.R., I, 16, 2, 95; HWH to EH, July 5, 1862, Schoff.

61. HWH to EH, July 5, 1862, Schoff.

62. AL to HWH, July 2, 1862, HWH to AL, July 2, 1862, O.R., I, 17, 2, 64.

63. David S. Sparks, ed., *Inside Lincoln's Army: The Diary of Marsena Rudolph Patrick, Provost Marshal General, Army of the Potomac* (New York: Thomas Yoseloff, 1964), July 5, 1862, 103; William Sprague to AL, July 5, 1862, AL Papers, LC; AL to HWH, July 6, 1862, HWH to AL, July 10, 1862, O.R., I, 17, 2, 76, 88; Peter Cozzens, *General John Pope: A Life for the Nation* (Urbana: University of Illinois Press, 2000), 74–78 (this is the standard biography); EMS to HWH, July 11, 1862, O.R., I, 17, 2, 90; Elliott, 755.

7. Supreme Commander

1. HWH to EMS, July 15, 1862, O.R., I, 17, 2, 97.

2. HWH to AL, July 11, 1862, HWH to EMS, July 12, 1862, O.R., I, 17, 2, 90, 91; HWH to EH, July 13, 1862, James Grant Wilson, "General Halleck: A Memoir," *Journal of the Military Service Institution of the United States* 37 (September-October, 1905): 556–557. Some historians argue that Halleck wanted to bypass Grant and name Quartermaster Officer Robert Allen to command instead. Brooks D. Simpson, *Ulysses S. Grant: Triumph over Adver-*

sity, 1822–1865 (Boston: Houghton, Mifflin, 2000), 140, cites Bruce Catton, *Grant Moves South* (Boston: Little Brown, 1960), 287–288, in making this assertion. Another recent book, Jean Edward Smith, *Grant* (New York: Simon and Schuster, 2001), 660n, finds the evidence lacking.

3. AL to HWH, July 11, 1862, O.R., I, 16, 2, 122; AL to Andrew Johnson, July 11, 1862, Basler, 5:313–314; AL to HWH, July 11, 13, 1862, O.R., I, 16, 2, 122, and I, 16, 1, 738; DCB to HWH, July 11, 1862, HWH to DCB, July 14, 1862, O.R., I, 16, 2, 122–123, 143.

4. The AL quote is in Otto Eisenschiml, *The Hidden Face of the Civil War* (Indianapolis: Bobbs-Merrill, 1961), 250; AL to HWH, July 14, 1862, HWH to AL, July 15, 1862, O.R., I, 17, 2, 97, 98; HWH to EMS, July 19, 1862, O.R., I, 13, 477.

5. The HWH quote is in Warren K, Hassler, *General George B. McClellan: Shield of the Union* (Baton Rouge: Louisiana State University Press, 1957), 187; Frank Southwick to HWH, July 14, 1862, HWH Papers, LC; John R. Martin to "Dear Father," July 17, 1862, HM 32131, HL.

6. Special Field Orders No. 162, Headquarters, Dept. of the Mississippi, July 16, 1862, HWH to WTS, July 16, 1862, O.R., I, 17, 2, 101, 100; HWH to DCB, July 15, 12, 1862, O.R., I, 16, 2, 151, 128; HWH to USG, July 11, 1862, O.R., I, 17, 2, 90.

7. WTS to HWH, July 16, 1862, O.R., I, 17, 2, 100–101; DCB to HWH, July 16, 1862, O.R., I, 16, 2, 159; the USG quote is in Herman Hattaway and Archer Jones, *Why the North Won: A Military History of the Civil War* (Urbana: University of Illinois Press, 1983), 237.

8. Philip Kinsley, *The Chicago Tribune*, 3 vols. (Chicago: Chicago Tribune, 1943), 1:243; Richard S. Fay to Benjamin F. Butler, July 29, 1862, in Benjamin F. Butler, *Private and Official Correspondence of Gen. Benjamin F. Butler during the Period of the Civil War*, 5 vols. (privately printed, 1917), 2:122.

9. Noah Brooks, *Washington in Lincoln's Time* (New York: Century, 1896), 2–3; William E. Doster, *Lincoln and Episodes of the Civil War* (New York: G. P. Putnam, 1915), 56.

10. Benjamin F. Thomas and Harold M. Hyman, *Stanton: The Life and Times of Lincoln's Secretary of War* (New York: Knopf, 1962), 215–216.

11. Herman Haupt, *Reminiscences* (Milwaukee: Wright and Jays, 1901), 302; George Alfred Townsend, *Rustics in Rebellion: A Yankee Reporter on the Road to Richmond, 1861–1865* (Chapel Hill: University of North Carolina Press, 1950), 189; Michael Burlingame, ed., *Lincoln's Journalist: John Hay's Anonymous Writings for the Press, 1860–1864* (Carbondale: Southern Illinois University Press, 1998), 288.

12. Brooks, 2.

13. Ibid., 28–29; James Harrison Wilson, *Under the Old Flag*, 2 vols. (New York: D. Appleton, 1912), 1:338; Thomas and Hyman, 150–151, 164.

14. Brooks, 33, 34; Frederick J. Blue, *Salmon P. Chase: A Life in Politics* (Kent: Kent State University Press, 1987).

15. Peter Cozzens and Robert I. Girardi, eds., *The Military Memoirs of General*

John Pope (Chapel Hill: University of North Carolina Press, 1998), 124. GBMc, *McClellan's Own Story* (New York: Charles L. Webster, 1887), 137; HWH to EH, January 15, 1862, Schoff.

16. SPC to Kate Chase, July 13, 1862, in John Niven, ed., *The Salmon P. Chase Papers,* 5 vols. (Kent: Kent State University Press, 1996), 3:226–228; Edward Bates to H. R. Gamble, July 24, 1862, Edward Bates Papers, Missouri Historical Society; Trustees Minutes, Book D, July 24, 1862, Union College; FL to HWH, July 23, 1862, in Richard Shelby Hartigan, *Lieber's Code and the Law of War* (Chicago: Precedent, 1983), 74–75.

17. SPC to AL, July 22, 1862, in Niven, *Chase Papers,* 1:350; William Thompson Lusk to his mother, July 28, 1862, in Lusk, *The War Letters of William Thompson Lusk* (privately printed, 1911), 170.

18. Theodore C. Pease and James G. Randall, eds., *The Diary of Orville Hickman Browning. Collections of the Illinois State Historical Library,* vol. 20, 563, July 25, 1862; Thomas and Hyman, 217.

19. Brooks, 14–15; GBMc to Samuel L. M. Barlow, July 23, 1862, in Stephen W. Sears, ed., *The Civil War Papers of George B. McClellan: Selected Correspondence, 1860–1865* (New York: Ticknor and Fields, 1989), 369. The standard biography is Stephen W. Sears, *George B. McClellan: The Young Napoleon* (New York: Ticknor and Fields, 1988).

20. HWH to EH, July 28, 1862, in Wilson, 557; "Memorandum for the Secretary of War," July 27, 1862, O.R., I, 2, 3, 337–338.

21. Sears, *George B. McClellan: The Young Napoleon,* 241; Pease and Randall, July 28, 1862, 565; GBMc to HWH, July 26, 1862, O.R., I, 2, 3, 333–334; GBMc to HWH, July 28, 1862, O.R., I, 11, 1, 75.

22. HWH to GBMc, July 30, 1862, O.R., I, 2, 3, 343.

23. HWH to EH, July 28, 1862, in Wilson, 557.

24. GBMc to HWH, July 30, 1862, O.R., I, 2, 3, 242; GBMc to HWH, August 1, 1862, O.R., I, 2, 3, 242, 345–346; July 31, 1862, "Excerpts from the Journal of Samuel P. Heintzelman, O.R. Supplement, I, 3, 100.

25. HWH to JP, August 1, 1862, O.R., I, 12, 3, 523.

26. Niven, *Chase Papers,* August 3, 1862, 1:357–361; Thomas and Hyman, 233, 243.

27. GBMc to HWH, August 4, 1862, O.R., I, 12, 2, 8–9.

28. GBMc to HWH, August 5, 1862, O.R., I, 12, 3, 355.

29. HWH to GBMc, August 6, 1862, O.R., I, 12, 2, 9–11.

30. HWH to GBMc, August 7, 1862, O.R., I, 12, 3, 359–360.

31. HWH to DCB, August 6, 1862, O.R., I, 16, 2, 266; HWH to USG, August 2, 1862, O R., I, 17, 2, 150; HWH to FL, August 6, 1862, in Hartigan, 78; T. J. Weed to EMS, August 6, 1862, O.R., III, 2, 312–313; Samuel Curtis to HWH, August 6, 1862, O.R., I, 13, 541; GWC to HWH, August 8, 1862, HWH Papers, USMA.

32. HWH to EH, August 9, 1862, Schoff.

33. JP to HWH, August 10, 1862, O.R., I, 12, 2, 132; GBMc to HWH, August 12,

1862, O.R., I, 11, 1, 87–88; GBMc to HWH, August 12, 1862, O.R., I, 2, 3, 372–373.

34. HWH to JP, August 14, 1862, Nathaniel P. Banks Papers, LC; regarding the recruitment process, see, for example, HWH to John Wool, August 13, 1862, O.R., III, 2, 370; John M. Schofield to HWH, August 12, 1862, HWH to Schofield, August 16, 1862, O.R., I, 13, 560–561, 574; DCB to HWH, August 18, 1862, O.R., I, 16, 2, 360; HWH to EH, August 13, 1862, in Wilson, 557–558.

35. Niven, *Chase Papers,* August 15, 1862, 1:363–364; August 17, 1862, GW, *Diary of GW, Secretary of the Navy under Lincoln and Johnson,* 3 vols. (Boston: Houghton Mifflin, 1909), 1:83.

36. Oliver O. Howard, *The Autobiography of Oliver Otis Howard,* 2 vols. (New York: Baker and Taylor, 1907), 1:266.

37. HWH to JP, August 19, August 30, 1862, O.R., I, 12, 3, 602; Speed [*sic*] to Dear Father, August 21, 1862, CHS; Burlingame, *Lincoln's Journalist,* August 24, 1862, 298–299.

38. JP to HWH, August 22, 25, 1862, O.R., I, 12, 2, 59, 65–66; HWH to JP, August 22, 23, 1862, O.R., I, 12, 3, 622, 630.

39. GBMc to HWH, August 18, 27, 1862, GBMc to wife, August 29, 1862, GBMc to AL, August 29, 1862, in GBMc, *McClellan's Own Story* (New York: Charles L. Webster, 1887), 506, 529, 530–531, 515; GBMc to HWH, August 24, 1862, O.R., I, 11, 1, 93–94.

40. GBMc to HWH, August 27, 1862, O.R., I, 11, 1, 96–97; HWH to GBMc, GBMc to HWH, August 27, 1862 (two letters), O.R., I, 12, 3, 691, 690, 692; August 28, 1862, in GBMc, *McClellan's Own Story,* 529–530; GBMc to HWH, August 28, 1862, O.R., I, 12, 3, 710.

41. HWH to JP, August 29, 1862, HWH to GBMc, August 29, 1862, O.R., I, 12, 3, 724, 722; GBMc, *McClellan's Own Story,* August 29, 1862, 531; Robert Goldthwaite Carter, *Four Brothers in Blue* (Austin: University of Texas Press, 1978), 93; HWH to GBMc, GBMc to HWH, August 29, 1862, O.R., I, 12, 3, 723, O.R., I, 12, 1, 99–100.

42. HWH to GBMc, August 30, 1862, HWH to JP, August 31, 1862, O.R., I, 12, 3, 749, 769; JP to HWH, August 31, 1862, O.R., I, 12, 2, 80; GBMc to HWH, August 31, 1862, O.R., I, 12, 3, 771; Bruce Tap, *Over Lincoln's Shoulder: The Committee on the Conduct of the War* (Lawrence; University Press of Kansas, 1998), 158; HWH to GBMc, August 31, 1862, GBMc to HWH, August 31, 1862, O.R., I, 11, 1, 102–103.

43. William R. Thayer, *The Life and Letters of John Hay,* 2 vols. (Boston: Houghton Mifflin, 1908), 126–129; Sears, 258–260; Thomas and Hyman, 220–222; Niven, *Chase Papers,* September 2, 1862, 1:368; JP to HWH, HWH to JP, September 2, 1862, O.R., I, 12, 3, 796, 797.

44. HWH to EH, September 2, 1862, Schoff; HWH to General McClellan's headquarters, September 1, 1862, O.R., 1, 12, 3, 787.

45. Sarah Butler to Benjamin F. Butler, September 1862, in Butler, 2:321; William

Lloyd Garrison to Oliver Johnson, September 9, 1862, in Walter M. Merrill, ed., *The Letters of William Lloyd Garrison,* 5 vols. (Cambridge: Harvard University Press, 1974), 5:112. As discussed in Irving Katz, *August Belmont: A Political Biography* (New York: Columbia University Press, 1968), 111–112, the banker August Belmont urged AL to make HWH his Secretary of War and GBMc the commanding general. John H. Brinton, *Personal Memoirs of John H. Brinton, Major and Surgeon U.S.V., 1861–1865,* (New York: Neale, 1914), September (?) 1862, 201; George Templeton Strong, *Diary of the Civil War, 1860–1865* (New York: Macmillan, 1962), September 11, 1862, 255.

46. HWH to EH, September 2, 1862, Schoff.

47. HWH to GBMc, EMS to HWH, September 3, 1862, HWH to JP, September 5, 1862, HWH to GBMc, September 5, 1862, O.R., I, 19, 2, 169, 183, 182; HWH to JP, September 23, 1862, O.R., I, 13, 663.

48. HWH to EH, September 5, 1862, in Wilson, 558.

49. Allen C. Clark, "Abraham Lincoln in the National Capital," *Records of the Columbia Historical Society, Washington D.C.* 27 (1925): 58; HWH to EH, September 9, 1862, Schoff; HWH to GBMc, September 23, 1862, O.R., I, 19, 2, 347.

50. Regarding McClellan's troop demands, see a number of letters to HWH on September 11, 1862, O.R., I, 19, 2, 252ff and September 13, 1862, O.R., 1, 19, 2, 282–283; HWH to GBMc, September 13, 1862, HWH to Lorenzo Thomas, September 22, 1862, O.R., I, 19, 2, 280–81, 801.

51. GBMc to HWH, September 13, 17, 22, 1862, O.R., I, 19, 2, 281–282, 312, 342–343.

52. HWH to DCB, September 20, 1862, HWH to J. C. McKibben, September 24, 1862, GHT to HWH, September 29, 1862, HWH to DCB and GHT, September 29, 1862, O.R., I, 16, 2, 530, 538–539, 555.

53. USG to HWH, September 20, 1872, Simon, 6:71–72.

54. SPC to Benjamin F. Butler, September 23, 1862, in Niven, *Chase Papers,* 3:284; GW, *Diary,* September 26, 1862, 1:153; Frank Moore, ed., *The Rebellion Record: A Diary of American Events,* 12 vols. (New York: D. Van Nostrand, 1861–1867), 6:19.

55. HWH to John M. Schofield, September 20, 1862, O.R., I, 13, 654.

56. Strong, September 24, 1862, 3:258.

57. GBMc to wife, September 20, 1862, in GBMc, *McClellan's Own Story,* 613–614; GBMc to HWH, September 20, 1862, HWH to GBMc, September 30, 1862, O.R., I, 19, 1, 68–69, 181–182.

58. GBMc to HWH, September 27, 1862, HWH to GBMc, October 14, 1862, O.R., I, 19, 1, 70–71, 155; AL to GBMc, October 24 [25], 1862, O.R. I, 19, 2, 485–486; GBMc to AL, October 25, 1862, O.R., I, 19, 2, 485; GBMc to Wife, September 25, 1862, in GBMc, *McClellan's Own Story,* 615.

59. HWH to GBMc, October 6, 1862, O.R., I, 19, 1, 10–11; GBMc to HWH, October 6, 1862, O.R., I, 19, 2, 387; GBMc to HWH, October 21, 1862, O.R., I, 19, 1, 81.

60. HWH to DCB, September 27, 1862, October 16, 1862, DCB to HWH, October 3, 16, 1862, O.R. I, 16, 2, 549, 564, 566, 619.

61. WSR to HWH, September 26, October 22, 1862, O.R., I, 17, 2, 239, 286–287; JP to HWH, October 30, 1862 (two letters), O.R., I, 12, 3, 823–824, 817.

62. Burlingame, *Lincoln's Journalist,* October 1, 1862, 317–318; Elizabeth Blair Lee to "Phil," October 7, 1862, in Virginia Jeans Laas, ed., *Wartime Washington: The Civil War Letters of Elizabeth Blair Lee* (Urbana: University of Illinois Press, 1991), 189–190; HWH to EH, October 7, 1862, Schoff.

63. HWH to EH, October 7, 1862, Schoff.

64. GW, *Diary,* November 4, 1862, 1:179–180; HWH to GBMc, October 26, 1862, in *Report of the Joint Committee on the Conduct of the War* (Washington, D.C.: Government Printing Office, 1865), part 1, 550.

65. T. J. Barnett to S. L. M. Barlow, October 12, 27, 1862, quoted in Michael Burlingame, *The Inner World of Abraham Lincoln* (Urbana: University of Illinois Press, 1994), 191; HWH to WSR, O.R., I, 16, 2, 640–642; AL to HWH, November 5, 1862, O.R., I, 19, 2, 545; HWH to Nathaniel P. Banks, November 9, 1862, O.R., I, 15, 590–591; USG to HWH, October 5, 1862 (two letters), O.R., I, 17, 1, 155.

66. HWH to H. R. Gamble, October 30, 1862, HWH to EMS, November 5, 1862, O.R., III, 2, 704, 877–878; J. C. Hamilton to HWH, December 7, 1862, EG 24, HL.

8. War by Washington Telegraph

1. E. W. Sheppard, "Generals of the American Civil War—I. The Northern Generals," *Army Quarterly and Defence Journal* (Great Britain) 86 (1963): 173; HWH to AEB, November 5, 1862, O.R., I, 19, 2, 546. See also William Marvel, *Burnside* (Chapel Hill: University of North Carolina Press, 1991), the modern biography.

2. AEB to GWC, November 9, 19, 22, 1862, O.R., I, 21, 99–104; HWH to AEB, November 14, 1862, O.R., I, 19, 2, 579; David S. Sparks, ed., *Inside Lincoln's Army: The Diary of Marsena Rudolph Patrick, Provost Marshall General, Army of the Potomac* (New York: Thomas Yoseloff, 1964), November 12, 1862, 175.

3. AL to HWH, November 27, 1862, Basler, 5:513–515; AEB to HWH, December 6, 1862, O.R., I, 21, 105.

4. HWH to AEB, December 10, 11, 1862, O.R., I, 21, 64, 65; HWH to JAD, December 13, 1862, JAD to HWH, December 13, 1862, O.R., I, 18, 479–480.

5. U.S. Congress, *Report of the Joint Committee on the Conduct of the War,* Senate Report No. 71, 37th Cong., 3rd Sess. 4 vols. (Washington, D.C.: Government Printing Office, 1863), I; HWH to AEB, November 23, 1862, O.R., I, 21, 792; David W. Miller, *Second Only to Grant: Quartermaster Montgomery C. Meigs* (Shippensburg, PA: White Mane, 2000), 187–189. The historian Ed-

ward J. Stackpole quotes from Halleck's book on military theory to demonstrate that Halleck well understood the importance of pontoons in a river crossing, yet did not act decisively in securing them: Stackpole, *Drama on the Rappahannock: The Fredericksburg Campaign* (Harrisburg: Stackpole, 1957), 91–93. For the definitive book see George C. Rable, *Fredericksburg! Fredericksburg!* (Chapel Hill: University of North Carolina Press, 2002).

6. Herman Haupt, *Reminiscences* (Milwaukee: Wright and Joyce, 1901), 177; GW, *Diary of GW, Secretary of the Navy under Lincoln and Johnson*, 3 vols. (Boston: Houghton Mifflin, 1909), December 14, 1862, January 5, 1863, 1:192, 216.

7. HWH to AEB, December 15, 1862, O.R., II, 21, 122.

8. Ralph R. Fahrney, *Horace Greeley and the Tribune in the Civil War* (Cedar Rapids, IA: Torch, 1936), 138–139; Bruce Tap, *Over Lincoln's Shoulder: The Committee on the Conduct of the War* (Lawrence: University Press of Kansas, 1998), 145–147; Michael Burlingame, ed., *Lincoln's Journalist: John Hay's Anonymous Writings for the Press, 1860–1864* (Carbondale: Southern Illinois University Press, 1998), December 21, 1862, 324–325; *Harper's Weekly*, January 10, 1863, 19.

9. HWH to HBW, December 24, 1862, HBW Papers, MHS; HWH to FL, November 23, 1862, in Richard Shelby Hartigan, *Lieber's Code and the Law of War* (Chicago: Precedent, 1983), 82–83.

10. WSR to HWH, November 2, 17, 18, 1862, O.R., I, 20, 2, 5, 69, 65; HWH to WSR, November 27, December 4, 1862, O.R., I, 20, 2, 102, 117–118. On Rosecrans, see William M. Lamers, *The Edge of Glory: A Biography of General William S. Rosecrans, U.S.A.* (New York: Harcourt Brace, 1961).

11. WSR to HWH, December 4, 1862, HWH to WSR, December 5, 1862, O.R., I, 20, 2, 118, 123–124.

12. WSR to HWH, December 24, 1862, O.R., I, 20, 2, 218. See Peter Cozzens, *No Better Place to Die: The Battle of Stones River* (Urbana: University of Illinois Press, 1990).

13. HWH to WSR, January 9, 8, 14, 30, 1862, O.R., I, 20, 1, 187, 186, O.R., I, 20, 2, 326, O.R., I, 23, 2, 22–23; HWH to WSR, January 30, 1862, O.R., I, 23, 2, 22–23.

14. USG to HWH, November 26, 1862, in Simon, 6:349.

15. JAMcC to HWH, November 10, 1862, O.R., I, 17, 2, 334–335; HWH to USG, November 3, 10, 11, 1862, O.R., I, 17, 1, 467, 468–469; JaMcC to HWH, December 16, 1862, O.R., I, 17, 2, 415; HWH to USG, December 18, 1862, O.R., I, 17, 1, 476; Elizabeth Blair Lee to Samuel Philip Lee, December 20, 1862, in Virginia Jean Laas, ed., *Wartime Washington: The Civil War Letters of Elizabeth Blair Lee* (Urbana: University of Illinois Press, 1991), 218. The standard biography is Richard L. Kiper, *Major General John Alexander McClernand, Politician in Uniform* (Kent: Kent State University Press, 1999).

16. HWH to Nathaniel Banks, January 4, 1863, O.R., I, 15, 636; HWH to Samuel Curtis, January 4, 1863, O.R., II, 3, 150.

17. JAMcC to AL, January 7, 1863, AL Papers, LC; HWH to USG, January 12, 1863, O.R., I, 17, 2, 555; Howard K. Beale, ed., *Diary of Edward Bates, 1859–1866: Annual Report of the American Historical Association, 1930,* February 28, 1863, 4:282–283.

18. Robert Goldthwaite Carter, ed., *Four Brothers in Blue* (Austin: University of Texas Press, 1978), November 10, 1862, 159; Charles S. Bartles to Benjamin F. Butler, December 14, 1862, in Benjamin F. Butler, *Private and Official Correspondence of Gen. Benjamin F. Butler during the Period of the Civil War,* 5 vols. (privately printed, 1917), 2:533; Stephen M. Weld to Mother, December 17, 1862, in Stephen Minot Weld, *Diary and Letters of Stephen M. Weld,* 2nd ed. (Boston: Massachusetts Historical Society, 1979), 154.

19. *New York Herald,* December 20, 1862 in Douglas Fermer, *James Gordon Bennett and the New York Herald: A Study of Editorial Opinion in the Civil War Era, 1854–1867* (Woodbridge, U.K.: Boydell, 1986), 226; John T. Metcalfe to HWH, December 20, 1862, EG 41, HL; A. J. Glover to (?) Wiley, December 21, 1862, in Scott J. Winslow Associates, Bedford, NH, Catalog No. 110; Weld to Father, December 21, 1862, Weld, 154–156; Henry Lea Graves to Cora Graves, January 22, 1863, in Richard Harwell, ed., *A Confederate Marine: A Sketch of Henry Lea Graves with Excerpts from the Graves Family Correspondence.* (Tuscaloosa: Confederate, 1973), 98.

20. An incisive biography of Count Adam Gurowski is LeRoy H. Fischer, *Lincoln's Gadfly, Adam Gurowski* (Norman: University of Oklahoma Press, 1964). AG, *Diary of AG, 1861–1865,* 3 vols. (New York: Burt Franklin, 1968), December 15, 1862, 2:30.

21. HWH to AEB, December 18, 1862, O.R., I, 21, 865; Charles M. Segal, ed., *Conversations with Lincoln* (New York: G.P. Putnam's Sons), 232–234.

22. AEB to AL, AL to HWH, January 1, 1863, O.R., I, 21, 940–941.

23. J. C. Hamilton to HWH, December 22, 1862, EG 23, HL; January 1, 1863, "Excerpts from the Journal of Samuel P. Heintzelman," O.R., Supplement, I, 3, 676; James A. Garfield to "Dear Crete," January 2, 1863, in Frederick D. Williams, ed., *The Wild Life of the Army: Civil War Letters of James A. Garfield* (East Lansing: Michigan State University Press, 1964), 206–207; Ben Perley Poore, *Perley's Reminiscences of Sixty Years in the National Metropolis,* 2 vols. (Philadelphia: Hubbard, 1886), 2:137; HWH to EMS, January 1, 1863, O.R., I, 21, 940–941.

24. AL to HWH, January 1, 1863, AEB to HWH, January 5, 1863, HWH to AEB (with AL endorsement), January 7, 1863, O.R., I, 21, 940, 945, 953–954; Noah Brooks, "Personal Reminiscences of Lincoln," *Scribner's Monthly,* March 1878, quoted in Segal, 266. Most historians are critical of HWH, but Herman Hattaway and Archer Jones argue that Halleck's attitude was perfectly reasonable, based on army precedent, historical examples of "too restrictive direction" by other historical figures, and HWH's own business experiences. Hattaway and Jones, *How the North Won: A Military History of the Civil War* (Urbana: University of Illinois Press, 1983), 328.

25. AEB to HWH, HWH to AEB, January 22, 1863, O.R., I, 21, 993.

26. AL to HWH, January 25, 1863, Basler, 6:77–78; HWH to William B. Franklin, May 29, 1863, O.R., I, 21, 1008–1009.

27. Frederick Bancroft and William A. Dunning, eds., *The Reminiscences of Carl Schurz . . .*, 3 vols. (New York: McClure, 1908), 2:403; the Adams quote is in Hattaway and Jones, 350; Walter H. Hebert, *Fighting Joe Hooker* (Indianapolis: Bobbs-Merrill, 1944), 166; Freeman Cleaves, *Meade of Gettysburg* (Norman: University of Oklahoma Press, 1960), 100–111.

28. AL to JH, January 26, 1863, Basler, 6:78–79.

29. JH to Samuel P. Bates, June 28, 1878, typescript, Samuel P. Bates Collection, Pennsylvania State Archives, Harrisburg); Hebert, 170.

30. The best source for biographical information on Lieber is Frank Freidel, *Francis Lieber, Nineteenth Century Liberal* (Baton Rouge: Louisiana State University Press, 1947). HWH to FL, February 3, 1862, LI 1643, HL; HWH to FL, July 30, 1862, Hartigan, 75–76; Freidel, 324–330.

31. FL to HWH, HWH to FL, November 13, 15, 1862, in Hartigan, 79–81.

32. HWH to Horatio G. Wright, November 18, 1862, O.R., I, 20, 2, 67–68. For an insightful study of the evolution of destructive war, see Mark Grimsley, *The Hard Hand of War: Union Military Policy toward Southern Civilians, 1861–1865* (Cambridge: Cambridge University Press, 1995).

33. FL to HWH, November 25, 1862, in Hartigan, 83; FL to HWH, December 4, 1862, LI 1767, HL; FL to HWH, December 7, 9, 1862, in Hartigan, 84, 84–85; S.O. No. 399, War Department, December 17, 1862, O.R., III, 2, 951.

34. HWH to D. Appleton and Company, November 29, 1862, BW 41, HL; FL to Samuel Austin Allibone, December 14, 1862, LI 679, HL; D. Van Nostrand to HWH, December 1, 1862, EG 61, HL; AG, *Diary,* January 10, 1863, 2:84.

35. HWH to WSR, February 1, 1863, O.R., I, 23, 2, 31; HWH to David Hunter, February 15, 1863, O.R., I, 14, 400–401; John A. Schofield to HWH, February 3, 1863, O.R., I, 22, 2, 94–95; Franz Sigel to JH, February 12, 1863, with endorsements, O.R., I, 22, 2, 70–71; Samuel Curtis to HWH, February 11, 1863, O.R., I, 22, 2, 107–108; USG to HWH, March 12, 1863, O.R., I, 24, 1, 19.

36. HWH to James B. McPherson, February 13, 1863, Parke Bernet Galleries, Sale 2988, No. 130, 1970; FL to HWH, March 4, 1863, LI 1778, HL.

37. HWH to JH, January 31, 1863, O.R., I, 25, 2, 12–13, with enclosed letter from HWH to AEB, January 7, 1863.

38. HWH to JH, February 8, 1863, O.R., I, 25, 2, 61; Hattaway and Jones, 350–351; HWH to JH, February 3, 1863, O.R., I, 25, 2, 44.

39. Hebert, 181; HWH to JH, March 27, 1863, O.R., I, 25, 2, 158; AG, *Diary,* April 20, 1863, 2:202–203; John Sedgwick to "My dear sister," April 20, 1863, in John Sedgwick, *Correspondence of John Sedgwick,* 2 vols. (New York: Battel, 1903), 2:90–91; "Excerpts from the Journal of Samuel P. Heintzelman," April 23, 1863, O.R., Supplement, I, 4, 463.

40. HWH to FL, April 30, 1863, LI 1661, HL; "Excerpts from the Journal of Samuel P. Heintzelman," May 1, 1863, O.R., Supplement, I, 4, 464–465.

41. An excellent book on the battle of Chancellorsville is Stephen W. Sears, *Chancellorsville* (Boston: Houghton Mifflin, 1996).

42. Weld, May 7, 1863, 193; Carl Sandburg, *Abraham Lincoln: The War Years,* 4 vols. (New York: Harcourt Brace, 1939), 2:98; Hebert, 226–227.

43. HWH to FL, May 9, 1863, LI 1663, HL; HWH to J. G. Foster, May 9, 1863, O.R., I, 18, 711; HWH to Nathaniel Banks, May 11, 1863, O.R., I, 15, 725–726.

44. Isaac N. Arnold to AL, May 18, 1863, Isaac Newton Arnold Papers, CHS; Lincoln's defense of HWH is found in AL to Arnold, May 26, 1863, Basler, 6:23–31; resolution enclosed in HWH to FL, June 3, 1863, LI 1078, HL; FL to HWH, June 5, 1863, LI 1801, HL; Caleb Cushing to Benjamin F. Butler, May 15, 1863, in Butler, 3:73; unnamed newspaper clipping, May 16, 1863, Bancroft Scraps, BL; Phillips quoted in Sandburg, 2:172.

45. "The Patriot's Catechism!" May 27, 1863, a broadside, Houghton Library, Harvard University; Beale, May 23, 1863, 293.

46. HWH to JAD, May 28, 1863, O.R., I, 18, 730–731; AL to JH, June 5, 1863, O.R., I, 27, 1, 31.

47. HWH to JH, June 5, 1863, O.R., I, 27, 1, 31–32; John F. Marszalek, "Second Union Misfire on the Peninsula," *America's Civil War* 14 (July 2001): 54–60.

48. JH to AL, HWH to JH (four letters), JH to HWH (three letters), AL to JH June 16, 1863 (two letters), O.R., I, 27, 1, 45–47.

49. JH to HWH (three letters), HWH to JH , June 17, 1862, O.R., I, 27, 1, 48–49; HWH to JH (two letters), June 18, 1862, JH to HWH, June 19, 1862 (three letters), HWH to JH, June 19, 1862, O.R., I, 27, 1, 51–52.

50. JH to HWH, June 24, 1863, O.R., I, 27, 1, 55–56; Hebert, 244–255; Haupt, 205–206.

51. JH to HWH, June 27, 1863, O.R., I, 27, 1, 60; Hebert, 247; JH to Samuel P. Bates, June 28, 1878, Samuel P. Bates Collection, Pennsylvania State Archives, Harrisburg; JH to William P. Fessenden, December 6, 1863, Parke-Bernet Galleries, Sale 1683, 1956.

52. Sheppard, 175; Carter, June 30, 1863, 293; J. Cutler Andrews, *The North Reports the Civil War* (Pittsburgh: University of Pittsburgh Press, 1955), 548. See Freeman Cleaves, *Meade of Gettysburg* (Norman: University of Oklahoma Press, 1960).

53. HWH to GGM, June 27, 1863, GGM to HWH, June 28, 1863, HWH to GGM, June 28, 1862, O.R., I, 27, 61–63.

54. HWH to USG, April 2, 1862, May 11, 1863, O.R., I, 24, 1, 25, 36.

55. HWH to Nathaniel Banks, May 23, 1863, O.R., I, 26, 1, 500–501; HWH to USG, March 20, 1863, O.R., I, 24, 22; USG to HWH, June 19, 1863, O.R., I, 24, 1, 43. See William L. Shea and Terrence Winschel, *Vicksburg Is the Key: The Struggle for the Mississippi River* (Lincoln: University of Nebraska Press, 2003).

56. HWH to WSR, April 20, 1863, O.R., I, 23, 2, 255–256; HWH to AEB, June 2, 1863, O.R., I, 24, 3, 376; HWH to John A. Schofield, June 2, 1863, O.R., I, 24, 3, 377; HWH to Banks, June 3, 1863, O.R., I, 26, 1, 534; HWH to WSR,

June 2, 1863, O.R., I, 24, 3, 376; WSR to HWH, June 2, 1863, O.R., I, 24, 3, 376–377; HWH to WSR, June 16, 1863, O.R., I, 23, 1, 10.

57. HWH to USG, JH, and WSR, March 1, 1863, O.R., I, 24, 1, 19; WSR to HWH, March 6, 1863, HWH to WSR, March 13, 1863, O.R., I, 23, 2, 111, 138.

58. General Order No. 100, April 24, 1863, O.R., III, 3, 148–164; FL to HWH, May 20, 1863, in Hartigan, 108; Friedel, 334–339.

59. HWH to USG, March 31, 1863, O.R., I, 24, 3, 157; HWH to James A. Roosevelt, April 5, 1863, *New York Times,* April 5, 1863.

60. GW, *Diary,* July 4, 1863, 1:358; Herman Haupt to HWH, July 4, 1863, O.R., I, 27, 3, 523; AL to HWH, July 6, 1863, Basler, 6:318; HWH to GGM, July 7, 1863, GGM to HWH, July 7, 1863, O.R., I, 27, 1, 81–83.

61. GW, *Diary,* July 7, 1863, 1:363–364; see, for example, HWH to GGM (two letters), July 8, 1863, O.R., I, 27, 1, 84–85; HWH to GGM, July 9, 1863, O.R., I, 27, 1, 88.

62. GGM to HWH, HWH to GGM, July 13, 1863, O.R. I, 27, 1, 91, 93; GW, *Diary,* July 13, 1863, 1:368.

63. GW, *Diary,* July 14, 1863, 1:370–371.

64. HWH to GGM (two letters), GGM to HWH, July 14, 1863, O.R., I, 27, 1, 92–94. AL to GGM, July 14, 1863, Basler, 6:327–329. For a less critical view of Meade, see Frank J. Williams, "Abraham Lincoln: The President and George Gordon Meade—An Evolving Commander in Chief," in *Judging Lincoln* (Carbonedale: Southern Illinois University Press, 2002), 80–92.

9. The Western Generals Bring Success

1. The best book on this topic is Iver Bernstein, *The New York City Draft Riot* . . . (New York: Oxford University Press, 1990).

2. HWH to Horatio Seymour, July 14, 1863, HWH to GGM, July 15, 1863, HWH to JAD, July 15, 1863, O.R., I, 27, 2, 915, 918, 920; JAD to HWH, August 16, 1863, in Morgan Dix, comp., *Memoirs of John Adams Dix,* 2 vols. (New York: Harper Brothers, 1883), 2:91; FL to HWH, August 2, July 25, 1863, LI 1808, LI 1807, HL.

3. HWH to FL, July 26, August 14, 1863, LI 1673, LI 1676, HL.

4. HWH to GGM, July 28, 1863, O.R., I, 27, 1, 105–106; GW, *Diary of GW, Secretary of the Navy under Lincoln and Johnson,* 3 vols. (Boston: Houghton Mifflin, 1909), July 26, 1863, 1:384.

5. HWH to USG, August 1, 1863, O.R., I, 24, 1, 63; HWH's reference was to Napoleon's 1805 encirclement of the Austrian army in the Bavarian city of Ulm, forcing it to surrender without a battle.

6. USG to HWH, July 24, 1863, O.R., I, 24, 3, 547; Nathaniel Banks to HWH, August 1, 1863, O.R., I, 26, 1, 666.

7. USG, *Personal Memoirs of U. S. Grant,* 2 vols. in 1(New York: The Library of America, 1990), 1:578–579.

8. HWH to WSR, WSR to HWH, July 24, 1863, O.R., I, 23, 2, 552, 555, HWH to WSR, July 25, 1863, O.R., I, 23, 2, 555.

9. WSR to HWH, September 9, 1863, HWH to AEB, HWH to USG or WTS, HWH to Stephen Hurlbut, September 13, 1863, O.R., I, 30, 3, 479, 617, 592, 594.

10. An excellent book on the battle of Chickamauga is Peter Cozzens, *This Terrible Sword: The Battle of Chickamauga* (Urbana: University of Illinois Press, 1992); AG, *Diary of AG, 1861–1865,* 3 vols. (New York: Burt Franklin, 1968), September 22, 1863, 2:329.

11. John Niven, ed., *The Salmon Chase Papers,* 5 vols. (Kent: Kent State University Press, 1993–), September 23, 1863, 1:450–453; Frank Abial Flower, *Edwin McMasters Stanton . . .* (Akron: Saalfield, 1905), 203–204.

12. GW, *Diary,* September 26, 29, 1863, 1:444, 448; HWH to USG, October 16, 1863, O.R., I, 30, 4, 404.

13. WTS to HWH, August 15, 1863, copy, SFP, UNDA; USG to Julia Dent Grant, April 30, 1862, USG, *Memoirs,* 1006.

14. Benjamin H. Thomas and Harold M. Hyman, *Stanton: The Life and Times of Lincoln's Secretary of War* (New York: Knopf, 1962), 290–291; an excellent book on the battle of Chattanooga is Peter Cozzens, *The Shipwreck of Their Hopes: The Battle of Chattanooga* (Urbana: University of Illinois Press, 1994); HWH to USG, November 26, 1863, O.R., I, 31, 2, 26.

15. John F. Marszalek, *Sherman: A Soldier's Passion for Order* (New York: The Free Press, 1993), 246.

16. HWH to USG, December 3, 1863, O.R., I, 31, 3, 315.

17. Certificate of Incorporation of the Halleck Gold and Silver Mining Company, No. 4200, CSA. See also folder 4174, CSA.

18. Two detailed studies of the New Almaden Civil War controversy, which form the basis of my discussion, are Leonard W. Ascher, "The Economic History of the New Almaden Quicksilver Mine, 1845–1863," Ph.D. diss., University of California, Berkeley, 1934, and Milton H. Shutes, "Abraham Lincoln and the New Almaden Mine," *California Historical Society Quarterly* 15 (1936): 3–20.

19. George Wright to HWH, July 9, 1863, O.R., I, 50, 2, 515; HWH to SPC, July 10, 1863, SPC Papers, LC.

20. John Parrott, to HWH, July 10, 1863, FB to HWH, July 11, 1863, O.R., I, 50, 2, 517, 518–519.

21. HWH to George Wright, July 11, 1863, HWH to FB, July 13, 1863, HWH to John Parrott, July 11, 1863, O.R., I, 50, 2, 518, 522, 518.

22. GW, *Diary,* August 11, 1863, 1:397–398; Howard K. Beale, ed., *Diary of Edward Bates, 1859–1866,* Annual Report of the American Historical Association, 4 vols. (Washington, D.C.: Government Office, 1932), August 11, 1863, 303–304; Edward Bates to HWH, August 11, 1863, Edward Bates Papers, Missouri Historical Society, excerpts also found in "Manuscripts," *The Bulletin of the Missouri Historical Society* 28 (October 1971): 62–63.

23. HWH to EH, November 9, 1862, Schoff; HWH to FL, August 4, 1863, LI 1674, FL to HWH, August 24, 1863, LI 1813, HL; HWH to FL, October 4, 24, 1863, LI 1681, LI 1684, HL; Charles J. Halpine to Samuel Francis DuPont, September 3, 1863, in Samuel F. Du Pont, *A Selection from His Civil War Letters,* 3 vols., ed. John D. Hayes (Ithaca: Cornell University Press for the Eleutherian Mills Historical Library, 1969), 3:231n.

24. FL to HWH, December 25, 24, 1863, LI 1826, LI 1686, HL; David Wager to HWH, March 30, 1863, EG 62, HL.

25. William E. Doster, *Lincoln and Episodes of the Civil War* (New York: G. P. Putnam, 1915), 180–181.

26. Otto Louis Hein, *Memories of Long Ago . . . by an Old Army Officer* (New York: Putnam's, 1925), 28–29; WTS to HWH, January 29, 1864, O.R., I, 32, 2, 261.

27. Richard Meade Bache, *Life of General George Gordon Meade* (Philadelphia: Henry T. Coates, 1897), 361; Edward K. Gould, *Major General Hiram G. Berry . . .* (Rockland, ME: Courier-Gazette, 1899), 271–273.

28. HWH to GWC, October 14, 1863, GWC Papers, USMA; S. O. Houghton to HWH, March 16, 1862, HWH Papers, LC; HWH to HBW, October 8, 1863, HBW Papers, MHS.

29. HWH to FL, December 24, 1863, January 5, 1864, LI 1686, LI 1689, HL.

30. USG to HWH, October 26, 1863, O.R., I, 31, 1, 740; HWH to USG, November 5, 1863, O.R., I, 31, 3, 48; USG to HWH, November 25, 1863, HWH to EMS, December 6, 1863, O.R., I, 31, 2, 25, 11–12.

31. USG to HWH, January 19, 1864, O.R., I, 33, 394–395; HWH to USG, February 17, 1864, HWH to USG, January 8, 1864, O.R., I, 32, 2, 411–413, 47.

32. HWH to WTS, August 29, 1863, WTS Papers, LC; WTS to HWH, September 17, 1863, USG to HWH, September 19, 1863, O.R., I, 30, 3, 694–700, 732; HWH to USG, January 17, February 17, 1864, O.R., I, 32, 2, 122–123, 411–413.

33. Thomas and Hyman, 285; USG to Charles A. Dana, August 5, 1863, Charles A. Dana Papers, LC.

34. John Hay Memorandum, December 7, 1863, in Helen Nicolay, *Lincoln's Secretary: A Biography of John G. Nicolay* (New York: Longman Green, 1949), 180–181.

35. WTS to JS, January 6, 1864, WTS Papers, LC.

36. AG, *Diary,* February 3, 1864, 2:91; *Harper's Weekly,* February 20, 1864, 126; Robert N. Scott to William C. Church, February 29, 1864, William C. Church Papers, New York Public Library; Christopher Dell, *Lincoln and the War Democrats: The Grand Erosion of Conservative Tradition* (Rutherford, NJ: Farleigh Dickinson Press, 1975), 276; HWH to USG, March 3, 1864, O.R., I, 32, 3, 13.

37. Noah Brooks, *Washington in Lincoln's Time* (New York: Century, 1896), 139–140.

38. HWH to WTS, February 16, 1864, O.R., I, 32, 2, 407–408.

39. HWH to Nathaniel Banks, March 5, 1864, O.R., I, 34, 2, 502; HWH to USG,

March 6, 1864, O.R., I, 32, 3, 26; HWH to FL, March 7, 1864, FL to HWH, March 10, 1864, LI 1694, LI 1835, HL.

40. HWH to EMS, March 9, 1864, O.R., I, 3, 4, 160; EMS, March 10, 1864, O.R., I, 33, 633.

41. General Orders No. 98, War Department, March 12, 1864, O.R., I, 32, 3, 58; William E. Marsh, "Lincoln and Henry W. Halleck," in Allan Nevins and Irving Stone, eds., *Lincoln: A Contemporary Portrait* (Garden City, NY: Doubleday, 1962), 75.

42. General Orders No. 98, War Department, March 12, 1864, O.R., I, 32, 3, 58; Brooks, 140; Tyler Dennett, ed., *Lincoln and the Civil War in the Diaries and Letters of John Hay* (New York: Dodd, Mead, 1939), March 24, 1864, 167.

43. AG, *Diary,* March 12, 1864, 2:136; George Templeton Strong, *Diary of the Civil War, 1860–1865,* 3 vols., ed. Allan Nevins (New York: Macmillan, 1962), March 14, 1864, 3:415; *New York Times,* March 15, 1864; Robert N. Scott to William C. Church, March 12, 1864, William C. Church Papers, New York Public Library; Matias Romero to Mexican Ministry of Foreign Relations, March 24, 1864, in Thomas Schoonover, ed., *A Mexican View of America in the 1860s: A Foreign Diplomat Describes the Civil War and Reconstruction* (Rutherford, NJ: Farleigh Dickinson Press, 1991), 161.

44. HWH to FL, March 14, 1864, GWC to FL, March 16, LI 1695, LI 1714, HL; Adam Badeau, *Military History of General Grant,* 2 vols. (New York: Appleton, 1868), 2:18; Shelby Foote, *The Civil War: A Narrative,* 3 vols. (New York: Random House, 1974), 3:24.

10. Chief of Staff under Grant

1. William E. Marsh, "Lincoln and Henry W. Halleck," in Allan Nevins and Irving Stone, eds., *Lincoln: A Contemporary Portrait* (Garden City, NY: Doubleday, 1962), 76.

2. HWH to EMS, November 15, 1863, O.R, III, 3, 1042; *New York Times,* December 17, 1863; John C. Gray Jr. to John C. Ropes, January 5, 1864, in John Chapman Gray and John Codman Ropes, *War Letters, 1861–1865* (Cambridge: Riverside Press for the Massachusetts Historical Society, 1927), 271; HWH to FL, April 24, 1864, LI 1699, HL; *Army and Navy Journal,* June 25, 1864, 725.

3. HWH to FL, December 27, 1863, LI 1687, HL.

4. USG to HWH, March 16, 17, 1864, O.R., I, 35, 2, 20 and 34, 2, 635; HWH to USG, March 25, 1864, O.R., I, 33, 729; HWH to Quincy A. Gillmore, April 1, 1864, O.R., I, 35, 2, 31.

5. HWH to USG, March 26, 1864, USG to HWH, March 28, 1864, O.R., I, 33, 741, 752–753.

6. USG backed off having HWH leave Washington by saying: "I am well aware of the importance of your remaining where you are at this time"; USG to HWH, April 29, 1864, O.R., I, 34, 3, 331. HWH agreed that he should stay in Washington because, he said, "there must be some military head here to keep

things from getting into a snarl"; HWH to USG, May 2, 1864, O.R., I, 36, 2, 329. Tyler Dennett, ed., *Lincoln and the Civil War in the Diaries and Letters of John Hay* (New York: Dodd, Mead, 1939), April 28, 1864, 176. On March 24, 1864, Lincoln said Halleck "shrunk from responsibility wherever it was possible"; Dennett, 167. HWH to FL, April 24, 1864, LI 1699, HL; HWH to WTS, April 29, 1864, O.R., I, 34, 3, 357; Robert N. Scott to William C. Church, April 24, March 20, 1864, William C. Church Papers, New York Public Library.

7. USG to HWH, April 22, 26, 1864, O.R., I, 34, 3, 252–253, 293–294; GW, *Diary of GW, Seretary of the Navy under Lincoln and Johnson,* 3 vols. (Boston: Houghton Mifflin, 1909), April 26, 1864, 2:18; HWH to USG, May 3, 1864, O.R., I, 34, 3, 409.

8. John F. Marszalek, *Sherman: A Soldier's Passion for Order* (New York: The Free Press, 1993), 257–258; Dennett, April 30, 1864, 178.

9. Benjamin P. Thomas and Harold M. Hyman, *Stanton: The Life and Times of Lincoln's Secretary of War* (New York: Knopf, 1962), 300; USG to HWH, May 10, 11, 1864, O.R., I, 36, 2, 595–596, 627.

10. HWH to FL, April 21, June 2, 1864, LI 1698, 1701, HL; Thomas and Hyman, 301.

11. HWH to FL, April 10, June 21, June 30, 1864, LI 1697, LI 1703, LI 1704, HL; Charles Francis Adams Jr. to Mother, August 27, 1864, in Worthington C. Ford, ed., *A Cycle of Adams Letters, 1861–1865,* 2 vols. (Boston: Houghton Mifflin, 1920), 2:186–187.

12. Charles G. Halpine to GWC, April 21, 1864, Barrett-Halpine Collection, University of Virginia Library; USG to HWH, May 26, 1864, O.R., I, 36, 3, 206–207; AG, *Diary of AG, 1861–1865,* 3 vols. (New York: Burt Franklin, 1968), April 15, 1864, 2:181.

13. WTS to HWH, June 11, 1864, O.R., I, 38, 4, 455.

14. HWH to USG, May 23, 1864, O.R., I, 36, 3, 114; USG to HWH, May 25, 1864, O.R., I, 36, 3, 183.

15. HWH to FL, June 21, 1864, LI 1703, HL; Horace Porter, *Campaigning with Grant* (New York: Century, 1897), 182; USG to HWH, June 23, 1864, O.R., I, 34, 4, 514–515; see, for example, HWH to Edward R. Canby, June 24, 1864, O.R., I, 34, 4, 528.

16. For a thorough overview of Early's raid, see Benjamin Franklin Cooling, *Jubal Early's Raid on Washington, 1864* (Baltimore: Nautical and Aviation Publishing Company of America, 1989), and Frank E. Vandiver Jr., *Jubal's Raid: General Early's Famous Attack on Washington in 1864* (New York: McGraw Hill, 1960); HWH to USG, July 3, 1864, O.R., I, 37, 2, 15; USG to HWH, July 4, 1864, O.R., I, 40, 2, 618; HWH to USG, July 5, 1864, O.R., I, 40, 3, 4.

17. USG to HWH, July 6, 1864, O.R., I, 40, 3, 31; HWH to USG, July 6, 1864, O.R., I, 40, 3, 31–32; B. S. Alexander to HWH, July 6, 1864, O.R., I, 37, 2, 83–85; J. G. Barnard to HWH, July 9, 1864, O.R., I, 37, 2, 140.

18. HWH to FL, July 7, 1864, LI 1705, HL.

19. Lew Wallace to HWH, July 7, 1864, O.R., I, 37, 2, 108–109; Robert E.

Morseberger, "The Battle That Saved Washington," *Civil War Times Illustrated* 13 (May 1974): 12–27.

20. HWH to USG, July 9, 1864, O.R., I, 40, 3, 93; Lew Wallace to HWH, HWH to Wallace, July 9, 1864, O.R., I, 37, 2, 145; HWH to USG, USG to HWH, July 9, 1864, O.R., I, 40, 3, 93, 92.

21. Thomas and Hyman, 319–320. For a detailed overview of Washington at the time of Early's raid, see Margaret Leech, *Reveille in Washington, 1860–1865* (New York: Harpers, 1941), 329–346.

22. Leech, 342; HWH to E. D. Townsend, HWH to Chief of Cavalry Bureau, July 9, 1864, HWH to W. W. Morris, HWH to George Cadwalader, HWH to JAD, July 10, 1864, O.R., I, 37, 2, 140, 159, 174, 188, 190; HWH to USG, July 10, 1864, O.R., I, 40, 3, 123.

23. AL to USG, July 10, 1864, Basler, 7:437.

24. GW, *Diary*, July 8, 1864, 2:70; AG, *Diary*, July 11, 1864, 2:280; Lew Wallace to HWH, July 11, 1864, O.R., I, 37, 2, 213; HWH to J. R. West, July 11, 1864, quoted in Vandiver, 142.

25. AG, *Diary*, July 12, 1864, 2:281.

26. Leech, 343.

27. HWH to USG, July 12, 1864, O.R., I, 37, 2, 22–23.

28. Charles A. Dana, *Recollections of the Civil War*, reprint (New York: Collier, 1964), 230; the Dana letter to Grant is quoted in James H. Wilson, *The Life of Charles A. Dana* (New York: Harper, 1907), 337; AG, *Diary*, July 13, 1864, 2:282.

29. GW, *Diary*, July 13, 1864, 2:76.

30. HWH to EMS, July 13, 1864, O.R, I, 37, 2, 260–261; AL to EMS, July 14, 1864, Basler, 7:439–440.

31. *United States Service Magazine* 2 (September 1864): 282; AG, *Diary*, July 15, 1864, 2:288. The October 1864 issue of the *North American Review*, which AG heavily quoted, even criticized Halleck for what AG called "the so pompously advertised *Notes*." AG, *Diary*, Appendix II, 3:408–413; George Agassiz, ed., *Meade's Headquarters, 1863–1865: Letters of Colonel Theodore Lyman from the Wilderness to Appomattox* (Boston: Atlantic Monthly, 1922), July 20, 1864, 193.

32. USG to HWH, July 26, 1864, O.R., I, 37, 2, 445; Thomas and Hyman, 320; EMS to HWH, July 27, 1864, O.R., I, 37, 2, 463; AG, *Diary*, July 27, 1864, 2:297. Italics are in the original.

33. HWH to WTS, July 16, 1864, O.R., I, 38, 5, 151; HWH to USG, July 19, 22, 1864, O.R., I, 37, 2, 384, 413.

34. An insightful article on the Chambersburg raid is Everard H. Smith, "Chambersburg: Anatomy of a Confederate Reprisal," *American Historical Review* 96 (1991): 432–455. A modern account of the siege at Petersburg is Noah Andre Trudeau, *The Last Citadel: Petersburg, Virginia, June 1864–April 1865* (Boston: Little Brown, 1991). USG to HWH, July 30, August 1, 1864, O.R., I, 40, 3, 636 and 1, 17–18; WTS to HWH, July 9, 23, 27 (two letters), 1864, O.R., I, 38, 5, 91–92, 234–235, 271–272.

35. USG to HWH, August 1, 1864, O.R., I, 37, 2, 558; HWH to USG, August 4, 1864, O.R., I, 43, 1, 681; USG to HWH, August 5, HWH to Philip Sheridan, August 6, 1864, O.R., I, 43, 1, 693, 709–710. See Roy Morris, *The Life and Wars of General Phil Sheridan* (New York: Crown, 1992), for the most detailed biography of Sheridan.

36. HWH to USG, August 11, 1864, USG to HWH, August 15, 1864, O.R., I, 42, 2, 111–112, 193–194; USG to EMS, August 15, 1864, USG to HWH, August 20, 1864, O.R., I, 50, 2, 945, 951.

37. FL to HWH, September 1, 1864, in Thomas S. Perry, ed., *Life and Letters of Francis Leiber* (Boston: J. R. Osgood, 1882), 350; HWH to FL, September 2, 1864, LI 1708, HL; HWH to FB, October 3, 1864, FBFM; HWH to Samuel P. Heintzelman, September 3, 1864, O.R., I, 39, 2, 341–342.

38. WTS to HWH, September 3, 1864, O.R., I, 38, 5, 777. See Chester G. Hearn, *Mobile Bay and the Mobile Campaign: The Last Great Battles of the Civil War* (Jefferson, NC: McFarland, 1993). For the best book on the Sherman-Johnston campaign, see Albert Castel, *Decision in the West: The Atlanta Campaign of 1864* (Lawrence: University Press of Kansas, 1992).

39. HWH to FL, September 12, 1864, LI 1709, HL; WTS to HWH, September 4, 1864, HWH to WTS, September 16, 1864, O.R., I, 38, 5, 791, 856; HWH to FL, October 22, 1864, LI 1713, HL; Dennett, September 29, 1864, 221; HWH to GWC, September 24, 1864, USMA.

40. HWH to FL, September 30, 1864, LI 1710, HL. HWH also believed that his nemesis, Montgomery Blair, had misspoken when he said that AL had been willing to offer GBMc another military command if he refused to run. "Politicians are *bad* enough for anything, but I think uncle Abe is too cunning to fall into such a trap"; HWH to GWC, October 4, 1864, GWC Papers, USMA; HWH to GWC, November 10, 1864, USMA; HWH to FL, November 12, 1864, LI 1716, HL.

41. HWH to WTS, September 26, 28, 1864, O.R., I, 39, 2, 470, 503. See Joseph T. Glatthaar, *The March to the Sea and Beyond: Sherman's Troops in the Savannah and Carolinas Campaign* (New York: New York University Press, 1985).

42. HWH to FL, December 11, 1864, LI 1718, HL; HWH to WTS, December 18, 1864, O.R,. I, 44, 741. See James L. McDonough and Thomas Lawrence Connelly, *Five Tragic Hours: The Battle of Franklin* (Knoxville: University of Tennessee Press, 1983).

43. There are no modern biographies of George H. Thomas. A modern essay by James L. Isemann may be found in David S. Heidler and Jeanne T. Heidler, *Encyclopedia of the American Civil War*, 5 vols. (Santa Barbara: ABC-CLIO, 2000), 4:1940–1944. WTS, "Grant, Thomas, Lee," *North American Review* 144 (1887): 444.

44. GHT to HWH, November 9, 1864, O.R., I, 39, 3, 718; GHT to HWH, November 27, 1864, O.R., I, 45, 1, 1083–1084; GHT to HWH, December 1, USG to HWH, December 2, HWH to USG, December 3, 1864, O.R., I, 45, 2, 3, 16–17, 28–29.

45. GHT to HWH, December 2, 5, 1864, HWH to GHT, December 6, 1864, GHT

to HWH, December 6, 1864, O.R., I, 45, 2, 18, 55, 71; USG to HWH, December 8, 1864, HWH to USG, December 8, 1864, O.R., I, 45, 2, 96.

46. USG to HWH, December 8, 1864, HWH to GHT, GHT to HWH, December 9, 1864, O.R., I, 45, 2, 96, 114.

47. USG to HWH, HWH to USG, USG to HWH, December 9, 1864, O.R., I, 45, 2, 115–116; GHT to HWH, December 11, 12, 13, 1864, HWH to GHT, GHT to HWH, December 14, 1864, O.R., I, 45, 2, 130, 143, 155, 168, 180.

48. GHT to HWH (two letters), HWH to GHT, December 21, 1864, O.R., I, 45, 2, 295, 296.

49. HWH to USG, December 30, 1864, HWH to GHT, December 31, 1864 (two letters) GHT to HWH, January 21, 24, 1865, O.R., I, 45, 2, 419–420, 441–442, 620–621, 628–629.

50. HWH to WTS, December 18, 1864, O.R., I, 44, 741.

51. HWH to GWC, September 13, 1864, GWC Papers, USMA; HWH to FL, August 24, 1864, LI 1707, HL; HWH to GWC, September 12, 1864, GWC Papers, USMA; HWH to FL, November 4, 1864, LI 1715, HL; HWH to GWC, November 17, 1864, USMA; HWH to FL, December 19, 1864, LI 1720, HL; HWH to "Mrs. Temple," October 13, 1864, HM 39957, HL; HWH to WTS, September 16, 1864, O.R., I, 38, 5, 856.

52. HWH to GWC, October 4, 1864, HWH to GWC, December 29, 1864, GWC Papers, USMA; HWH to HBW, March 14, 1864, HBW Papers, MHS; HWH to GWC, January 29, 1865, USMA.

53. HWH to GWC, December 29, 1864, GWC Papers, USMA; HWH to H. E. Paine, January 4, 1865, O.R., II, 8, 21; HWH to GWC, January 16, 1865, GWC Papers, USMA.

54. Congressional Globe, 38th Cong., 2nd Sess., January 25, February 27, 1865, 419, 1148; "Letter from the Secretary of War [January 28, 1865]" House of Representatives, 38th Cong., 2nd Sess., Exec. Doc. No. 41.

55. Report of the Joint Committee on the Conduct of the War, 38th Cong., 2nd Sess., 2:227–228; Howard K. Beale, ed., Diary of Edward Bates, 1859–1866: Annual Report of the American Historical Association, 1930 (Washington, D.C.: Government Printing Office, 1933), March 28, 1865, 4:468.

56. HWH to USG, October 2, 1865, O.R., I, 39, 3, 25; HWH to GWC, December 29, 1864, USMA; HWH to WTS, December 30, 1864, O.R., I, 44, 836–837.

57. WTS to HWH, January 12, 1865, O.R., I, 47, 2, 36–37; Marszalek, 314.

58. WTS to HWH, December 24, 1864, O.R., I, 44, 800; HWH to WTS, January 1, 1865, O.R., I, 47, 2, 3–4; HWH to FL, February 18, March 5, 1865, LI 1723, LI 1725, HL. See John G. Barrett, Sherman's March through the Carolinas (Chapel Hill: University of North Carolina Press, 1966, 1995).

59. HWH to FL, March 5, 1865, LI 1725, HL; Hannibal Hamlin to unknown, Inaugural Ball Invitation, 1865, Inaugural Ball Collection, LC; Ben Perley Poore, Perley's Reminiscences of Sixty Years in the National Metropolis, 2 vols. (Philadelphia: Hubbard, 1886), 2:162; HWH to HBW, March 14, 1865, HBW Papers, MHS.

60. HWH to WTS, April 10, 1865, O.R., I, 47, 3, 150–151.

61. HWH to EMS, March 15, 1865, HWH to GWC, March 31, 1865, GWC Papers, USMA.

62. FL to HWH, April 22, 1865, LI 1894, HL; Thomas and Hyman, 399.

63. HWH to E. O. C. Ord, HWH to Winfield Scott Hancock, HWH to C. C. Augur, April 15, 1865, O.R., I, 46, 3, 762, 765, 766; HWH to WTS, April 15, 1865, O.R., I, 47, 3, 221; HWH to FL, April 16, 1865, LI 1729, HL.

64. General Order No. 65, War Department, April 16, 1865, O.R., I, 46, 3, 788; HWH to GWC, April 17, 1865, GWC Papers, USMA.

65. WTS to USG or HWH, April 18, 1865, O.R., I, 47, 3, 243–244. See Mark Bradley, *This Astounding Close: The Road to Bennett Place* (Chapel Hill: University of North Carolina Press, 2000).

66. EMS to HWH, April 21, 1865, USG to HWH, April 22, 1865, O.R., I, 47, 3, 264, 276–277; HWH to EMS, April 22, 1865, O.R., I, 47, 3, 277.

67. EMS to HWH, April 22, 1865, O.R., I, 47, 3, 277; David S. Sparks, ed., *Inside Lincoln's Army: The Diary of Marsena Rudolph Patrick, Provost Marshal General, Army of the Potomac* (New York: Thomas Yoseloff, 1964), April 24, 1865, 500.

68. HWH to EMS, USG to HWH, April 26, 1865, O.R., I, 47, 3, 311, 312; HWH to GGM, April 26, 27, 1865, O.R., I, 46, 3, 955, 968; HWH to GWC, April 27, 1865, GWC Papers, USMA.

69. Madeleine V. Dahlgren, *Memoir of John A. Dahlgren* (Boston: James R. Osgood, 1882), May 3, 1865, 510–511.

70. HWH to WTS or John A. Schofield, May 3, 1865, O.R., I, 47, 3, 380; USG to WTS, May 6, 1865, *North American Review* 143 (November 1886): 499; HWH to WTS, May 8, 1865, O.R., I, 47, 3, 435.

71. HWH to WTS, May 9, 1865, O.R., I, 47, 3, 454.

72. WTS to HWH, HWH to WTS, May 9, 1865, O.R., I, 47, 3, 446; WTS to Ellen Sherman, May 10, 1865, SFP, UNDA; HWH to GWC, May 11, 1865, GWC Papers, USMA; HWH to FL, June 3, 1865, LI 1733, HL; HWH to EMS, June 7, 1865, O.R., I, 47, 3, 634–637.

73. WTS to John A. Logan, May 12, 1865, O.R., I, 47, 3, 478; the Missouri soldier's quote is found in Leslie Anders, *The Eighteenth Missouri* (Indianapolis: Bobbs-Merrill, 1968), 330; Sylvia G. L. Dannett, ed., *Noble Women of the North* (New York: T. Yoseloff, 1959), May 14, 1865, 358–359.

74. Harold Adams Small, ed., *The Road to Richmond: The Civil War Memoirs of Abner R. Small of the Sixteenth Maine Volunteers* (Berkeley: University of California Press, 1939), 182.

11. From War to Peace

1. HWH to FL, April 18, 1865, LI 1730, HL.

2. Warren F. Spencer, "A French View of the Fall of Richmond: Alfred Paul's Report to Drouyn de Llys, April 11, 1865," *Virginia Magazine of History and Biography* 73 (April 1965): 178–188; Mary A. Fontaine to "My Dear Cousin," April 30, 1865, in Katherine Jones, *Ladies of Richmond, Confederate Capi-*

tal (Indianapolis: Bobbs-Merrill, 1962), 293–296; Michael B. Chesson, *Richmond after the War, 1865–1890* (Richmond: Virginia State Library, 1981), 57–59; Joseph P. Cullen, "Richmond Falls!" *American History Illustrated* 8 (January 1974): 10–21.

3. Chesson, 80–81; William E. Rachal, ed., "The Occupation of Richmond, April, 1865: The Memorandum of Events of Colonel Christopher Q. Tompkins," *Virginia Magazine of History and Biography* 73 (April 1965): 192; Charles C. Coffin, *Four Years of Fighting,* reprint (New York: Arno, 1970), 508–511.

4. HWH to EMS, April 22, 1865, O.R., I, 46, 3, 888; HWH to GWC, April 24, 1865, GWC Papers, USMA; HWH to FL, April 27, 1865, LI 1731, HL: HWH to EMS, April 22, 1865, HWH to R. D. Cutts, April 22, 1865, HWH to Montgomery Meigs, April 24, 1865, O.R., I, 46, 3, 888, 889, 916.

5. Rachal, 196; R. J. M. Blackett, ed., *Thomas Morris Chester, Black Civil War Correspondent: His Dispatches from the Virginia Front* (Baton Rouge: Louisiana State University Press, 1989), April 26, 1865, 323–324.

6. Chesson, 68; General Order No. 5, May 3, 1865, HWH to E. O. C. Ord, June 7, 1865, RG 94, NARA.

7. HWH to USG, May 5, 1865, O.R., II, 8, 534; *New York Times,* May 7, 1865; HWH to GGM, April 30, 1865, O.R., I, 46, 3, 1016; William B. Hesseltine, *Civil War Prisons: A Study in War Psychology* (Columbus: Ohio State University Press, 1930), 235–236; Chesson, 90; HWH to EMS, April 28, 26, 1865, O.R., I, 46, 3, 990–991, 953.

8. Chesson, 119, 74.

9. HWH to USG, April 29, 1865, O.R., I, 46, 3, 1005; General Order No. 6, Military Division of the James, May 5, 1865, HL; Chesson, 90.

10. General Order No. 8, Military Division of the James, May 27, 1865, printed in *Army and Navy Journal* 2 (June 10, 1865): 667–668.

11. Chesson, 89, 75.

12. James R. Gilmore, ed., *Letters of a War Correspondent by Charles A. Page, Special Correspondent of the New York Tribune during the Civil War* (Boston: L. C. Page, 1899), 330; General Order No. 3, April 25, 1865, Military Division of the James, HL; Carol Reardon, *Soldiers and Scholars: The U.S. Army and the Uses of Military History, 1865–1920* (Lawrence: University Press of Kansas, 1990), 159; HWH to E. O. C. Ord, April 22, 1865, O.R., I, 46, 3, 896.

13. HWH to EMS, May 11, 1865, O.R., I, 46, 3, 1132; John M. Schofield to HWH, May 16, 17, 1865, HWH to Schofield, May 16, 1865, O.R., I, 47, 3, 510–511, 519; Frank Freidel, *Francis Leiber, Nineteenth-Century Liberal* (Baton Rouge: Louisiana State University Press, 1947), 370–373.

14. Marie Tyler-McGraw, *At the Falls: Richmond Virginia and Its People* (Chapel Hill: University of North Carolina Press for the Valentine, the Museum of the Life and History of Richmond, 1994), 172; HWH to GWC, April 27, 1865, GWC Papers, USMA; HWH to EMS, June 8, 1865 with an endorsement by Charles A. Dana, June 14, 1865, O.R., I, 46, 3, 1264–1266.

15. HWH to EMS, May 13, 1865, O.R., I, 49, 2, 741; HWH to USG, EMS to HWH, May 14, 19, 1865, O.R., I, 49, 2, 759, 836–837; HWH to EMS, May 20, 1865, copybook, RG 94, NARA; HWH to Nelson Miles, May 22, 1865, (two letters), O.R., I, 49, 2, 881, and O.R., II, 8, 564–565; Charles A. Dana to EMS, May 22, 1865, EMS Papers, LC.

16. HWH to EMS, June 8, 1865, RG 94, NARA.

17. Blackett, 44–45; Peter Rachleff, *Black Labor in Richmond, 1865–1890* (Urbana: University of Illinois Press, 1989), 13–15, 34–37.

18. HWH to Daniel H. Rucker, April 30, 1865, copybook, RG 94, NARA; HWH to GWC, May 11, 1865, GWC Papers, USMA; EMS to HWH, May 17, 1865, O.R., I, 46, 3, 1162; HWH to USG, May 17, 1865, USG to HWH, May 18, 1865, O.R., I, 46, 3, 1162, 1169; HWH to GWC, April 27, 1865, GWC Papers, USMA.

19. EMS to HWH, June 10, 1865, O.R., I, 50, 2, 1258; General Order No. 118, June 27, 1865, O.R., I, 46, 3, 1298–1299.

20. HWH to EMS, June 26, 1865, O.R., I, 46, 3, 1295–1297.

21. HWH to FL, June 14, 1865, LI 1735, HL.

22. *Alta California,* August 26, 1865.

23. *New York Times,* August 11, 1865.

24. *Alta California,* August 26, 1865.

25. HWH to GWC, September 5, 1865, GWC Papers, USMA.

26. Charles A. Murdock, *A Backward Glance at Eighty Recolllections and Comments* (San Francisco: Elder, 1921), 130. An interesting personal account of San Francisco during these years is James F. Rusling, *Across America . . .* (New York: Sheldon, 1874), 276–299.

27. James F. Carson, "Gold to Finance the War," *Journal of the West* 14 (January 1975): 25–40; DeWitt C. Thompson, *California in the Rebellion: A Paper Prepared and Read before the California Commandery of the Military Order of the Loyal Legion of the United States, July 1891* (San Francisco: Bacus, 1891).

28. HWH to William H. Seward, November 6, 1865, Seward Papers, University of Rochester; see also HWH to James A. Hardie, November 6, 1865, Hardie Papers, LC; HWH to E. D. Townsend, April 7, June 11, 1866, RG 94, NARA.

29. Report of Major General Halleck, September 18, 1867, 40th Cong., 2nd Sess., House Exec. Doc. 1, Serial 1324.

30. General Order No. 6, September 18, 1865, Military Division of the Pacific, HL; HWH to Ad Gen, September 8, 1865, R G. 94, NARA

31. HWH to JFG, October 27, 1865, JFG Papers, USMA; HWH to FL, April 16, 1866, LI 1741, HL; HWH to John Wilson, May 23, 1867, RG 94, NARA.

32. JP to HWH, July 3, 1865, HWH to JP, JP to HWH, July 5, 1865, O.R.. I, 10, 2, 635, 636–637; JP to Adam Badeau, JP to USG, December 30, 1867, Simon, 16:509n and 18:95.

33. General Order No. 127, War Department, July 21, 1865, Richard Shelby Hartigan, *Lieber's Code and the Law of War* (Chicago: Precedent, 1983), 146; FL to HWH, September 10, 1865, Thomas Sergeant Perry, ed., *The Life and*

Letters of Francis Lieber (Boston: J. R. Osgood, 1882), 359–360; HWH to FL, December 5, 1865, April 16, 1866, LI 1739, LI 1741, HL.

34. Undated, unnamed newspaper clipping on HWH, Special Collections, UCLA; *New York Times,* July 15, 1869; John M. Schofield, *Forty-Six Years in the Army* (New York, 1897), 293–298.

35. HWH to FL, December 15, 1865, April 16, 1866, LI 1740, LI 1741, HL.

36. HWH to FL, December 15, 1865, March 15, 1868, LI 1740, LI 1746, HL.

37. HWH to JFG, July 29, November 29, 1865, JFG Papers, USMA.

38. HWH to Frederick Steele, April 4, 1866; HWH to E. D. Townsend, October 18, 1866; HWH to H. G. Blasdel, ca. February 1866, RG 94, NARA; HWH to GWC, February 27, 1866, GWC Papers, USMA.

39. HWH to E. D. Townsend, February 14, 1867, Simon, 17:272–273n; HWH to E. D. Townsend, May 22, 1867, RG 94, NARA.

40. USG to HWH, May 28, 1867, Simon, 17:281–282; GW, *Diary of GW, Secretary of the Navy under Lincoln and Johnson,* 3 vols. (Boston: Houghton Mifflin, 1909), July 5, 1867, 3:129; HWH to FL, July 5, 1867, LI 1744, HL; Elizabeth Shafer, "Rousseau, Lovell Harrison," in David S. Heidler and Jeanne T. Heidler, *Encyclopedia of the Civil War,* 5 vols. (New York: ABC-CLIO, 2000), 4:1681; Orville E. Babcock to Elihu B. Washburne, August 13, 1867, Simon, 17:291.

41. HWH to Jefferson C. Davis, September 6, 1867, Davis Papers, Newberry Library, Chicago. The definitive biography of Davis is Nathaniel Cheairs Hughes Jr. and Gordon D. Whitney, *Jefferson Davis in Blue: The Life of Sherman's Relentless Warrior* (Baton Rouge: Louisiana State University Press, 2002).

42. HWH to FL, January 28, 1868, LI 1745, HL; HWH to Ad Gen, February 14, 1868, RG 94, NARA.

43. For a detailed discussion of the army in Alaska, see Valerie K. Stubbs, "The United States Army in Alaska, 1867–1877: An Experiment in Military Government," MA thesis, American University, 1956; for a briefer version covering the early years to the 1950s statehood, see U.S. Army, *Building Alaska with the United States Army, 1867–1965* (Seattle: Hq., U.S. Army Alaska, 1965). HWH to Ad Gen, November 21, 18, 1867, HWH to A. H. Nickerson, September 26, 1868, RG 94, NARA.

44. Circular, June 4, 1865, General Order No. 12, November 6, 1865, Military Division of the Pacific, HL; HWH to Montgomery C. Meigs, January 6, 1866, HWH to Ad Gen, August 22, 1866, RG 94, NARA; Stephen J. Field, *Personal Reminiscences of Early Days in California,* reprint (New York: Da Capo Press, 1968), 146–150.

45. HWH to FL, October 15, 1865, LI 1737, HL; HWH to GWC, November 9, 1865, GWC Papers, USMA; HWH to FL, November 9, 1865, LI 1738, HL; HWH to GWC, February 27, 1866, GWC Papers, USMA; HWH to FL, August 2, 1866, LI 1742, HL; HWH, *Elements of International Law and Laws of War: Prepared for the Use of Colleges and Private Students* (Philadelphia: J. B. Lippincott, 1866).

46. HWH to JFG, October 27, November 29, 1865, JFG Papers, USMA; Albert Shumate, *Rincon Hill and South Park, San Francisco's Early Fashionable Neighborhood* (Sausalito, CA: Windgate, 1988); *Alta California,* December 18, 1868.

47. HWH to FL, April 16, 1866, January 27, July 5, 1867, March 15, 1868, LI 1741, 1743, 1744, 1746, HL; HWH to JFG, November 29, 1865, JFG Papers, USMA.

48. *Alta California,* January 12, 1872; HWH to H. J. Tilden, June 21, 1867, RG 94, NARA; *San Francisco Chronicle,* September 7, 1890; E. P. Oberholtzer, *History of the United States since the Civil War,* 5 vols. (New York: Macmillan, 1917–1937), 2:508.

49. HWH to JFG, August 7, 1866, JFG Papers, USMA; WSR to Ann Eliza Rosecrans, August 28, 1867, WSR Papers, UCLA.

50. *Alta California,* March 18, June 9, 1869; General Order No. 21, Military Division of the Pacific, June 1, 1869, HL.

51. *Alta California,* June 9, 1869; unnamed June 8, 1869, newspaper clipping, Bancroft Scraps, "Educated Men of California," 127, BL; *New York Times,* June 19, 1869.

52. HWH to Ad Gen, June 13, 21, 1869, M-619, Roll 750, NARA; "Report of Major General H. W. Halleck," November 6, 1869, 41st Cong., 2nd Sess., House Exec. Doc. 1, Serial 1412. The division's territory was changed in 1870, with Texas added, and West Virginia, North Carolina, and Arkansas transferred to other jurisdictions.

53. See, for example, Special Order No. 14, Military Division of the South, August 22, 1869, M-619, Roll 750, NARA; HWH to Ad Gen, May 20, 1870, HWH to Ad Gen, November 30, 1870, RG 94, NARA.

54. Report of HWH, November 6, 1869, Serial 1412.

55. Ibid.

56. Report of HWH, October 24, 1870, ibid.; A. K. Lakin to WTS, January 15, 1870, in James E. Sefton, *The United States Army and Reconstruction, 1865–1877* (Baton Rouge: Louisiana State University Press, 1967), 221.

57. HWH to John M. Schofield, June 1, 1870, HB 18, HL; HWH to Ellen W. Cogswell, December 13, 1870, SP.

58. HWH to GWC, February 15, 1865, GWC Papers, USMA, and December 16, 1869, EG 23, HL. See also HWH to "My Dear Sister," December 16, 1869, SP; *Chicago Tribune,* January 12, 1872. Having no training in medicine or psychology, I called upon professionals in these fields to take the information about Halleck I had discovered to see if they could provide a diagnosis at a distance that might throw light on the direction of his life. Hampered as they were by their inability to examine or interview Halleck, they each, individually, insisted on the hypothetical nature of their findings. Using their modern training and experience, however, they nonetheless provided me with valuable insights that I have incorporated into this book. My comments on physical and mental health throughout this book and my conclusions in this chapter are based on their observations. My four consultants were, in alphabetical order:

Robert K. Collins, M.D.; John F. Marszalek III, Ph.D.; Robert L. Singer, M.D.; and Linda K. Sherby, Ph.D. R. Robinson Baker, M.D., provided information on mercury poisoning. I alone am responsible for the use made of the information these professionals gave me.

59. Alfred H. Terry to Ad Gen, January 9, 1872, HWH Personnel File, M-1395, NARA.

60. *Army and Navy Journal,* January 27, February 3, 1872; *New York Post,* January 10, 1872.

61. *New York Tribune, Chicago Tribune,* January 11, 1872; Jane Cuccurullo, Secretary, The Green-Wood Cemetery, to the author, October 28, 1999, with enclosed a computer printout of burials in Lot 20293, Section 185, of the cemetery, hereafter cited as Green-Wood Cemetery printout; *Alta California,* January 11, 1872.

62. EH to Elizabeth W. Halleck, January 17, 1872, SP; *Chicago Tribune,* January 12, 1872; HBW to Elizabeth W. Halleck, January 2, 1874, SP; EH to FB, January 29, March 8, 1872, FBFM.

63. Typescript of essay by Henry V. Boynton, Ezra A. Carmen Papers, New York Public Library; see also WTS to EH, March 16, 1873, copy, WTS Papers, LC.

64. *Alta California,* February 16, 1872; Probate of the Will of HWH, City and County of San Francisco, May 30, 1872, SP; *Alta California,* April 24, 1873.

65. EH to Elizabeth W. Halleck, September 20, 1875, SP; *Alta California,* December 9, 1875; G. W. Granniss to Ellen Cogswell, January 6, 1885, SP.

66. Undated, untitled newspaper clipping, SP; Green-Wood Cemetery printout; *San Francisco Call,* November 4, 1882.

67. Green-Wood Cemetery printout; "Program for Laying of Cornerstone, The New York Cancer Hospital, May 13, 1884," SP; Last Will and Testament of Elizabeth Halleck Cullum, undated, SP.

68. Last Will and Testament of GWC, November 20, 1891, GWC Papers, USMA; Harold Holzer, vice president of the Metropolitan Museum of Art, New York, email to the author, November 9, 1999, in the author's possession.

69. Jeff Richman, *Brooklyn's Green-wood Cemetery, New York's Buried Treasure* (Brooklyn: The Cemetery, 1998), 87–88; Works Progress Administration, Writers' Program, *San Francisco: The Bay and Its Cities* (New York: Hasting House, 1947), 336; Shumate, 10, 50.

Acknowledgments

IN RESEARCHING and writing this biography, I have incurred many debts. John Y. Simon, the editor of the U. S. Grant Papers, enthusiastically encouraged my work, even though he had already written several essays on Halleck. Other historians were kind enough to help me acquire pertinent documentation. They include Jonathan Earle of the University of Kansas, Stephen Engle of Florida Atlantic University, Joseph Glatthaar of the University of Houston, the independent scholar David S. Heidler, Harold Holzer of the Metropolitan Museum of Art, New York, the independent scholar Lee Kennett, T. Michael Parrish of Baylor University, the independent scholar Stephen W. Sears, Virginia Syers of Harvard University, Rhode Island Supreme Court Chief Justice Frank J. Williams, R. Hal Williams of Southern Methodist University, and Donald Wisnoski of the Oneida County Historical Society (Utica, New York).

Historians, archivists, and librarians who aided me include the following, listed alphabetically by their institutions: Bancroft Library, University of California, Berkeley: Dean Smith, David Kessler, and Anthony Lise; Billings Farm and Museum Library, Woodstock, Vermont: Esther Munroe Swift; Brown University: Mary Jo Kline; California Historical Society, San Francisco: Tanya Hollis and Peggy Zeigler; California State Archives, Sacramento: Jeff Crawford; California State Library, Sacramento: Sibylle Zemitis; California State Railroad Museum, Sacramento: Ellen Halteman; Casa Grande, Parks and Recreation Department, County of Santa Clara, California: John J. Slenter; Colton Hall Museum, Monterey, California: Dorothea Sallee; Filson Club, Louisville: Jim Holmberg; Herkimer County (New York) Historian James M. Greiner; Herkimer County Historical Society: Susan R. Perkins; Huntington Library, San Marino, California: Christopher Adde, Jill Cogen, Kristin Cooper, Bill Frank, S. Krasnoo, Lisa Ann Libby, Anne Marr, Mona Nourelden, and Olga Tsapina; Indiana Historical Society,

Indianapolis: Paul Brockman; Indiana State Library, Indianapolis: Jill Costill; University of Iowa Libraries, Ames: Kathryn Hodson; Library of Congress, Manuscript Division: Haley Barnett, Frederick W. Bauman, Ernest J. Emrich, Jeffrey M. Flannery, Bradley E. Gernand, Heather Klein, Mary W. Wolfskill; University of Michigan, William L. Clements Library: Barbara DeWolfe; Minnesota Historical Society, St. Paul: Steve Nielsen; Missouri Historical Society, St Louis: Dennis Northcott; National Archives and Records Administration: Wayne de Caesar, Michael P. Musick, Trevor Plante; The Newberry Library, Chicago: Christine Colburn; University of New Hampshire, Durham: Roland Goodbody; Ohio Historical Center, Archives/Library Division, Columbus: Gary J. Arnold; Onondaga Historical Association, Syracuse: Judy Haven; Historical Society of Quincy and Adams County (Illinois): Barbara Lieber; Rome (New York) Historical Society: Polly Henderson; Santa Barbara Mission Archive Library: Virgilio Biasiol, O.F.M.; Society of California Pioneers, San Francisco: Herb Garcia and Susan Hoff; Tennessee State Library and Archives, Nashville: Tom Kanon; Union College, Schaffer Library: Betty Allen; United States Army Military History Institute, Carlisle, Pennsylvania: Richard Sommers; United States Military Academy Library, West Point: Alan Aimone, Suzanne Christoff, Susan Lintelmann, Deborah McKeon-Pogue; University of Washington, University Libraries, Seattle: Gary A. Lundell; Vermont Historical Society, Montpelier: Paul A. Carnahan and Marjorie J. Strong; University of Virginia Library, Charlottesville: Margaret Hrabe; Wells Fargo Bank, Historical Services, San Francisco: Robert J. Chandler.

Numerous other people provided answers to my questions. These include Frank E. Bourne of Knoxville; R. Larry Comstock of San Jose; Stephen K. Laird of Rowayton, Connecticut; John Londres of Whiting, New Jersey; and David W. Palmer of Clifton Heights, Pennsylvania. University of Maryland History Professor Emeritus George H. Callcott put me in touch with the retired historian and administrator David S. Sparks, a long-time Halleck researcher, who offered helpful advice. Marylou Symonds of Annapolis, Maryland, suggested the book's title.

To understand Halleck's health and personality, I asked several medical and mental health professionals for advice, and they graciously went out of their way to be helpful: Robert K. Collins, M.D., the director of the Longest Student Health Center at Mississippi State University and my personal physician for nearly thirty years; John F. Marszalek III, Ph.D., Xavier University, New Orleans, and my son; Linda B. Sherby, Ph.D., Boca Raton, Florida, psychologist; and Robert L. Singer, M.D., Fremont California, ophthalmologist. R. Robinson Baker, M.D., the Warfield M. Firor Emeritus Professor of Surgery, Johns Hopkins University, furnished information on mercury poisoning.

At Mississippi State University, the History Department secretaries Patsy Humphrey and Lonna Reinecke provided a variety of essential services. Peggy Bonner formatted the final manuscript and, as always, gave insightful advice and steady encouragement. The late Fred Y. Faulk, a renowned Mississippi State University photographer, prepared numerous photographs for this book.

One of the high points in researching this book was the time my wife and I spent in Westernville, New York, Halleck's birthplace. Eleanor Sexton, who inherited the

Halleck family material from her aunt Eleanor H. Pillmore, welcomed us into her home and made available essential documents. Douglas and Linda White hosted our visit and held a reception for us with the historically minded citizens of the community. Floyd Olney and all the officials at Olney and Floyd Company allowed us to monopolize their copying machine for several days. Stephen M. Smits gave us a copy of the 1990 paper he had prepared about Halleck.

I was fortunate to receive a Humanities and Arts Research Program Grant from Mississippi State University and held a Mayers Fellowship at the Huntington Library during August 1999. Good friends, Michael and Maureen Zukernick of Orinda, California, hosted my wife and me for several weeks while we conducted research at Berkeley.

As I have done in the past, I asked several widely published historians to comment on my manuscript: Dr. Michael B. Ballard, Dr. Charles D. Lowery, and Dr. William E. Parrish, all of Mississippi State University. This time, too, I was fortunate to have the evaluation of three other important scholars: the leading Civil War biographer Dr. Craig L. Symonds, of the United States Naval Academy, the late preeminent military historian Russell F. Weigley of Temple University, and Rhode Island Chief Justice Frank J. Williams, the president of the Lincoln Forum. I am most grateful to all of them for their forthright advice. Nancy N. Clemente's editorial skills saved me from numerous faux pas. Joyce Seltzer, as always, was editor and friend throughout the process. There is no better professional in the business.

My family again provided important support: our three sons and their two mates, John, Chris, Jamie, Michael, and Shannon; our two grandchildren, Will and Emily; my mother, Regina Marszalek; my mother-in-law, Martha Kozmer; and my brother, three sisters, and their families. My brother, Stanley T. Marszalek, successfully searched the New York State Library in Albany for information on Halleck's father's term in the state legislature.

My wife, Jeanne, not only worked with me, side by side, at all the libraries we visited, but she also took care of all the details that made our research trips productive and then read the completed manuscript several times. Without her hard work, support, patience, and love, this biography would never have been completed.

Finally, I dedicate this book to all the students I taught at Mississippi State University during my thirty-year career there, the thousands of undergraduates, especially the Schillig Scholars I mentored, and the special group of graduate students. In particular, I want to remember here several generations of undergraduate work-student assistants. Particularly helpful in the research for this book were four of these outstanding people: Ross Crumbley, Deanna Davis, Bridgette Neely, and Lindley Carruth Shedd. I hope my many students learned from me. I know I benefitted enormously from my association with them. This dedication is but a token of my esteem.

Illustration Credits

1. Samuel W. Durant, *History of Oneida County, New York* (Philadelphia: Everts and Fariss, 1878).
2. Town of Western (New York) Historical Society.
3. *History of Columbia County, New York* . . . (Philadelphia: J. B. Lippincott, 1878).
4. Morris Schaff, *The Spirit of Old West Point, 1858–1862* (Boston: Houghton Mifflin, 1907).
5. Library of Congress.
6. In the author's possession.
7. California State Library, Sacramento.
8. California State Library, Sacramento.
9. Library of Congress.
10. Library of Congress.
11. Billings Family Archives, The Woodstock (Vermont) Foundation, Inc.
12. Library of Congress.
13. Library of Congress.
14. Town of Western (New York) Historical Society
15. Massachusetts Commandery, Military Order of the Loyal Legion and the U.S. Army Military History Institute.
16. Library of Congress.
17. Library of Congress.
18. Library of Congress.
19. Library of Congress.
20. Benson J. Lossing, *Pictorial History of the Civil War* (Hartford: T. Belknaps, 1868).

21. Lewis R. Harley, *Frances Lieber: His Life and Political Philosophy* (New York: Columbia University Press, 1899).
22. *Harpers Weekly,* January 10, 1863.
23. Library of Congress.
24. Library of Congress.
25. Library of Congress.
26. National Archives and Records Administration, College Park, MD.
27. Photograph by Jeanne A. Marszalek.

Index